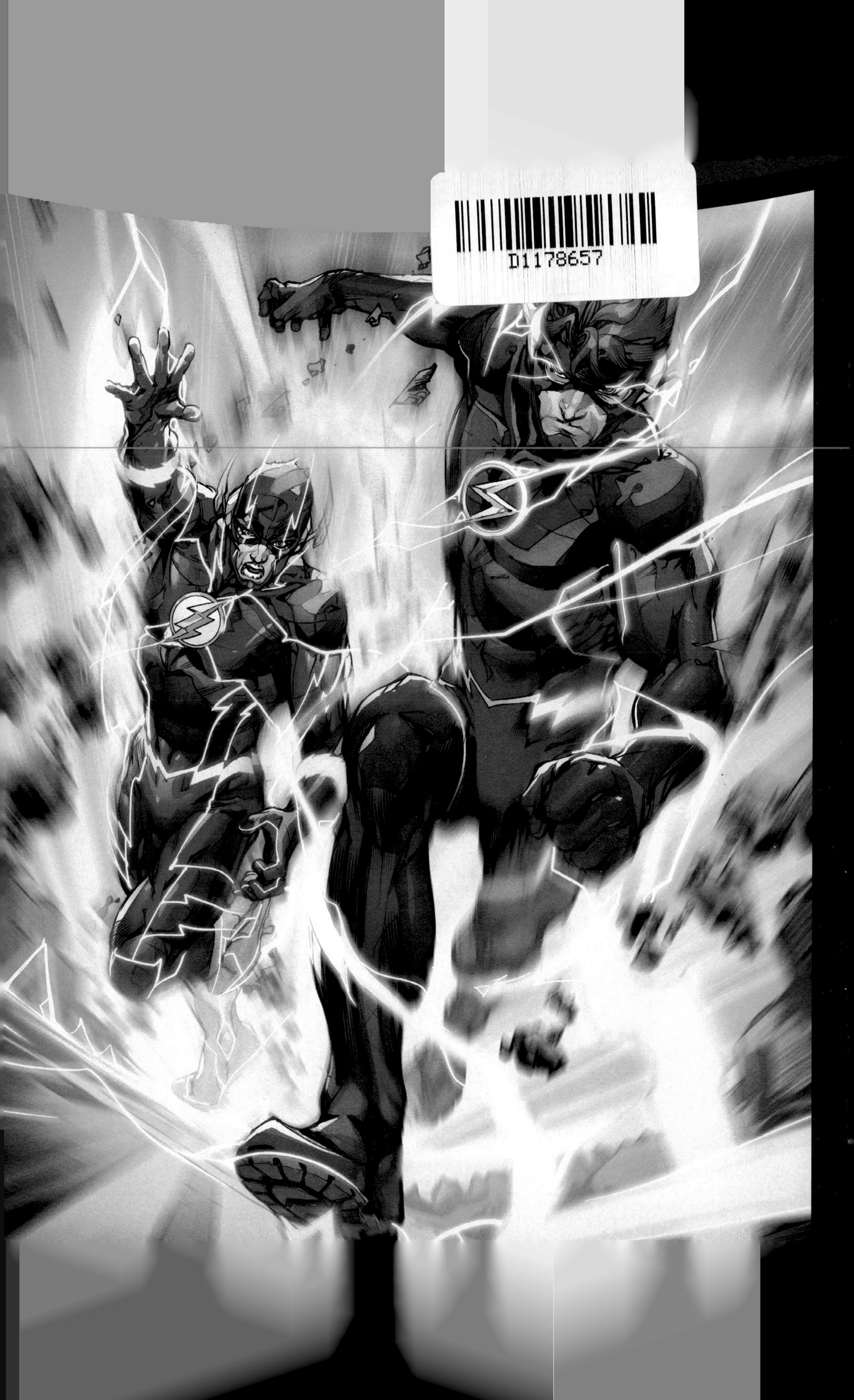

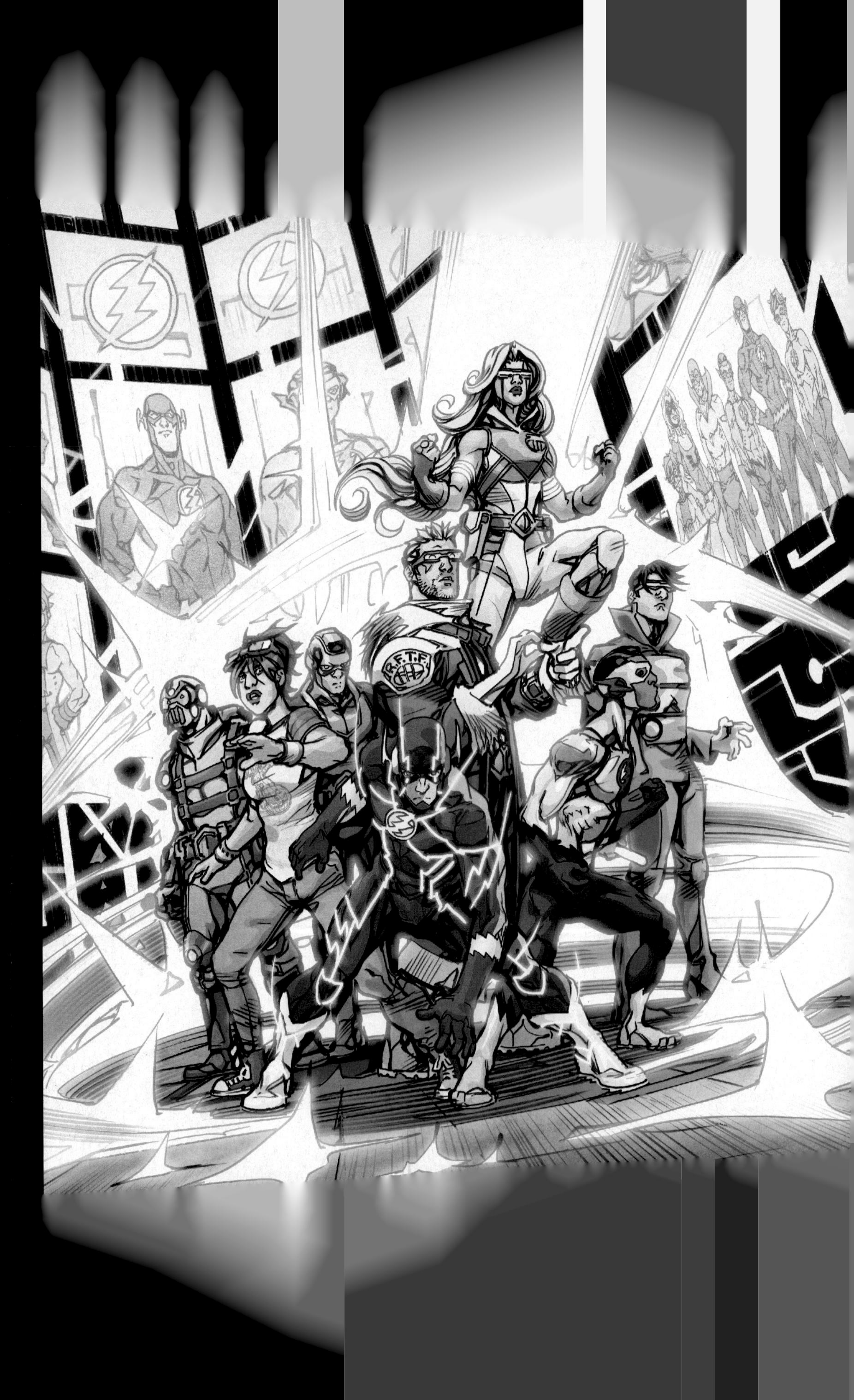
R.F.T.F.

THE FLASH
VOL.8 FLASH WAR

JOSHUA WILLIAMSON
writer

HOWARD PORTER
SCOTT KOLINS
artists

HI-FI
LUIS GUERRERO
colorists

STEVE WANDS
TRAVIS LANHAM ✳ CARLOS M. MANGUAL
letterers

HOWARD PORTER and HI-FI
collection cover artists

SUPERMAN created by **JERRY SIEGEL** and **JOE SHUSTER**
By special arrangement with the Jerry Siegel family

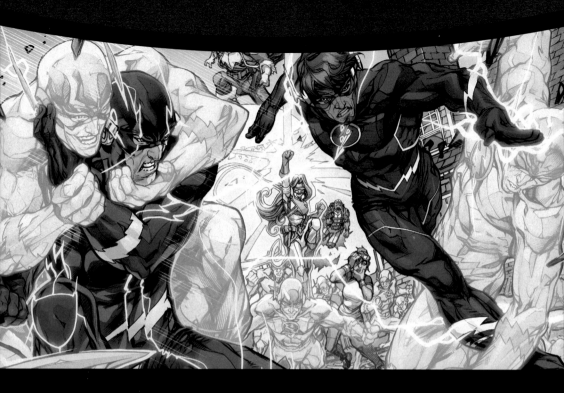

REBECCA TAYLOR Editor - Original Series ✷ **ANDREW MARINO** Assistant Editor - Original Series
JEB WOODARD Group Editor - Collected Editions ✷ **ERIKA ROTHBERG** Editor - Collected Edition
STEVE COOK Design Director - Books ✷ **MONIQUE NARBONETA** Publication Design

BOB HARRAS Senior VP - Editor-in-Chief, DC Comics
PAT McCALLUM Executive Editor, DC Comics

DAN DiDIO Publisher ✷ **JIM LEE** Publisher & Chief Creative Officer
AMIT DESAI Executive VP - Business & Marketing Strategy, Direct to Consumer & Global Franchise Management
BOBBIE CHASE VP & Executive Editor, Young Reader & Talent Development ✷ **MARK CHIARELLO** Senior VP - Art, Design & Collected Editions
JOHN CUNNINGHAM Senior VP - Sales & Trade Marketing ✷ **BRIAR DARDEN** VP - Business Affairs
ANNE DePIES Senior VP - Business Strategy, Finance & Administration ✷ **DON FALLETTI** VP - Manufacturing Operations
LAWRENCE GANEM VP - Editorial Administration & Talent Relations ✷ **ALISON GILL** Senior VP - Manufacturing & Operations
JASON GREENBERG VP - Business Strategy & Finance ✷ **HANK KANALZ** Senior VP - Editorial Strategy & Administration
JAY KOGAN Senior VP - Legal Affairs ✷ **NICK J. NAPOLITANO** VP - Manufacturing Administration
LISETTE OSTERLOH VP - Digital Marketing & Events ✷ **EDDIE SCANNELL** VP - Consumer Marketing
COURTNEY SIMMONS Senior VP - Publicity & Communications ✷ **JIM (SKI) SOKOLOWSKI** VP - Comic Book Specialty Sales & Trade Marketing
NANCY SPEARS VP - Mass, Book, Digital Sales & Trade Marketing ✷ **MICHELE R. WELLS** VP - Content Strategy

THE FLASH VOL. 8: FLASH WAR

DC Comics, 2900 West Alameda Ave., Burbank, CA 91505
Printed by LSC Communications, Kendallville, IN, USA. 11/9/18. First Printing.
ISBN: 978-1-4012-8350-6

Library of Congress Cataloging-in-Publication Data is available.

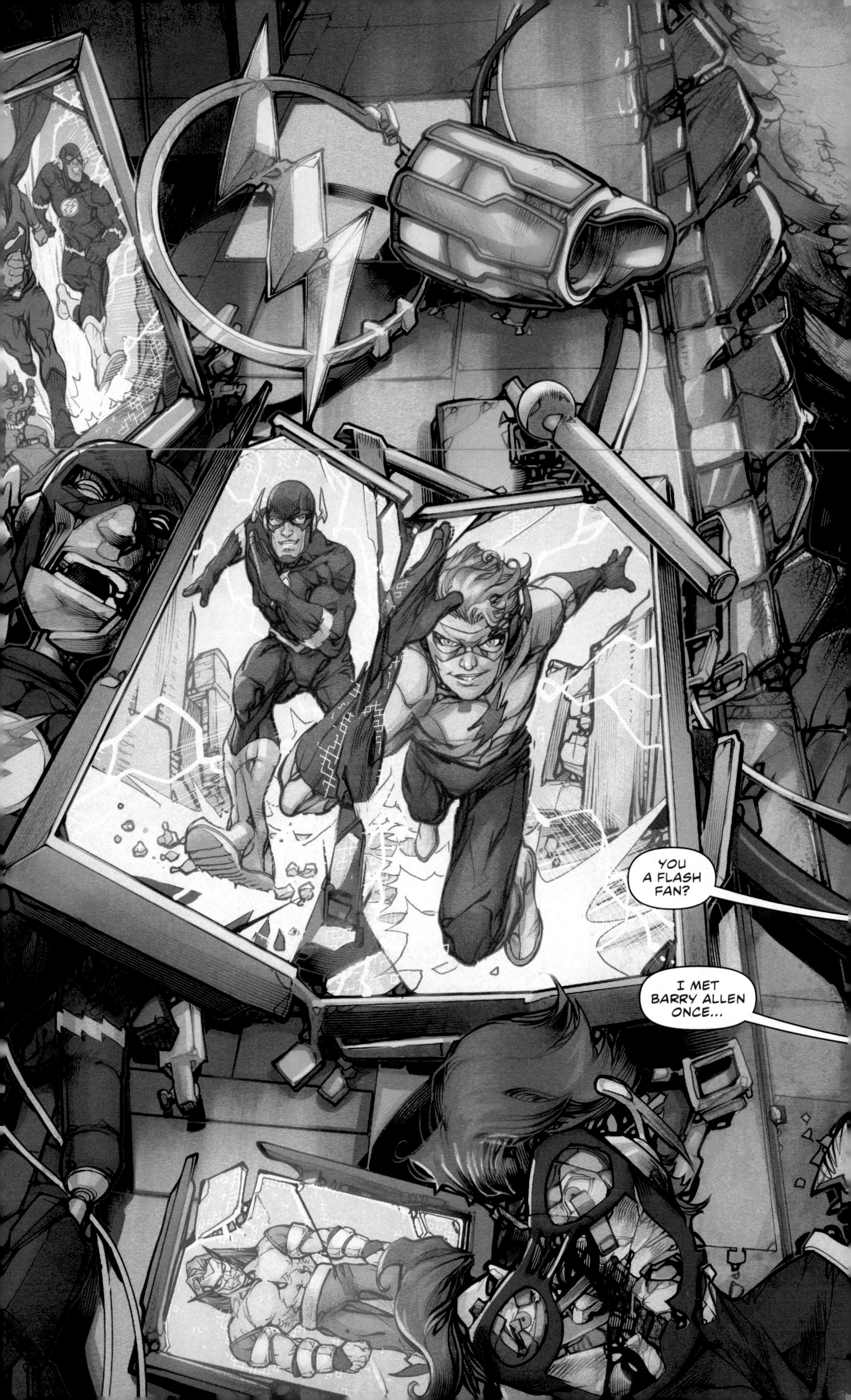
YOU A FLASH FAN?
I MET BARRY ALLEN ONCE...

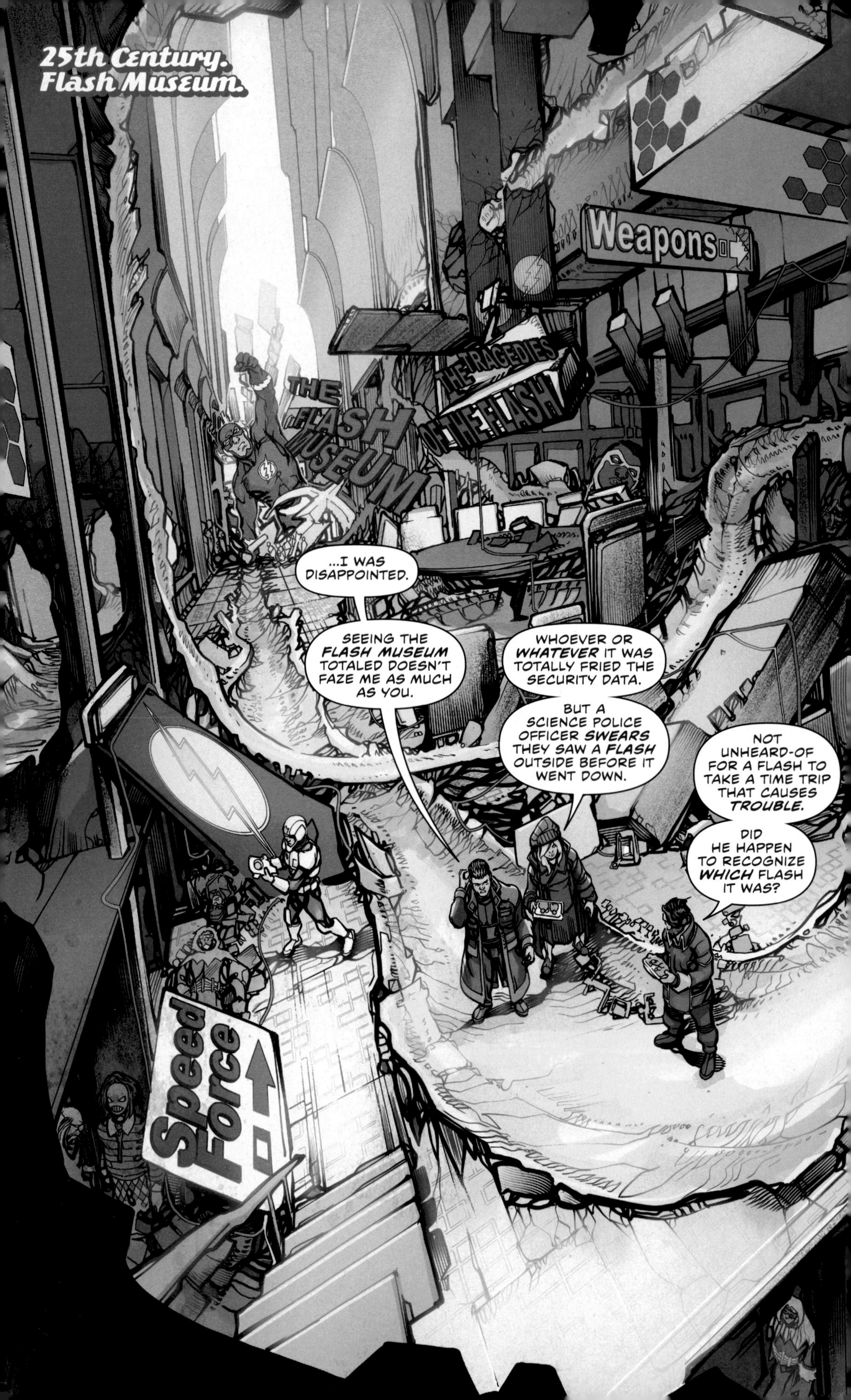
25th Century. Flash Museum.
Weapons
THE FLASH MUSEUM
THE TRAGEDIES OF THE FLASH
...I WAS DISAPPOINTED.
SEEING THE FLASH MUSEUM TOTALED DOESN'T FAZE ME AS MUCH AS YOU.
WHOEVER OR WHATEVER IT WAS TOTALLY FRIED THE SECURITY DATA.
BUT A SCIENCE POLICE OFFICER SWEARS THEY SAW A FLASH OUTSIDE BEFORE IT WENT DOWN.
NOT UNHEARD-OF FOR A FLASH TO TAKE A TIME TRIP THAT CAUSES TROUBLE.
DID HE HAPPEN TO RECOGNIZE WHICH FLASH IT WAS?
Speed Force

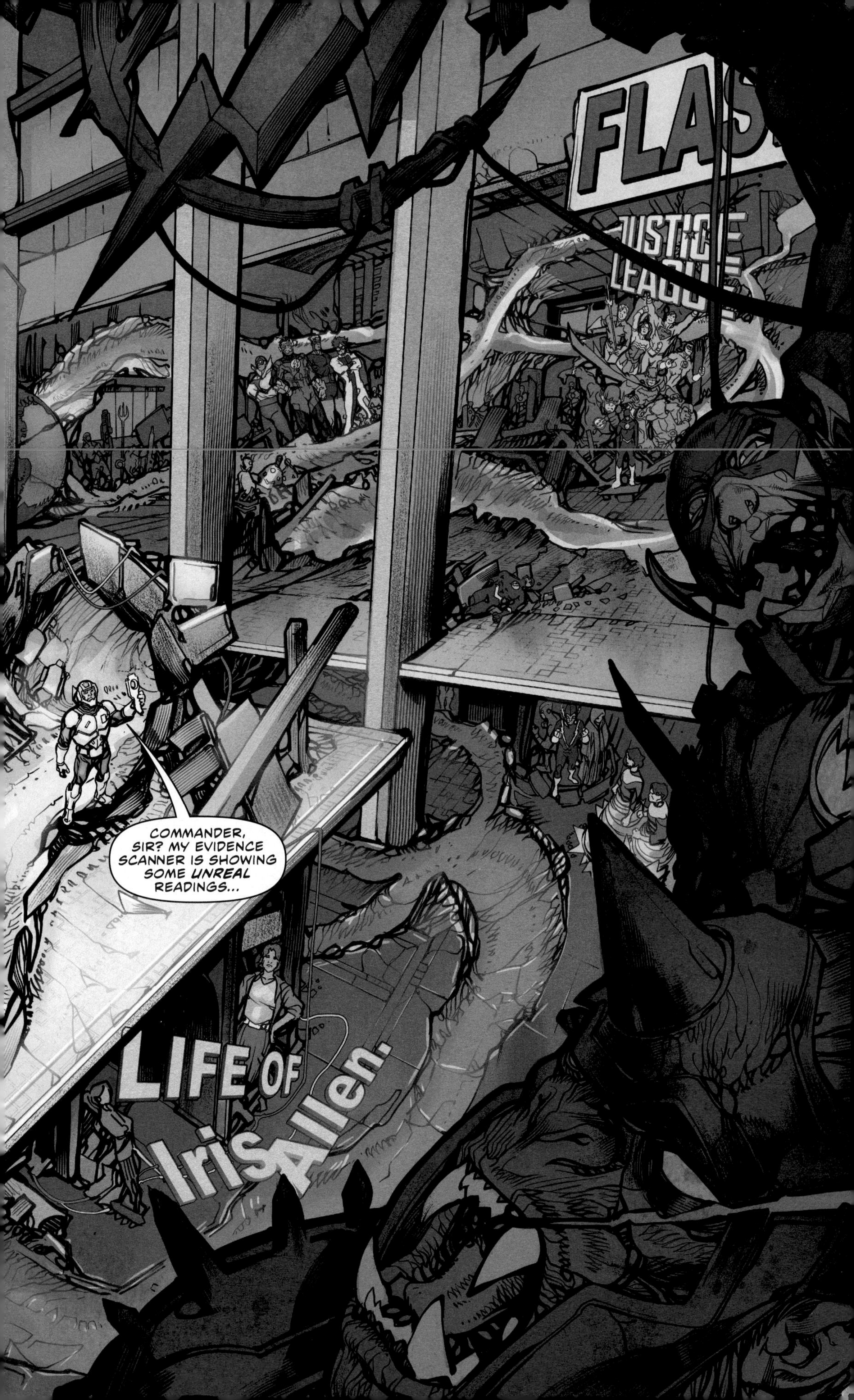
FLAS
JUSTICE LEAGUE
COMMANDER, SIR? MY EVIDENCE SCANNER IS SHOWING SOME UNREAL READINGS...
LIFE OF Iris Allen.

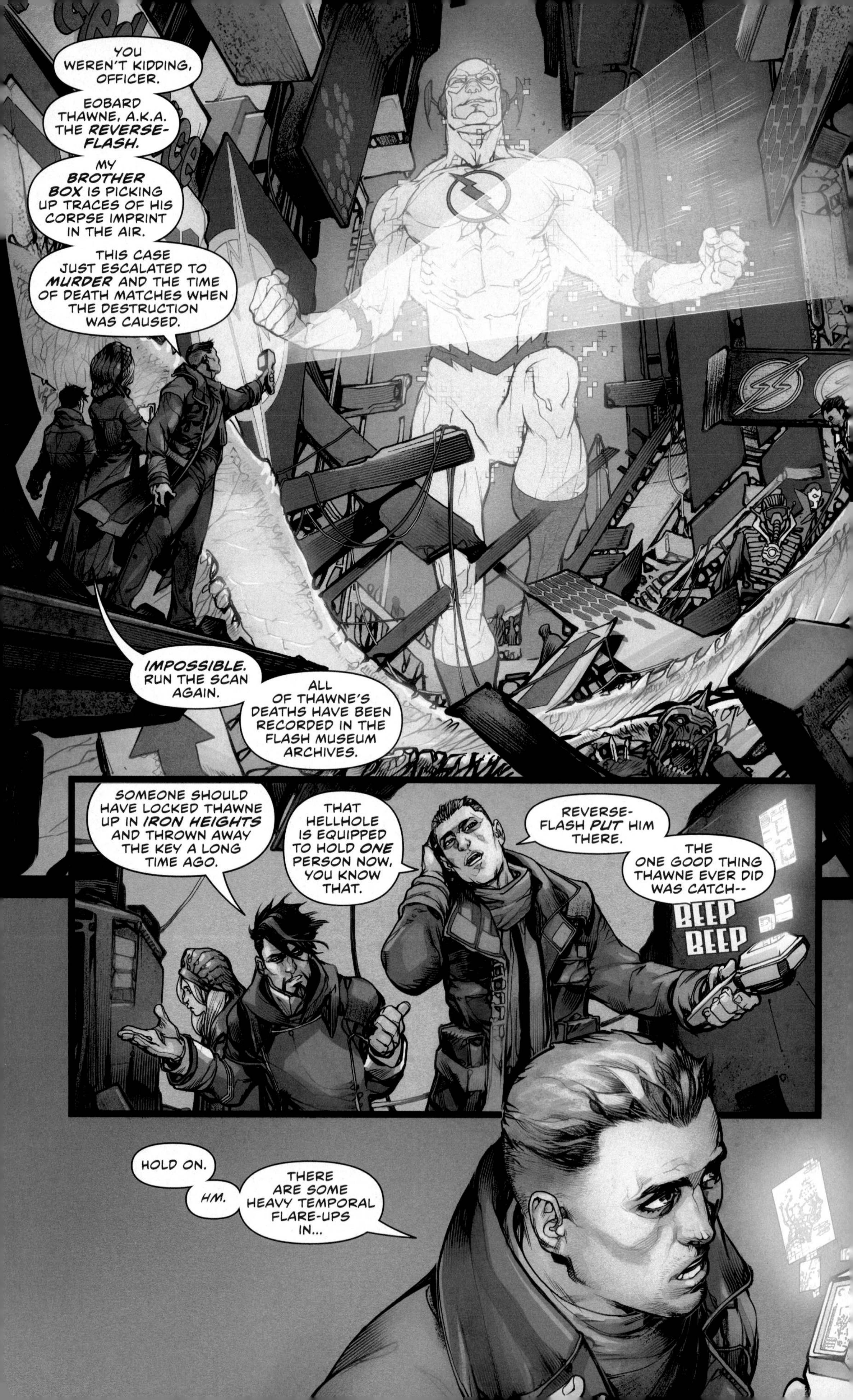
YOU WEREN'T KIDDING, OFFICER.
EOBARD THAWNE, A.K.A. THE REVERSE-FLASH.
MY BROTHER BOX IS PICKING UP TRACES OF HIS CORPSE IMPRINT IN THE AIR.
THIS CASE JUST ESCALATED TO MURDER AND THE TIME OF DEATH MATCHES WHEN THE DESTRUCTION WAS CAUSED.
IMPOSSIBLE. RUN THE SCAN AGAIN.
ALL OF THAWNE'S DEATHS HAVE BEEN RECORDED IN THE FLASH MUSEUM ARCHIVES.
SOMEONE SHOULD HAVE LOCKED THAWNE UP IN IRON HEIGHTS AND THROWN AWAY THE KEY A LONG TIME AGO.
THAT HELLHOLE IS EQUIPPED TO HOLD ONE PERSON NOW, YOU KNOW THAT.
REVERSE-FLASH PUT HIM THERE.
THE ONE GOOD THING THAWNE EVER DID WAS CATCH--
BEEP BEEP
HOLD ON.
HM.
THERE ARE SOME HEAVY TEMPORAL FLARE-UPS IN...

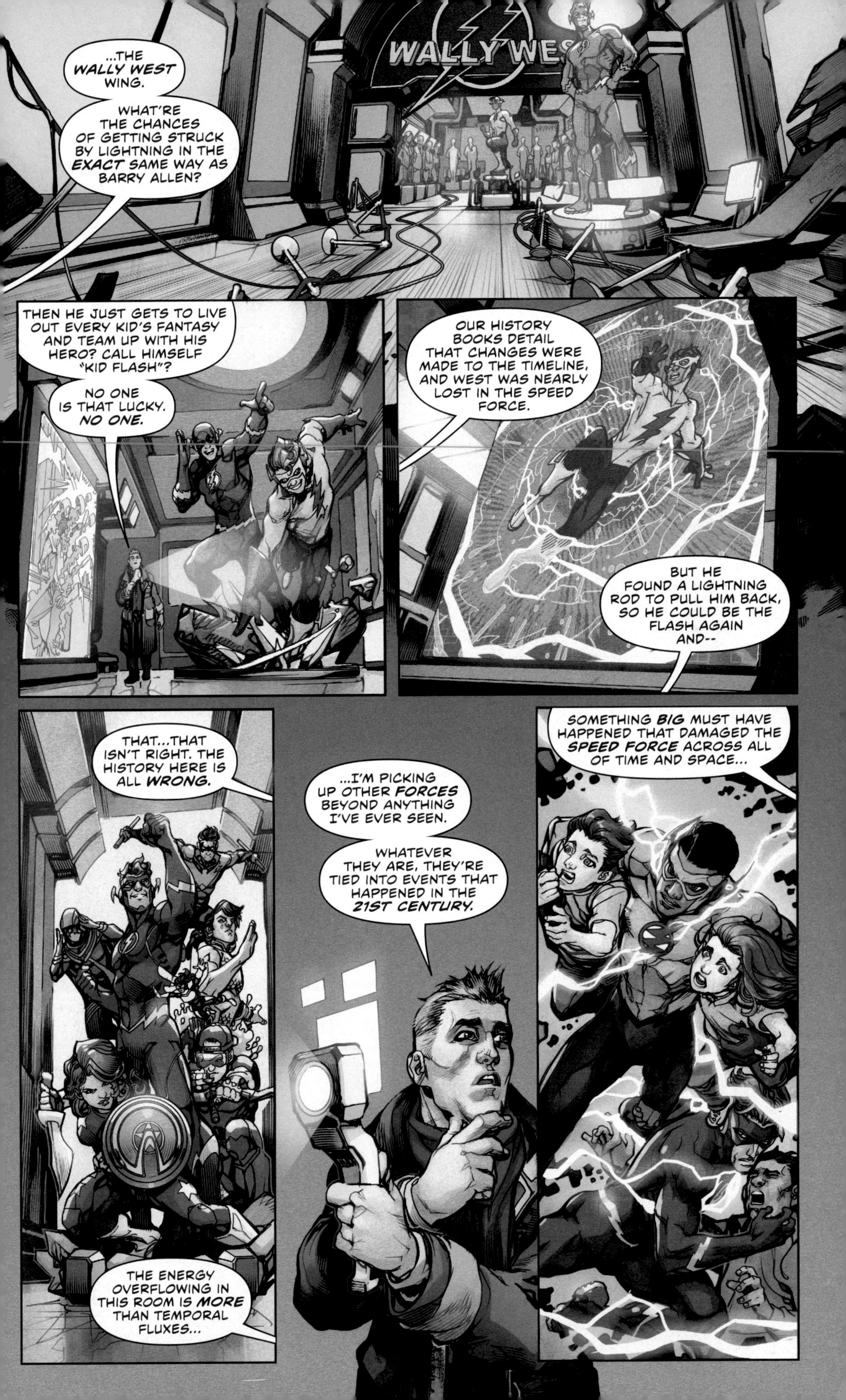

WALLY WEST
...THE WALLY WEST WING.
WHAT'RE THE CHANCES OF GETTING STRUCK BY LIGHTNING IN THE EXACT SAME WAY AS BARRY ALLEN?
THEN HE JUST GETS TO LIVE OUT EVERY KID'S FANTASY AND TEAM UP WITH HIS HERO? CALL HIMSELF "KID FLASH"?
NO ONE IS THAT LUCKY. NO ONE.
OUR HISTORY BOOKS DETAIL THAT CHANGES WERE MADE TO THE TIMELINE, AND WEST WAS NEARLY LOST IN THE SPEED FORCE.
BUT HE FOUND A LIGHTNING ROD TO PULL HIM BACK, SO HE COULD BE THE FLASH AGAIN AND--
THAT...THAT ISN'T RIGHT. THE HISTORY HERE IS ALL WRONG.
THE ENERGY OVERFLOWING IN THIS ROOM IS MORE THAN TEMPORAL FLUXES...
...I'M PICKING UP OTHER FORCES BEYOND ANYTHING I'VE EVER SEEN.
WHATEVER THEY ARE, THEY'RE TIED INTO EVENTS THAT HAPPENED IN THE 21ST CENTURY.
SOMETHING BIG MUST HAVE HAPPENED THAT DAMAGED THE SPEED FORCE ACROSS ALL OF TIME AND SPACE...

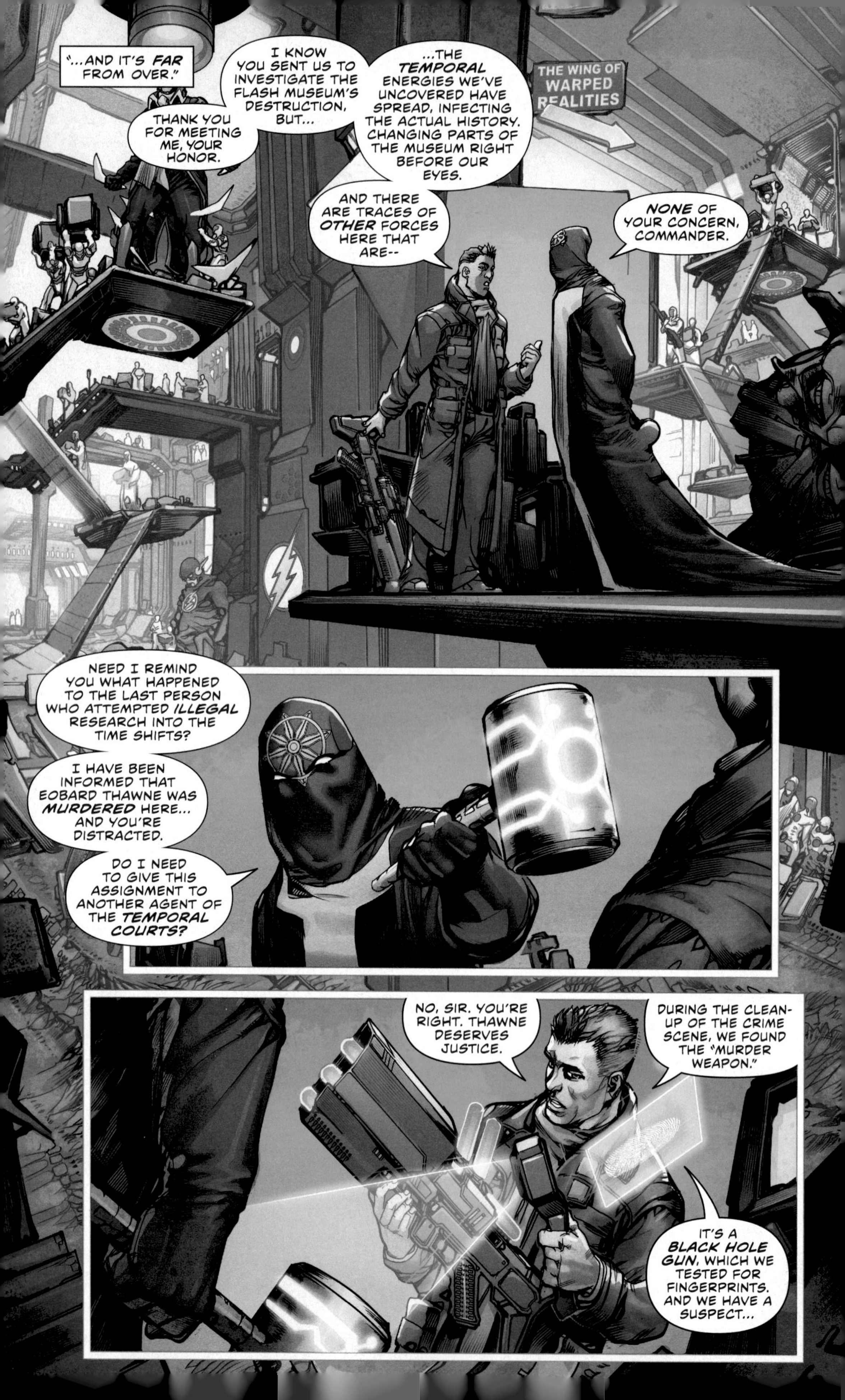
"...AND IT'S FAR FROM OVER."
THANK YOU FOR MEETING ME, YOUR HONOR.
I KNOW YOU SENT US TO INVESTIGATE THE FLASH MUSEUM'S DESTRUCTION, BUT...
...THE TEMPORAL ENERGIES WE'VE UNCOVERED HAVE SPREAD, INFECTING THE ACTUAL HISTORY. CHANGING PARTS OF THE MUSEUM RIGHT BEFORE OUR EYES.
THE WING OF WARPED REALITIES
AND THERE ARE TRACES OF OTHER FORCES HERE THAT ARE--
NONE OF YOUR CONCERN, COMMANDER.
NEED I REMIND YOU WHAT HAPPENED TO THE LAST PERSON WHO ATTEMPTED ILLEGAL RESEARCH INTO THE TIME SHIFTS?
I HAVE BEEN INFORMED THAT EOBARD THAWNE WAS MURDERED HERE... AND YOU'RE DISTRACTED.
DO I NEED TO GIVE THIS ASSIGNMENT TO ANOTHER AGENT OF THE TEMPORAL COURTS?
NO, SIR. YOU'RE RIGHT. THAWNE DESERVES JUSTICE.
DURING THE CLEAN-UP OF THE CRIME SCENE, WE FOUND THE "MURDER WEAPON."
IT'S A BLACK HOLE GUN, WHICH WE TESTED FOR FINGERPRINTS. AND WE HAVE A SUSPECT...

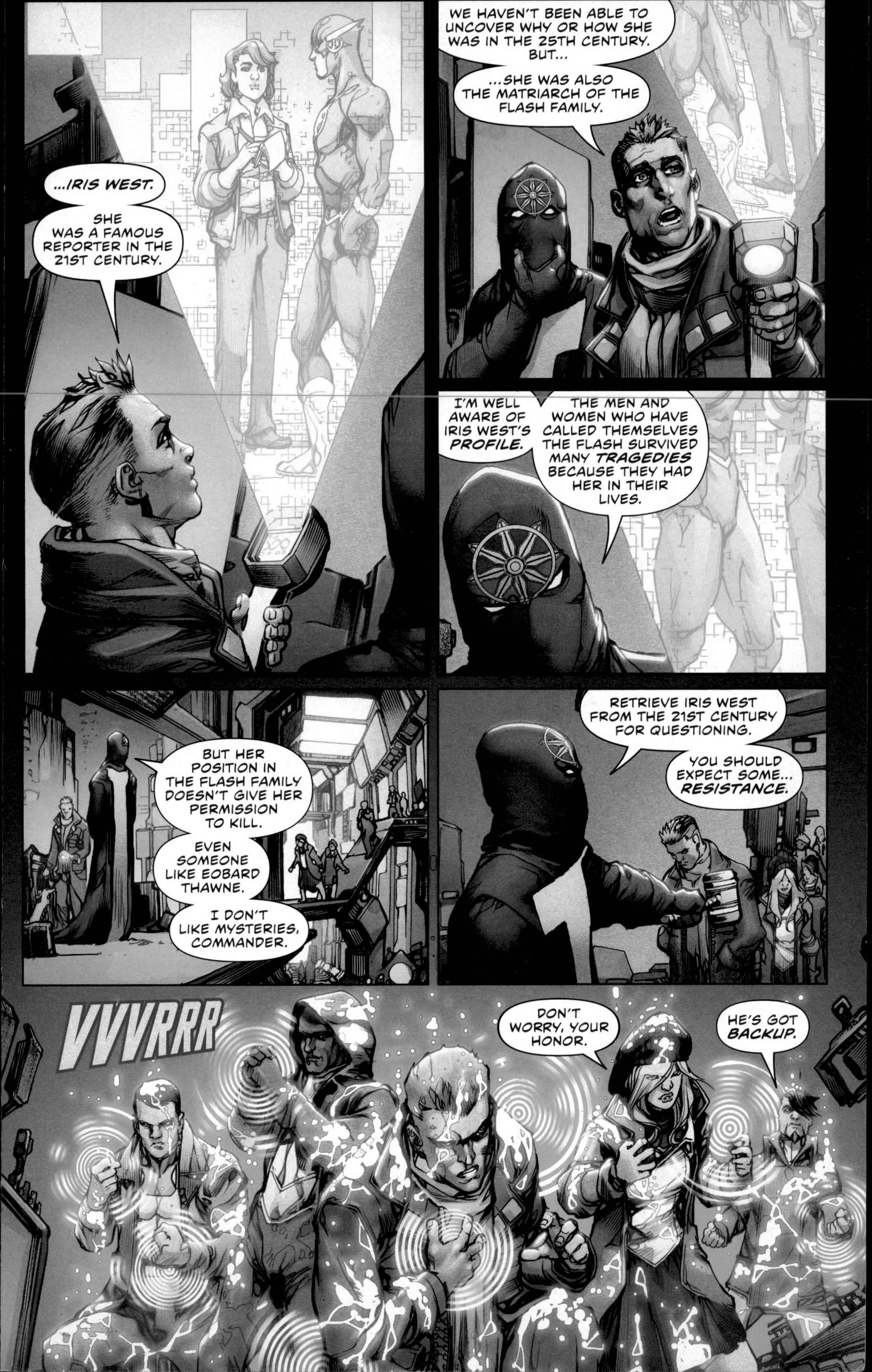
...IRIS WEST.
SHE WAS A FAMOUS REPORTER IN THE 21ST CENTURY.
WE HAVEN'T BEEN ABLE TO UNCOVER WHY OR HOW SHE WAS IN THE 25TH CENTURY. BUT...
...SHE WAS ALSO THE MATRIARCH OF THE FLASH FAMILY.
I'M WELL AWARE OF IRIS WEST'S PROFILE.
THE MEN AND WOMEN WHO HAVE CALLED THEMSELVES THE FLASH SURVIVED MANY TRAGEDIES BECAUSE THEY HAD HER IN THEIR LIVES.
BUT HER POSITION IN THE FLASH FAMILY DOESN'T GIVE HER PERMISSION TO KILL.
EVEN SOMEONE LIKE EOBARD THAWNE.
I DON'T LIKE MYSTERIES, COMMANDER.
RETRIEVE IRIS WEST FROM THE 21ST CENTURY FOR QUESTIONING.
YOU SHOULD EXPECT SOME... RESISTANCE.
VVVRRR
DON'T WORRY, YOUR HONOR.
HE'S GOT BACKUP.

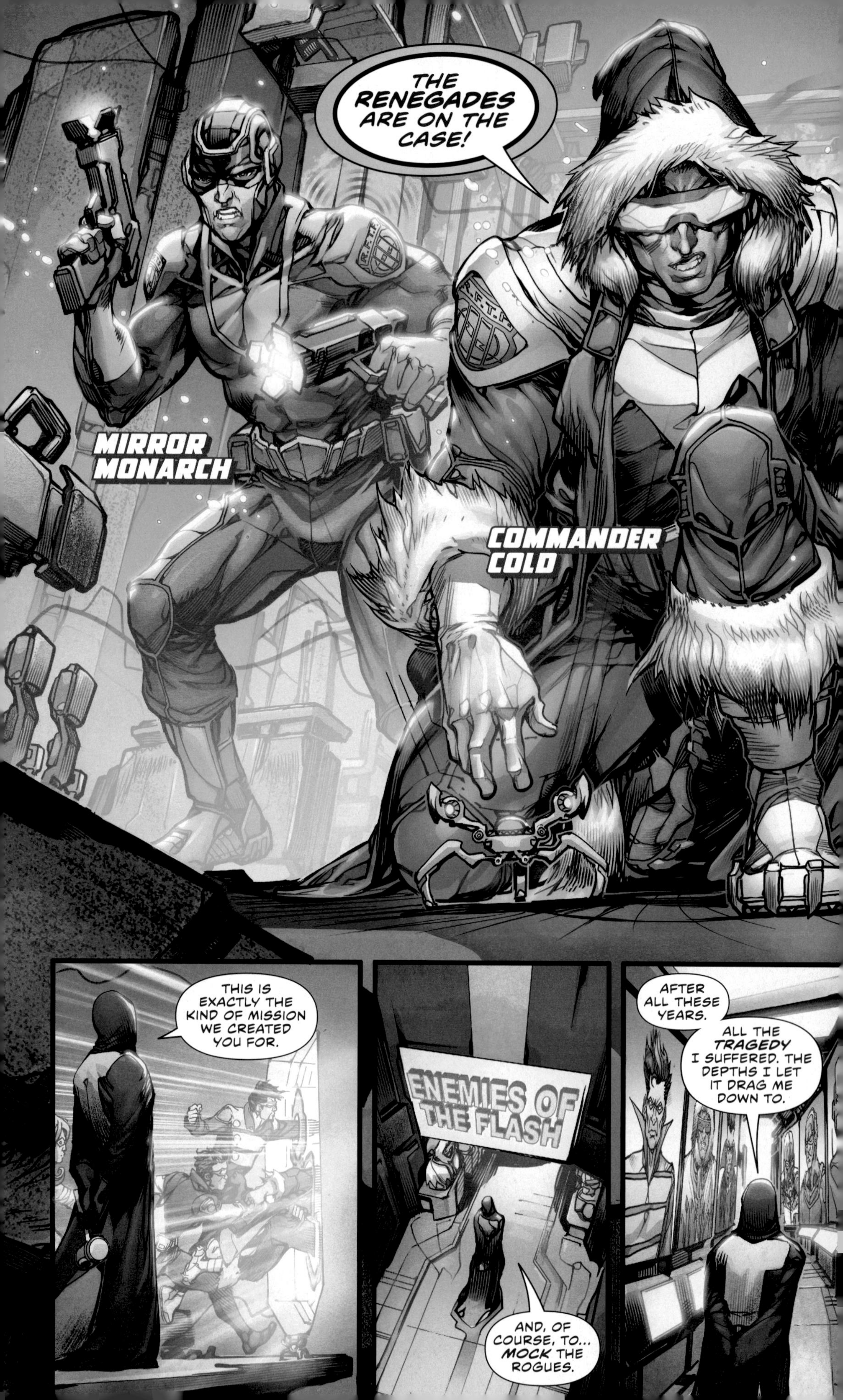
THE RENEGADES ARE ON THE CASE!
MIRROR MONARCH
COMMANDER COLD
THIS IS EXACTLY THE KIND OF MISSION WE CREATED YOU FOR.
ENEMIES OF THE FLASH
AND, OF COURSE, TO... MOCK THE ROGUES.
AFTER ALL THESE YEARS.
ALL THE TRAGEDY I SUFFERED. THE DEPTHS I LET IT DRAG ME DOWN TO.

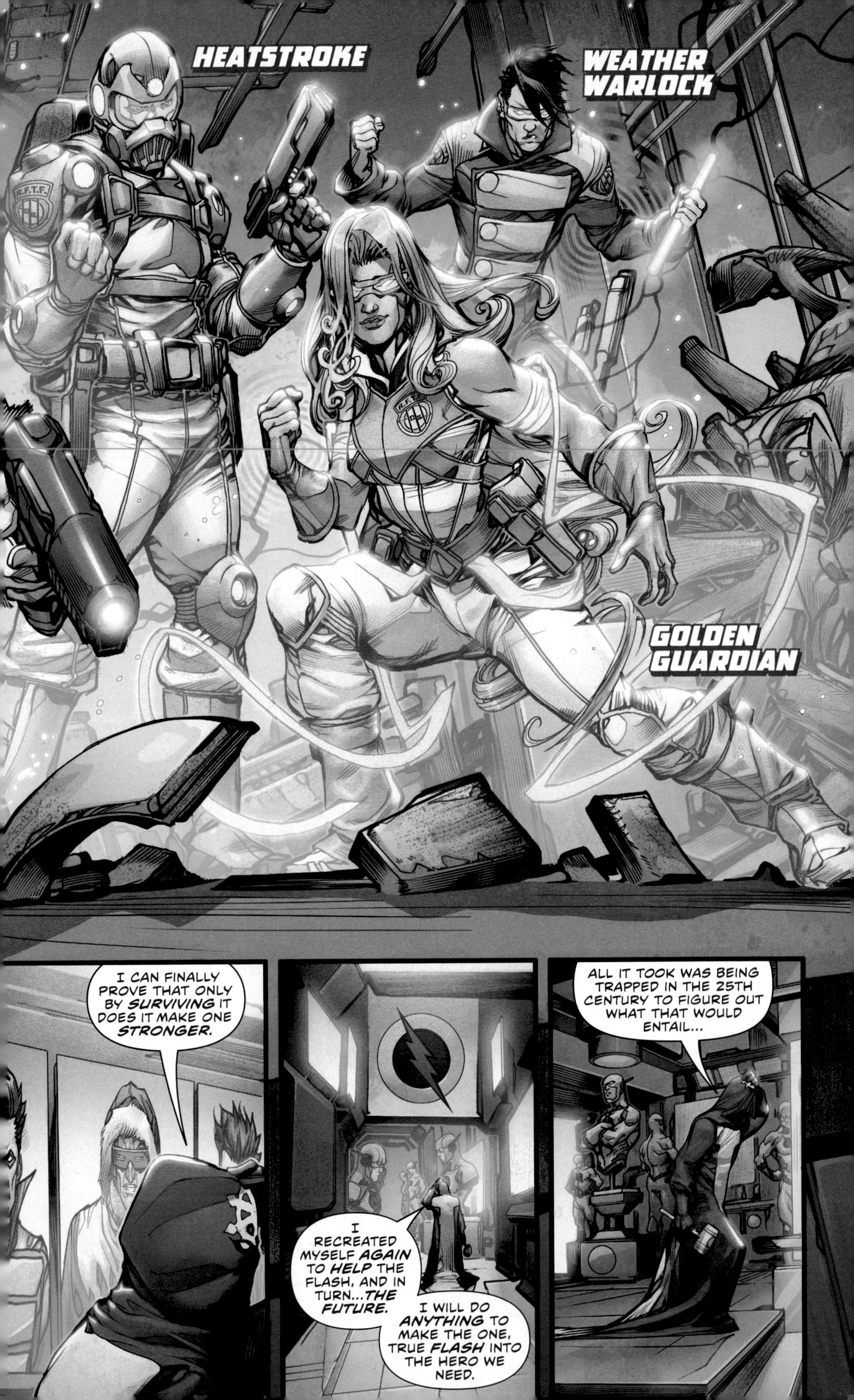
HEATSTROKE
WEATHER WARLOCK
GOLDEN GUARDIAN
I CAN FINALLY PROVE THAT ONLY BY SURVIVING IT DOES IT MAKE ONE STRONGER.
I RECREATED MYSELF AGAIN TO HELP THE FLASH, AND IN TURN...THE FUTURE.
I WILL DO ANYTHING TO MAKE THE ONE, TRUE FLASH INTO THE HERO WE NEED.
ALL IT TOOK WAS BEING TRAPPED IN THE 25TH CENTURY TO FIGURE OUT WHAT THAT WOULD ENTAIL...

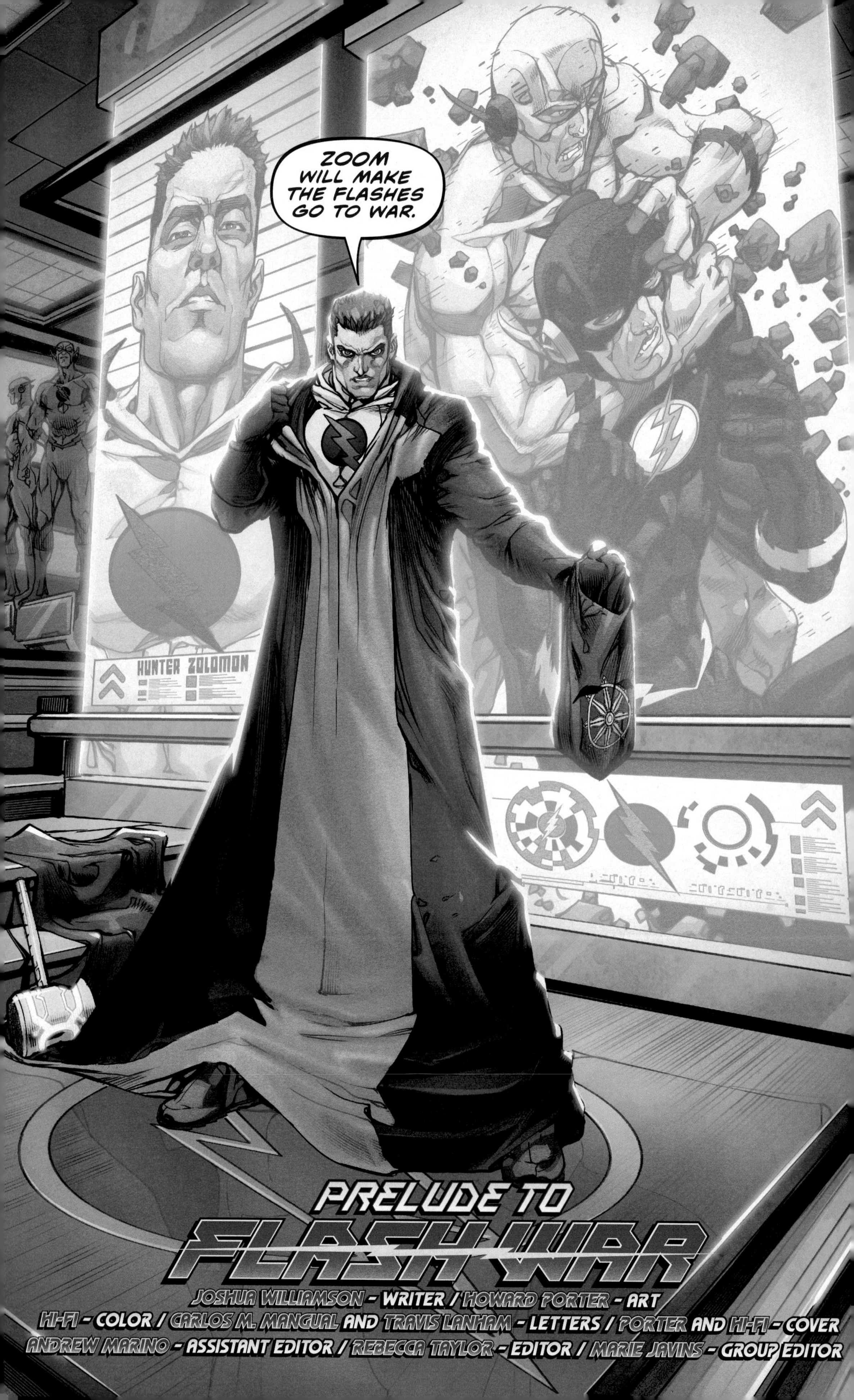
ZOOM WILL MAKE THE FLASHES GO TO WAR.
HUNTER ZOLOMON
PRELUDE TO
FLASH WAR
JOSHUA WILLIAMSON - WRITER / HOWARD PORTER - ART
HI-FI - COLOR / CARLOS M. MANGUAL AND TRAVIS LANHAM - LETTERS / PORTER AND HI-FI - COVER
ANDREW MARINO - ASSISTANT EDITOR / REBECCA TAYLOR - EDITOR / MARIE JAVINS - GROUP EDITOR

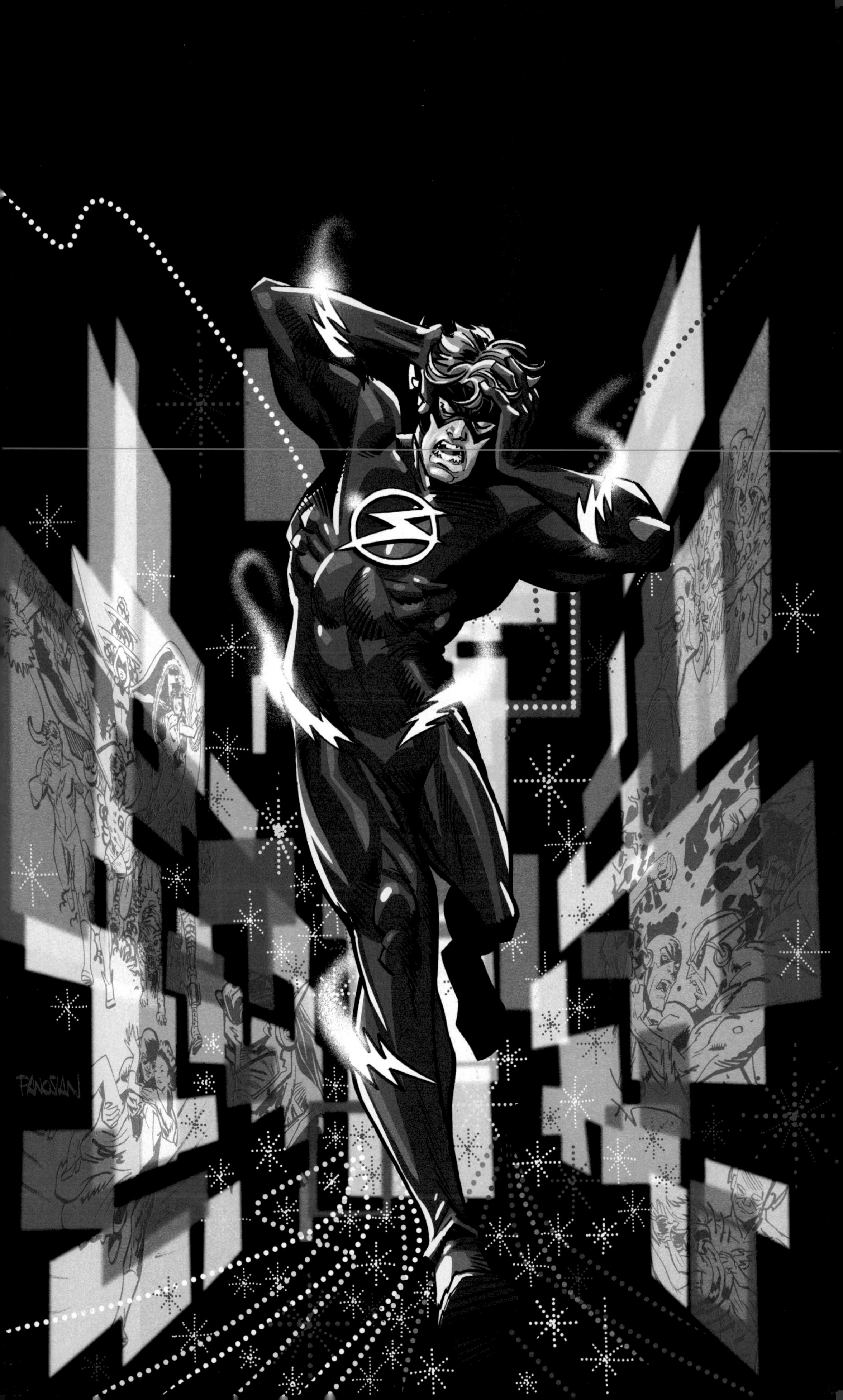
PANOSIAN

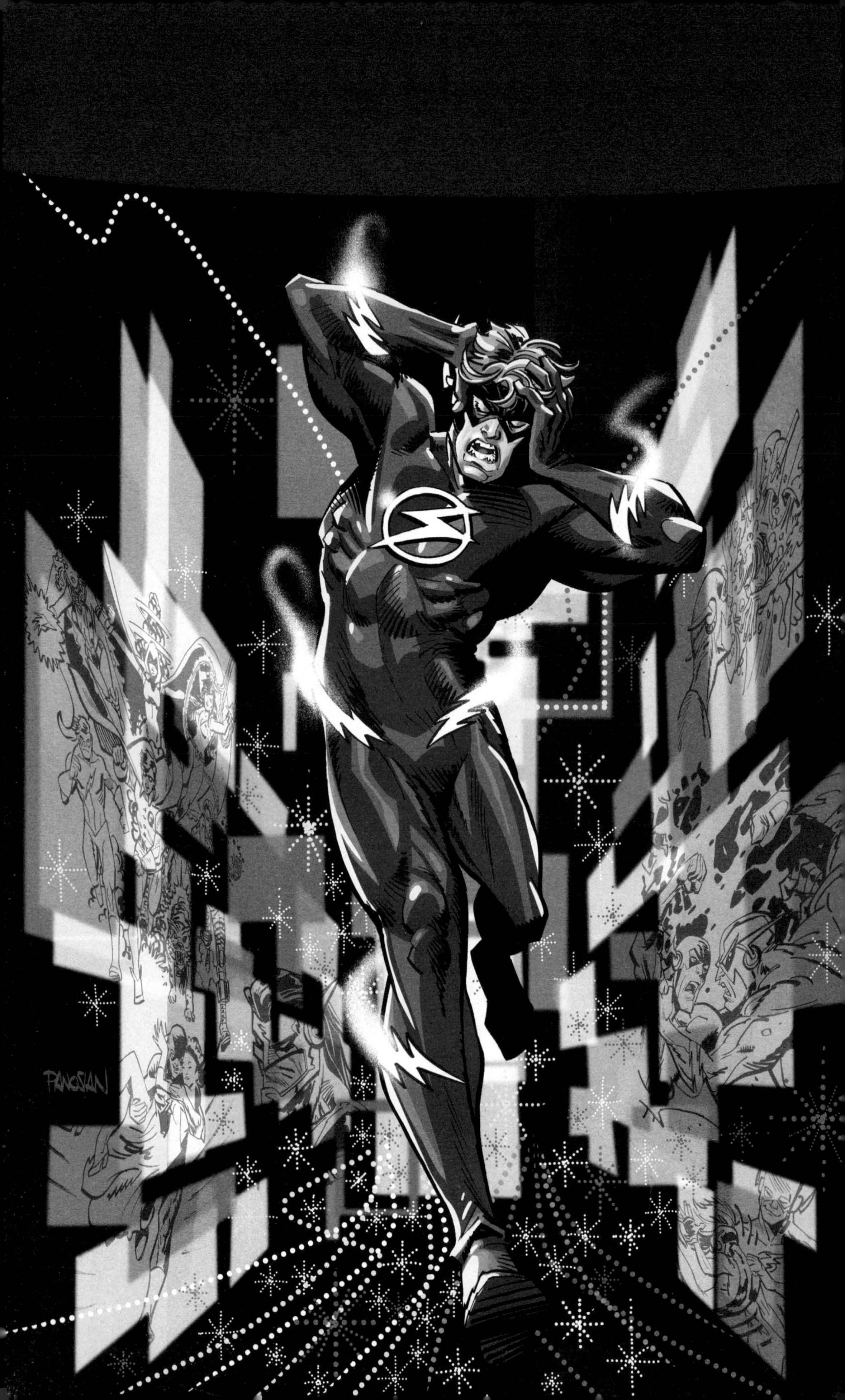
PANOSIAN

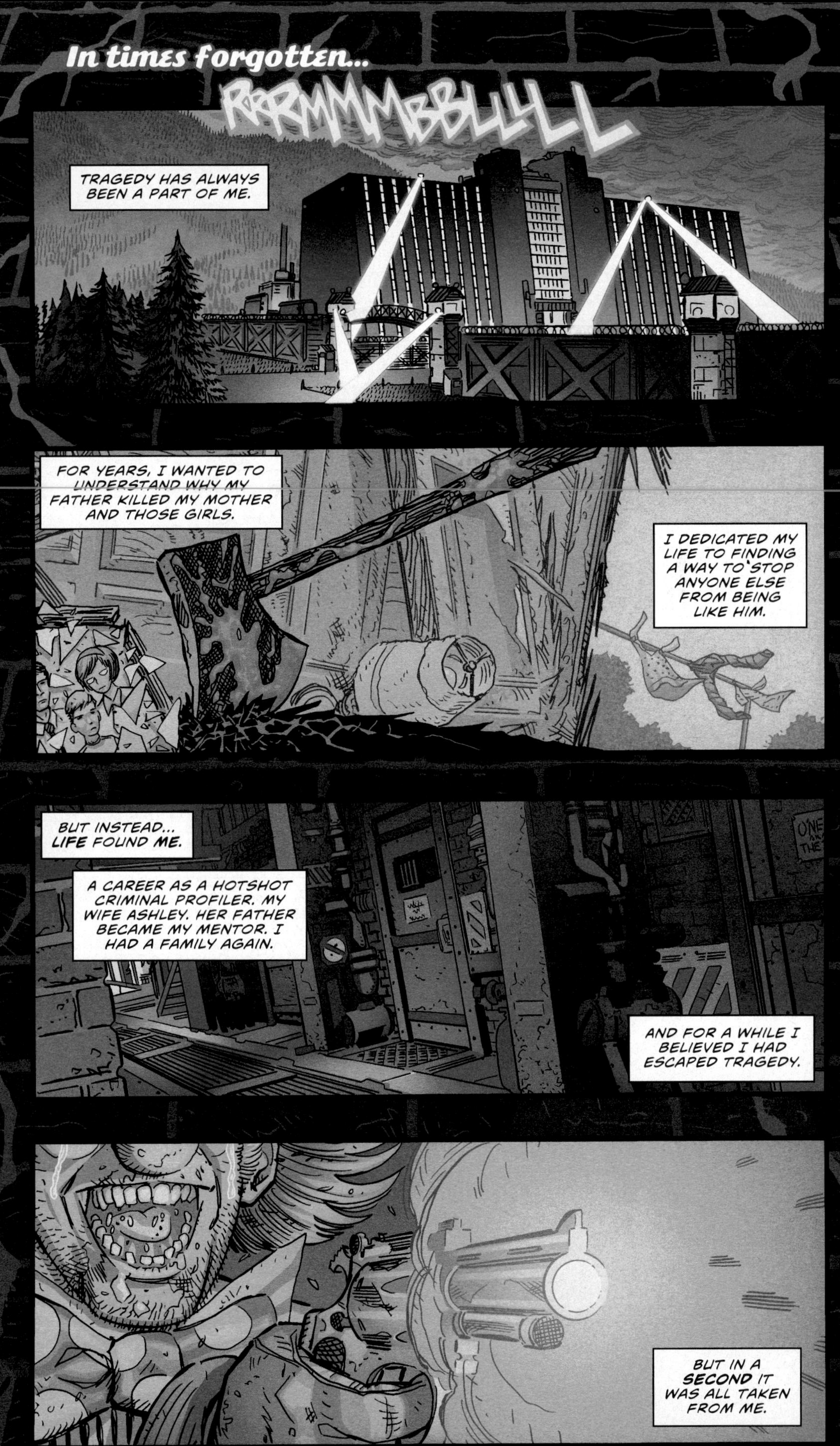
In times forgotten...
RRRRMMMMBBLLLLL
TRAGEDY HAS ALWAYS BEEN A PART OF ME.
FOR YEARS, I WANTED TO UNDERSTAND WHY MY FATHER KILLED MY MOTHER AND THOSE GIRLS.
I DEDICATED MY LIFE TO FINDING A WAY TO STOP ANYONE ELSE FROM BEING LIKE HIM.
BUT INSTEAD... **LIFE** FOUND **ME**.
A CAREER AS A HOTSHOT CRIMINAL PROFILER. MY WIFE ASHLEY. HER FATHER BECAME MY MENTOR. I HAD A FAMILY AGAIN.
AND FOR A WHILE I BELIEVED I HAD ESCAPED TRAGEDY.
BUT IN A **SECOND** IT WAS ALL TAKEN FROM ME.

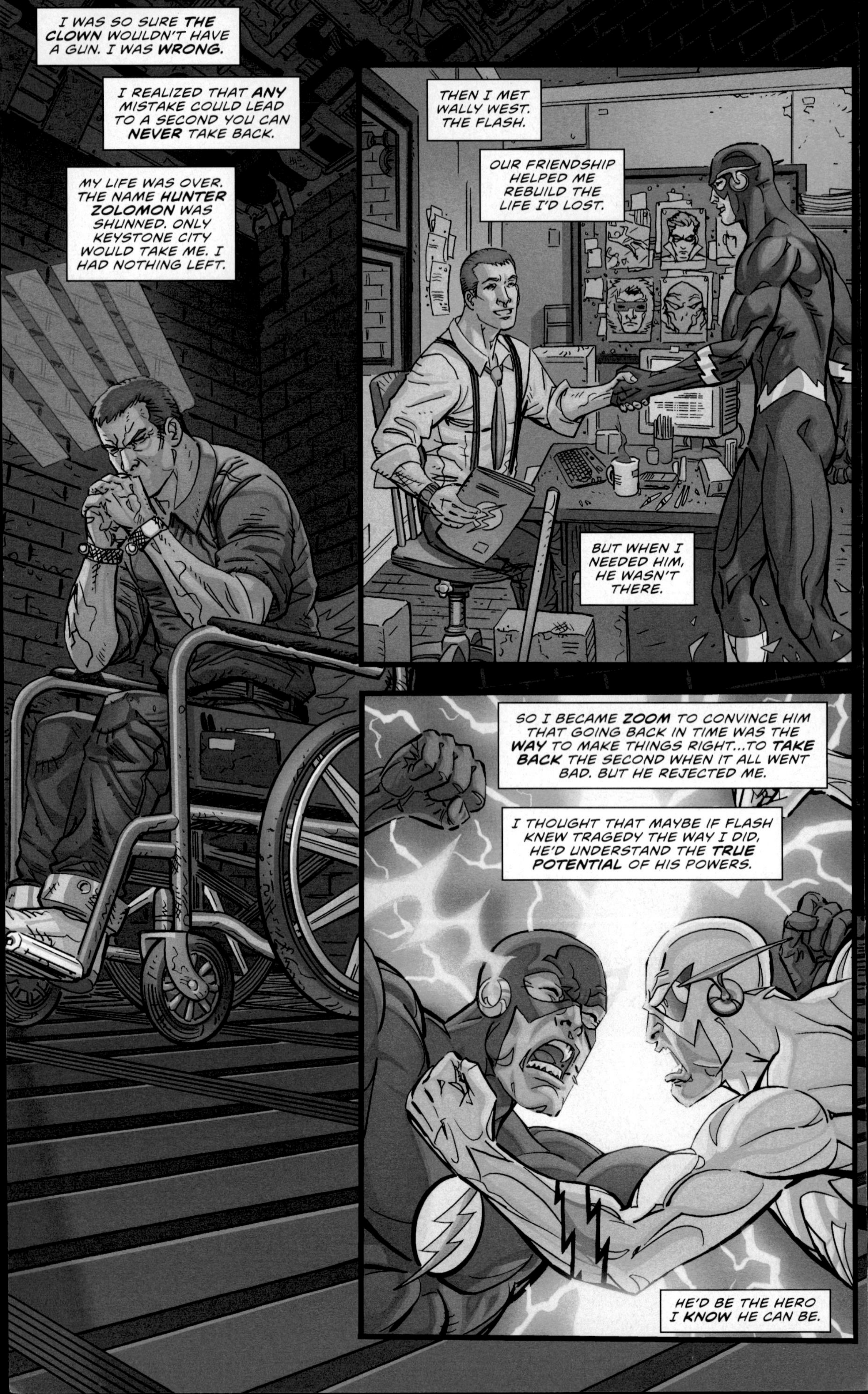
I WAS SO SURE THE CLOWN WOULDN'T HAVE A GUN. I WAS WRONG.
I REALIZED THAT ANY MISTAKE COULD LEAD TO A SECOND YOU CAN NEVER TAKE BACK.
MY LIFE WAS OVER. THE NAME HUNTER ZOLOMON WAS SHUNNED. ONLY KEYSTONE CITY WOULD TAKE ME. I HAD NOTHING LEFT.
THEN I MET WALLY WEST. THE FLASH.
OUR FRIENDSHIP HELPED ME REBUILD THE LIFE I'D LOST.
BUT WHEN I NEEDED HIM, HE WASN'T THERE.
SO I BECAME ZOOM TO CONVINCE HIM THAT GOING BACK IN TIME WAS THE WAY TO MAKE THINGS RIGHT...TO TAKE BACK THE SECOND WHEN IT ALL WENT BAD. BUT HE REJECTED ME.
I THOUGHT THAT MAYBE IF FLASH KNEW TRAGEDY THE WAY I DID, HE'D UNDERSTAND THE TRUE POTENTIAL OF HIS POWERS.
HE'D BE THE HERO I KNOW HE CAN BE.

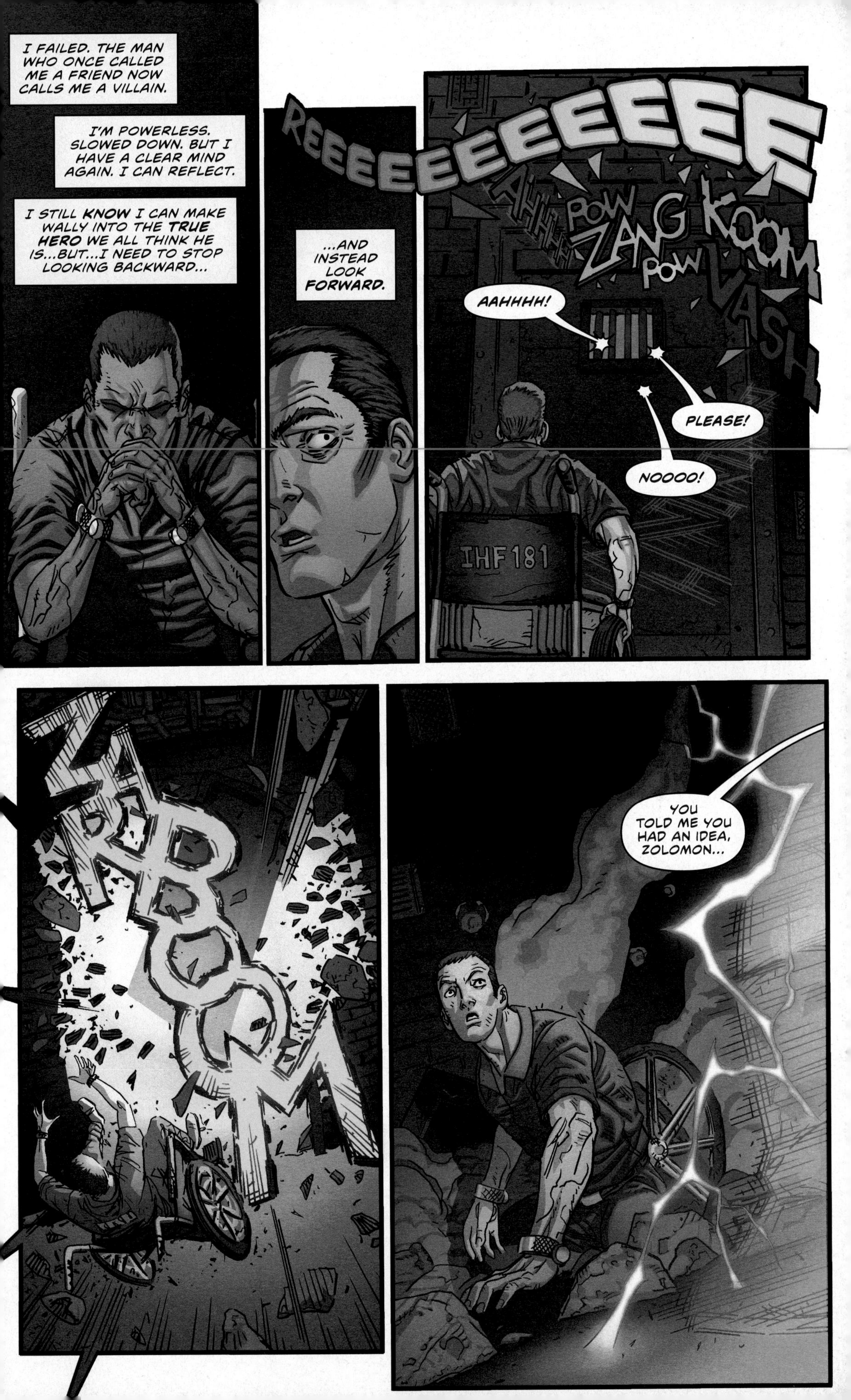
I FAILED. THE MAN WHO ONCE CALLED ME A FRIEND NOW CALLS ME A VILLAIN.
I'M POWERLESS. SLOWED DOWN. BUT I HAVE A CLEAR MIND AGAIN. I CAN REFLECT.
I STILL KNOW I CAN MAKE WALLY INTO THE TRUE HERO WE ALL THINK HE IS...BUT...I NEED TO STOP LOOKING BACKWARD...
...AND INSTEAD LOOK FORWARD.
REEEEEEEEEEEEF
AHHHH POW ZANG KOOM POW VASH!
AAHHHH!
PLEASE!
NOOOO!
IHF 181
KABOOM
YOU TOLD ME YOU HAD AN IDEA, ZOLOMON...

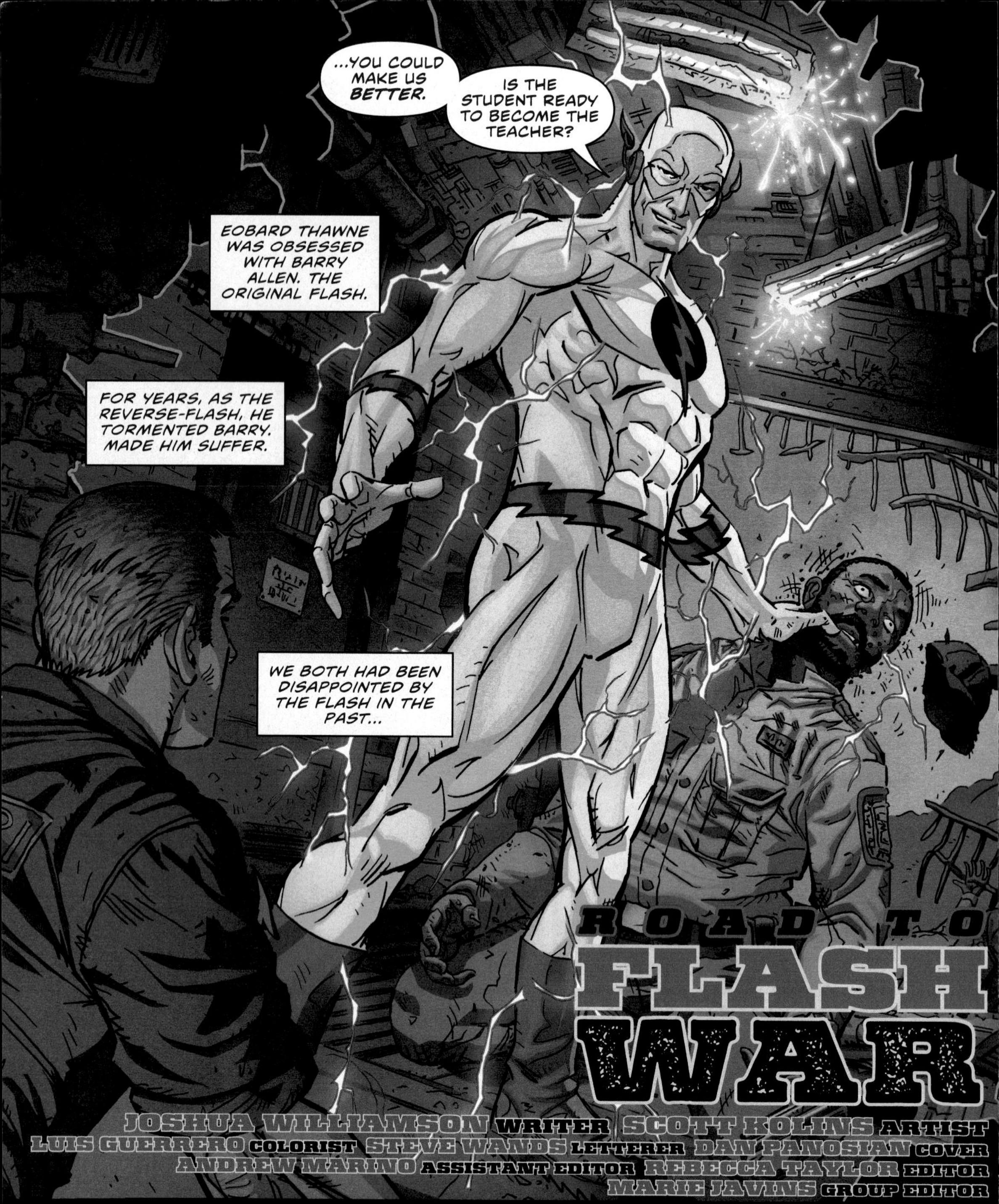

...YOU COULD MAKE US BETTER.
IS THE STUDENT READY TO BECOME THE TEACHER?
EOBARD THAWNE WAS OBSESSED WITH BARRY ALLEN. THE ORIGINAL FLASH.
FOR YEARS, AS THE REVERSE-FLASH, HE TORMENTED BARRY. MADE HIM SUFFER.
WE BOTH HAD BEEN DISAPPOINTED BY THE FLASH IN THE PAST...
ROAD TO FLASH WAR
JOSHUA WILLIAMSON WRITER SCOTT KOLINS ARTIST
LUIS GUERRERO COLORIST STEVE WANDS LETTERER DAN PANOSIAN COVER
ANDREW MARINO ASSISTANT EDITOR REBECCA TAYLOR EDITOR
MARIE JAVINS GROUP EDITOR

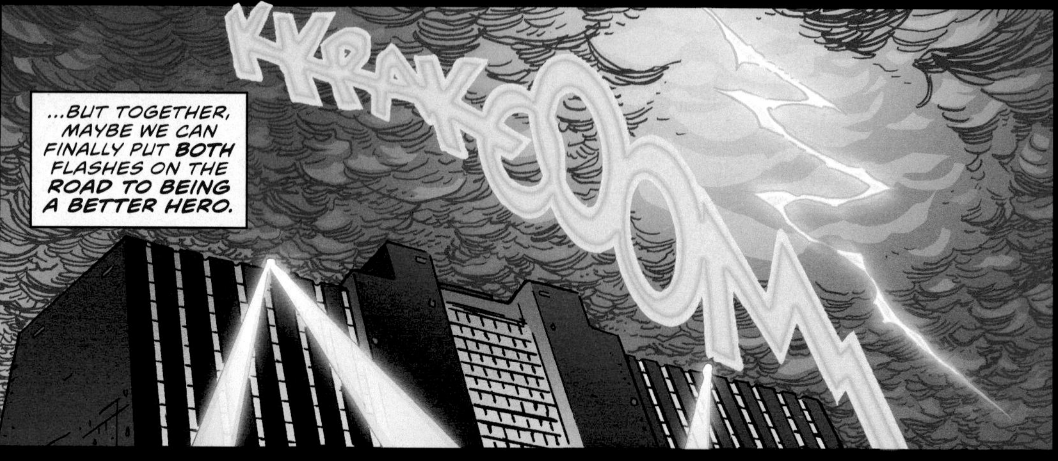

KKRAKKOOOOM
...BUT TOGETHER, MAYBE WE CAN FINALLY PUT BOTH FLASHES ON THE ROAD TO BEING A BETTER HERO.

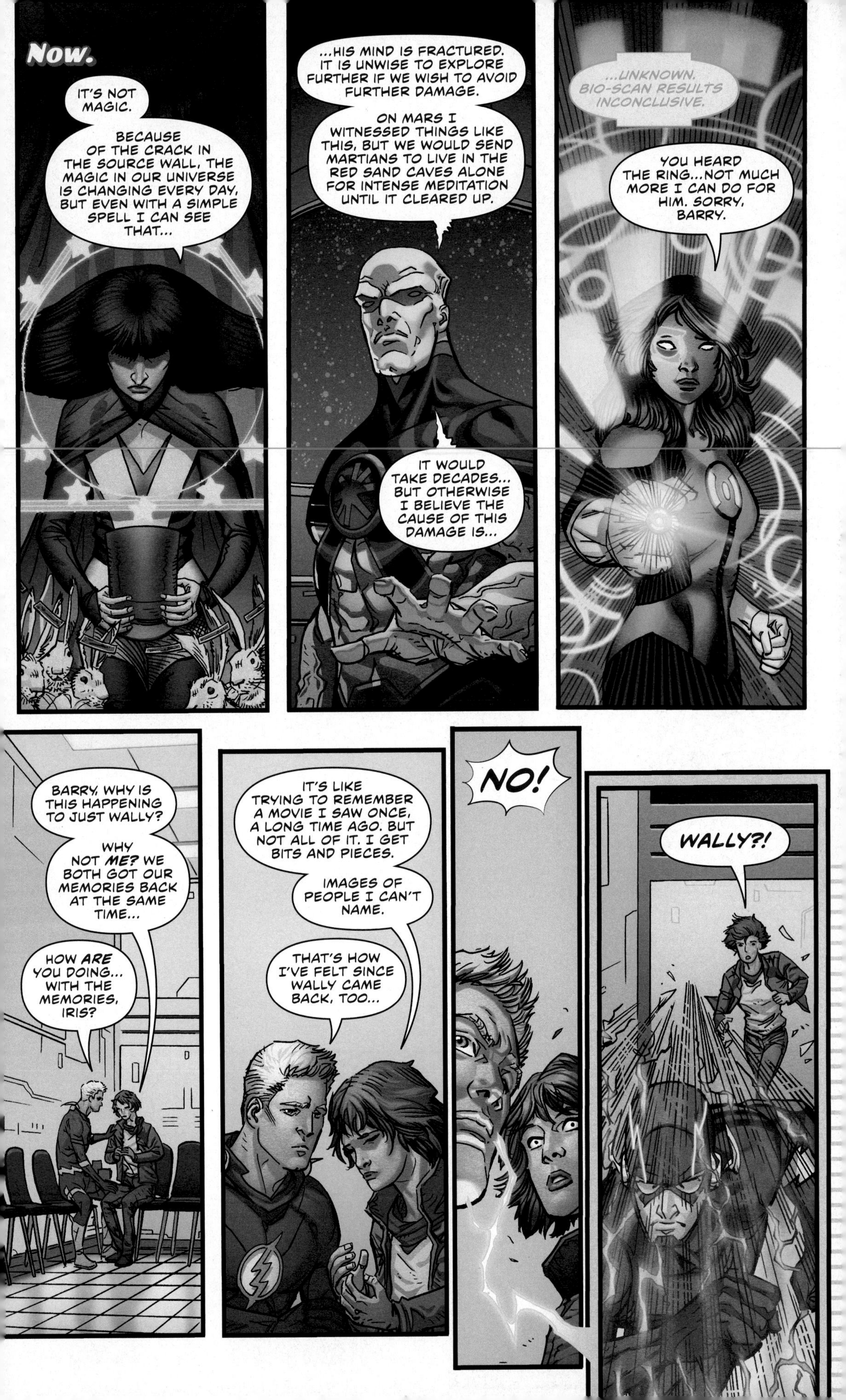
Now.
IT'S NOT MAGIC.
BECAUSE OF THE CRACK IN THE SOURCE WALL, THE MAGIC IN OUR UNIVERSE IS CHANGING EVERY DAY, BUT EVEN WITH A SIMPLE SPELL I CAN SEE THAT...
...HIS MIND IS FRACTURED. IT IS UNWISE TO EXPLORE FURTHER IF WE WISH TO AVOID FURTHER DAMAGE.
ON MARS I WITNESSED THINGS LIKE THIS, BUT WE WOULD SEND MARTIANS TO LIVE IN THE RED SAND CAVES ALONE FOR INTENSE MEDITATION UNTIL IT CLEARED UP.
IT WOULD TAKE DECADES... BUT OTHERWISE I BELIEVE THE CAUSE OF THIS DAMAGE IS...
...UNKNOWN. BIO-SCAN RESULTS INCONCLUSIVE.
YOU HEARD THE RING...NOT MUCH MORE I CAN DO FOR HIM. SORRY, BARRY.
BARRY, WHY IS THIS HAPPENING TO JUST WALLY?
WHY NOT ME? WE BOTH GOT OUR MEMORIES BACK AT THE SAME TIME...
HOW ARE YOU DOING... WITH THE MEMORIES, IRIS?
IT'S LIKE TRYING TO REMEMBER A MOVIE I SAW ONCE, A LONG TIME AGO. BUT NOT ALL OF IT. I GET BITS AND PIECES.
IMAGES OF PEOPLE I CAN'T NAME.
THAT'S HOW I'VE FELT SINCE WALLY CAME BACK, TOO...
NO!
WALLY?!

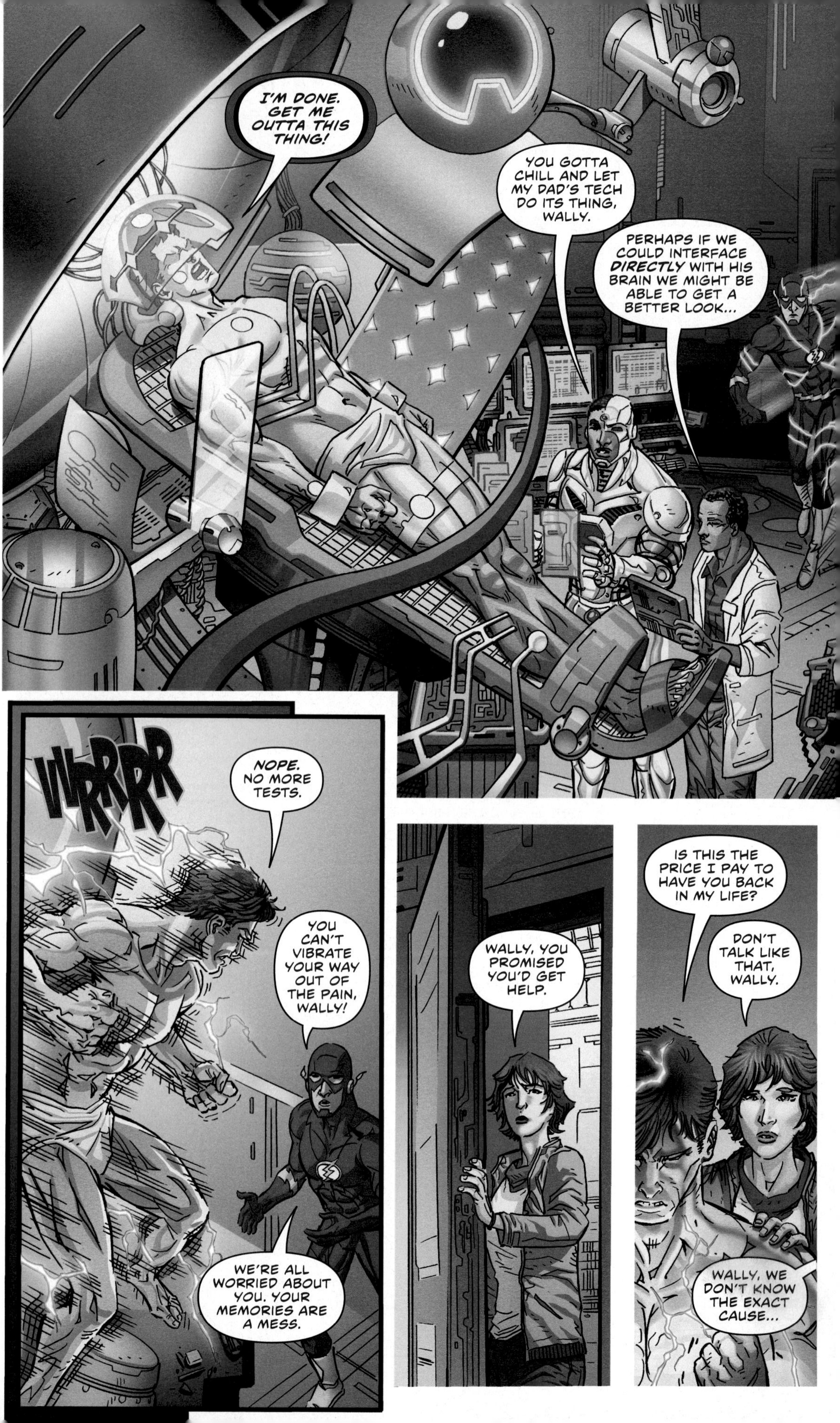
I'M DONE. GET ME OUTTA THIS THING!
YOU GOTTA CHILL AND LET MY DAD'S TECH DO ITS THING, WALLY.
PERHAPS IF WE COULD INTERFACE DIRECTLY WITH HIS BRAIN WE MIGHT BE ABLE TO GET A BETTER LOOK...
VVRRRR
NOPE. NO MORE TESTS.
YOU CAN'T VIBRATE YOUR WAY OUT OF THE PAIN, WALLY!
WE'RE ALL WORRIED ABOUT YOU. YOUR MEMORIES ARE A MESS.
WALLY, YOU PROMISED YOU'D GET HELP.
IS THIS THE PRICE I PAY TO HAVE YOU BACK IN MY LIFE?
DON'T TALK LIKE THAT, WALLY.
WALLY, WE DON'T KNOW THE EXACT CAUSE...

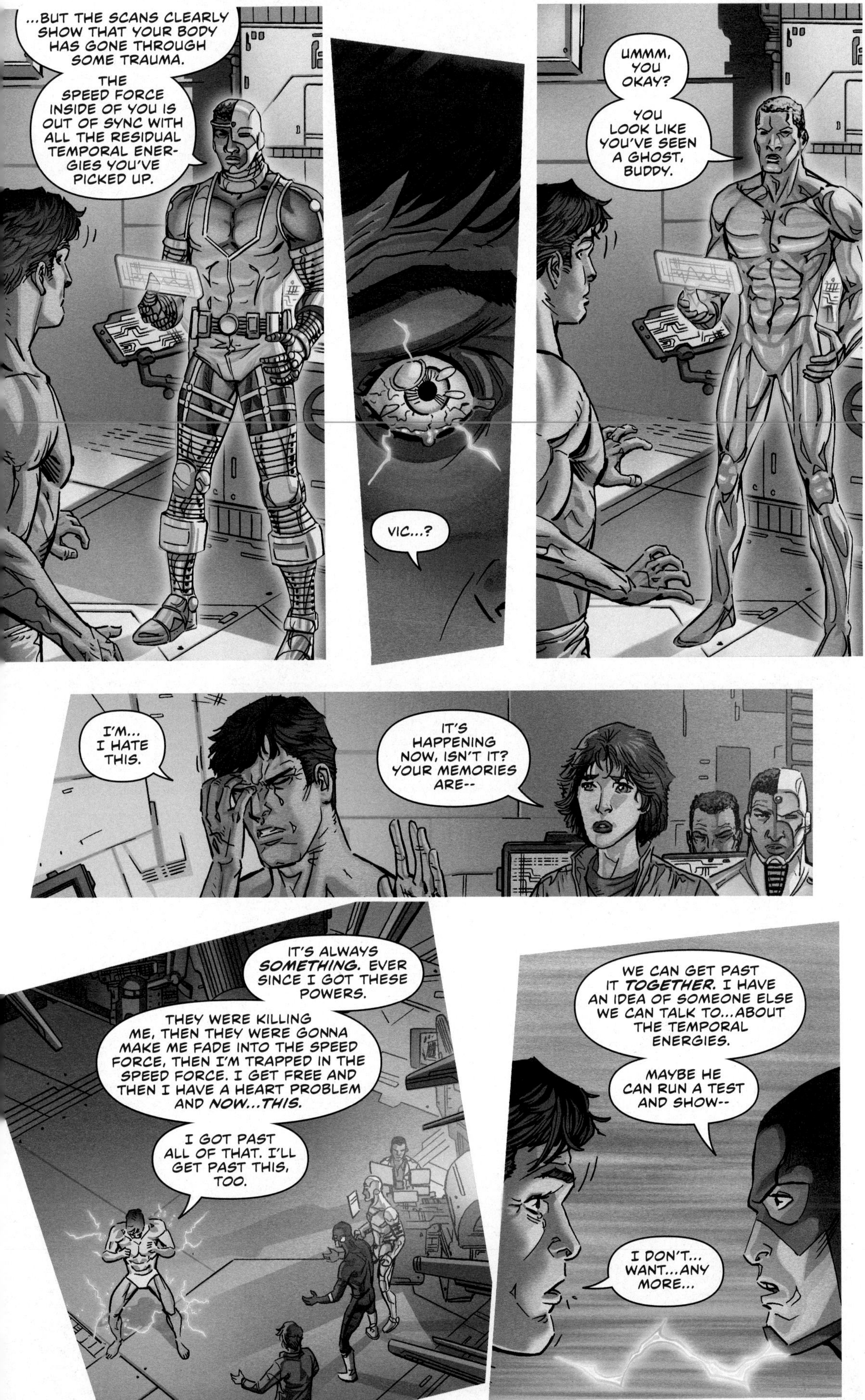
...BUT THE SCANS CLEARLY SHOW THAT YOUR BODY HAS GONE THROUGH SOME TRAUMA.
THE SPEED FORCE INSIDE OF YOU IS OUT OF SYNC WITH ALL THE RESIDUAL TEMPORAL ENERGIES YOU'VE PICKED UP.
VIC...?
UMMM, YOU OKAY?
YOU LOOK LIKE YOU'VE SEEN A GHOST, BUDDY.
I'M... I HATE THIS.
IT'S HAPPENING NOW, ISN'T IT? YOUR MEMORIES ARE--
IT'S ALWAYS *SOMETHING.* EVER SINCE I GOT THESE POWERS.
THEY WERE KILLING ME, THEN THEY WERE GONNA MAKE ME FADE INTO THE SPEED FORCE, THEN I'M TRAPPED IN THE SPEED FORCE. I GET FREE AND THEN I HAVE A HEART PROBLEM AND *NOW...THIS.*
I GOT PAST ALL OF THAT. I'LL GET PAST THIS, TOO.
WE CAN GET PAST IT *TOGETHER.* I HAVE AN IDEA OF SOMEONE ELSE WE CAN TALK TO...ABOUT THE TEMPORAL ENERGIES.
MAYBE HE CAN RUN A TEST AND SHOW--
I DON'T... WANT...ANY MORE...

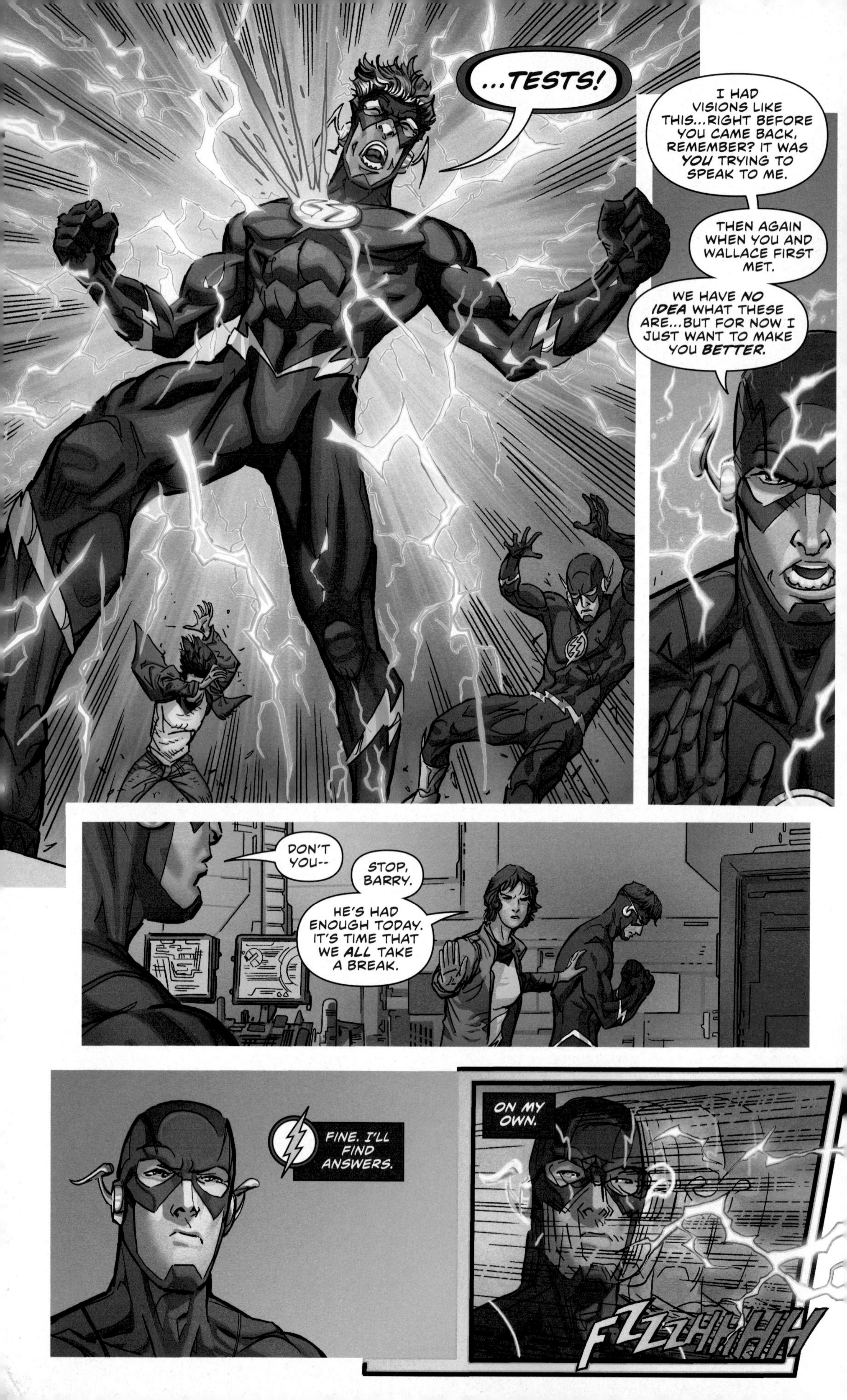
...TESTS!
I HAD VISIONS LIKE THIS...RIGHT BEFORE YOU CAME BACK, REMEMBER? IT WAS YOU TRYING TO SPEAK TO ME.
THEN AGAIN WHEN YOU AND WALLACE FIRST MET.
WE HAVE NO IDEA WHAT THESE ARE...BUT FOR NOW I JUST WANT TO MAKE YOU BETTER.
DON'T YOU--
STOP, BARRY.
HE'S HAD ENOUGH TODAY. IT'S TIME THAT WE ALL TAKE A BREAK.
FINE. I'LL FIND ANSWERS.
ON MY OWN.
FZZZHHHHH

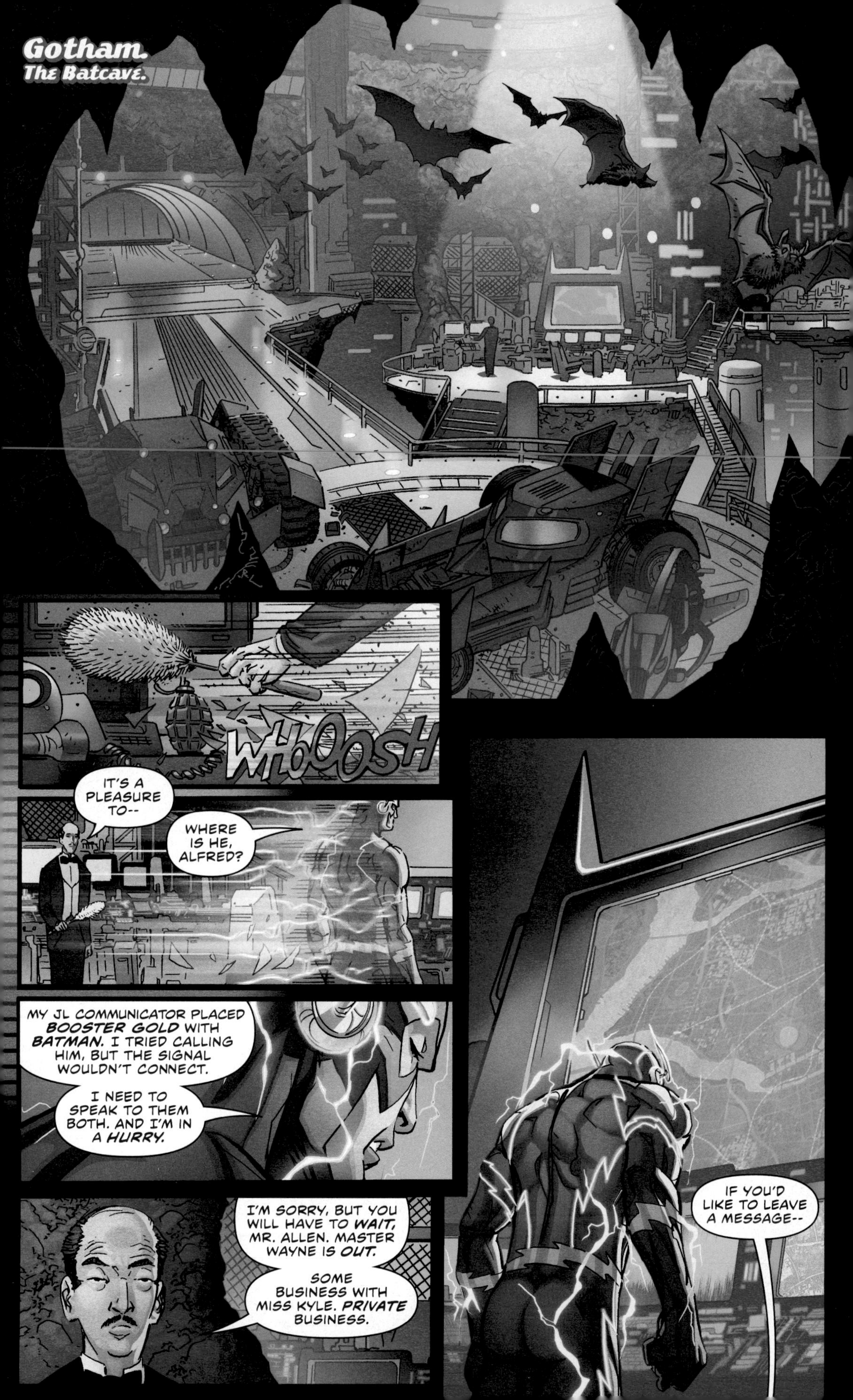
Gotham.
The Batcave.
WHOOSH
IT'S A PLEASURE TO--
WHERE IS HE, ALFRED?
MY JL COMMUNICATOR PLACED BOOSTER GOLD WITH BATMAN. I TRIED CALLING HIM, BUT THE SIGNAL WOULDN'T CONNECT.
I NEED TO SPEAK TO THEM BOTH. AND I'M IN A HURRY.
I'M SORRY, BUT YOU WILL HAVE TO WAIT, MR. ALLEN. MASTER WAYNE IS OUT.
SOME BUSINESS WITH MISS KYLE. PRIVATE BUSINESS.
IF YOU'D LIKE TO LEAVE A MESSAGE--

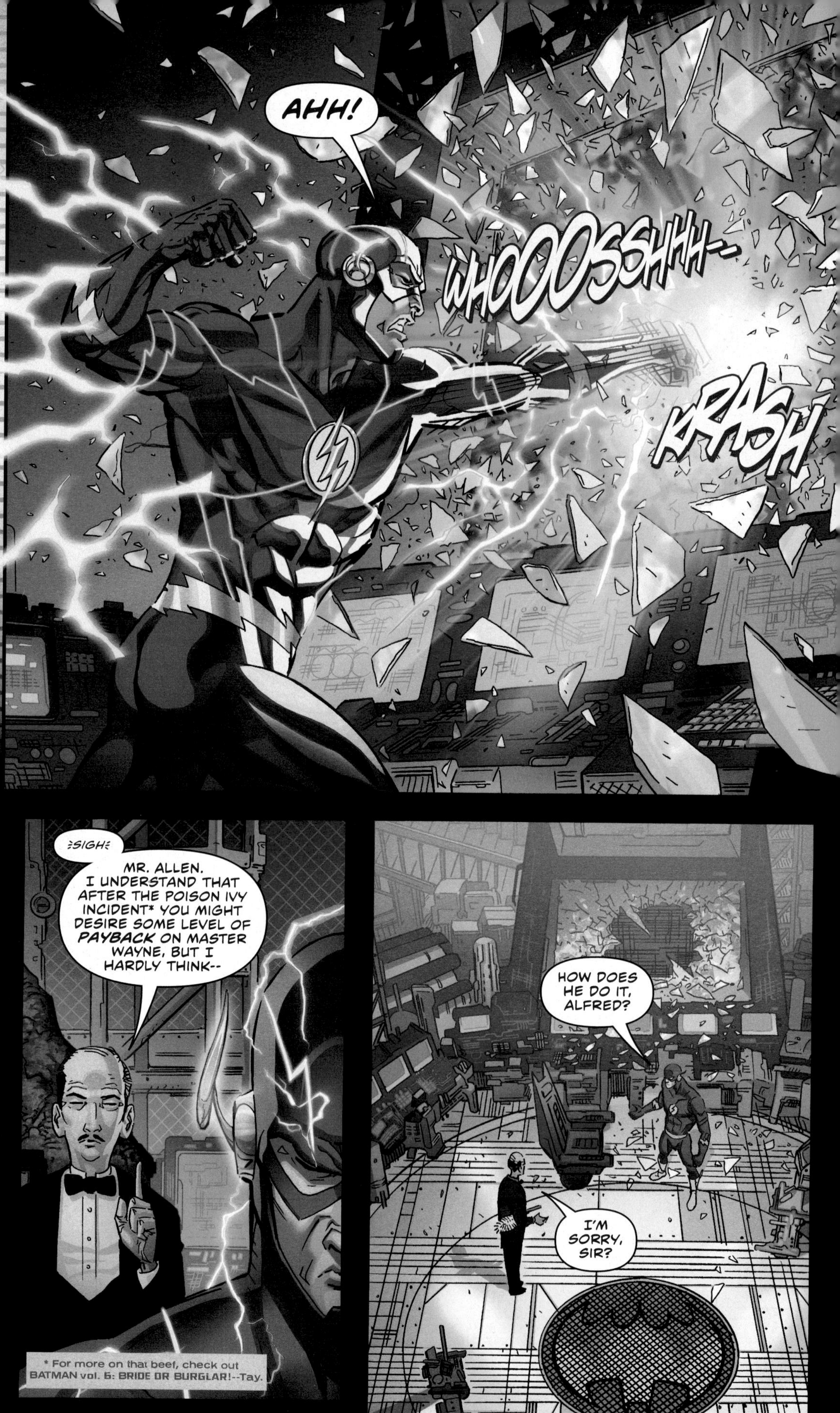
AHH!
WHOOOOSSHHH--
KRASH
SIGH
MR. ALLEN. I UNDERSTAND THAT AFTER THE POISON IVY INCIDENT* YOU MIGHT DESIRE SOME LEVEL OF PAYBACK ON MASTER WAYNE, BUT I HARDLY THINK--
* For more on that beef, check out BATMAN vol. 6: BRIDE OR BURGLAR!--Tay.
HOW DOES HE DO IT, ALFRED?
I'M SORRY, SIR?

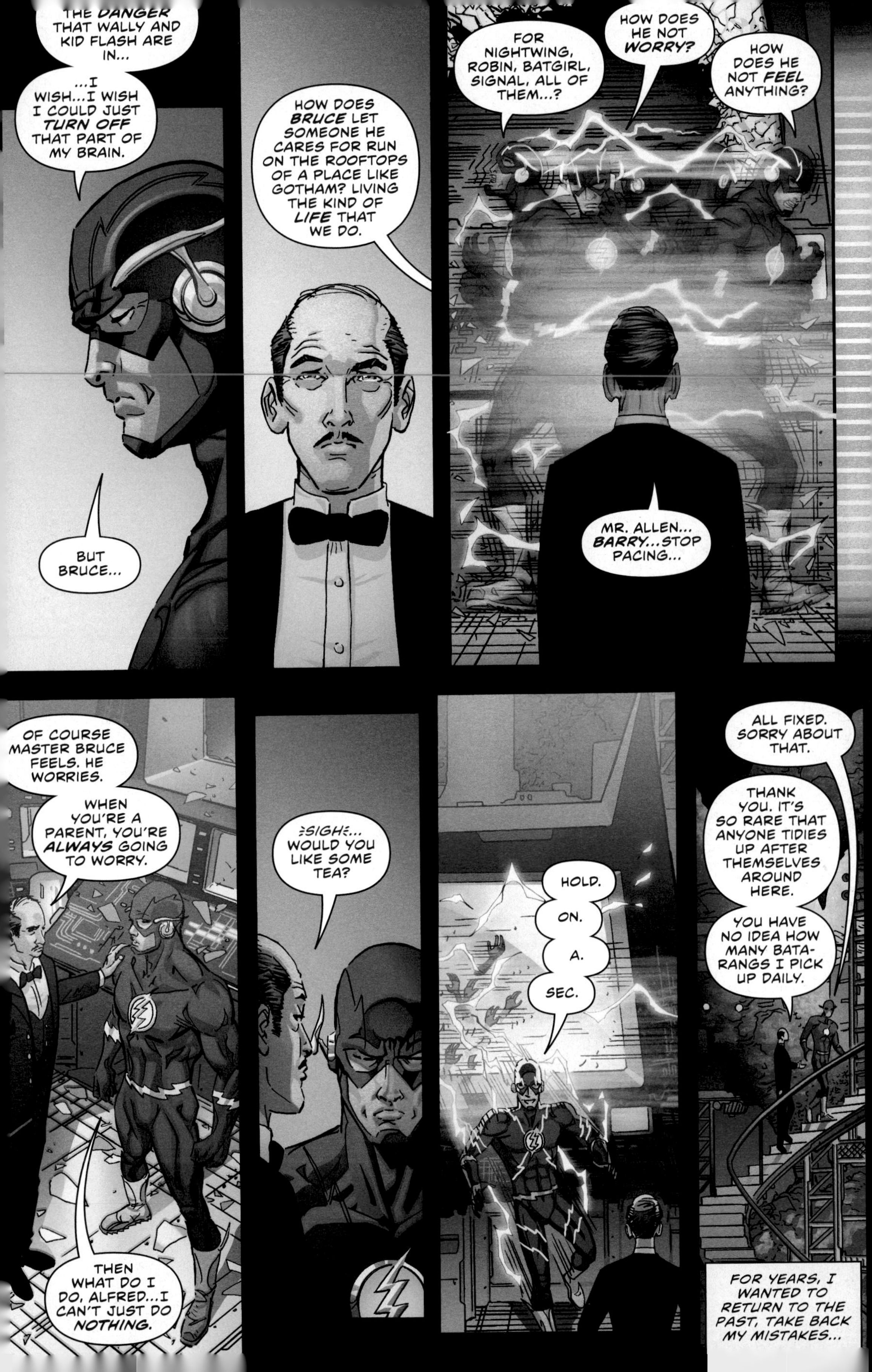
THE DANGER THAT WALLY AND KID FLASH ARE IN...
...I WISH...I WISH I COULD JUST TURN OFF THAT PART OF MY BRAIN.
BUT BRUCE...
HOW DOES BRUCE LET SOMEONE HE CARES FOR RUN ON THE ROOFTOPS OF A PLACE LIKE GOTHAM? LIVING THE KIND OF LIFE THAT WE DO.
FOR NIGHTWING, ROBIN, BATGIRL, SIGNAL, ALL OF THEM...?
HOW DOES HE NOT WORRY?
HOW DOES HE NOT FEEL ANYTHING?
MR. ALLEN... BARRY...STOP PACING...
OF COURSE MASTER BRUCE FEELS. HE WORRIES.
WHEN YOU'RE A PARENT, YOU'RE ALWAYS GOING TO WORRY.
THEN WHAT DO I DO, ALFRED...I CAN'T JUST DO NOTHING.
SIGH... WOULD YOU LIKE SOME TEA?
HOLD.
ON.
A.
SEC.
ALL FIXED. SORRY ABOUT THAT.
THANK YOU. IT'S SO RARE THAT ANYONE TIDIES UP AFTER THEMSELVES AROUND HERE.
YOU HAVE NO IDEA HOW MANY BATA-RANGS I PICK UP DAILY.
FOR YEARS, I WANTED TO RETURN TO THE PAST, TAKE BACK MY MISTAKES...

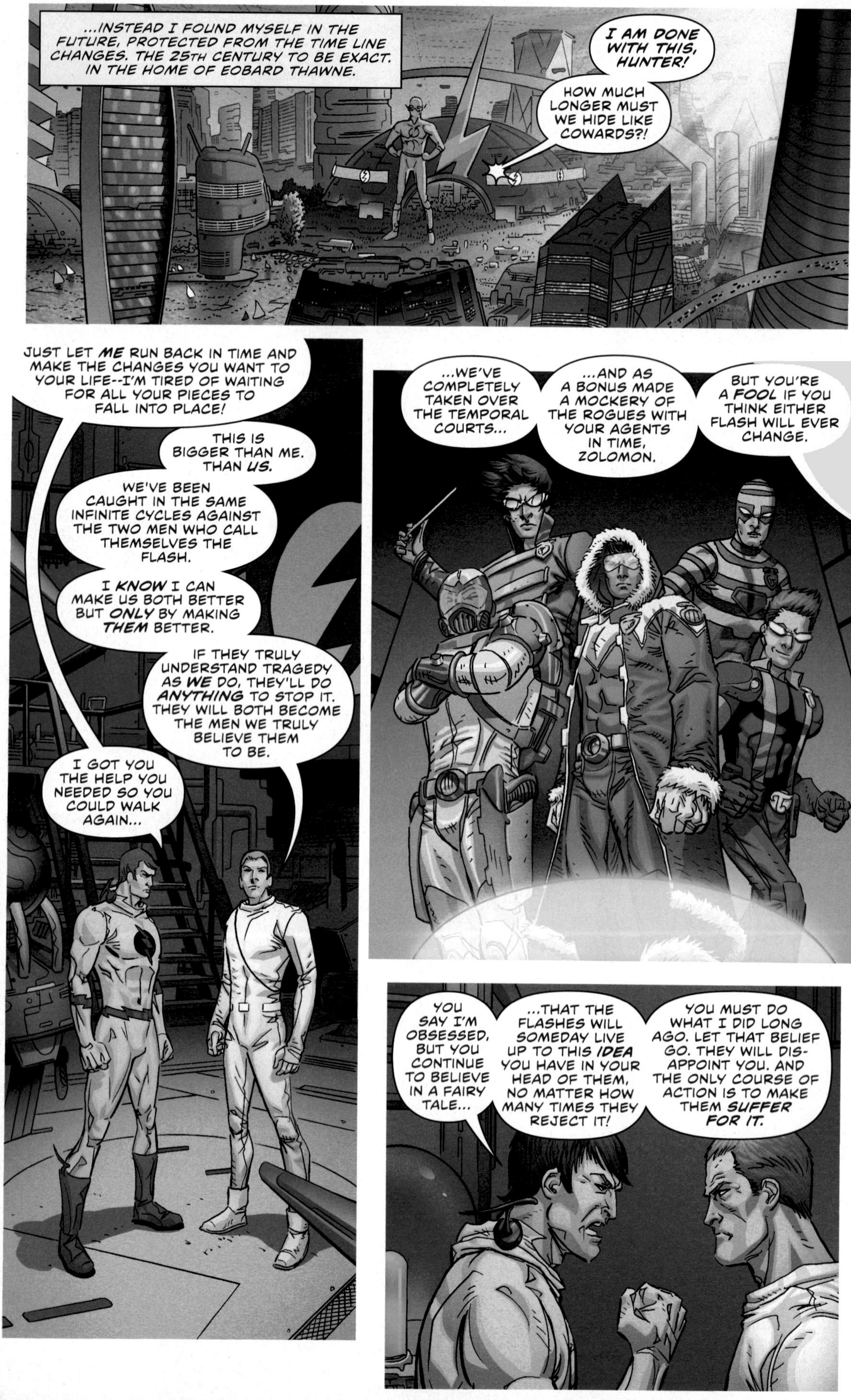

...INSTEAD I FOUND MYSELF IN THE FUTURE, PROTECTED FROM THE TIME LINE CHANGES. THE 25TH CENTURY TO BE EXACT. IN THE HOME OF EOBARD THAWNE.
I AM DONE WITH THIS, HUNTER!
HOW MUCH LONGER MUST WE HIDE LIKE COWARDS?!
JUST LET ME RUN BACK IN TIME AND MAKE THE CHANGES YOU WANT TO YOUR LIFE--I'M TIRED OF WAITING FOR ALL YOUR PIECES TO FALL INTO PLACE!
THIS IS BIGGER THAN ME. THAN US.
WE'VE BEEN CAUGHT IN THE SAME INFINITE CYCLES AGAINST THE TWO MEN WHO CALL THEMSELVES THE FLASH.
I KNOW I CAN MAKE US BOTH BETTER BUT ONLY BY MAKING THEM BETTER.
IF THEY TRULY UNDERSTAND TRAGEDY AS WE DO, THEY'LL DO ANYTHING TO STOP IT. THEY WILL BOTH BECOME THE MEN WE TRULY BELIEVE THEM TO BE.
I GOT YOU THE HELP YOU NEEDED SO YOU COULD WALK AGAIN...
...WE'VE COMPLETELY TAKEN OVER THE TEMPORAL COURTS...
...AND AS A BONUS MADE A MOCKERY OF THE ROGUES WITH YOUR AGENTS IN TIME, ZOLOMON.
BUT YOU'RE A FOOL IF YOU THINK EITHER FLASH WILL EVER CHANGE.
YOU SAY I'M OBSESSED, BUT YOU CONTINUE TO BELIEVE IN A FAIRY TALE...
...THAT THE FLASHES WILL SOMEDAY LIVE UP TO THIS IDEA YOU HAVE IN YOUR HEAD OF THEM, NO MATTER HOW MANY TIMES THEY REJECT IT!
YOU MUST DO WHAT I DID LONG AGO. LET THAT BELIEF GO. THEY WILL DISAPPOINT YOU. AND THE ONLY COURSE OF ACTION IS TO MAKE THEM SUFFER FOR IT.

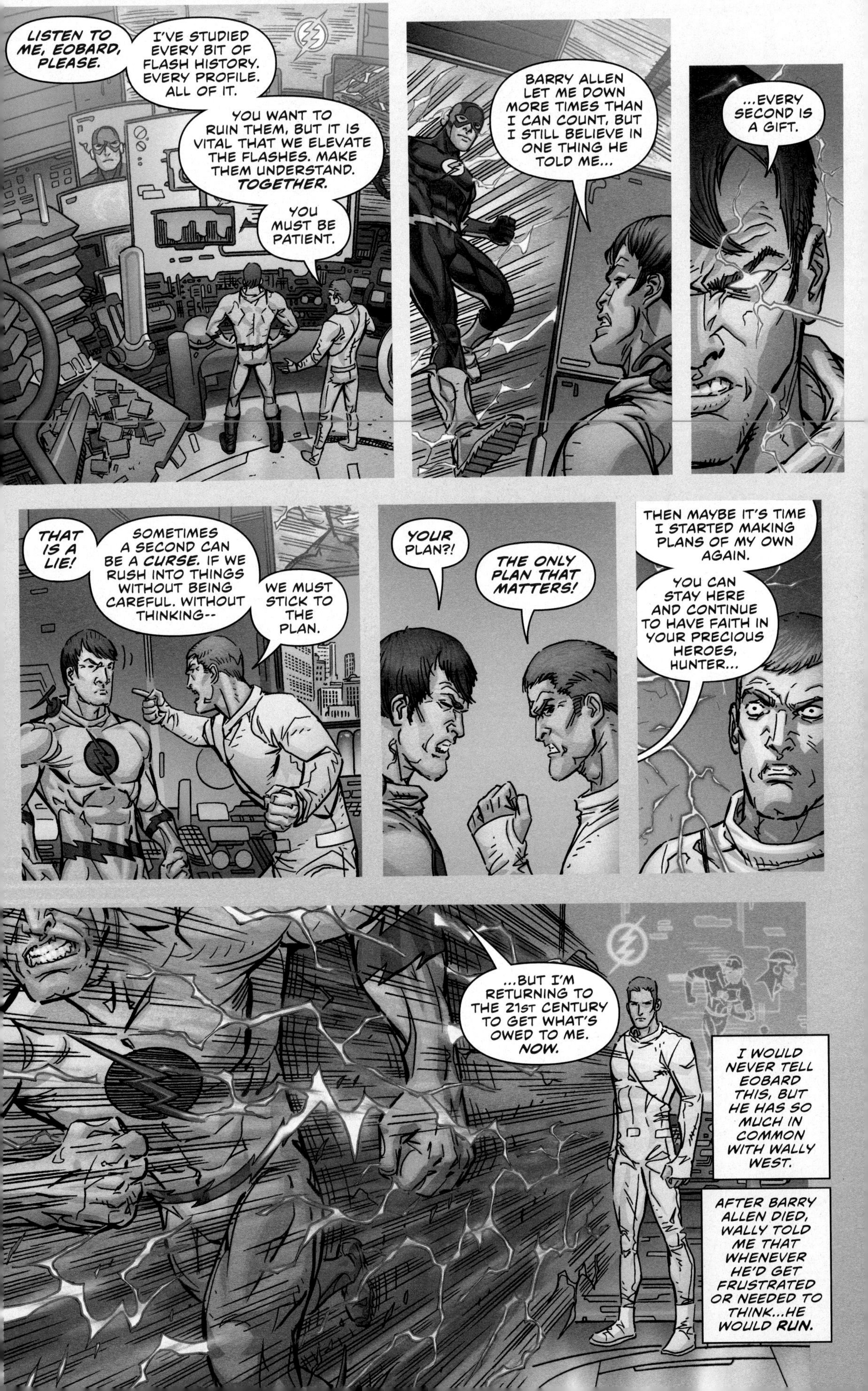
LISTEN TO ME, EOBARD, PLEASE.
I'VE STUDIED EVERY BIT OF FLASH HISTORY. EVERY PROFILE. ALL OF IT.
YOU WANT TO RUIN THEM, BUT IT IS VITAL THAT WE ELEVATE THE FLASHES. MAKE THEM UNDERSTAND. TOGETHER.
YOU MUST BE PATIENT.
BARRY ALLEN LET ME DOWN MORE TIMES THAN I CAN COUNT, BUT I STILL BELIEVE IN ONE THING HE TOLD ME...
...EVERY SECOND IS A GIFT.
THAT IS A LIE!
SOMETIMES A SECOND CAN BE A CURSE. IF WE RUSH INTO THINGS WITHOUT BEING CAREFUL. WITHOUT THINKING--
WE MUST STICK TO THE PLAN.
YOUR PLAN?!
THE ONLY PLAN THAT MATTERS!
THEN MAYBE IT'S TIME I STARTED MAKING PLANS OF MY OWN AGAIN.
YOU CAN STAY HERE AND CONTINUE TO HAVE FAITH IN YOUR PRECIOUS HEROES, HUNTER...
...BUT I'M RETURNING TO THE 21ST CENTURY TO GET WHAT'S OWED TO ME. NOW.
I WOULD NEVER TELL EOBARD THIS, BUT HE HAS SO MUCH IN COMMON WITH WALLY WEST.
AFTER BARRY ALLEN DIED, WALLY TOLD ME THAT WHENEVER HE'D GET FRUSTRATED OR NEEDED TO THINK...HE WOULD RUN.

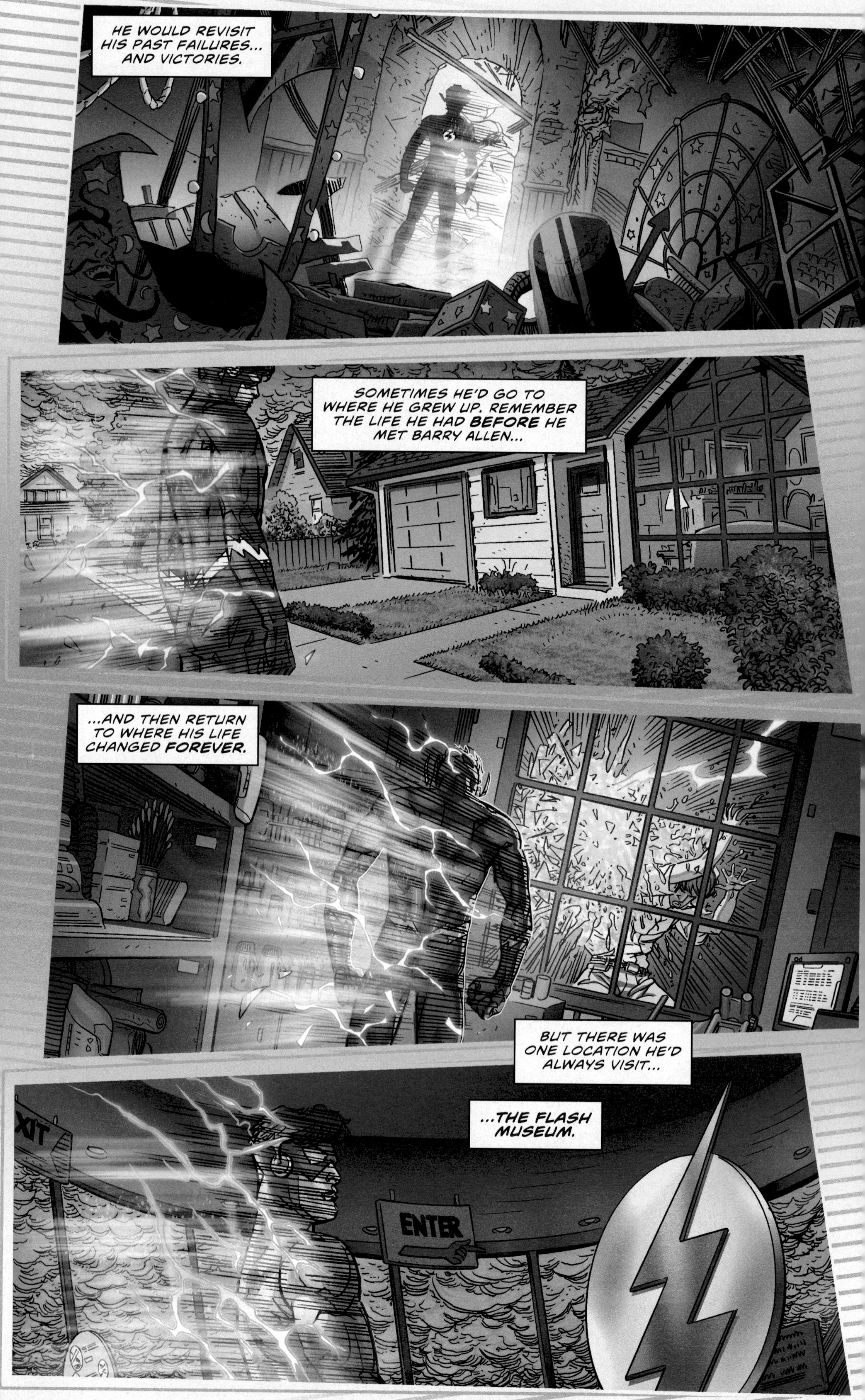
HE WOULD REVISIT HIS PAST FAILURES... AND VICTORIES.
SOMETIMES HE'D GO TO WHERE HE GREW UP. REMEMBER THE LIFE HE HAD BEFORE HE MET BARRY ALLEN...
...AND THEN RETURN TO WHERE HIS LIFE CHANGED FOREVER.
BUT THERE WAS ONE LOCATION HE'D ALWAYS VISIT...
...THE FLASH MUSEUM.
XIT
ENTER

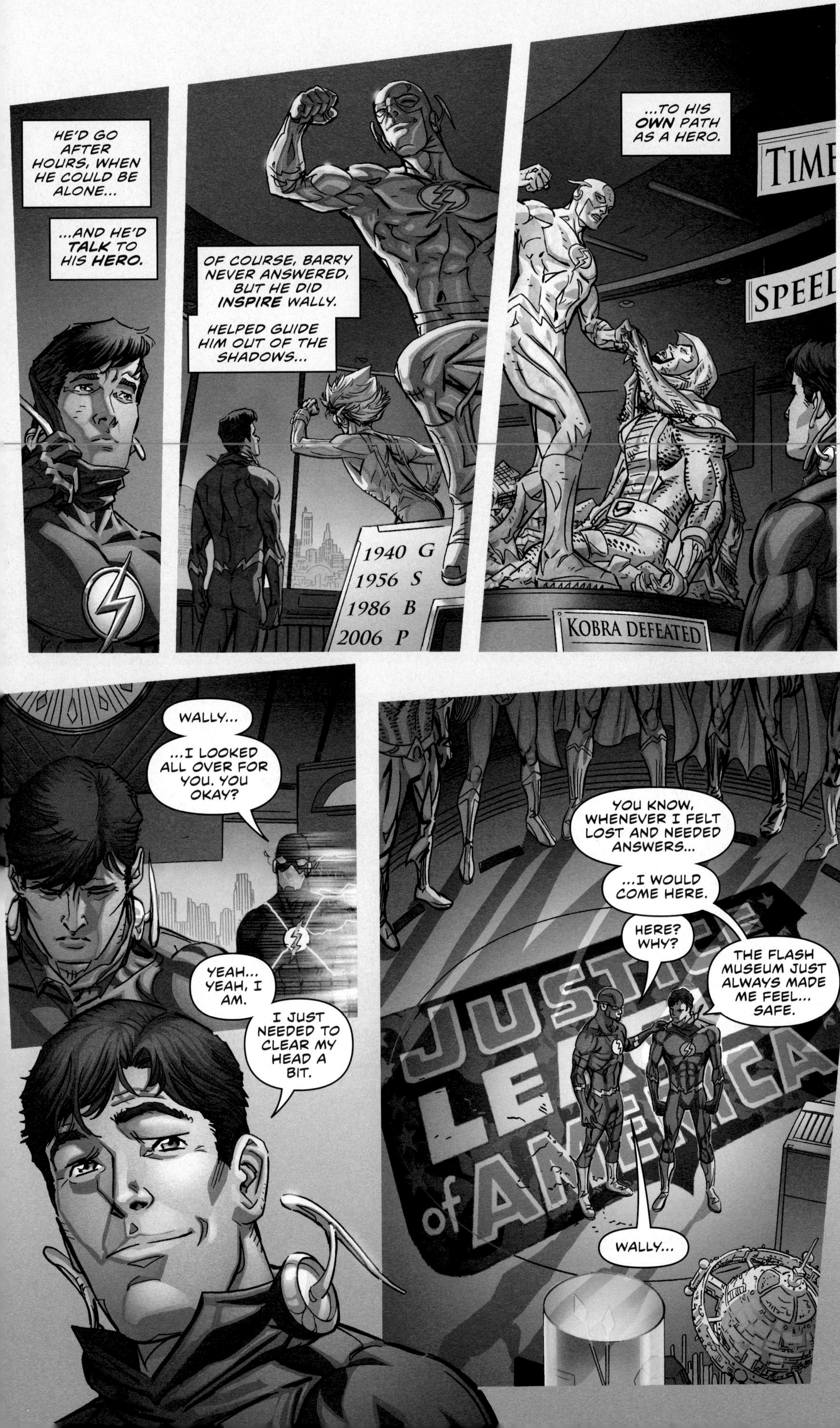
HE'D GO AFTER HOURS, WHEN HE COULD BE ALONE...
...AND HE'D TALK TO HIS HERO.
OF COURSE, BARRY NEVER ANSWERED, BUT HE DID INSPIRE WALLY.
HELPED GUIDE HIM OUT OF THE SHADOWS...
1940 G
1956 S
1986 B
2006 P
...TO HIS OWN PATH AS A HERO.
TIME
SPEED
KOBRA DEFEATED
WALLY...
...I LOOKED ALL OVER FOR YOU. YOU OKAY?
YEAH... YEAH, I AM.
I JUST NEEDED TO CLEAR MY HEAD A BIT.
YOU KNOW, WHENEVER I FELT LOST AND NEEDED ANSWERS...
...I WOULD COME HERE.
HERE? WHY?
THE FLASH MUSEUM JUST ALWAYS MADE ME FEEL... SAFE.
WALLY...

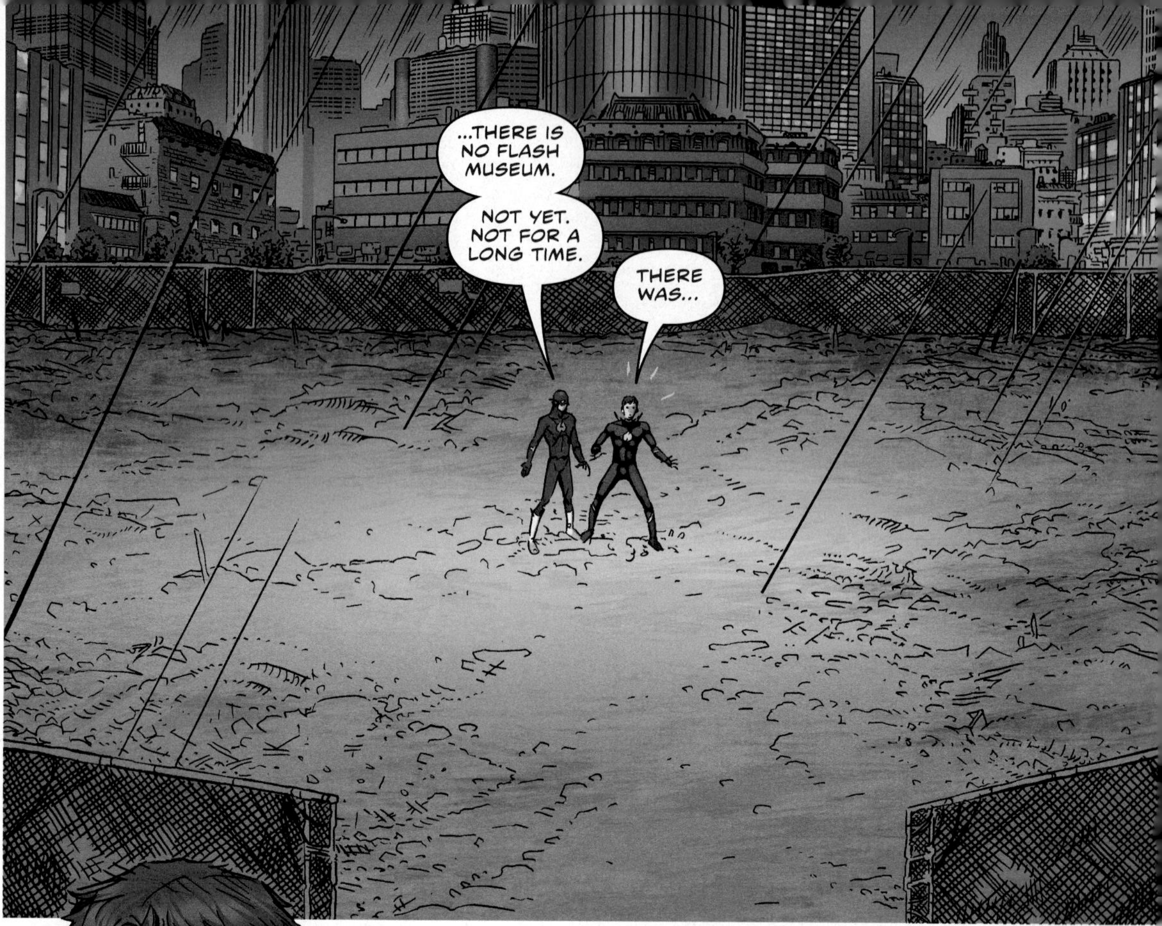
...THERE IS NO FLASH MUSEUM.
NOT YET. NOT FOR A LONG TIME.
THERE WAS...

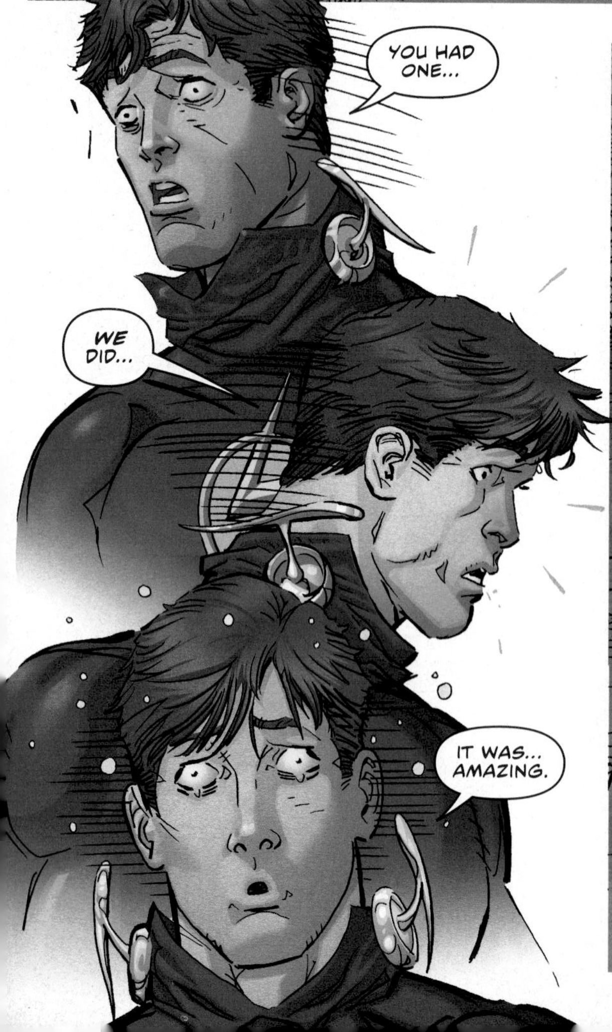
YOU HAD ONE...
WE DID...
IT WAS... AMAZING.

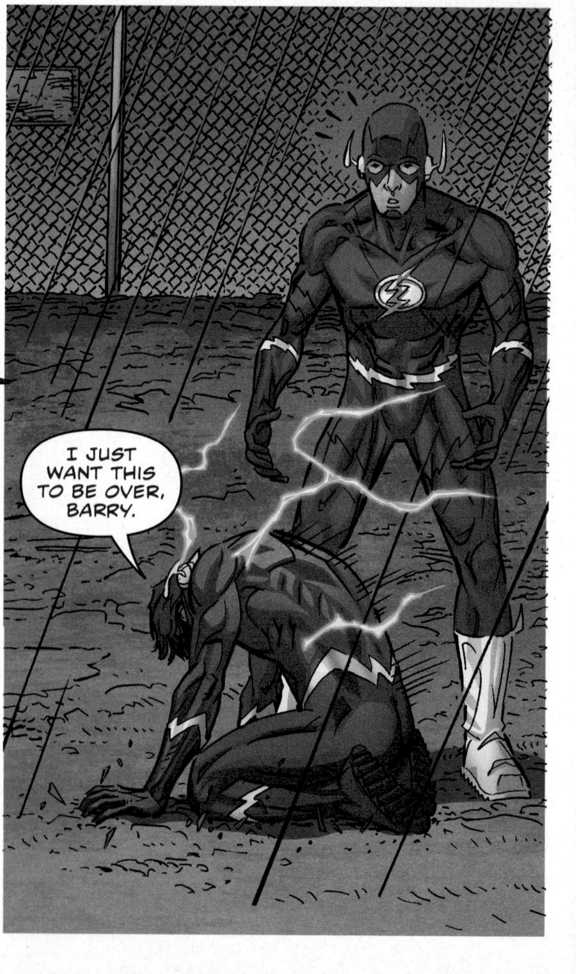
I JUST WANT THIS TO BE OVER, BARRY.

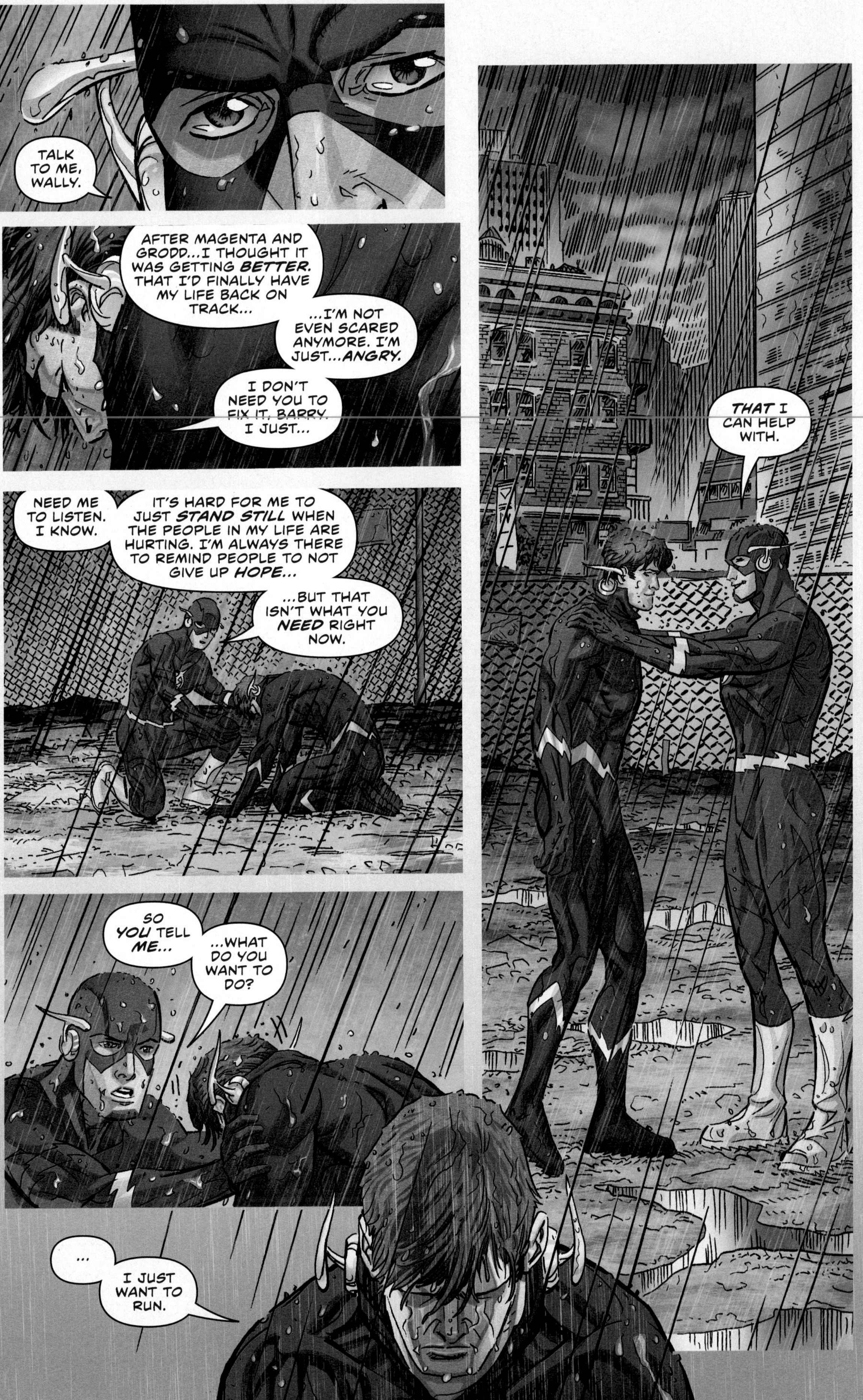
TALK TO ME, WALLY.
AFTER MAGENTA AND GRODD...I THOUGHT IT WAS GETTING BETTER. THAT I'D FINALLY HAVE MY LIFE BACK ON TRACK...
...I'M NOT EVEN SCARED ANYMORE. I'M JUST...ANGRY.
I DON'T NEED YOU TO FIX IT, BARRY. I JUST...
NEED ME TO LISTEN. I KNOW.
IT'S HARD FOR ME TO JUST STAND STILL WHEN THE PEOPLE IN MY LIFE ARE HURTING. I'M ALWAYS THERE TO REMIND PEOPLE TO NOT GIVE UP HOPE...
...BUT THAT ISN'T WHAT YOU NEED RIGHT NOW.
SO YOU TELL ME...
...WHAT DO YOU WANT TO DO?
...
I JUST WANT TO RUN.
THAT I CAN HELP WITH.

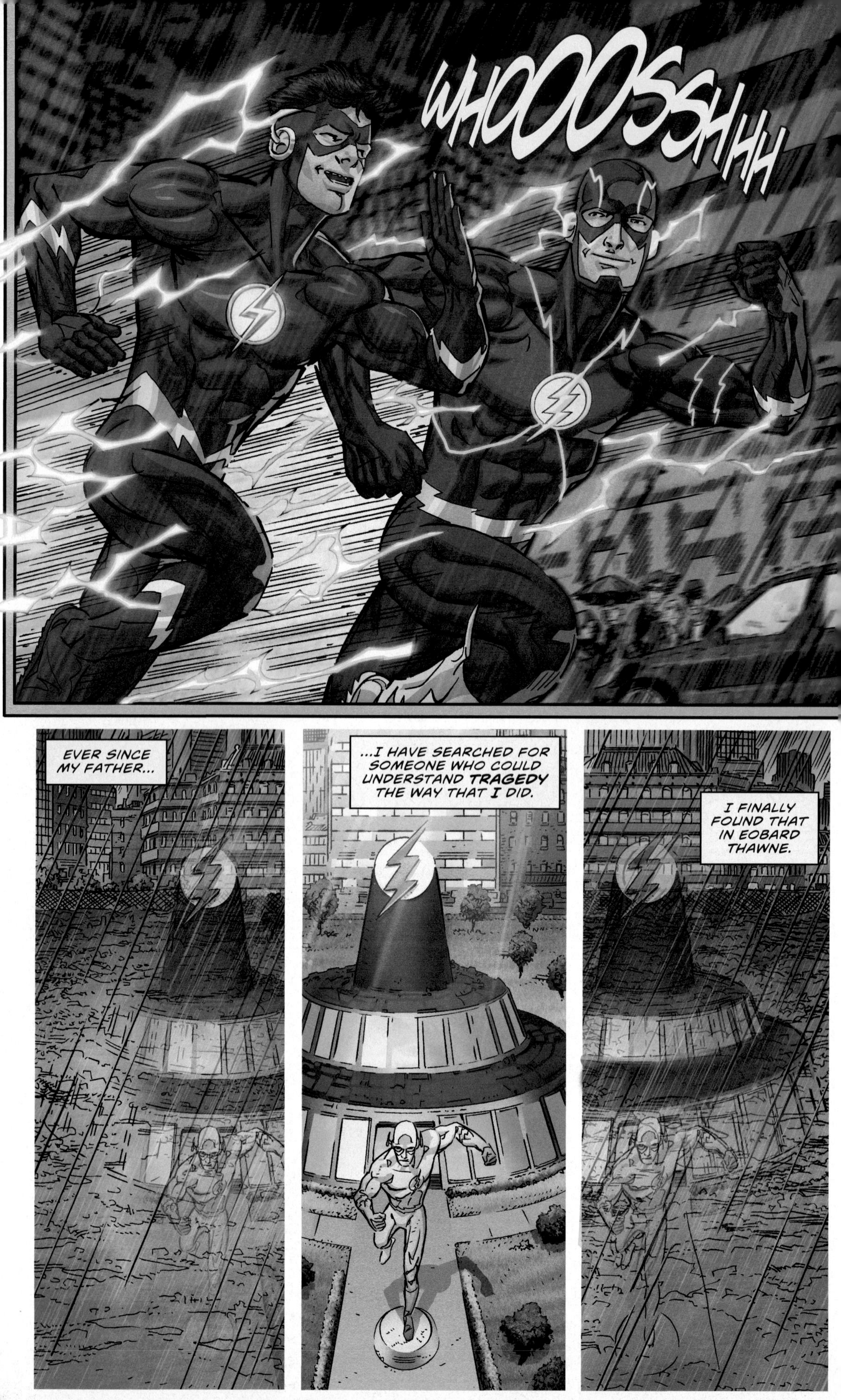
WHOOOOSSHHH
EVER SINCE MY FATHER...
...I HAVE SEARCHED FOR SOMEONE WHO COULD UNDERSTAND **TRAGEDY** THE WAY THAT I DID.
I FINALLY FOUND THAT IN EOBARD THAWNE.

BUT THIS TIME...*TRAGEDY FOUND HIM.*

I SHOULDN'T HAVE LET EOBARD GO BACK ALONE.

I SHOULD HAVE RUN ALONGSIDE HIM.

ALL BECAUSE HE WOULDN'T LISTEN TO ME!

I WAS SO SURE I COULD MAKE WALLY AND BARRY FINALLY LIVE UP TO OUR EXPECTATIONS...

NOW...I WATCH HIM DIE AGAIN, AND AGAIN AND *AGAIN.*

...BUT I WAS WRONG.

AND JUST LIKE BEFORE...SOMEONE WHO HELPED ME ESCAPE THE TRAGEDY OF MY LIFE WAS DEAD.

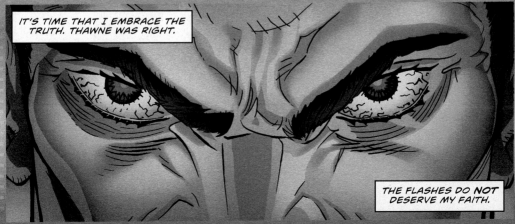

IT'S TIME THAT I EMBRACE THE TRUTH. THAWNE WAS RIGHT.

THE FLASHES DO *NOT* DESERVE MY FAITH.

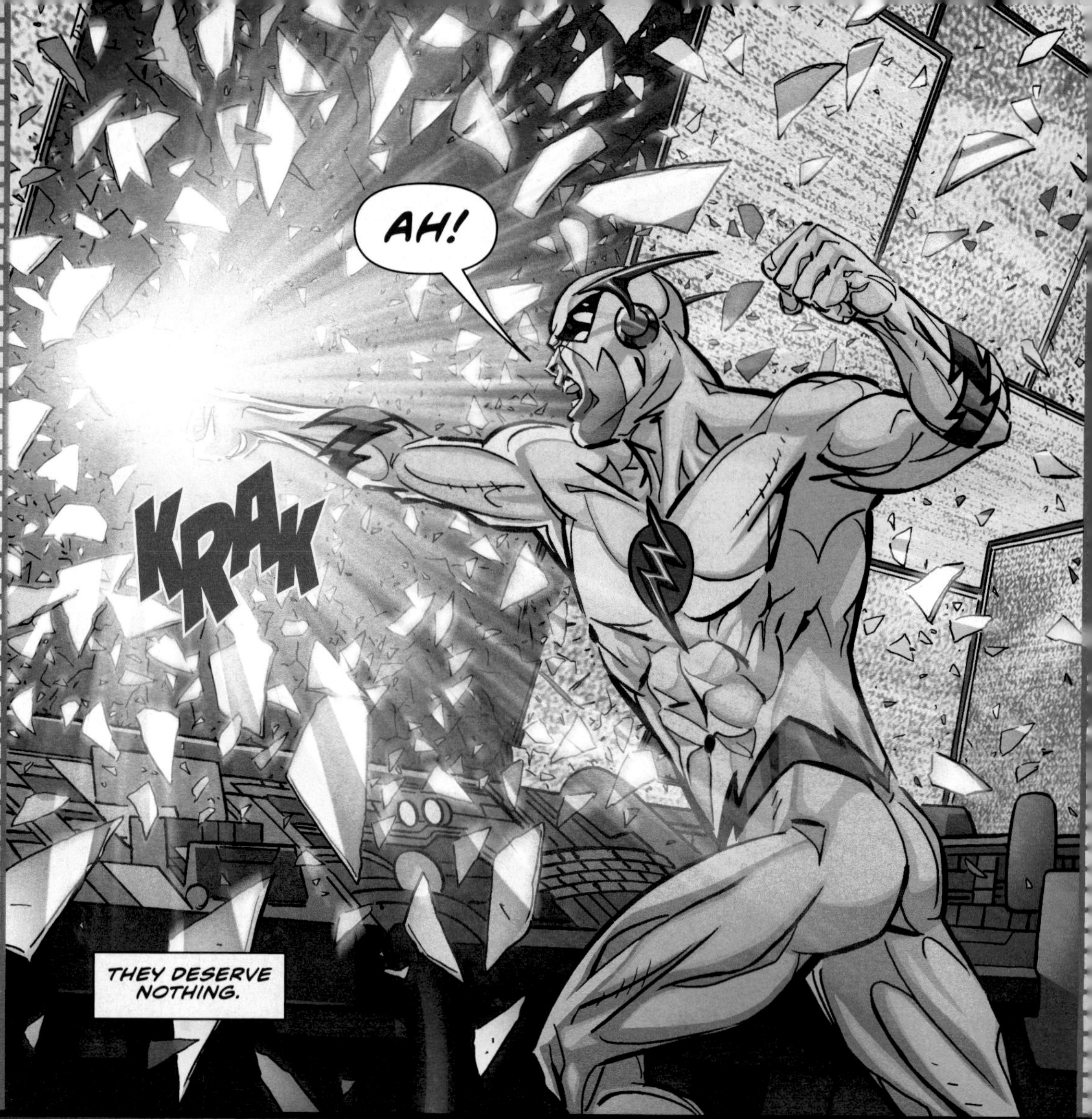
AH!
KRAK
THEY DESERVE NOTHING.

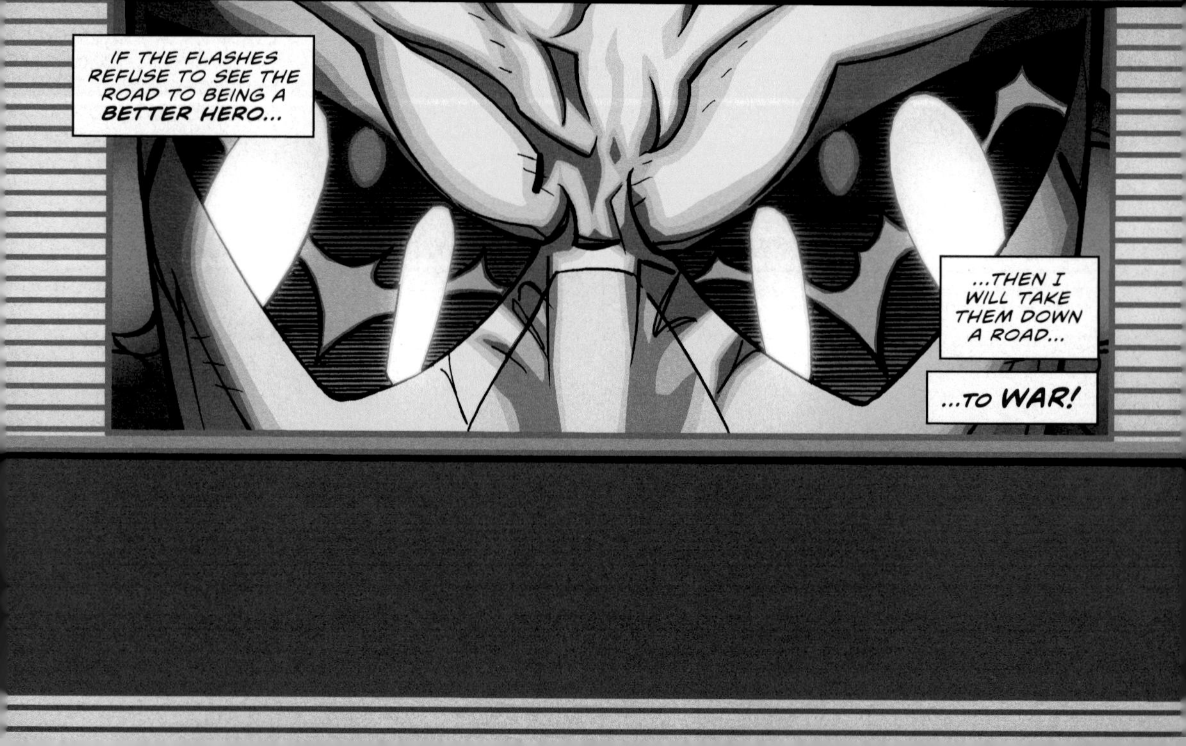
IF THE FLASHES REFUSE TO SEE THE ROAD TO BEING A BETTER HERO...
...THEN I WILL TAKE THEM DOWN A ROAD...
...TO WAR!

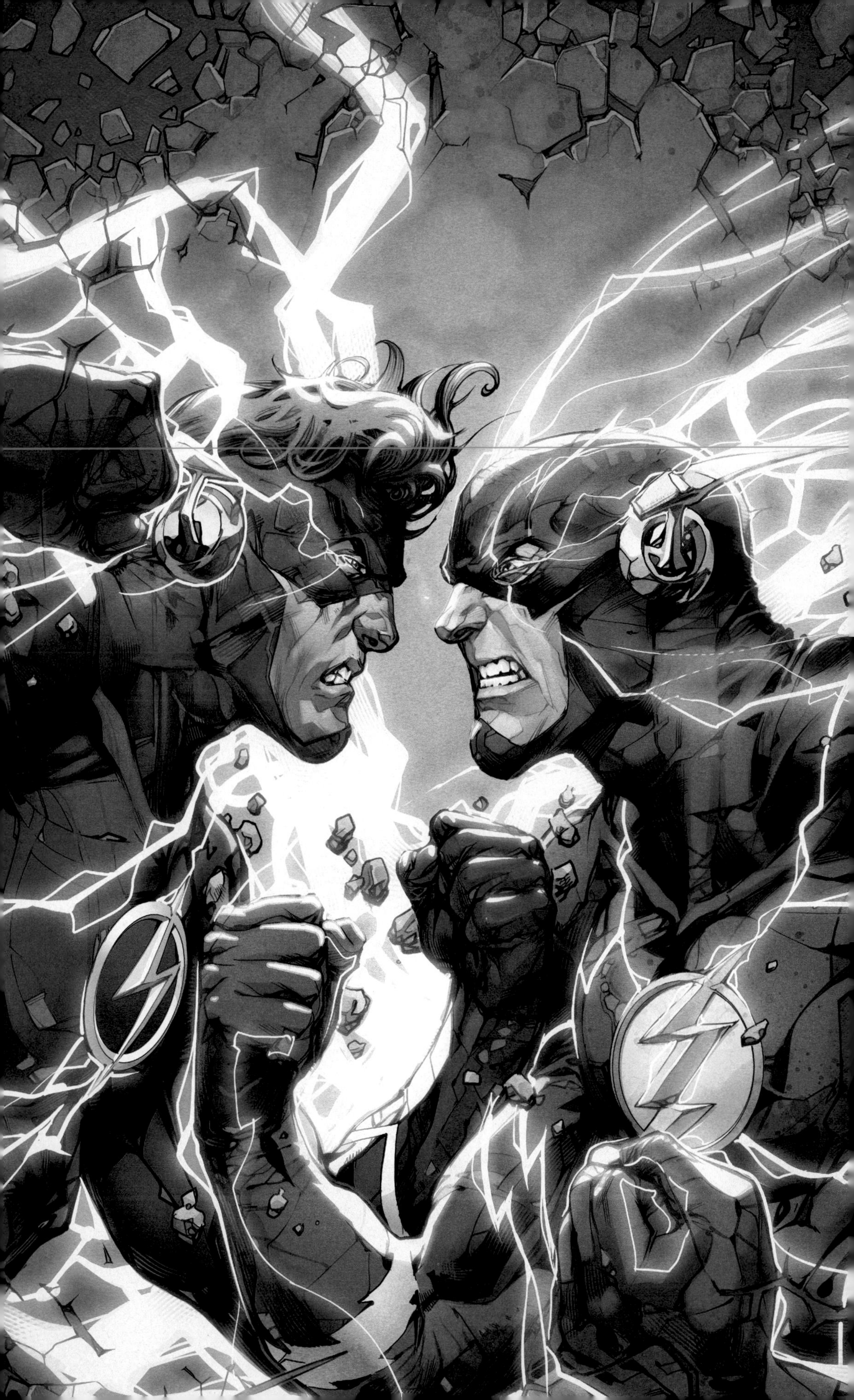

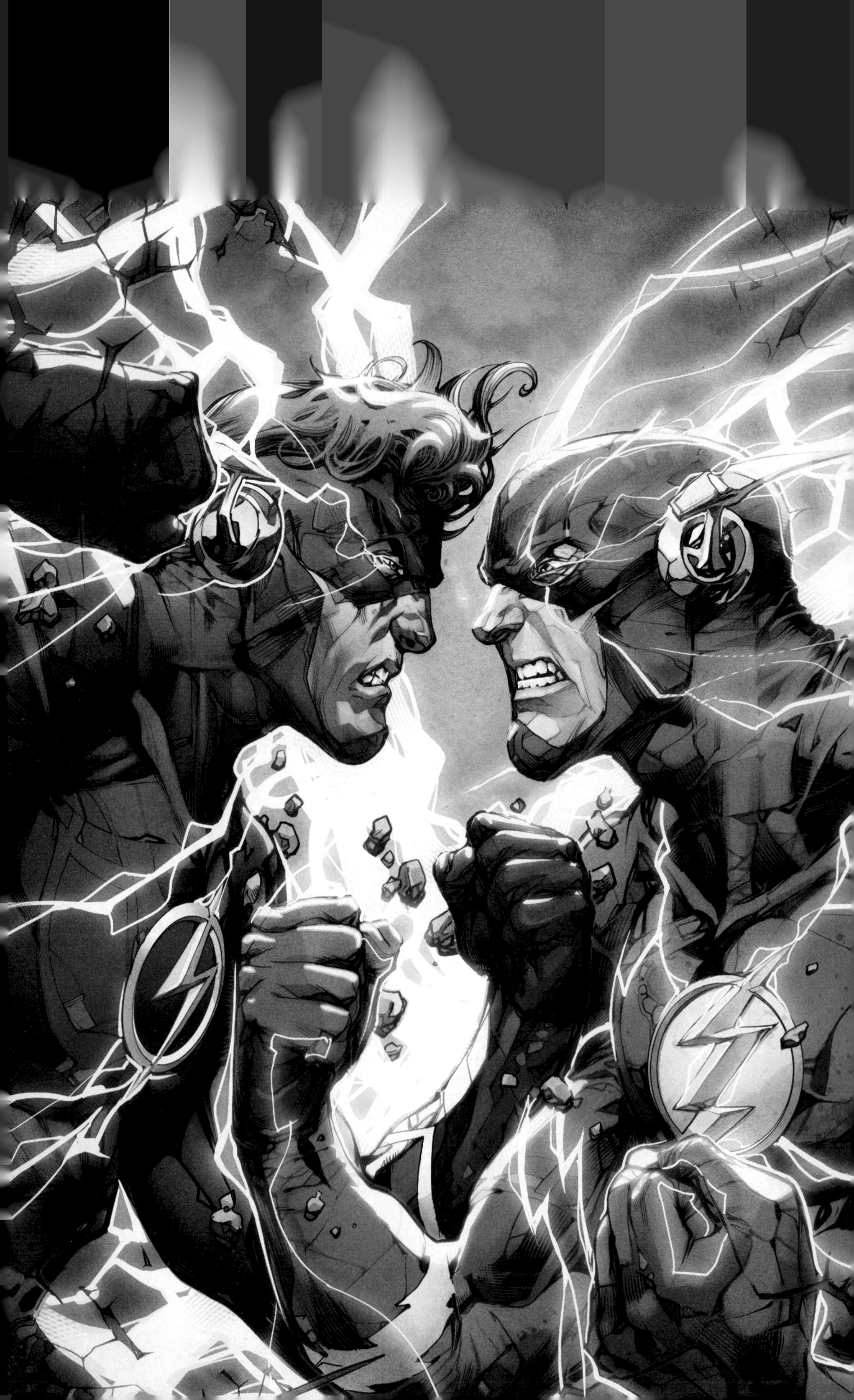

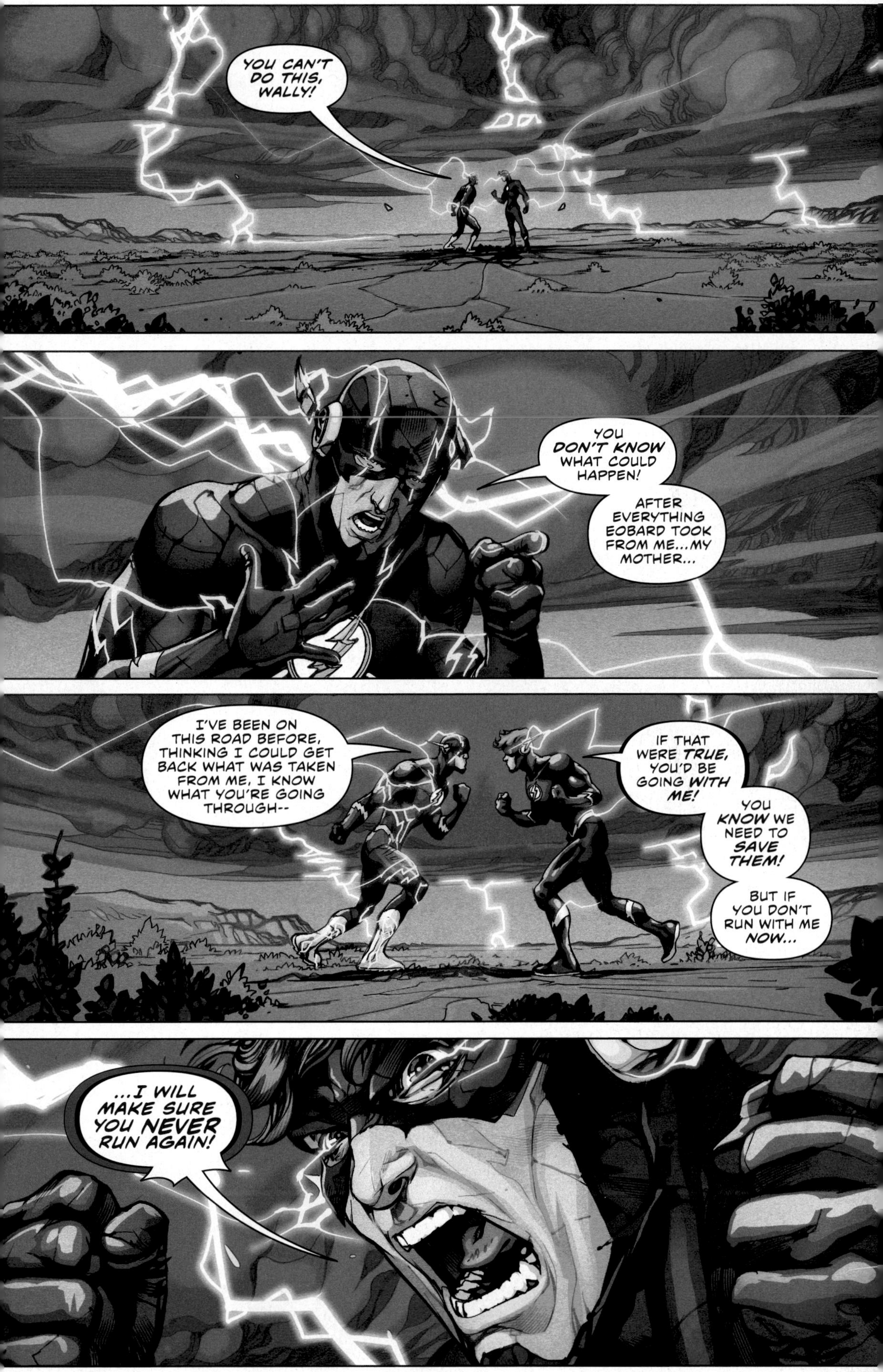
YOU CAN'T DO THIS, WALLY!
YOU DON'T KNOW WHAT COULD HAPPEN!
AFTER EVERYTHING EOBARD TOOK FROM ME...MY MOTHER...
I'VE BEEN ON THIS ROAD BEFORE, THINKING I COULD GET BACK WHAT WAS TAKEN FROM ME, I KNOW WHAT YOU'RE GOING THROUGH--
IF THAT WERE TRUE, YOU'D BE GOING WITH ME!
YOU KNOW WE NEED TO SAVE THEM!
BUT IF YOU DON'T RUN WITH ME NOW...
...I WILL MAKE SURE YOU NEVER RUN AGAIN!

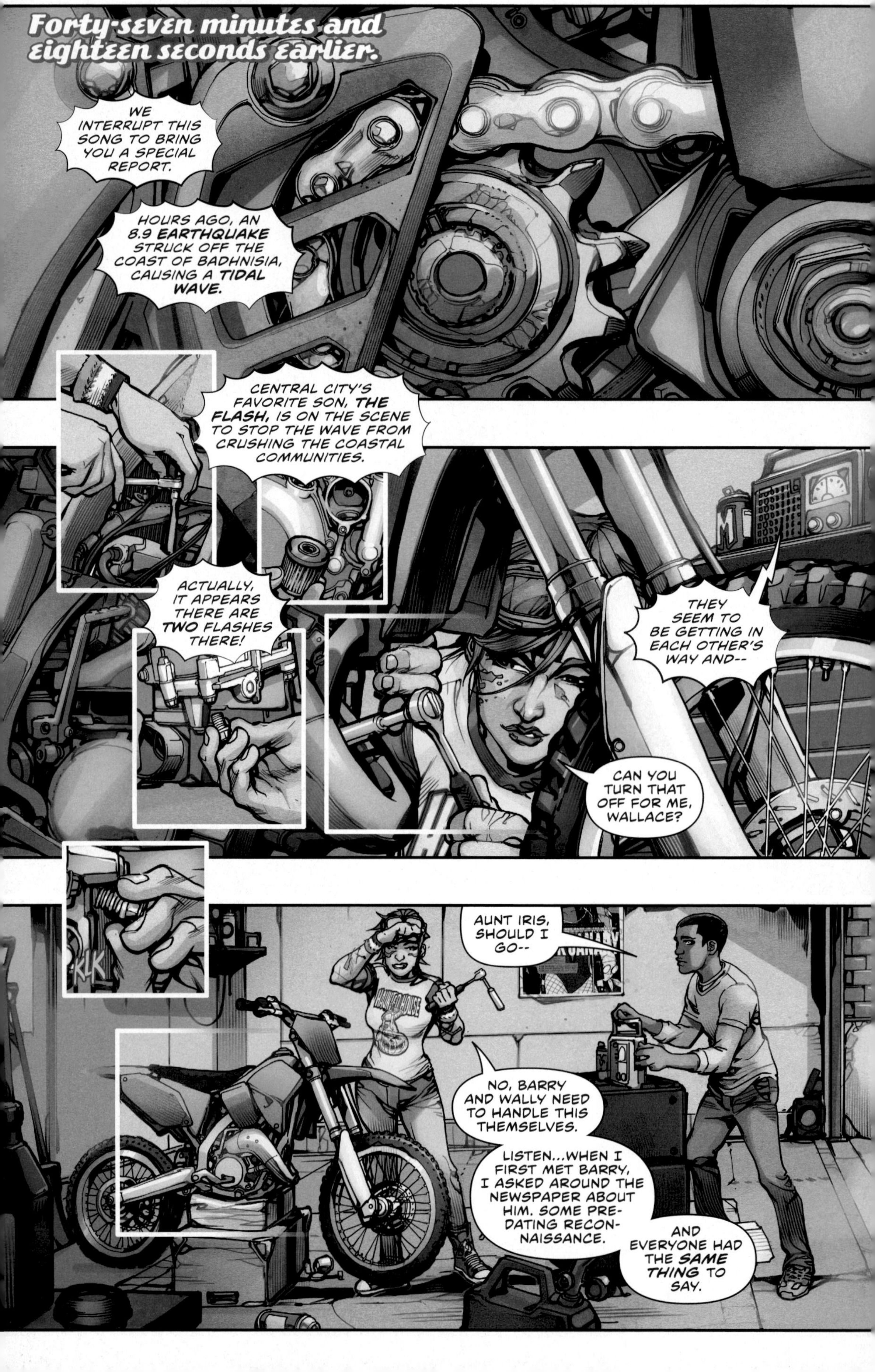
Forty-seven minutes and eighteen seconds earlier.
WE INTERRUPT THIS SONG TO BRING YOU A SPECIAL REPORT.
HOURS AGO, AN 8.9 EARTHQUAKE STRUCK OFF THE COAST OF BADHNISIA, CAUSING A TIDAL WAVE.
CENTRAL CITY'S FAVORITE SON, THE FLASH, IS ON THE SCENE TO STOP THE WAVE FROM CRUSHING THE COASTAL COMMUNITIES.
ACTUALLY, IT APPEARS THERE ARE TWO FLASHES THERE!
THEY SEEM TO BE GETTING IN EACH OTHER'S WAY AND--
CAN YOU TURN THAT OFF FOR ME, WALLACE?
KLIK
AUNT IRIS, SHOULD I GO--
NO, BARRY AND WALLY NEED TO HANDLE THIS THEMSELVES.
LISTEN...WHEN I FIRST MET BARRY, I ASKED AROUND THE NEWSPAPER ABOUT HIM. SOME PRE-DATING RECON-NAISSANCE.
AND EVERYONE HAD THE SAME THING TO SAY.

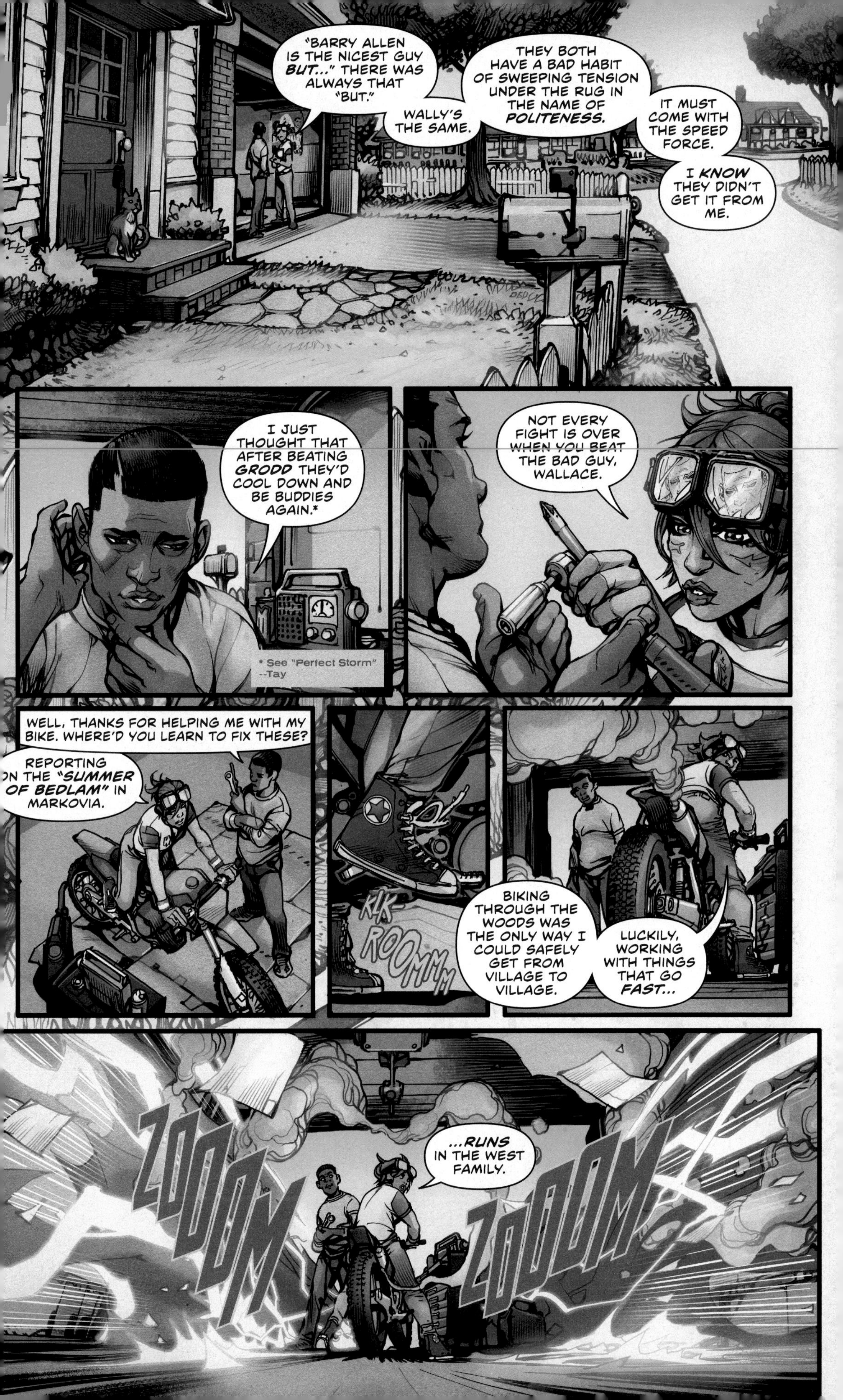
"BARRY ALLEN IS THE NICEST GUY BUT..." THERE WAS ALWAYS THAT "BUT."
WALLY'S THE SAME.
THEY BOTH HAVE A BAD HABIT OF SWEEPING TENSION UNDER THE RUG IN THE NAME OF POLITENESS.
IT MUST COME WITH THE SPEED FORCE.
I KNOW THEY DIDN'T GET IT FROM ME.
I JUST THOUGHT THAT AFTER BEATING GRODD THEY'D COOL DOWN AND BE BUDDIES AGAIN.*
* See "Perfect Storm" --Tay
NOT EVERY FIGHT IS OVER WHEN YOU BEAT THE BAD GUY, WALLACE.
WELL, THANKS FOR HELPING ME WITH MY BIKE. WHERE'D YOU LEARN TO FIX THESE?
REPORTING ON THE "SUMMER OF BEDLAM" IN MARKOVIA.
KLK-ROOOMMM
BIKING THROUGH THE WOODS WAS THE ONLY WAY I COULD SAFELY GET FROM VILLAGE TO VILLAGE.
LUCKILY, WORKING WITH THINGS THAT GO FAST...
ZOOOM
...RUNS IN THE WEST FAMILY.
ZOOOOM

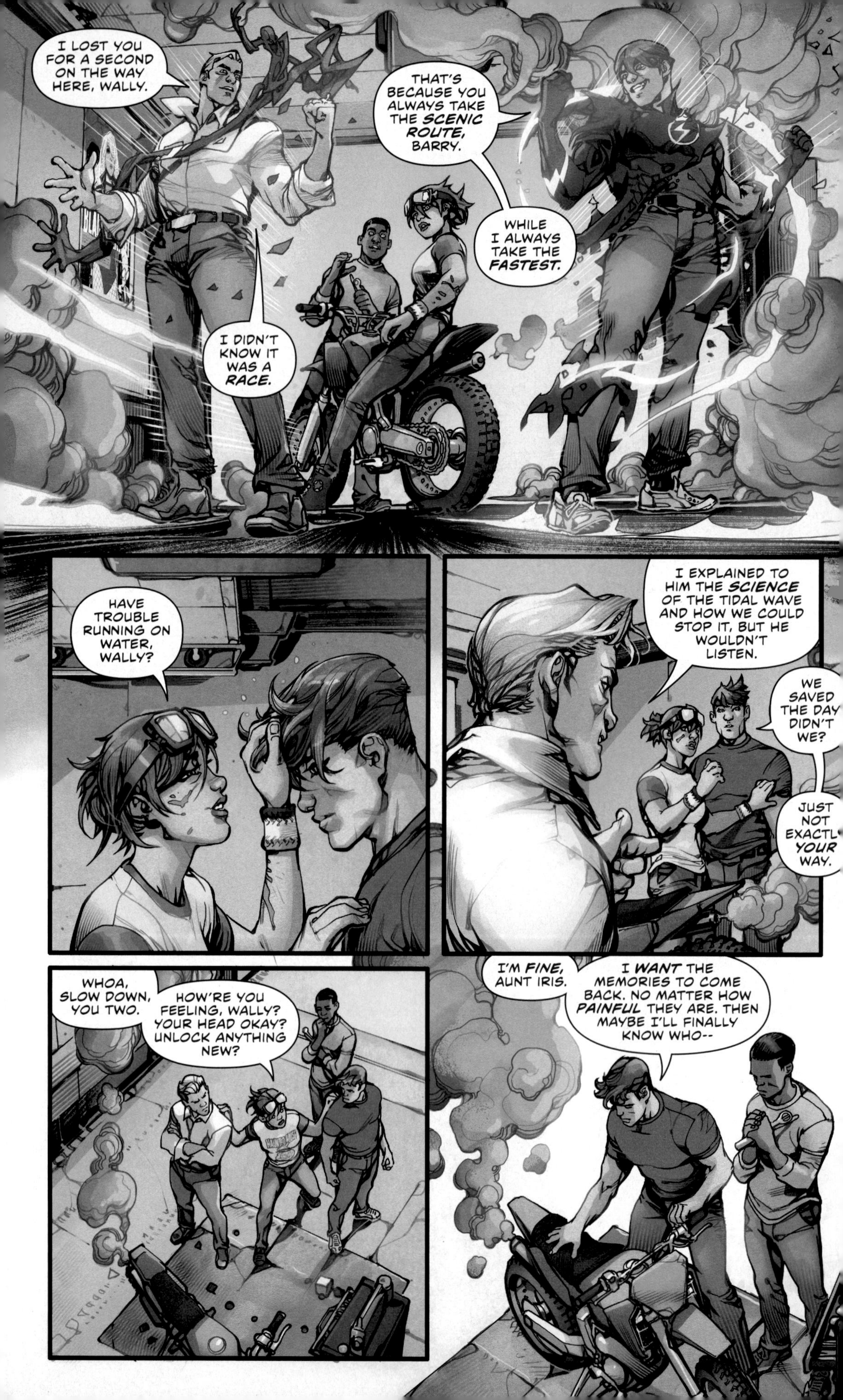
I LOST YOU FOR A SECOND ON THE WAY HERE, WALLY.
THAT'S BECAUSE YOU ALWAYS TAKE THE SCENIC ROUTE, BARRY.
WHILE I ALWAYS TAKE THE FASTEST.
I DIDN'T KNOW IT WAS A RACE.
HAVE TROUBLE RUNNING ON WATER, WALLY?
I EXPLAINED TO HIM THE SCIENCE OF THE TIDAL WAVE AND HOW WE COULD STOP IT, BUT HE WOULDN'T LISTEN.
WE SAVED THE DAY DIDN'T WE?
JUST NOT EXACTL YOUR WAY.
WHOA, SLOW DOWN, YOU TWO.
HOW'RE YOU FEELING, WALLY? YOUR HEAD OKAY? UNLOCK ANYTHING NEW?
I'M FINE, AUNT IRIS.
I WANT THE MEMORIES TO COME BACK. NO MATTER HOW PAINFUL THEY ARE. THEN MAYBE I'LL FINALLY KNOW WHO--

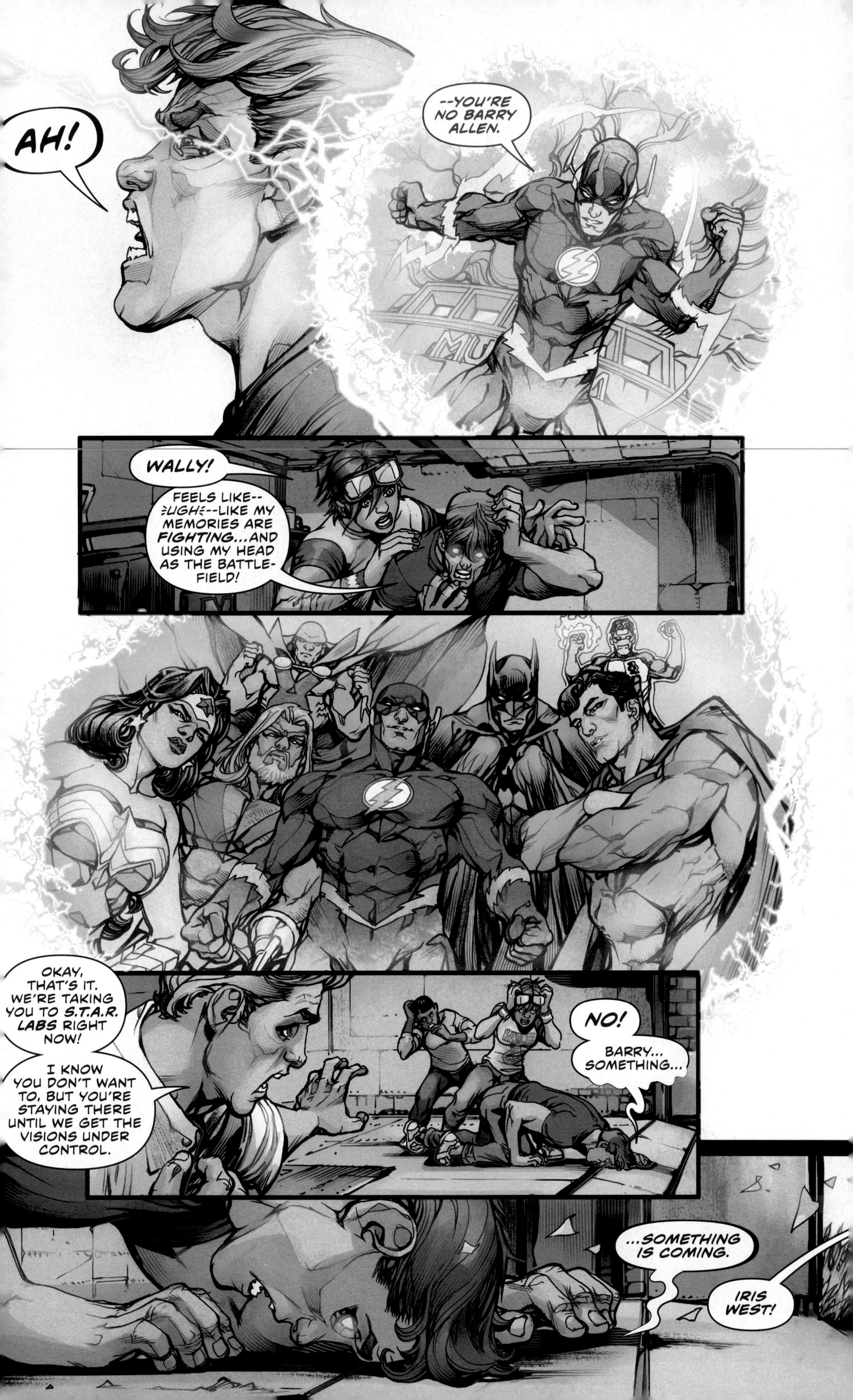
AH!
--YOU'RE NO BARRY ALLEN.
WALLY!
FEELS LIKE-- UGH--LIKE MY MEMORIES ARE FIGHTING...AND USING MY HEAD AS THE BATTLE-FIELD!
OKAY, THAT'S IT. WE'RE TAKING YOU TO S.T.A.R. LABS RIGHT NOW!
I KNOW YOU DON'T WANT TO, BUT YOU'RE STAYING THERE UNTIL WE GET THE VISIONS UNDER CONTROL.
NO!
BARRY... SOMETHING...
...SOMETHING IS COMING.
IRIS WEST!

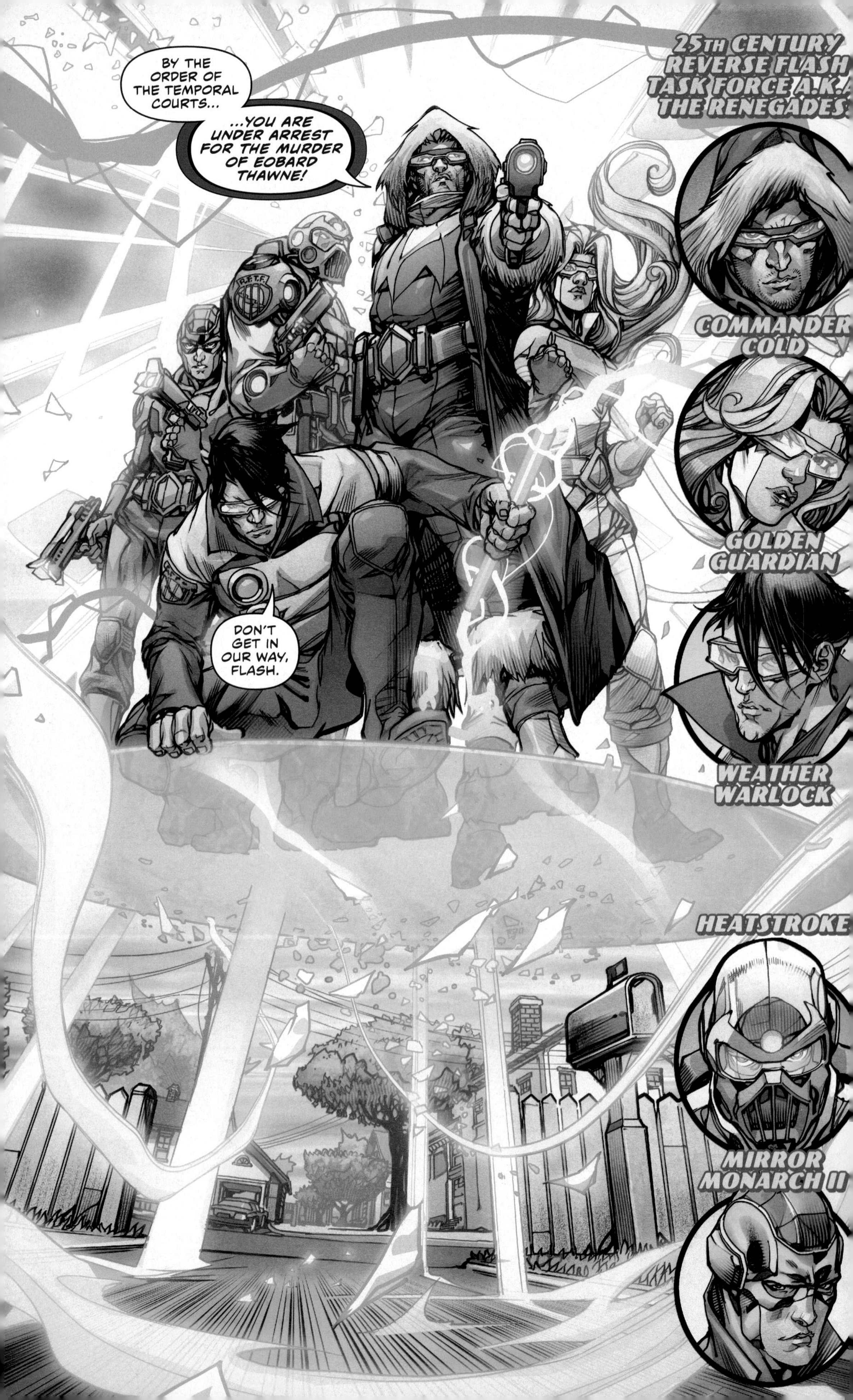
BY THE ORDER OF THE TEMPORAL COURTS...
...YOU ARE UNDER ARREST FOR THE MURDER OF EOBARD THAWNE!
25TH CENTURY REVERSE FLASH TASK FORCE A.K.A. THE RENEGADES
COMMANDER COLD
GOLDEN GUARDIAN
WEATHER WARLOCK
DON'T GET IN OUR WAY, FLASH.
HEATSTROKE
MIRROR MONARCH II

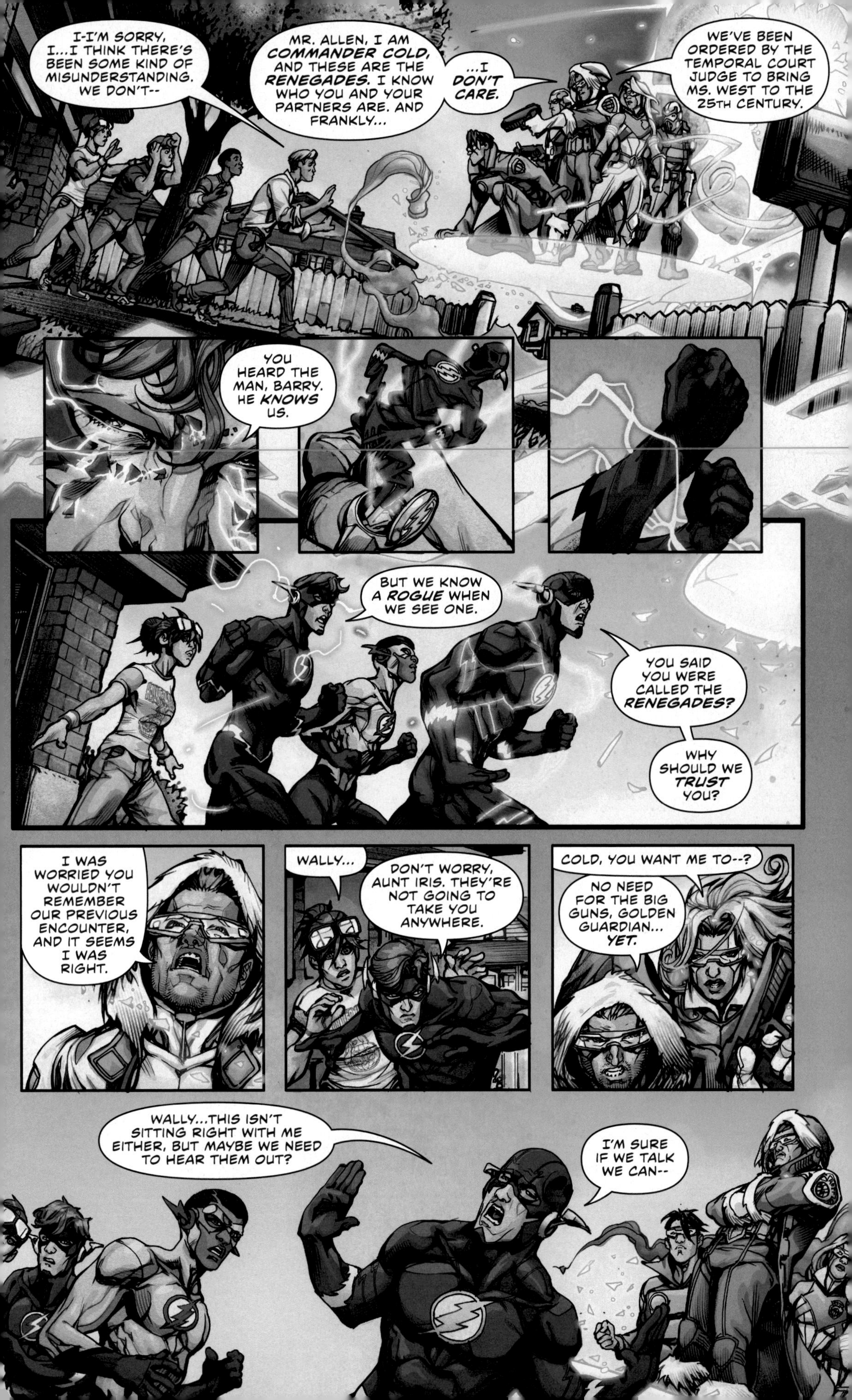

I-I'M SORRY, I...I THINK THERE'S BEEN SOME KIND OF MISUNDERSTANDING. WE DON'T--
MR. ALLEN, I AM COMMANDER COLD, AND THESE ARE THE RENEGADES. I KNOW WHO YOU AND YOUR PARTNERS ARE. AND FRANKLY...
...I DON'T CARE.
WE'VE BEEN ORDERED BY THE TEMPORAL COURT JUDGE TO BRING MS. WEST TO THE 25TH CENTURY.
YOU HEARD THE MAN, BARRY. HE KNOWS US.
BUT WE KNOW A ROGUE WHEN WE SEE ONE.
YOU SAID YOU WERE CALLED THE RENEGADES?
WHY SHOULD WE TRUST YOU?
I WAS WORRIED YOU WOULDN'T REMEMBER OUR PREVIOUS ENCOUNTER, AND IT SEEMS I WAS RIGHT.
WALLY...
DON'T WORRY, AUNT IRIS. THEY'RE NOT GOING TO TAKE YOU ANYWHERE.
COLD, YOU WANT ME TO--?
NO NEED FOR THE BIG GUNS, GOLDEN GUARDIAN... YET.
WALLY...THIS ISN'T SITTING RIGHT WITH ME EITHER, BUT MAYBE WE NEED TO HEAR THEM OUT?
I'M SURE IF WE TALK WE CAN--

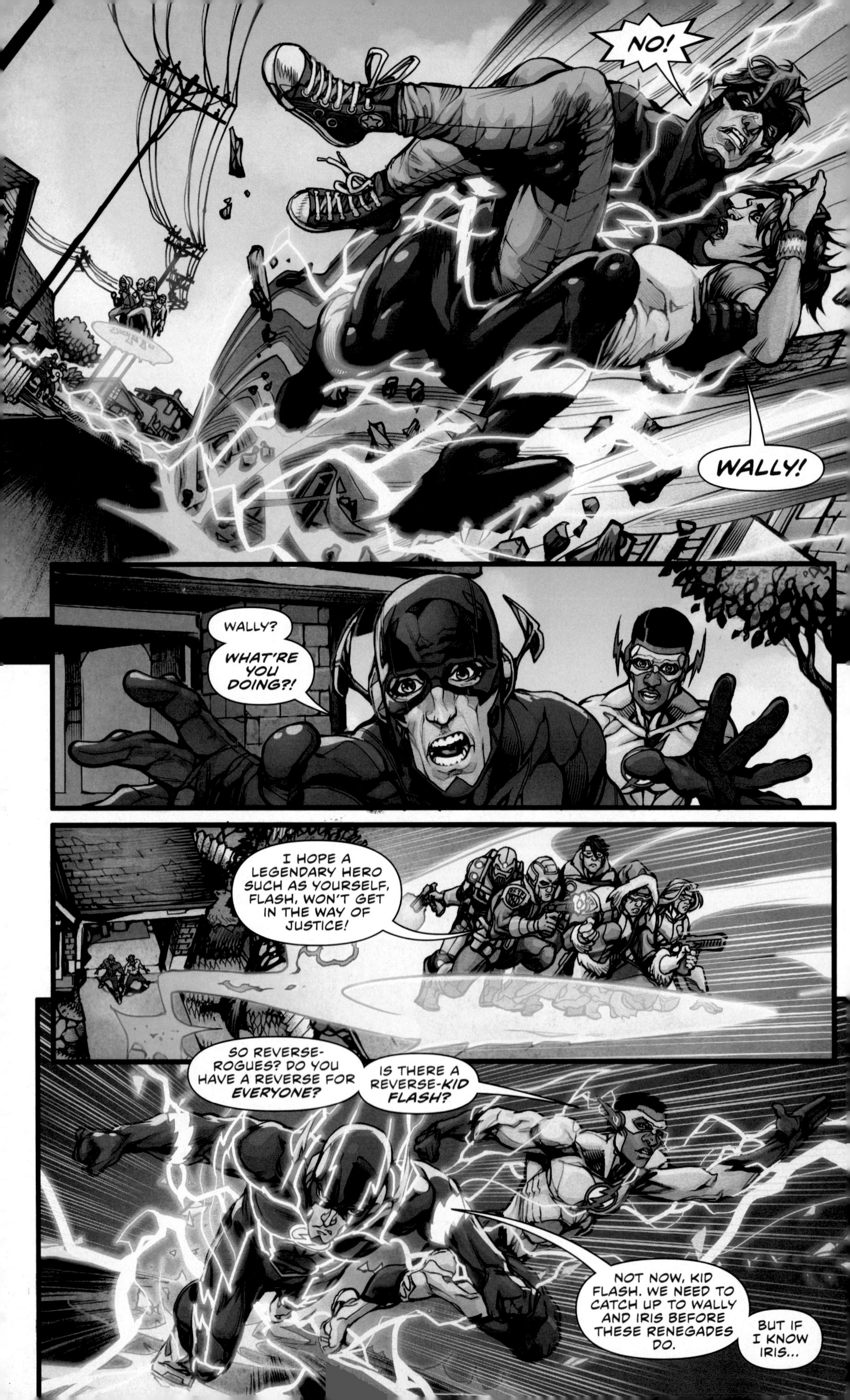
NO!
WALLY!
WALLY?
WHAT'RE YOU DOING?!
I HOPE A LEGENDARY HERO SUCH AS YOURSELF, FLASH, WON'T GET IN THE WAY OF JUSTICE!
SO REVERSE-ROGUES? DO YOU HAVE A REVERSE FOR EVERYONE?
IS THERE A REVERSE-KID FLASH?
NOT NOW, KID FLASH. WE NEED TO CATCH UP TO WALLY AND IRIS BEFORE THESE RENEGADES DO.
BUT IF I KNOW IRIS...

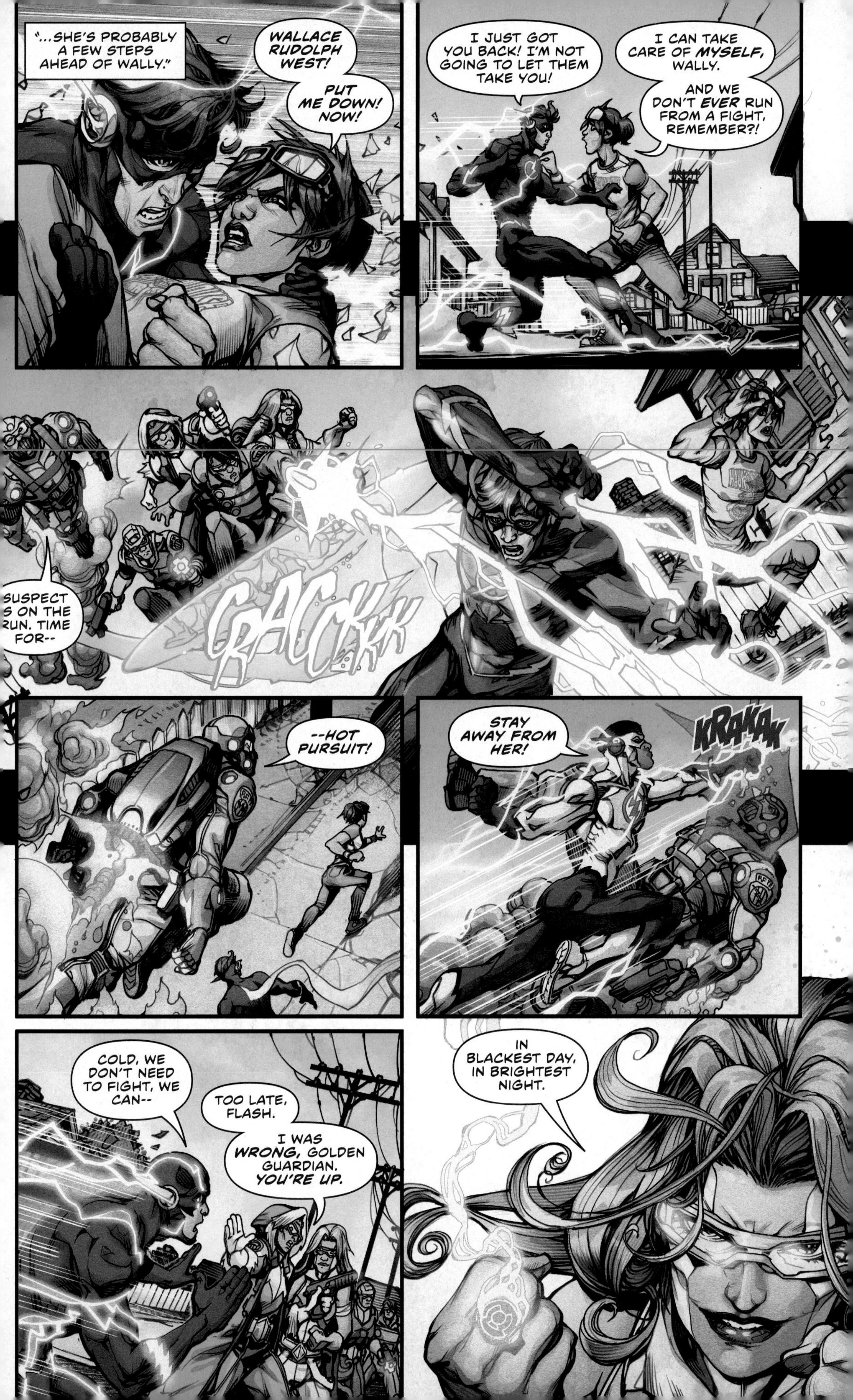

"...SHE'S PROBABLY A FEW STEPS AHEAD OF WALLY."
WALLACE RUDOLPH WEST!
PUT ME DOWN! NOW!
I JUST GOT YOU BACK! I'M NOT GOING TO LET THEM TAKE YOU!
I CAN TAKE CARE OF MYSELF, WALLY.
AND WE DON'T EVER RUN FROM A FIGHT, REMEMBER?!
SUSPECT S ON THE RUN. TIME FOR--
CRACKKK
--HOT PURSUIT!
STAY AWAY FROM HER!
KRAKAK
COLD, WE DON'T NEED TO FIGHT, WE CAN--
TOO LATE, FLASH.
I WAS WRONG, GOLDEN GUARDIAN. YOU'RE UP.
IN BLACKEST DAY, IN BRIGHTEST NIGHT.

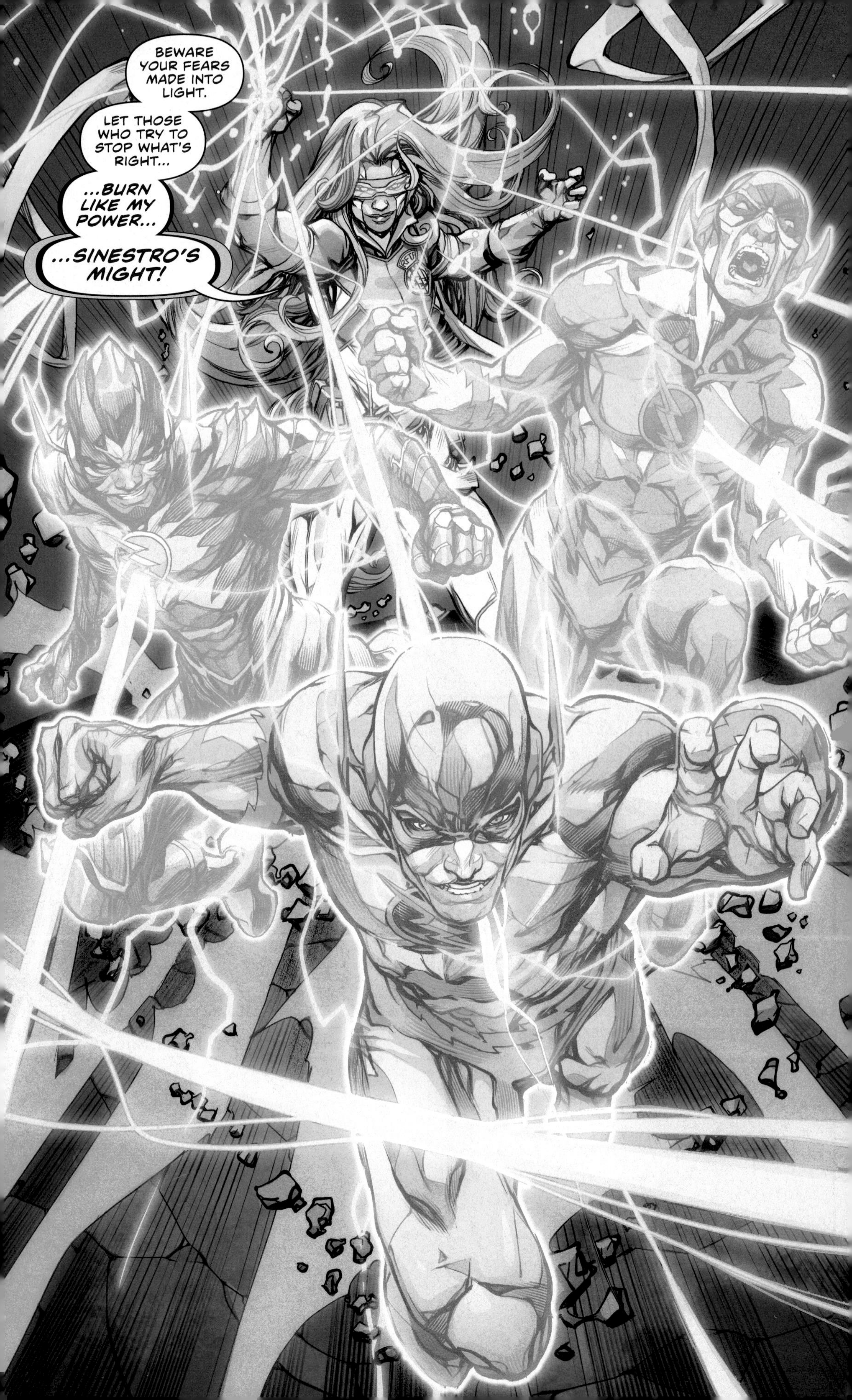
BEWARE YOUR FEARS MADE INTO LIGHT.
LET THOSE WHO TRY TO STOP WHAT'S RIGHT...
...BURN LIKE MY POWER...
...SINESTRO'S MIGHT!

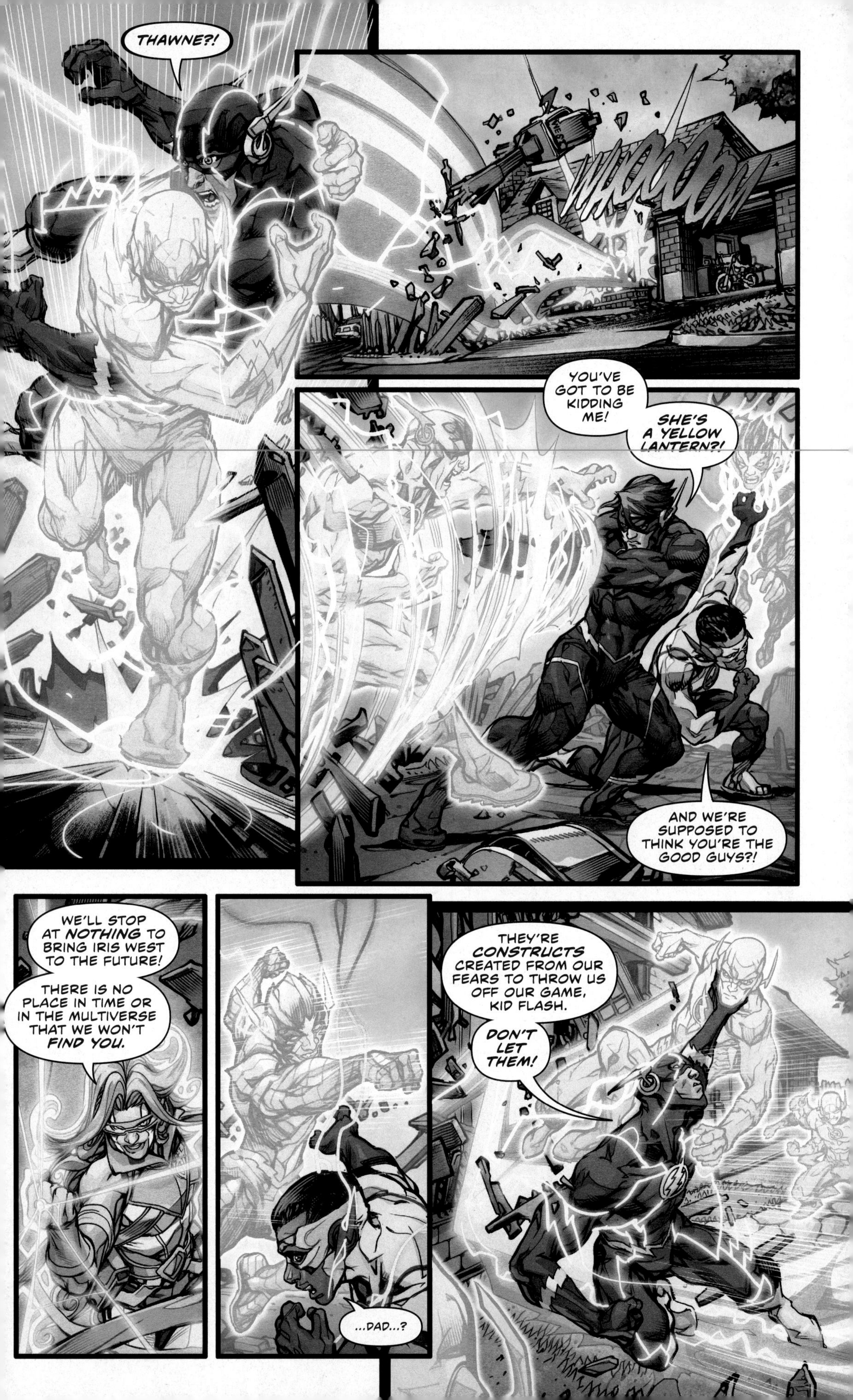
THAWNE?!
WHOOOOM
YOU'VE GOT TO BE KIDDING ME!
SHE'S A YELLOW LANTERN?!
AND WE'RE SUPPOSED TO THINK YOU'RE THE GOOD GUYS?!
WE'LL STOP AT NOTHING TO BRING IRIS WEST TO THE FUTURE!
THERE IS NO PLACE IN TIME OR IN THE MULTIVERSE THAT WE WON'T FIND YOU.
...DAD...?
THEY'RE CONSTRUCTS CREATED FROM OUR FEARS TO THROW US OFF OUR GAME, KID FLASH.
DON'T LET THEM!

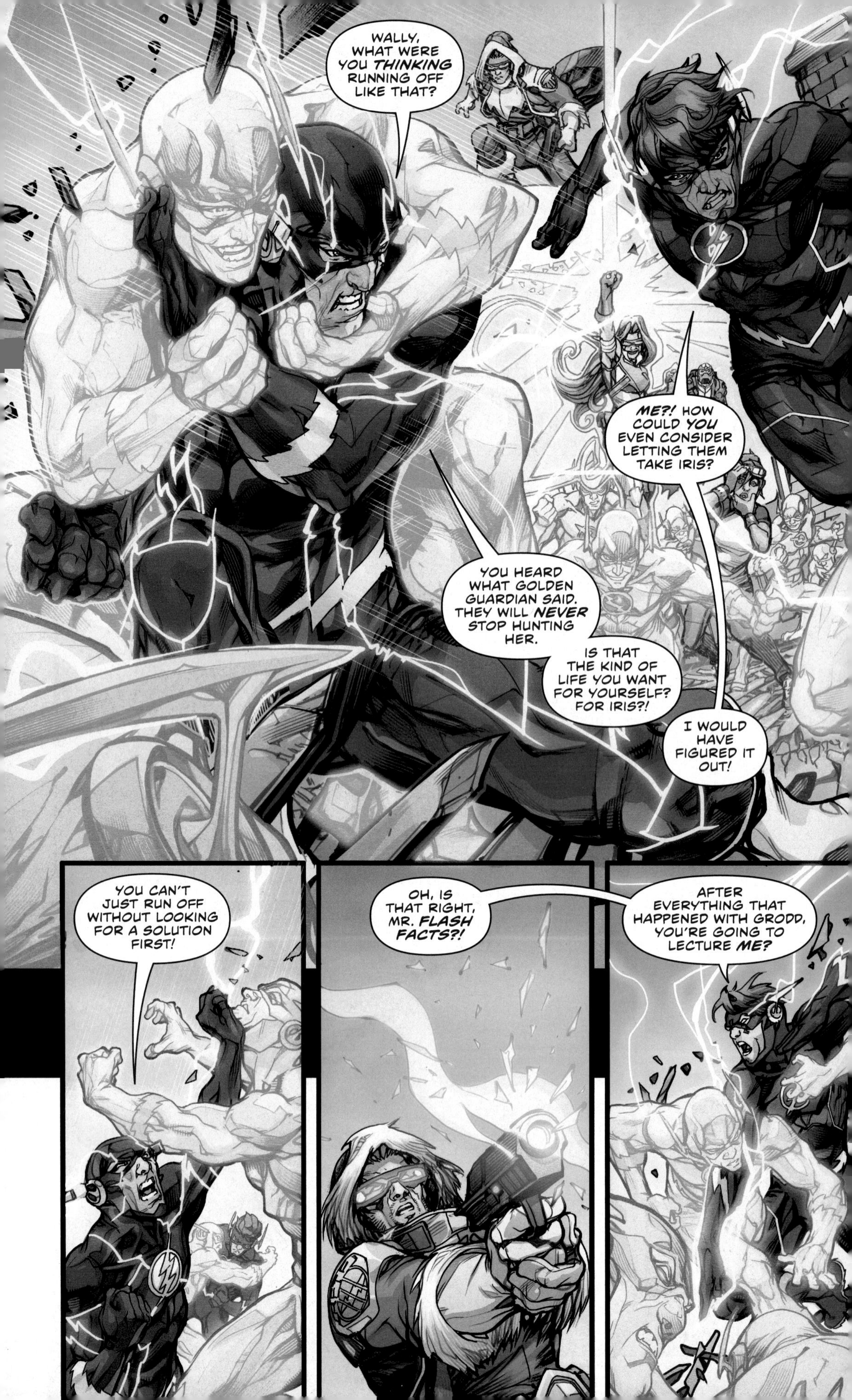
WALLY, WHAT WERE YOU THINKING RUNNING OFF LIKE THAT?
ME?! HOW COULD YOU EVEN CONSIDER LETTING THEM TAKE IRIS?
YOU HEARD WHAT GOLDEN GUARDIAN SAID. THEY WILL NEVER STOP HUNTING HER.
IS THAT THE KIND OF LIFE YOU WANT FOR YOURSELF? FOR IRIS?!
I WOULD HAVE FIGURED IT OUT!
YOU CAN'T JUST RUN OFF WITHOUT LOOKING FOR A SOLUTION FIRST!
OH, IS THAT RIGHT, MR. FLASH FACTS?!
AFTER EVERYTHING THAT HAPPENED WITH GRODD, YOU'RE GOING TO LECTURE ME?

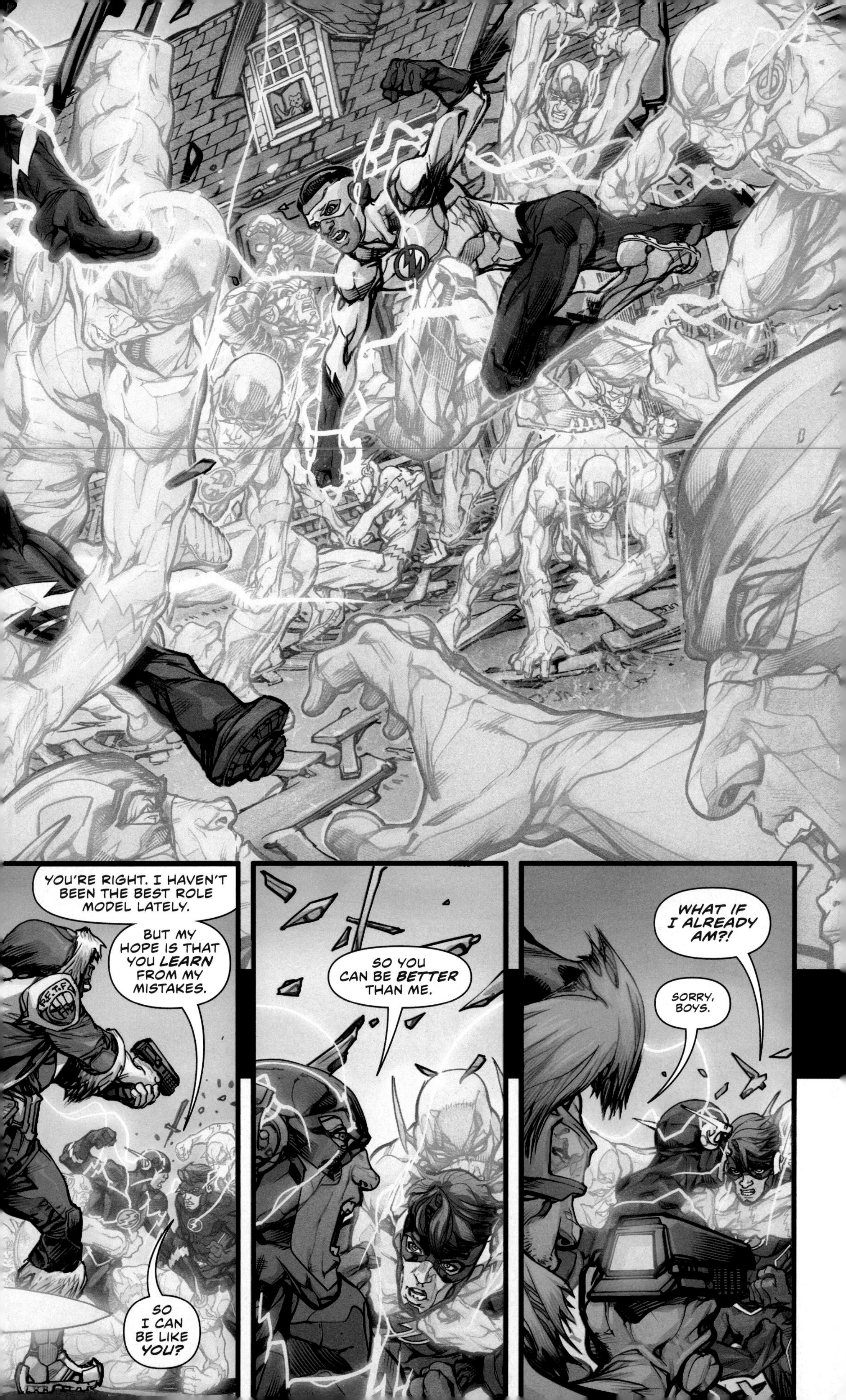
YOU'RE RIGHT. I HAVEN'T BEEN THE BEST ROLE MODEL LATELY.
BUT MY HOPE IS THAT YOU LEARN FROM MY MISTAKES.
SO I CAN BE LIKE YOU?
SO YOU CAN BE BETTER THAN ME.
WHAT IF I ALREADY AM?!
SORRY, BOYS.

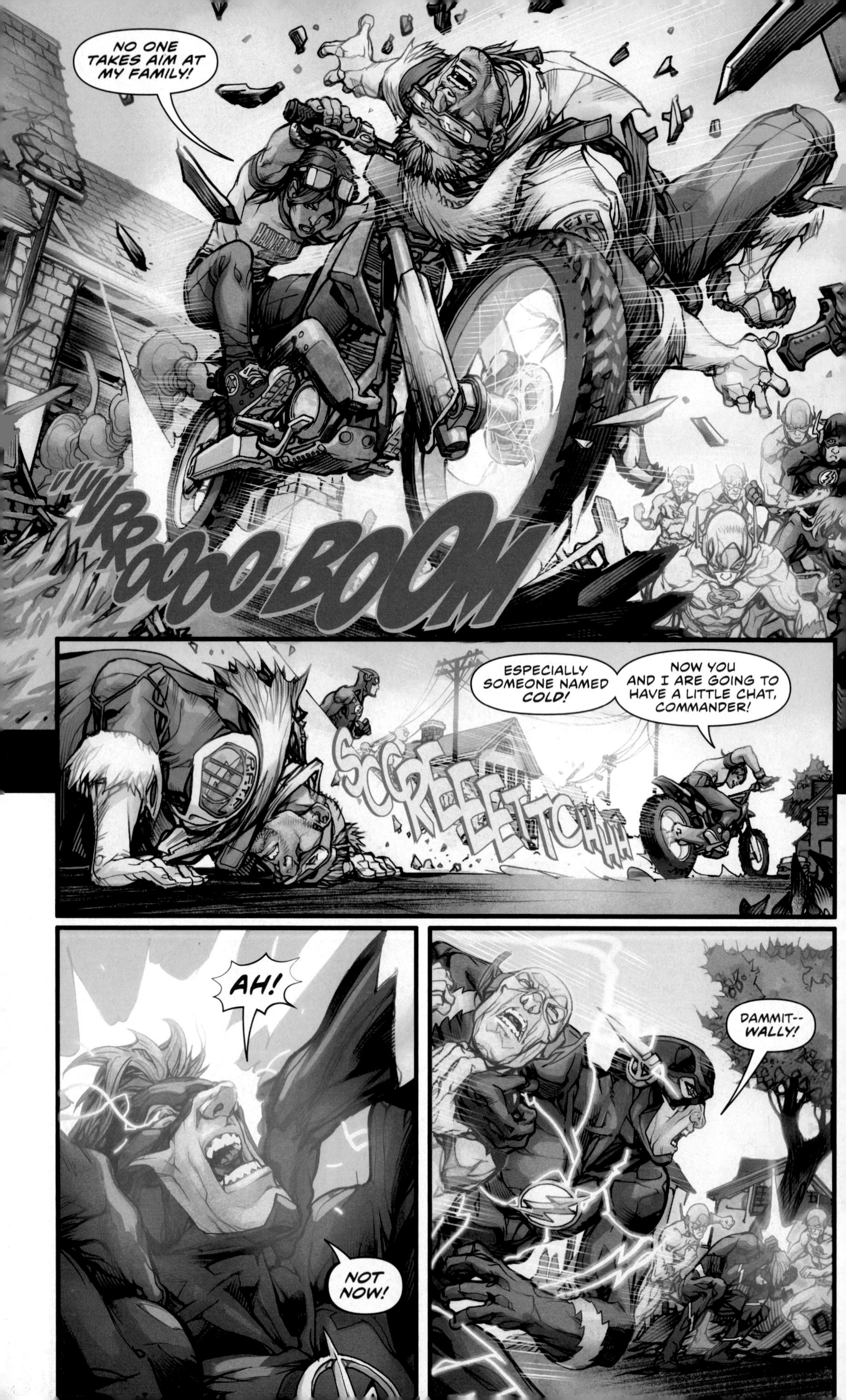
NO ONE TAKES AIM AT MY FAMILY!
VVVRROOOO-BOOM
ESPECIALLY SOMEONE NAMED COLD!
NOW YOU AND I ARE GOING TO HAVE A LITTLE CHAT, COMMANDER!
SCCREEETTCHHH
AH!
NOT NOW!
DAMMIT-- WALLY!

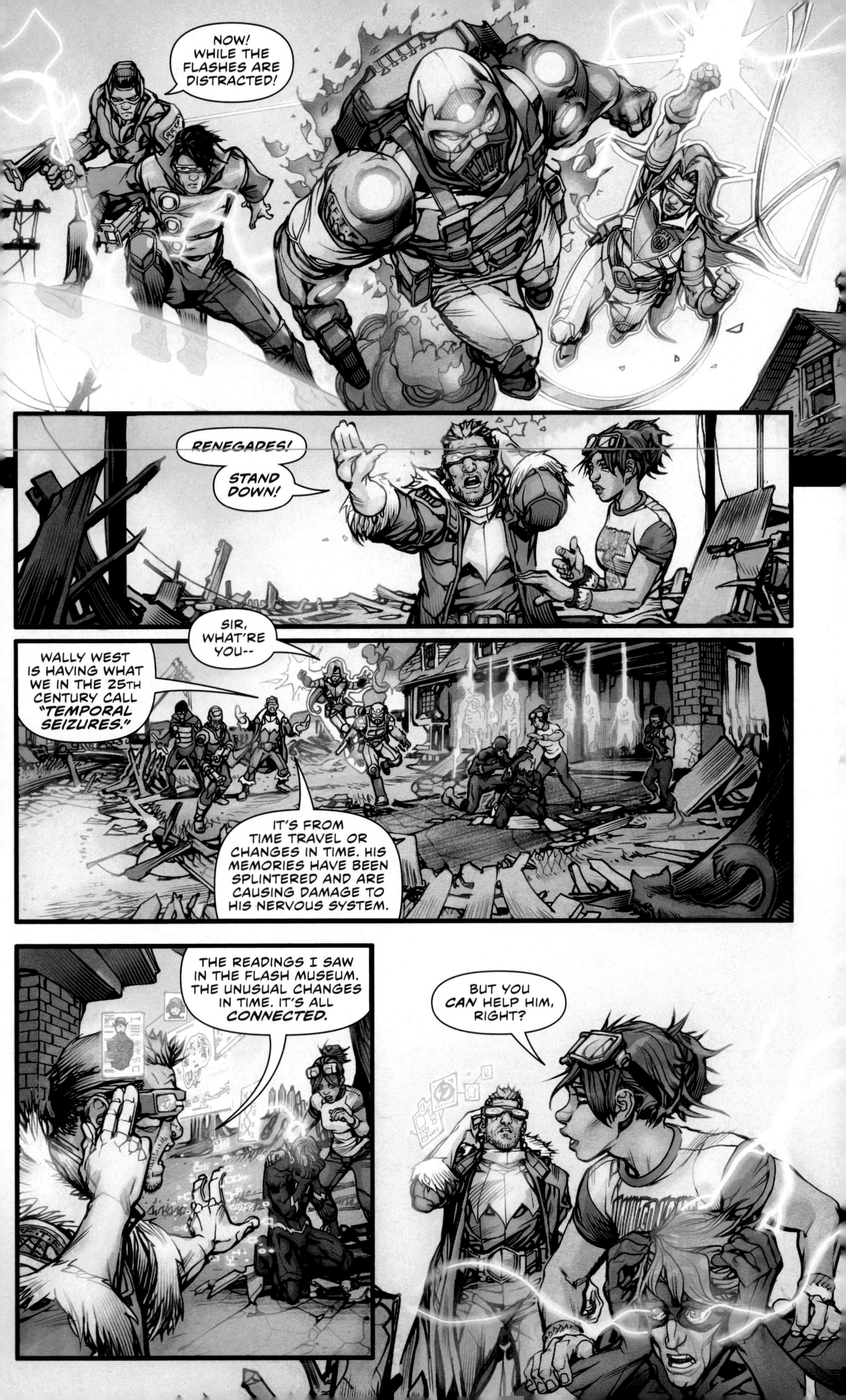
NOW! WHILE THE FLASHES ARE DISTRACTED!
RENEGADES!
STAND DOWN!
SIR, WHAT'RE YOU--
WALLY WEST IS HAVING WHAT WE IN THE 25TH CENTURY CALL "TEMPORAL SEIZURES."
IT'S FROM TIME TRAVEL OR CHANGES IN TIME. HIS MEMORIES HAVE BEEN SPLINTERED AND ARE CAUSING DAMAGE TO HIS NERVOUS SYSTEM.
THE READINGS I SAW IN THE FLASH MUSEUM. THE UNUSUAL CHANGES IN TIME. IT'S ALL CONNECTED.
BUT YOU CAN HELP HIM, RIGHT?

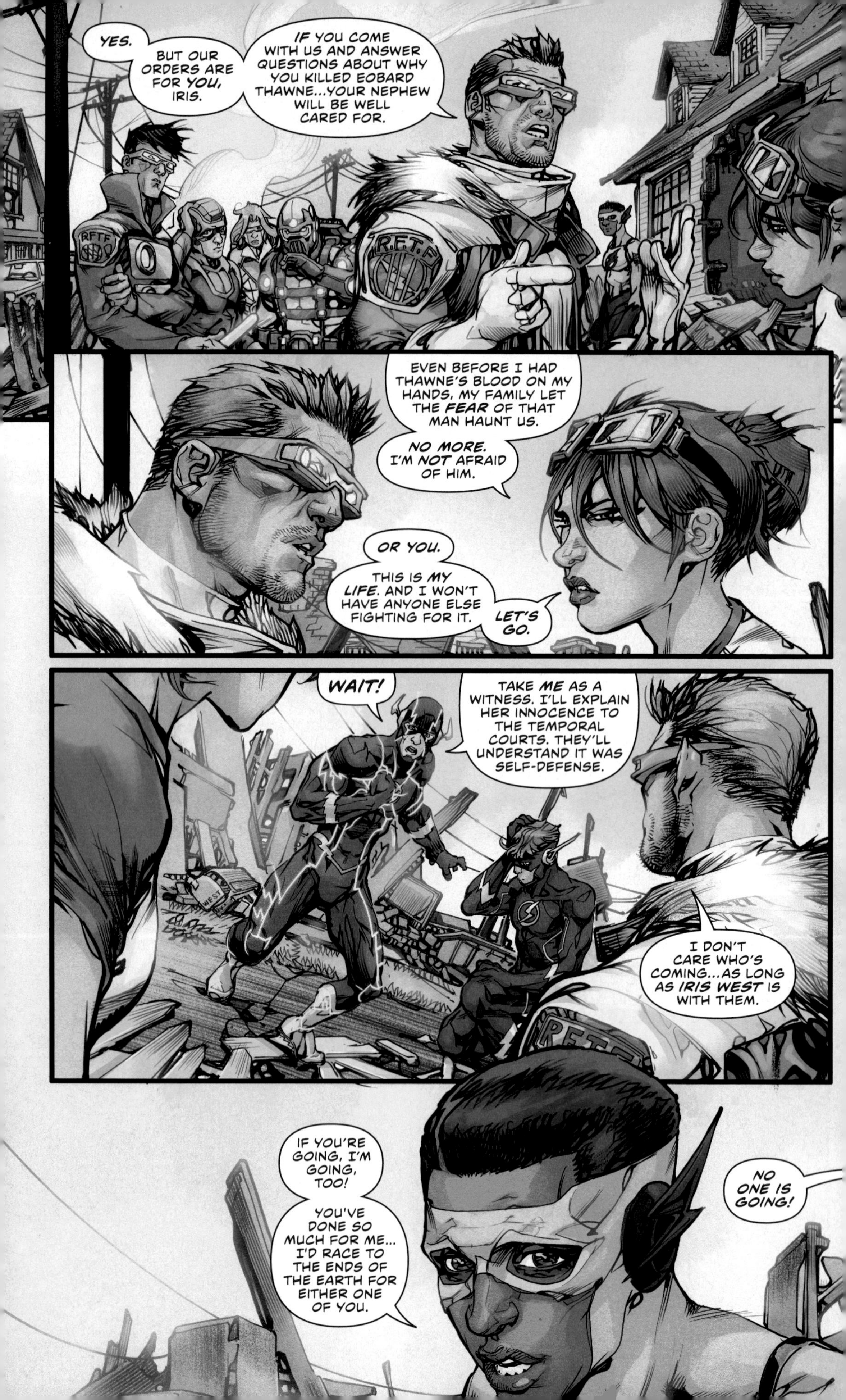
YES.
BUT OUR ORDERS ARE FOR YOU, IRIS.
IF YOU COME WITH US AND ANSWER QUESTIONS ABOUT WHY YOU KILLED EOBARD THAWNE...YOUR NEPHEW WILL BE WELL CARED FOR.
R.F.T.F
EVEN BEFORE I HAD THAWNE'S BLOOD ON MY HANDS, MY FAMILY LET THE FEAR OF THAT MAN HAUNT US.
NO MORE. I'M NOT AFRAID OF HIM.
OR YOU.
THIS IS MY LIFE. AND I WON'T HAVE ANYONE ELSE FIGHTING FOR IT.
LET'S GO.
WAIT!
TAKE ME AS A WITNESS. I'LL EXPLAIN HER INNOCENCE TO THE TEMPORAL COURTS. THEY'LL UNDERSTAND IT WAS SELF-DEFENSE.
I DON'T CARE WHO'S COMING...AS LONG AS IRIS WEST IS WITH THEM.
IF YOU'RE GOING, I'M GOING, TOO!
YOU'VE DONE SO MUCH FOR ME... I'D RACE TO THE ENDS OF THE EARTH FOR EITHER ONE OF YOU.
NO ONE IS GOING!

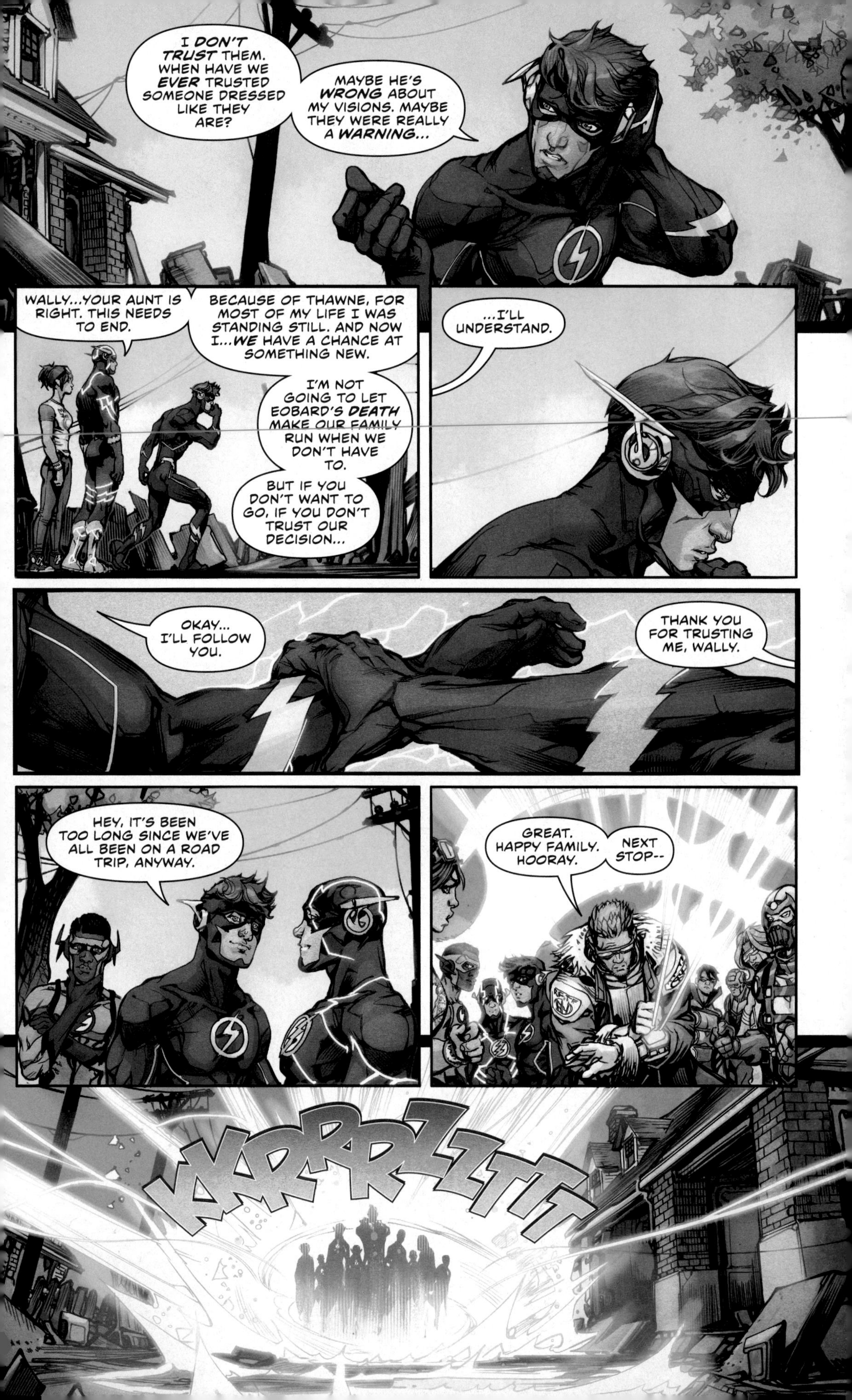
I DON'T TRUST THEM. WHEN HAVE WE EVER TRUSTED SOMEONE DRESSED LIKE THEY ARE?
MAYBE HE'S WRONG ABOUT MY VISIONS. MAYBE THEY WERE REALLY A WARNING...
WALLY...YOUR AUNT IS RIGHT. THIS NEEDS TO END.
BECAUSE OF THAWNE, FOR MOST OF MY LIFE I WAS STANDING STILL. AND NOW I...WE HAVE A CHANCE AT SOMETHING NEW.
I'M NOT GOING TO LET EOBARD'S DEATH MAKE OUR FAMILY RUN WHEN WE DON'T HAVE TO.
BUT IF YOU DON'T WANT TO GO, IF YOU DON'T TRUST OUR DECISION...
...I'LL UNDERSTAND.
OKAY... I'LL FOLLOW YOU.
THANK YOU FOR TRUSTING ME, WALLY.
HEY, IT'S BEEN TOO LONG SINCE WE'VE ALL BEEN ON A ROAD TRIP, ANYWAY.
GREAT. HAPPY FAMILY. HOORAY.
NEXT STOP--
KKRRZZTTT

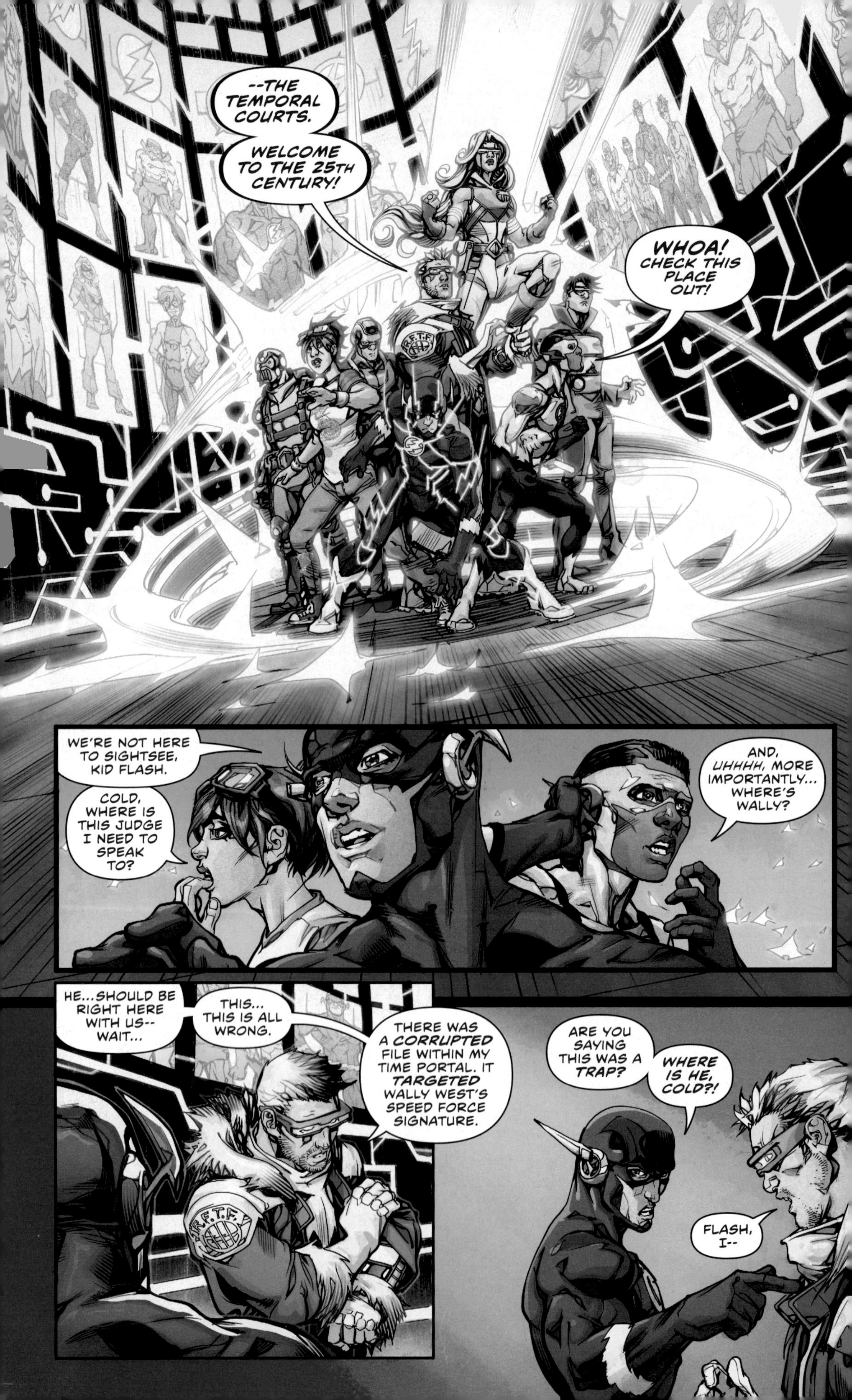
--THE TEMPORAL COURTS.
WELCOME TO THE 25TH CENTURY!
WHOA! CHECK THIS PLACE OUT!
WE'RE NOT HERE TO SIGHTSEE, KID FLASH.
COLD, WHERE IS THIS JUDGE I NEED TO SPEAK TO?
AND, UHHHH, MORE IMPORTANTLY... WHERE'S WALLY?
HE...SHOULD BE RIGHT HERE WITH US-- WAIT...
THIS... THIS IS ALL WRONG.
THERE WAS A CORRUPTED FILE WITHIN MY TIME PORTAL. IT TARGETED WALLY WEST'S SPEED FORCE SIGNATURE.
ARE YOU SAYING THIS WAS A TRAP?
WHERE IS HE, COLD?!
FLASH, I--

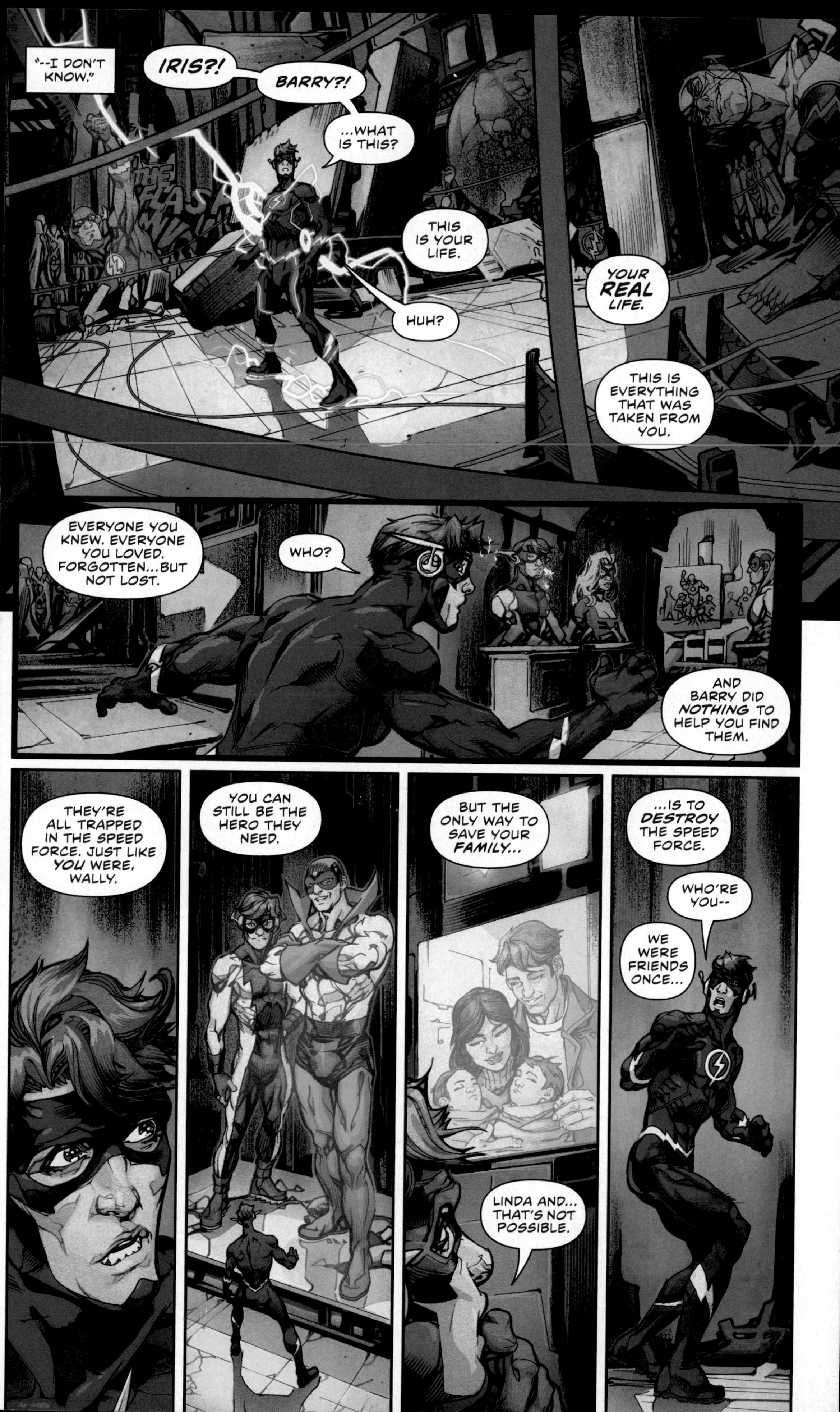
"--I DON'T KNOW."
IRIS?!
BARRY?!
...WHAT IS THIS?
THIS IS YOUR LIFE.
HUH?
YOUR REAL LIFE.
THIS IS EVERYTHING THAT WAS TAKEN FROM YOU.
EVERYONE YOU KNEW. EVERYONE YOU LOVED. FORGOTTEN...BUT NOT LOST.
WHO?
AND BARRY DID NOTHING TO HELP YOU FIND THEM.
THEY'RE ALL TRAPPED IN THE SPEED FORCE. JUST LIKE YOU WERE, WALLY.
YOU CAN STILL BE THE HERO THEY NEED.
BUT THE ONLY WAY TO SAVE YOUR FAMILY...
LINDA AND... THAT'S NOT POSSIBLE.
...IS TO DESTROY THE SPEED FORCE.
WHO'RE YOU--
WE WERE FRIENDS ONCE...

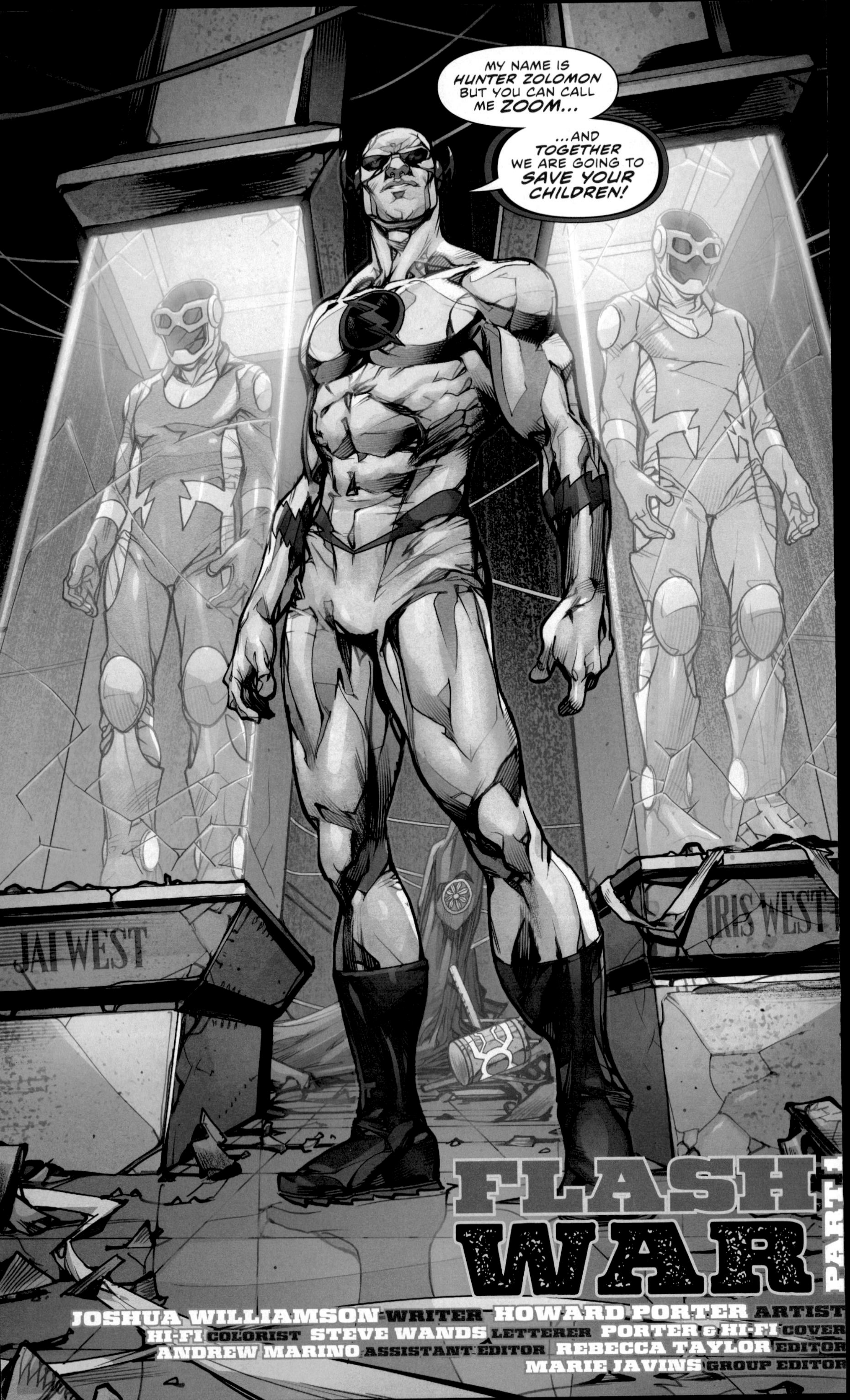
MY NAME IS HUNTER ZOLOMON BUT YOU CAN CALL ME ZOOM...
...AND TOGETHER WE ARE GOING TO SAVE YOUR CHILDREN!
JAI WEST
IRIS WEST
FLASH WAR
PART 1
JOSHUA WILLIAMSON WRITER HOWARD PORTER ARTIST
HI-FI COLORIST STEVE WANDS LETTERER PORTER & HI-FI COVER
ANDREW MARINO ASSISTANT EDITOR REBECCA TAYLOR EDITOR
MARIE JAVINS GROUP EDITOR

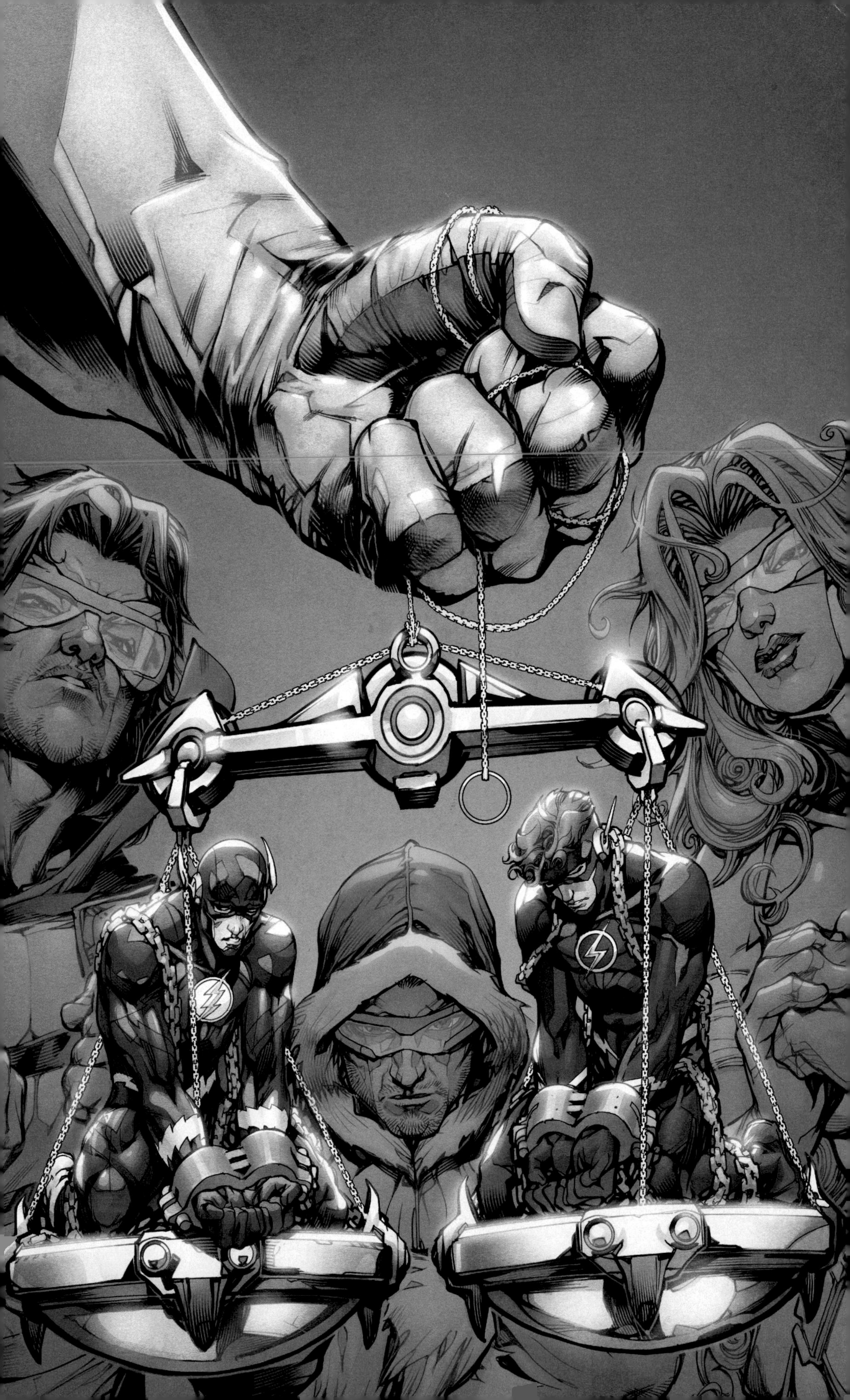

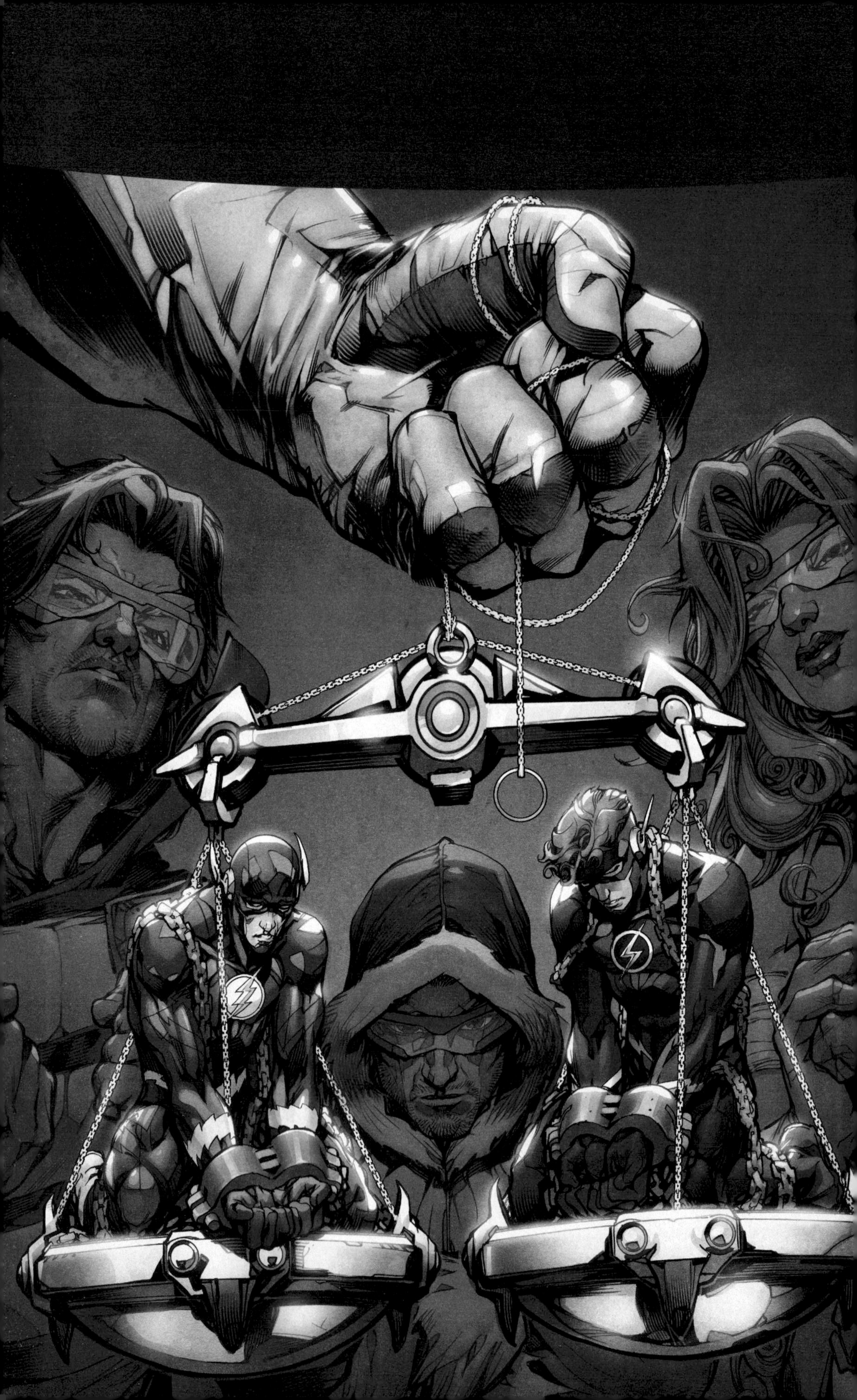

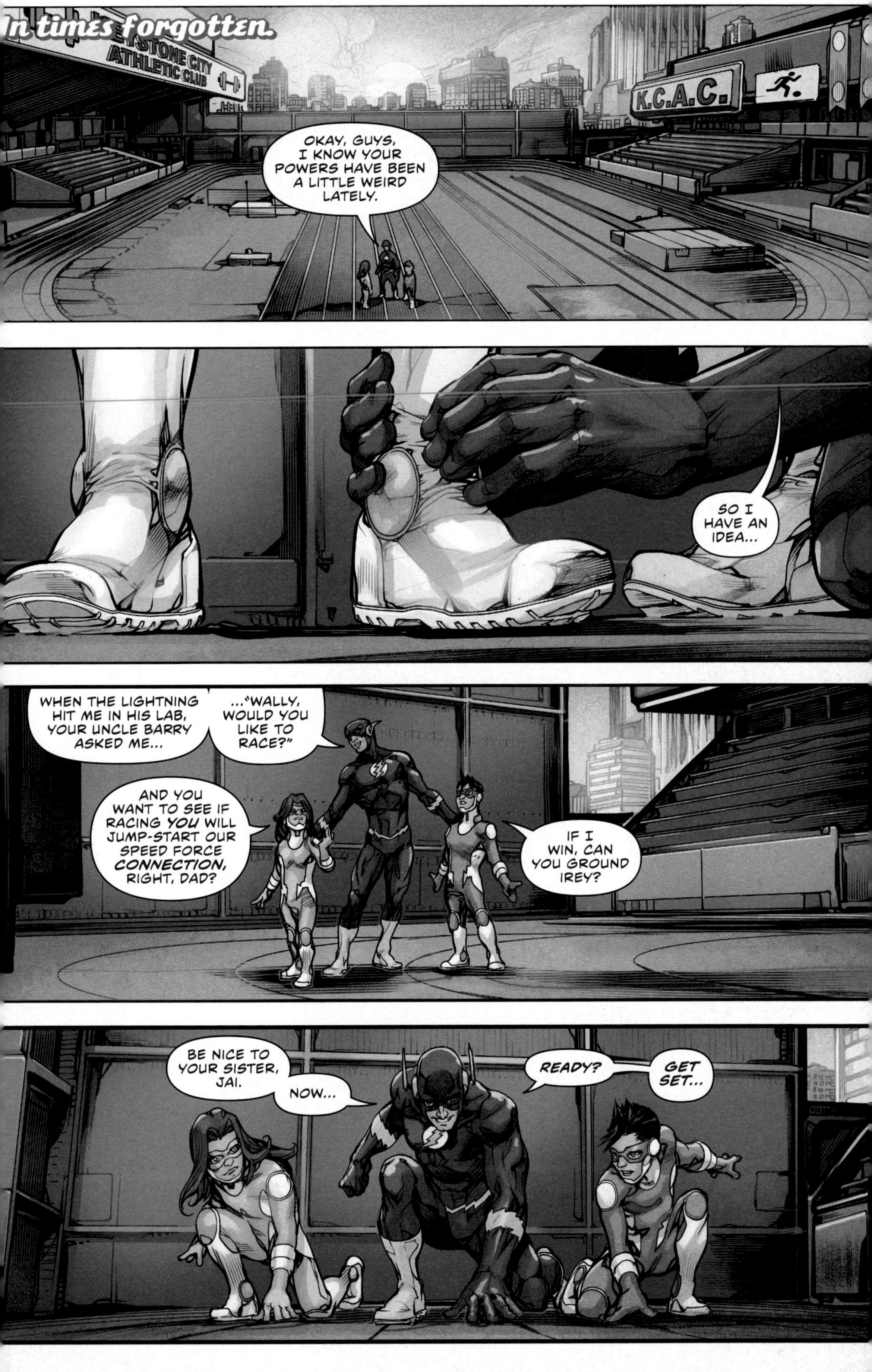
n times forgotten.
KEYSTONE CITY ATHLETIC CLUB
K.C.A.C.
OKAY, GUYS, I KNOW YOUR POWERS HAVE BEEN A LITTLE WEIRD LATELY.
SO I HAVE AN IDEA...
WHEN THE LIGHTNING HIT ME IN HIS LAB, YOUR UNCLE BARRY ASKED ME...
..."WALLY, WOULD YOU LIKE TO RACE?"
AND YOU WANT TO SEE IF RACING *YOU* WILL JUMP-START OUR SPEED FORCE *CONNECTION*, RIGHT, DAD?
IF I WIN, CAN YOU GROUND IREY?
BE NICE TO YOUR SISTER, JAI.
NOW...
READY?
GET SET...

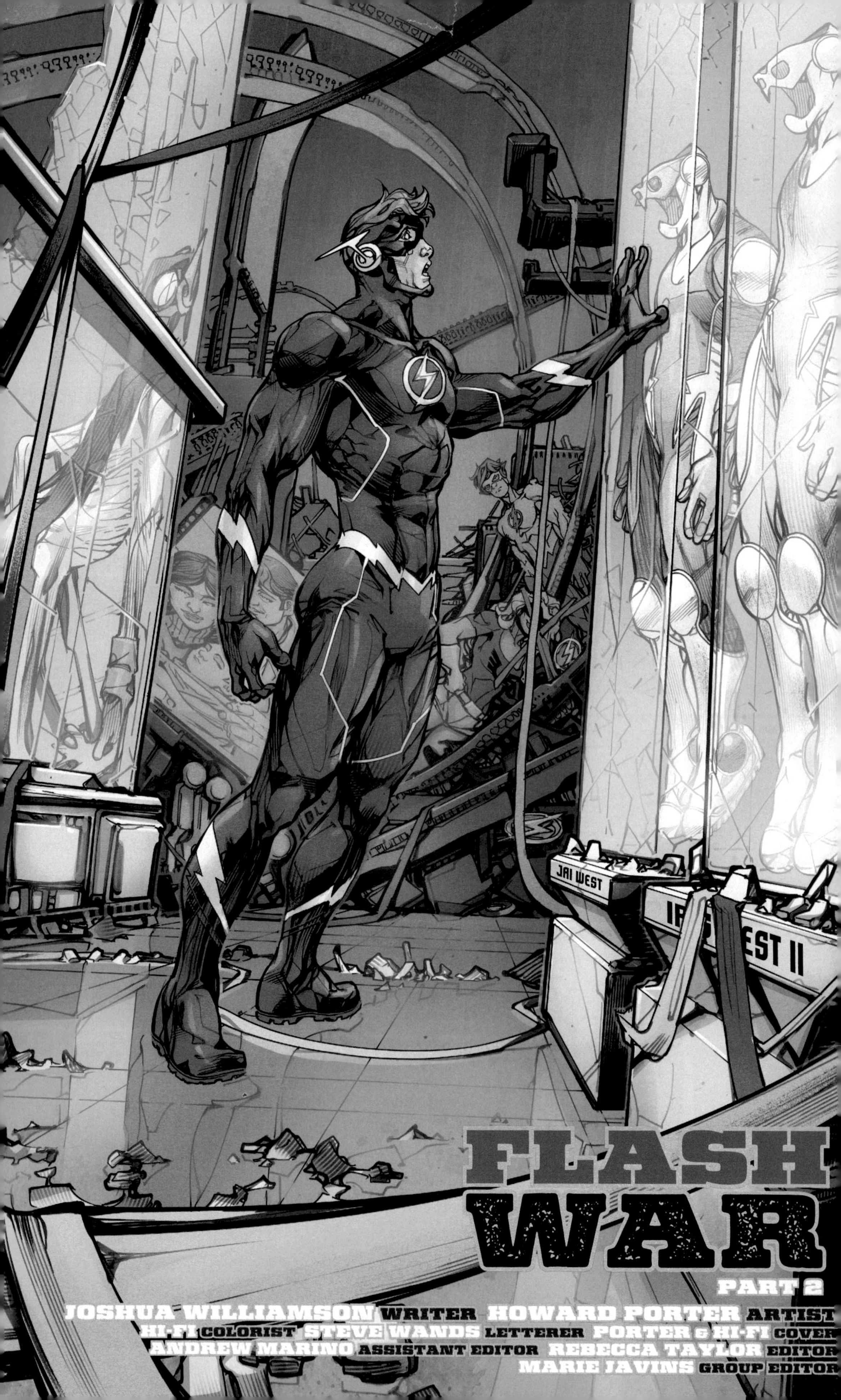
JAI WEST
FLASH
WAR
PART 2
JOSHUA WILLIAMSON WRITER HOWARD PORTER ARTIST
HI-FI COLORIST STEVE WANDS LETTERER PORTER & HI-FI COVER
ANDREW MARINO ASSISTANT EDITOR REBECCA TAYLOR EDITOR
MARIE JAVINS GROUP EDITOR

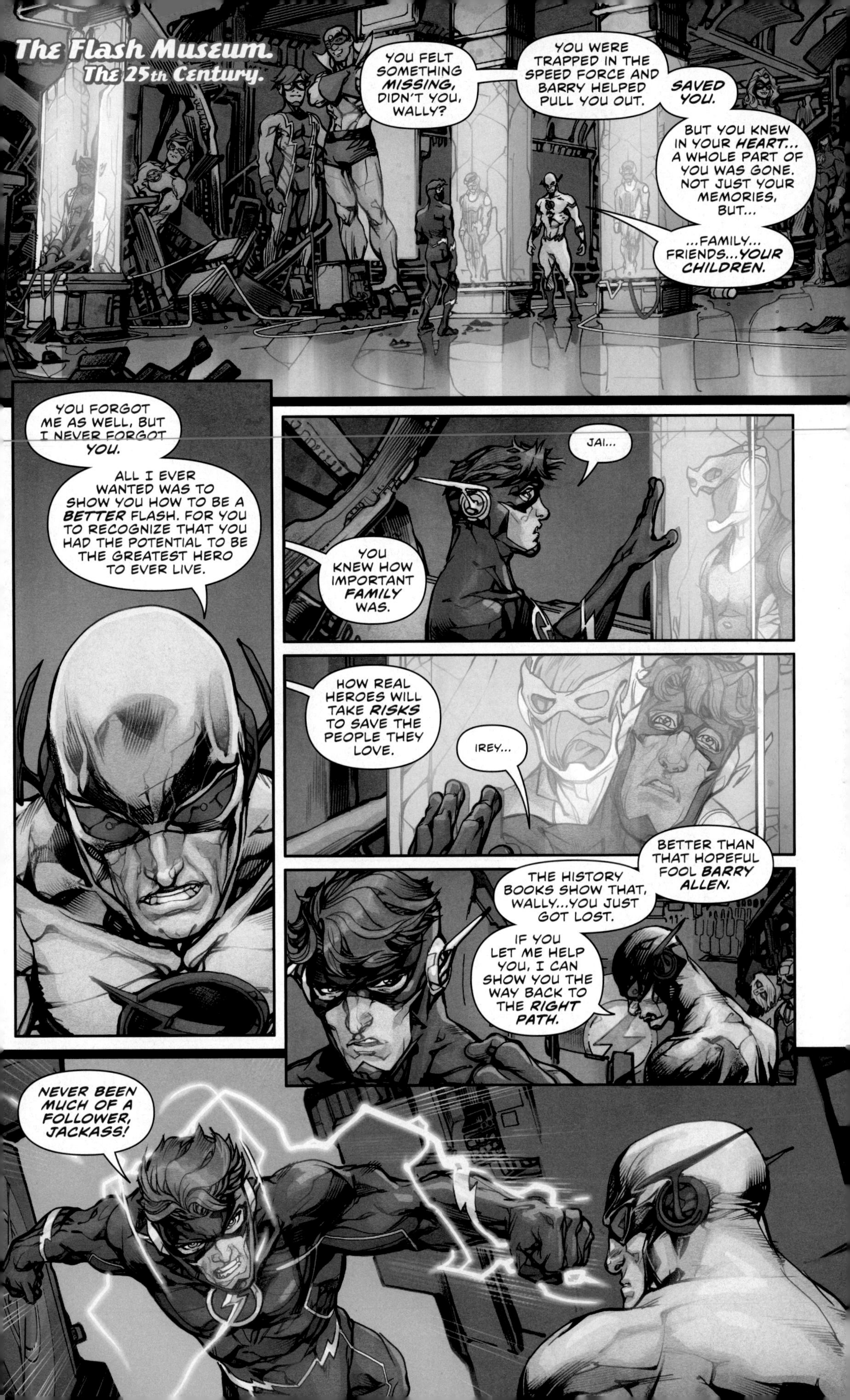

The Flash Museum.
The 25th Century.
YOU FELT SOMETHING MISSING, DIDN'T YOU, WALLY?
YOU WERE TRAPPED IN THE SPEED FORCE AND BARRY HELPED PULL YOU OUT.
SAVED YOU.
BUT YOU KNEW IN YOUR HEART... A WHOLE PART OF YOU WAS GONE. NOT JUST YOUR MEMORIES, BUT...
...FAMILY... FRIENDS...YOUR CHILDREN.
YOU FORGOT ME AS WELL, BUT I NEVER FORGOT YOU.
ALL I EVER WANTED WAS TO SHOW YOU HOW TO BE A BETTER FLASH. FOR YOU TO RECOGNIZE THAT YOU HAD THE POTENTIAL TO BE THE GREATEST HERO TO EVER LIVE.
JAI...
YOU KNEW HOW IMPORTANT FAMILY WAS.
HOW REAL HEROES WILL TAKE RISKS TO SAVE THE PEOPLE THEY LOVE.
IREY...
THE HISTORY BOOKS SHOW THAT, WALLY...YOU JUST GOT LOST.
BETTER THAN THAT HOPEFUL FOOL BARRY ALLEN.
IF YOU LET ME HELP YOU, I CAN SHOW YOU THE WAY BACK TO THE RIGHT PATH.
NEVER BEEN MUCH OF A FOLLOWER, JACKASS!

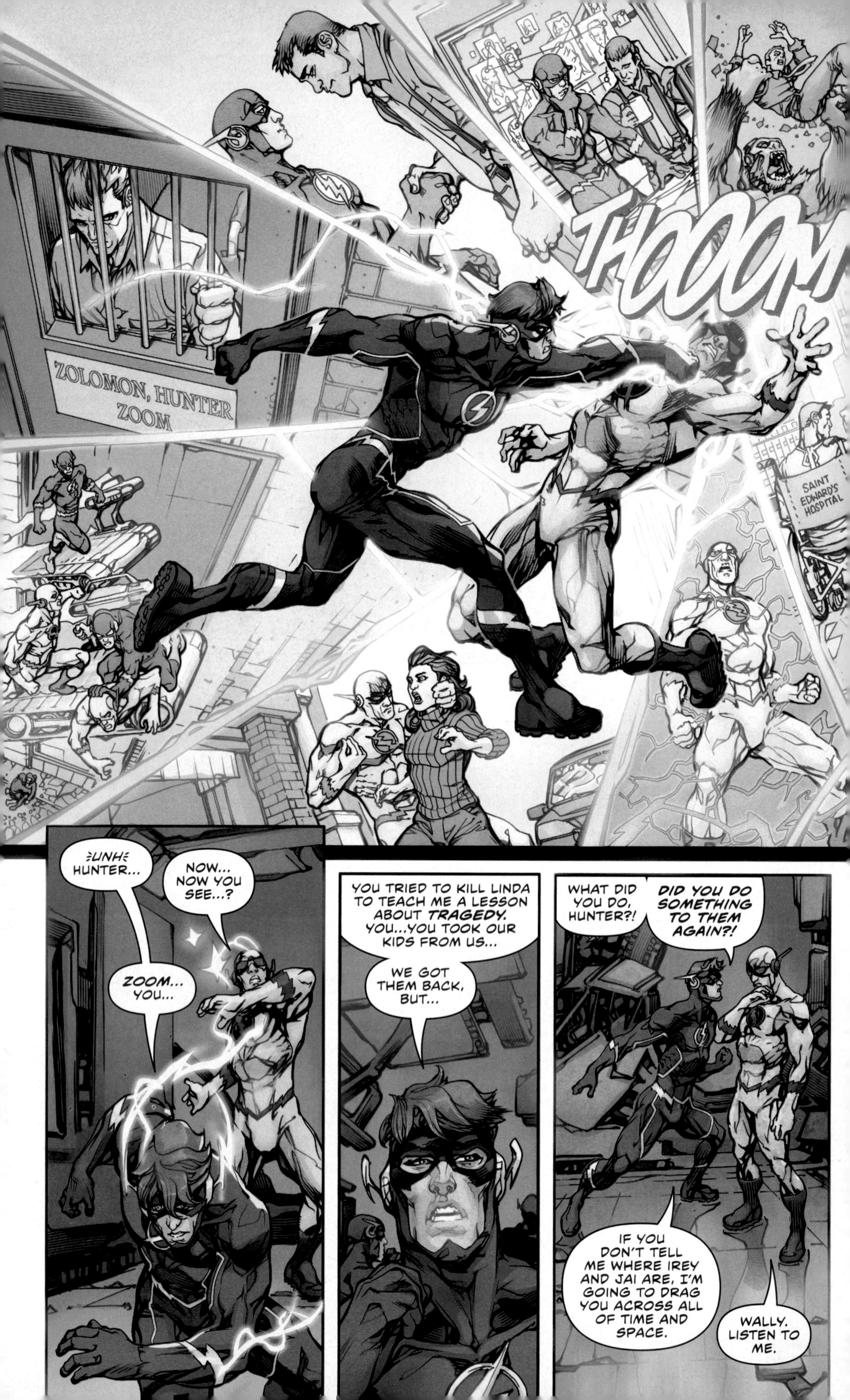
ZOLOMON, HUNTER
ZOOM
THOOOM
SAINT EDWARD'S HOSPITAL
UNH HUNTER...
NOW... NOW YOU SEE...?
ZOOM... YOU...
YOU TRIED TO KILL LINDA TO TEACH ME A LESSON ABOUT TRAGEDY. YOU...YOU TOOK OUR KIDS FROM US...
WE GOT THEM BACK, BUT...
WHAT DID YOU DO, HUNTER?!
DID YOU DO SOMETHING TO THEM AGAIN?!
IF YOU DON'T TELL ME WHERE IREY AND JAI ARE, I'M GOING TO DRAG YOU ACROSS ALL OF TIME AND SPACE.
WALLY. LISTEN TO ME.

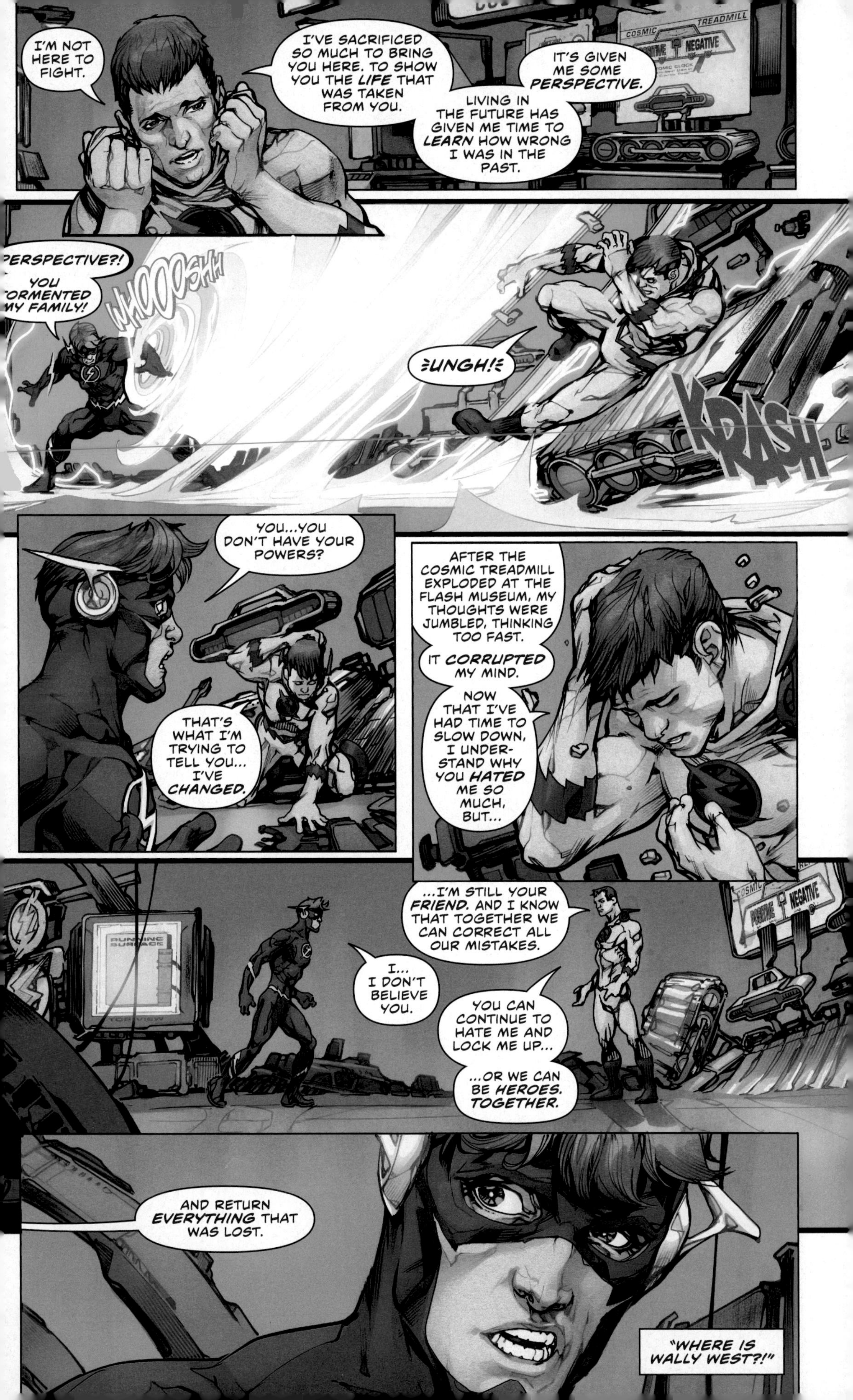

I'M NOT HERE TO FIGHT.
I'VE SACRIFICED SO MUCH TO BRING YOU HERE. TO SHOW YOU THE *LIFE* THAT WAS TAKEN FROM YOU.
IT'S GIVEN ME SOME *PERSPECTIVE.*
LIVING IN THE FUTURE HAS GIVEN ME TIME TO *LEARN* HOW WRONG I WAS IN THE PAST.
COSMIC TREADMILL
POSITIVE NEGATIVE
PERSPECTIVE?! YOU TORMENTED MY FAMILY!
WHOOOSHH
UNGH!
KRASH
YOU...YOU DON'T HAVE YOUR POWERS?
THAT'S WHAT I'M TRYING TO TELL YOU... I'VE *CHANGED.*
AFTER THE COSMIC TREADMILL EXPLODED AT THE FLASH MUSEUM, MY THOUGHTS WERE JUMBLED, THINKING TOO FAST.
IT *CORRUPTED* MY MIND.
NOW THAT I'VE HAD TIME TO SLOW DOWN, I UNDERSTAND WHY YOU *HATED* ME SO MUCH, BUT...
...I'M STILL YOUR *FRIEND.* AND I KNOW THAT TOGETHER WE CAN CORRECT ALL OUR MISTAKES.
I... I DON'T BELIEVE YOU.
YOU CAN CONTINUE TO HATE ME AND LOCK ME UP...
...OR WE CAN BE *HEROES. TOGETHER.*
RUNNING SURFACE
COSMIC
POSITIVE NEGATIVE
AND RETURN *EVERYTHING* THAT WAS LOST.
"WHERE IS WALLY WEST?!"

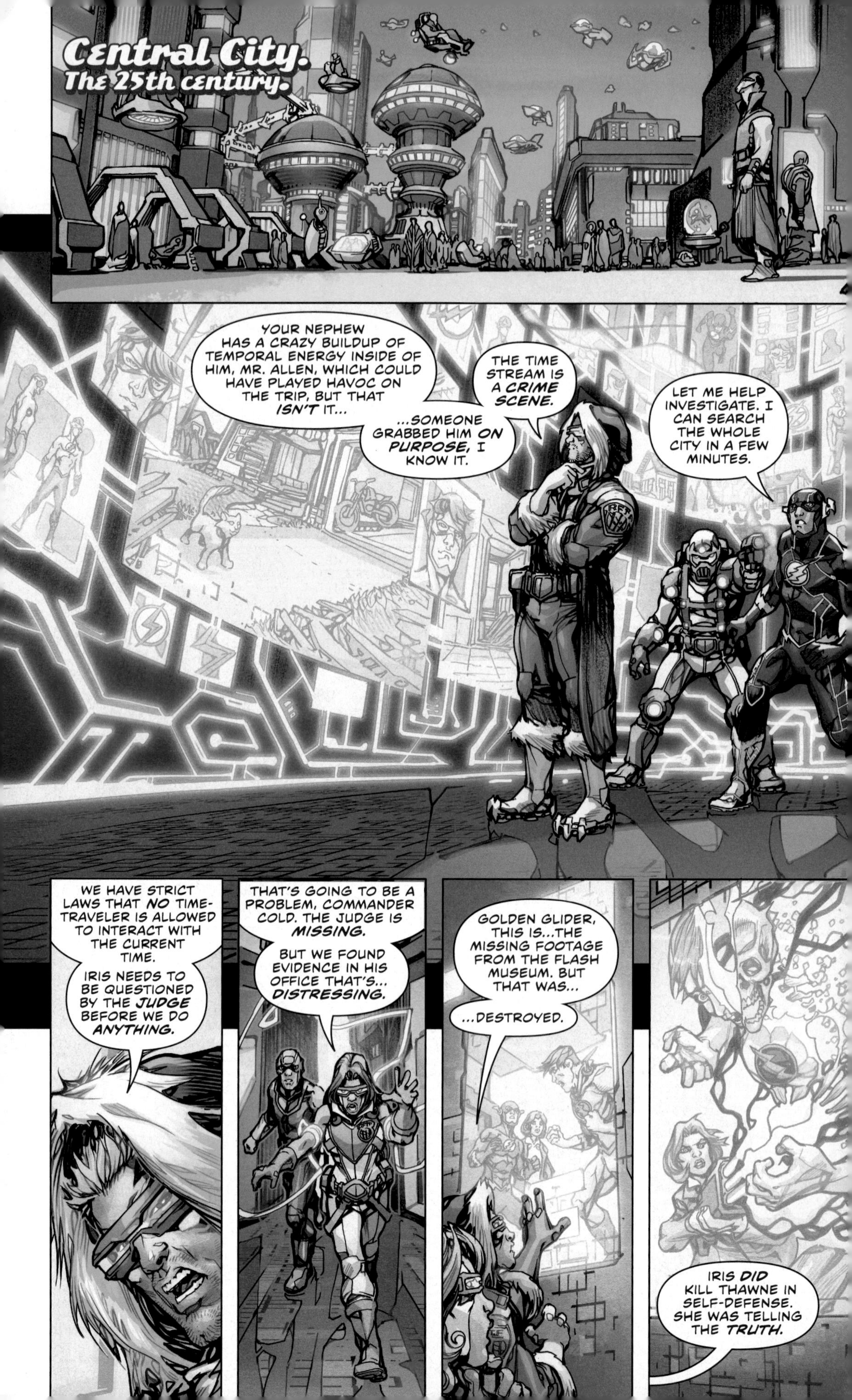
Central City.
The 25th century.
YOUR NEPHEW HAS A CRAZY BUILDUP OF TEMPORAL ENERGY INSIDE OF HIM, MR. ALLEN, WHICH COULD HAVE PLAYED HAVOC ON THE TRIP, BUT THAT ISN'T IT...
...SOMEONE GRABBED HIM ON PURPOSE, I KNOW IT.
THE TIME STREAM IS A CRIME SCENE.
LET ME HELP INVESTIGATE. I CAN SEARCH THE WHOLE CITY IN A FEW MINUTES.
WE HAVE STRICT LAWS THAT NO TIME-TRAVELER IS ALLOWED TO INTERACT WITH THE CURRENT TIME.
IRIS NEEDS TO BE QUESTIONED BY THE JUDGE BEFORE WE DO ANYTHING.
THAT'S GOING TO BE A PROBLEM, COMMANDER COLD. THE JUDGE IS MISSING.
BUT WE FOUND EVIDENCE IN HIS OFFICE THAT'S... DISTRESSING.
GOLDEN GLIDER, THIS IS...THE MISSING FOOTAGE FROM THE FLASH MUSEUM. BUT THAT WAS...
...DESTROYED.
IRIS DID KILL THAWNE IN SELF-DEFENSE. SHE WAS TELLING THE TRUTH.

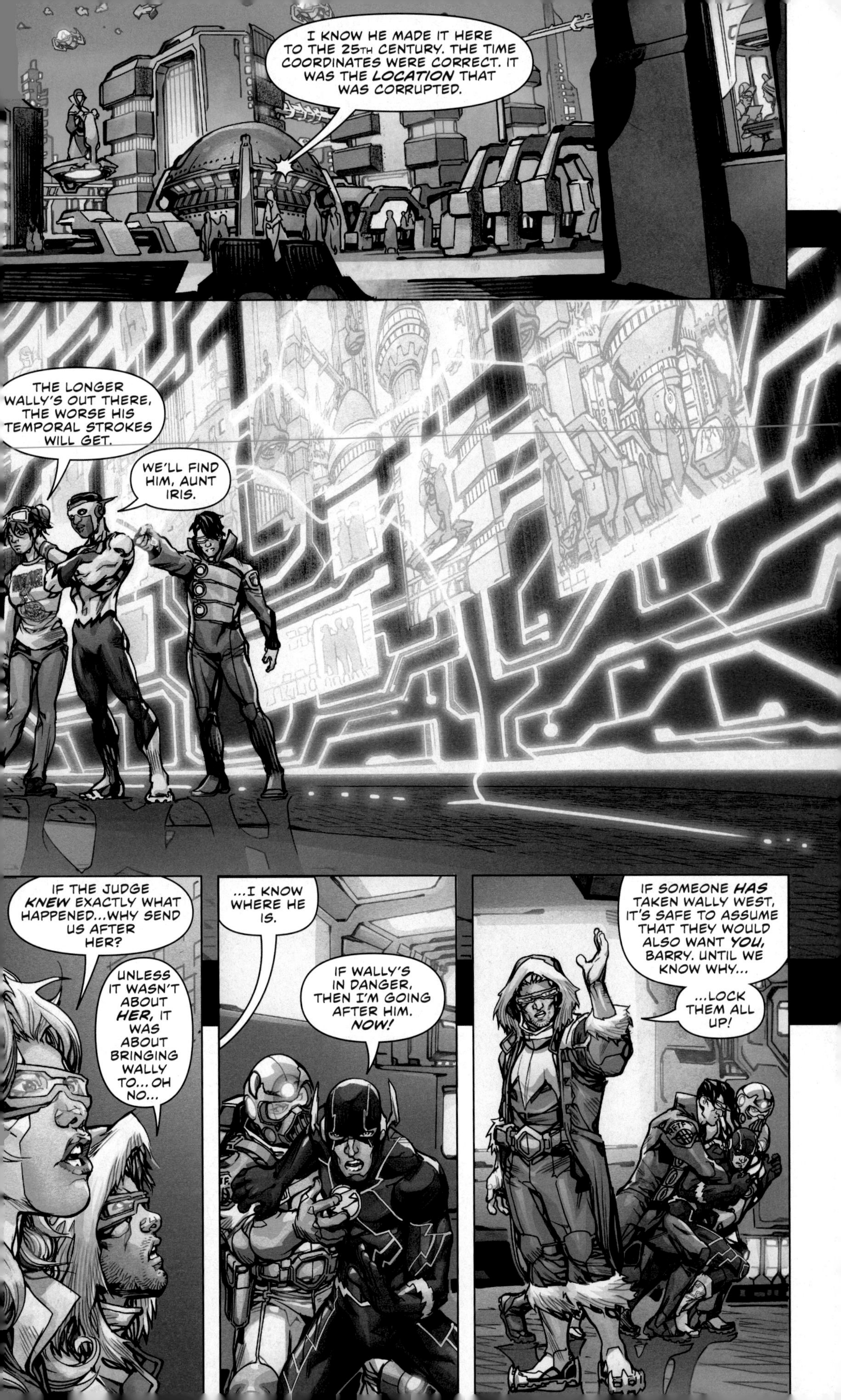

I KNOW HE MADE IT HERE TO THE 25TH CENTURY. THE TIME COORDINATES WERE CORRECT. IT WAS THE *LOCATION* THAT WAS CORRUPTED.
THE LONGER WALLY'S OUT THERE, THE WORSE HIS TEMPORAL STROKES WILL GET.
WE'LL FIND HIM, AUNT IRIS.
IF THE JUDGE *KNEW* EXACTLY WHAT HAPPENED...WHY SEND US AFTER HER?
UNLESS IT WASN'T ABOUT *HER*, IT WAS ABOUT BRINGING WALLY TO...OH NO...
...I KNOW WHERE HE IS.
IF WALLY'S IN DANGER, THEN I'M GOING AFTER HIM. *NOW!*
IF SOMEONE *HAS* TAKEN WALLY WEST, IT'S SAFE TO ASSUME THAT THEY WOULD ALSO WANT *YOU*, BARRY. UNTIL WE KNOW WHY...
...LOCK THEM ALL UP!

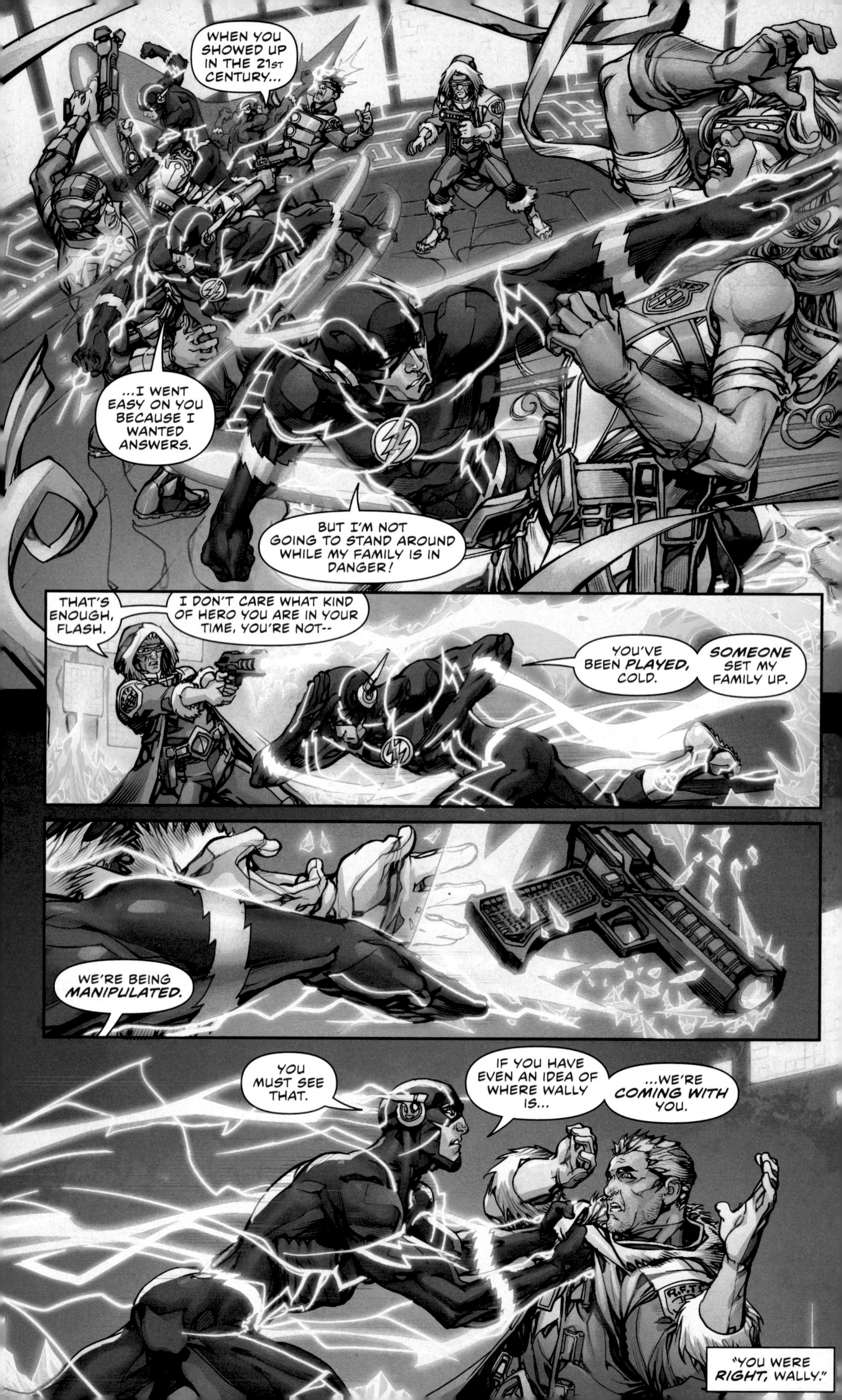
WHEN YOU SHOWED UP IN THE 21st CENTURY...
...I WENT EASY ON YOU BECAUSE I WANTED ANSWERS.
BUT I'M NOT GOING TO STAND AROUND WHILE MY FAMILY IS IN DANGER!
THAT'S ENOUGH, FLASH.
I DON'T CARE WHAT KIND OF HERO YOU ARE IN YOUR TIME, YOU'RE NOT--
YOU'VE BEEN PLAYED, COLD.
SOMEONE SET MY FAMILY UP.
WE'RE BEING MANIPULATED.
YOU MUST SEE THAT.
IF YOU HAVE EVEN AN IDEA OF WHERE WALLY IS...
...WE'RE COMING WITH YOU.
"YOU WERE RIGHT, WALLY."

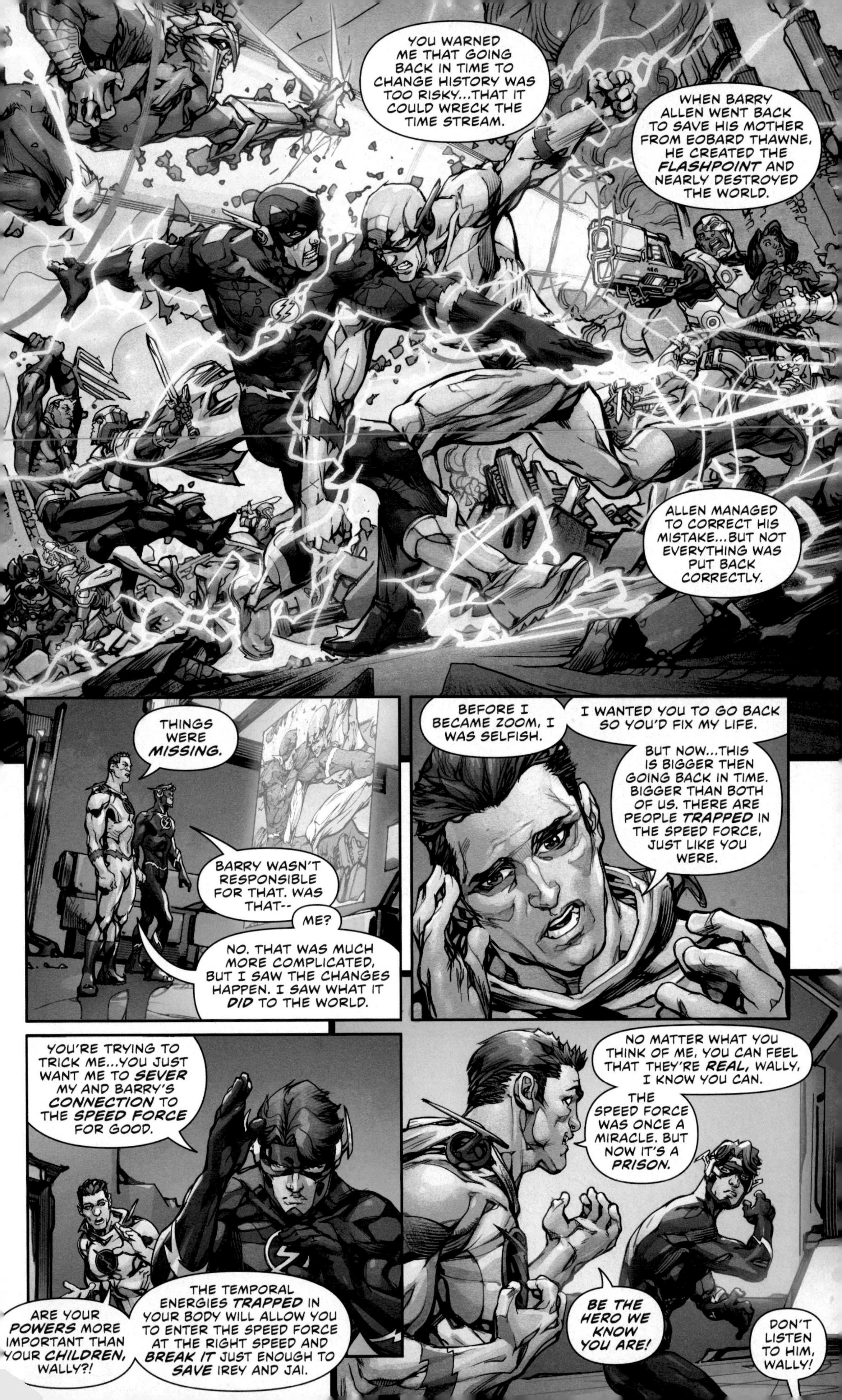

YOU WARNED ME THAT GOING BACK IN TIME TO CHANGE HISTORY WAS TOO RISKY...THAT IT COULD WRECK THE TIME STREAM.
WHEN BARRY ALLEN WENT BACK TO SAVE HIS MOTHER FROM EOBARD THAWNE, HE CREATED THE FLASHPOINT AND NEARLY DESTROYED THE WORLD.
ALLEN MANAGED TO CORRECT HIS MISTAKE...BUT NOT EVERYTHING WAS PUT BACK CORRECTLY.
THINGS WERE MISSING.
BARRY WASN'T RESPONSIBLE FOR THAT. WAS THAT--
ME?
NO. THAT WAS MUCH MORE COMPLICATED, BUT I SAW THE CHANGES HAPPEN. I SAW WHAT IT DID TO THE WORLD.
BEFORE I BECAME ZOOM, I WAS SELFISH.
I WANTED YOU TO GO BACK SO YOU'D FIX MY LIFE.
BUT NOW...THIS IS BIGGER THEN GOING BACK IN TIME. BIGGER THAN BOTH OF US. THERE ARE PEOPLE TRAPPED IN THE SPEED FORCE, JUST LIKE YOU WERE.
YOU'RE TRYING TO TRICK ME...YOU JUST WANT ME TO SEVER MY AND BARRY'S CONNECTION TO THE SPEED FORCE FOR GOOD.
ARE YOUR POWERS MORE IMPORTANT THAN YOUR CHILDREN, WALLY?!
THE TEMPORAL ENERGIES TRAPPED IN YOUR BODY WILL ALLOW YOU TO ENTER THE SPEED FORCE AT THE RIGHT SPEED AND BREAK IT JUST ENOUGH TO SAVE IREY AND JAI.
NO MATTER WHAT YOU THINK OF ME, YOU CAN FEEL THAT THEY'RE REAL, WALLY, I KNOW YOU CAN.
THE SPEED FORCE WAS ONCE A MIRACLE. BUT NOW IT'S A PRISON.
BE THE HERO WE KNOW YOU ARE!
DON'T LISTEN TO HIM, WALLY!

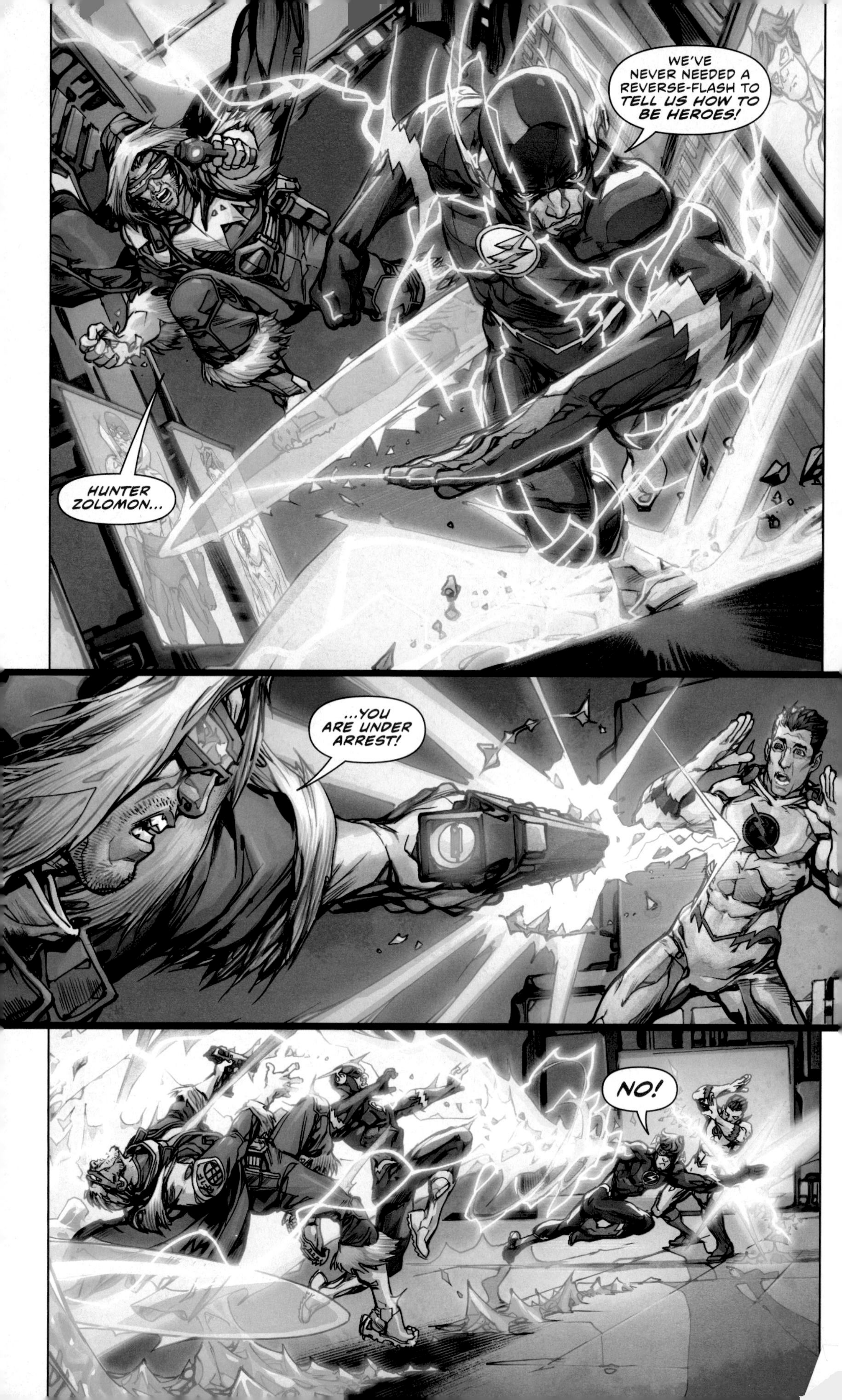
WE'VE NEVER NEEDED A REVERSE-FLASH TO TELL US HOW TO BE HEROES!
HUNTER ZOLOMON...
...YOU ARE UNDER ARREST!
NO!

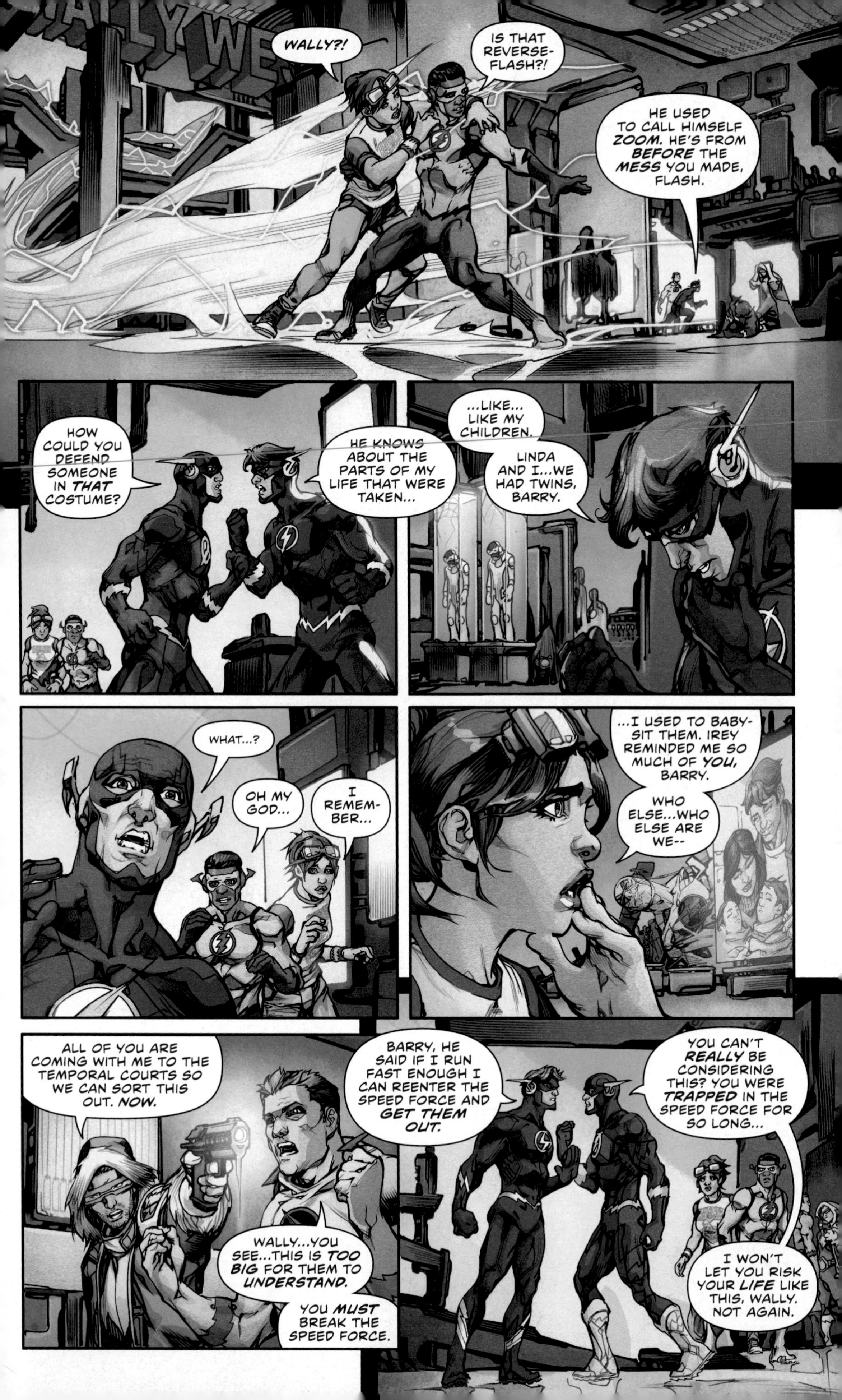

WALLY?!
IS THAT REVERSE-FLASH?!
HE USED TO CALL HIMSELF ZOOM. HE'S FROM BEFORE THE MESS YOU MADE, FLASH.
HOW COULD YOU DEFEND SOMEONE IN THAT COSTUME?
HE KNOWS ABOUT THE PARTS OF MY LIFE THAT WERE TAKEN...
...LIKE... LIKE MY CHILDREN.
LINDA AND I...WE HAD TWINS, BARRY.
WHAT...?
OH MY GOD...
I REMEMBER...
...I USED TO BABY-SIT THEM. IREY REMINDED ME SO MUCH OF YOU, BARRY.
WHO ELSE...WHO ELSE ARE WE--
ALL OF YOU ARE COMING WITH ME TO THE TEMPORAL COURTS SO WE CAN SORT THIS OUT. NOW.
WALLY...YOU SEE...THIS IS TOO BIG FOR THEM TO UNDERSTAND.
YOU MUST BREAK THE SPEED FORCE.
BARRY, HE SAID IF I RUN FAST ENOUGH I CAN REENTER THE SPEED FORCE AND GET THEM OUT.
YOU CAN'T REALLY BE CONSIDERING THIS? YOU WERE TRAPPED IN THE SPEED FORCE FOR SO LONG...
I WON'T LET YOU RISK YOUR LIFE LIKE THIS, WALLY. NOT AGAIN.

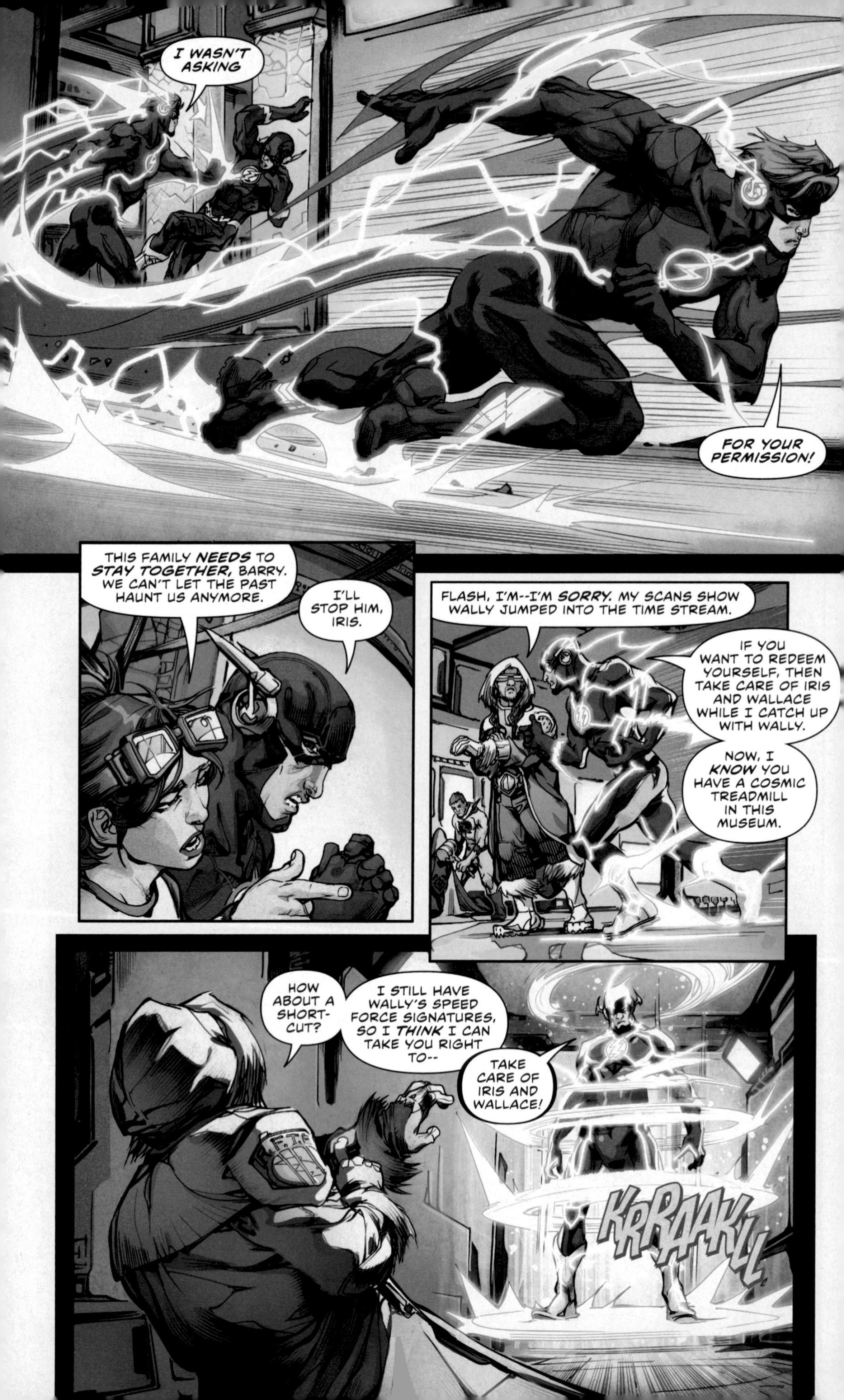
I WASN'T ASKING
FOR YOUR PERMISSION!
THIS FAMILY NEEDS TO STAY TOGETHER, BARRY. WE CAN'T LET THE PAST HAUNT US ANYMORE.
I'LL STOP HIM, IRIS.
FLASH, I'M--I'M SORRY. MY SCANS SHOW WALLY JUMPED INTO THE TIME STREAM.
IF YOU WANT TO REDEEM YOURSELF, THEN TAKE CARE OF IRIS AND WALLACE WHILE I CATCH UP WITH WALLY.
NOW, I KNOW YOU HAVE A COSMIC TREADMILL IN THIS MUSEUM.
HOW ABOUT A SHORT-CUT?
I STILL HAVE WALLY'S SPEED FORCE SIGNATURES, SO I THINK I CAN TAKE YOU RIGHT TO--
TAKE CARE OF IRIS AND WALLACE!
KRRAAKLL

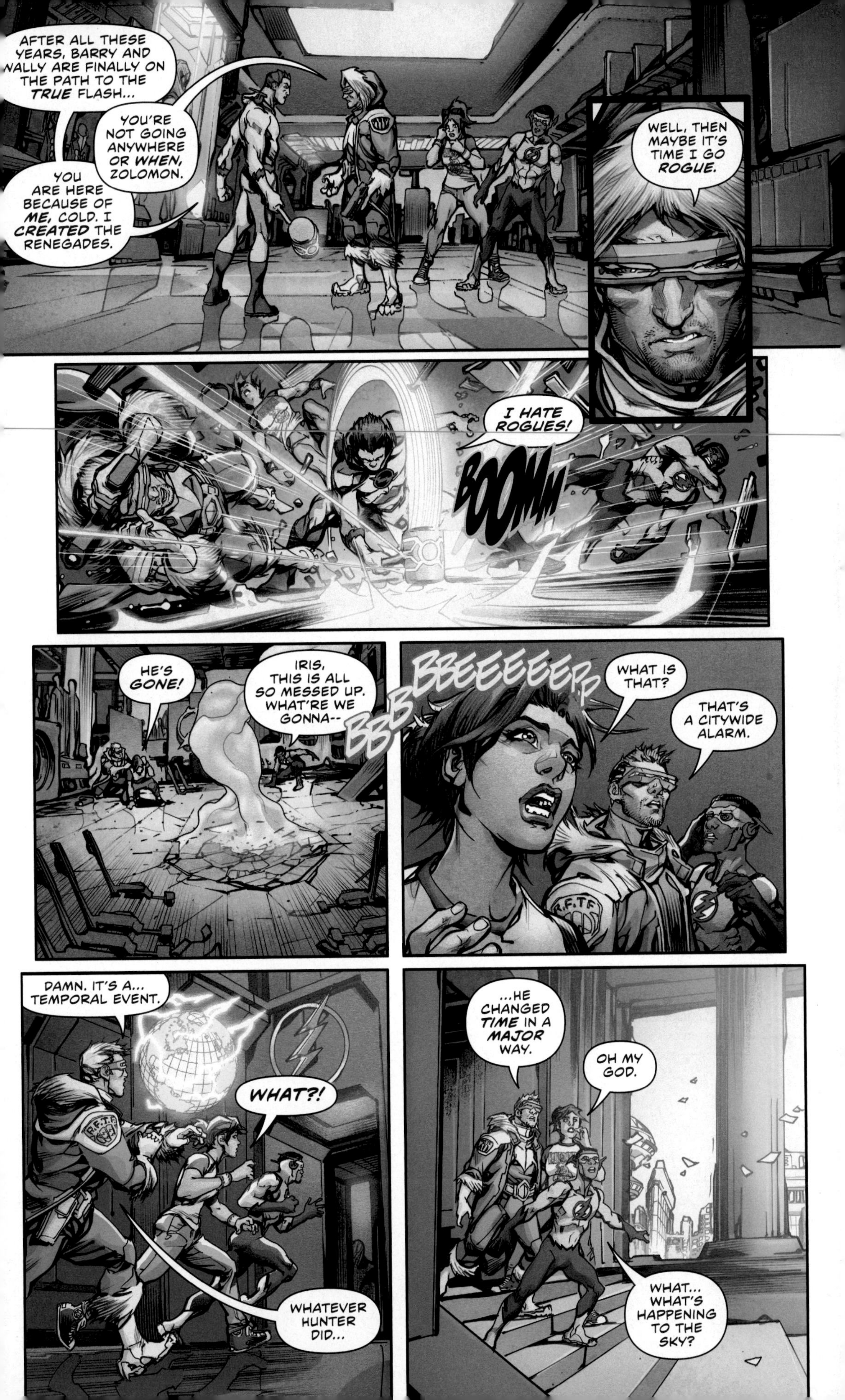
AFTER ALL THESE YEARS, BARRY AND WALLY ARE FINALLY ON THE PATH TO THE TRUE FLASH...
YOU'RE NOT GOING ANYWHERE OR WHEN, ZOLOMON.
YOU ARE HERE BECAUSE OF ME, COLD. I CREATED THE RENEGADES.
WELL, THEN MAYBE IT'S TIME I GO ROGUE.
I HATE ROGUES!
BOOMM
HE'S GONE!
IRIS, THIS IS ALL SO MESSED UP. WHAT'RE WE GONNA--
BBBBBEEEEEEPP
WHAT IS THAT?
THAT'S A CITYWIDE ALARM.
DAMN. IT'S A... TEMPORAL EVENT.
WHAT?!
WHATEVER HUNTER DID...
...HE CHANGED TIME IN A MAJOR WAY.
OH MY GOD.
WHAT... WHAT'S HAPPENING TO THE SKY?

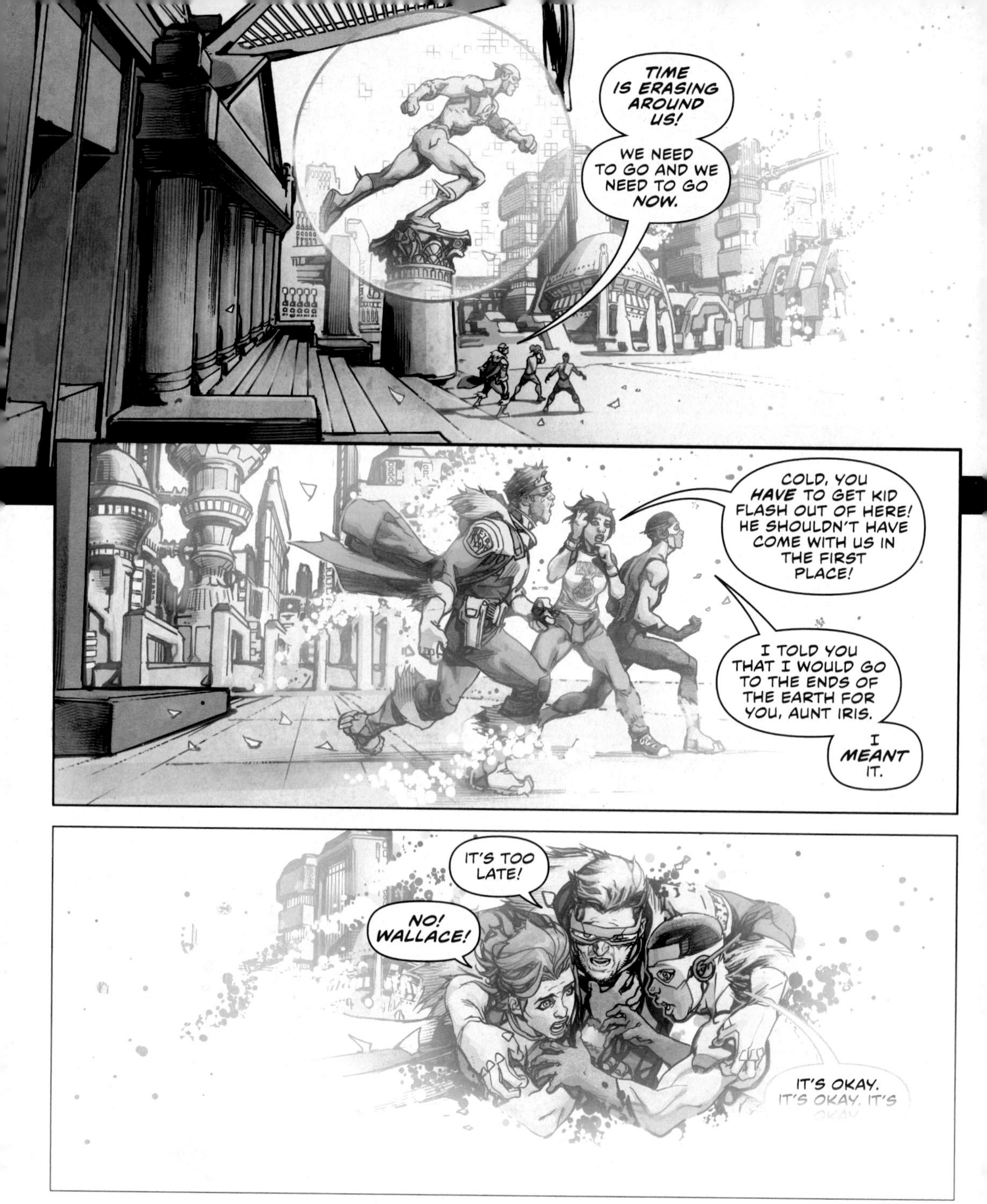
TIME IS ERASING AROUND US!
WE NEED TO GO AND WE NEED TO GO NOW.
COLD, YOU HAVE TO GET KID FLASH OUT OF HERE! HE SHOULDN'T HAVE COME WITH US IN THE FIRST PLACE!
I TOLD YOU THAT I WOULD GO TO THE ENDS OF THE EARTH FOR YOU, AUNT IRIS.
I MEANT IT.
IT'S TOO LATE!
NO! WALLACE!
IT'S OKAY. IT'S OKAY. IT'S

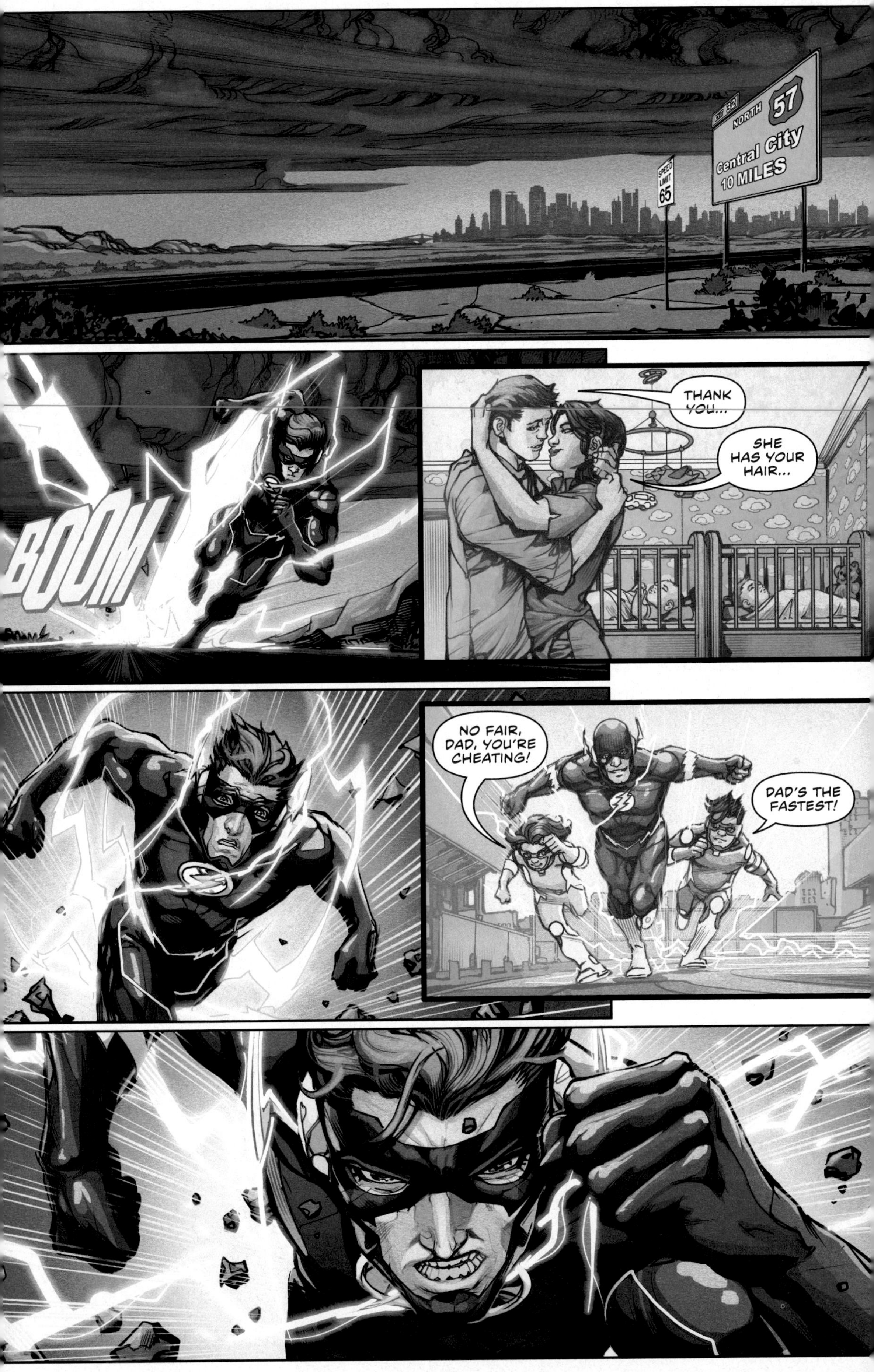

SPEED LIMIT 65
NORTH 57
Central City
10 MILES
BOOM
THANK YOU...
SHE HAS YOUR HAIR...
NO FAIR, DAD, YOU'RE CHEATING!
DAD'S THE FASTEST!

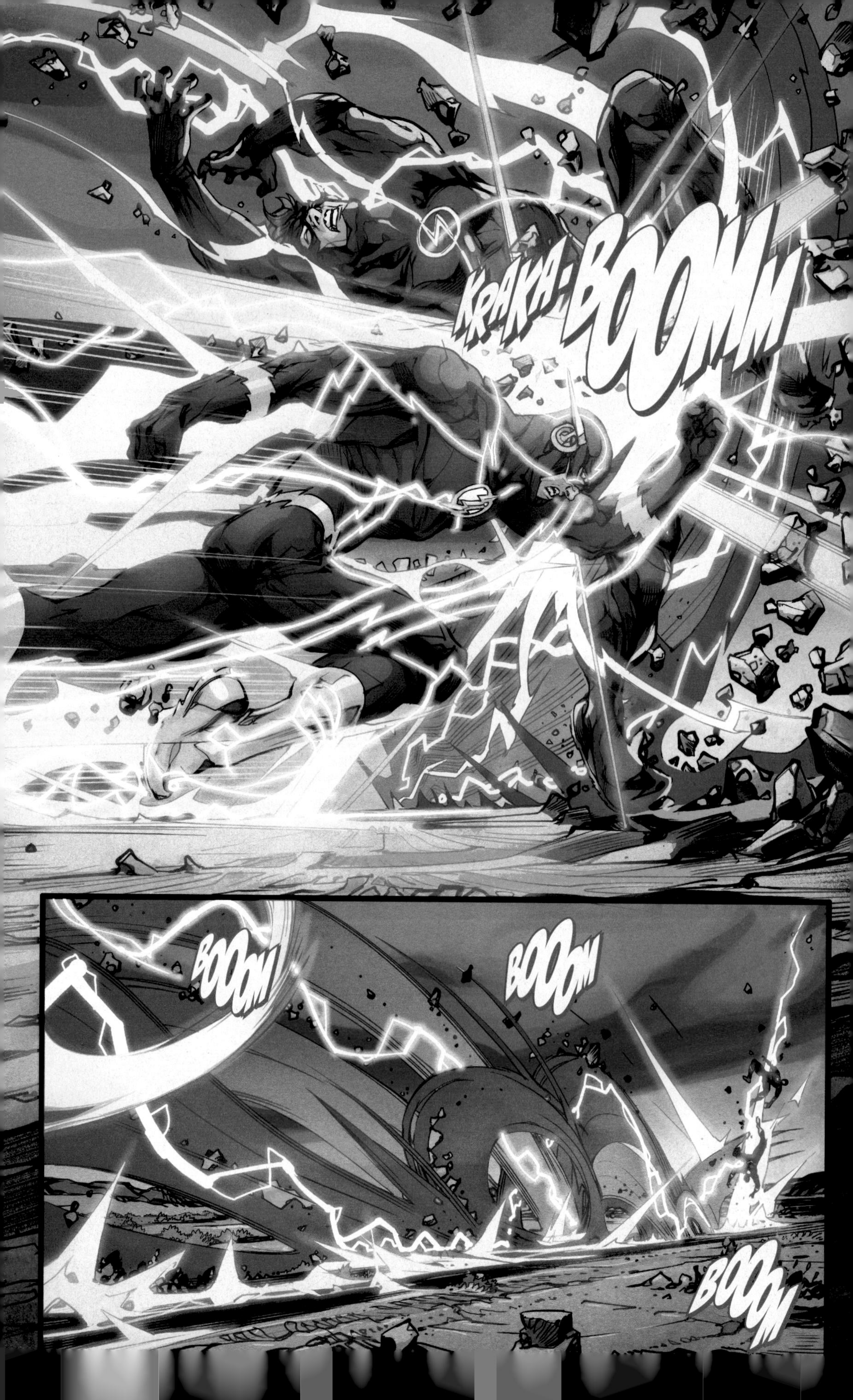
KRAKA-BOOMM
BOOOM
BOOOM
BOOOM

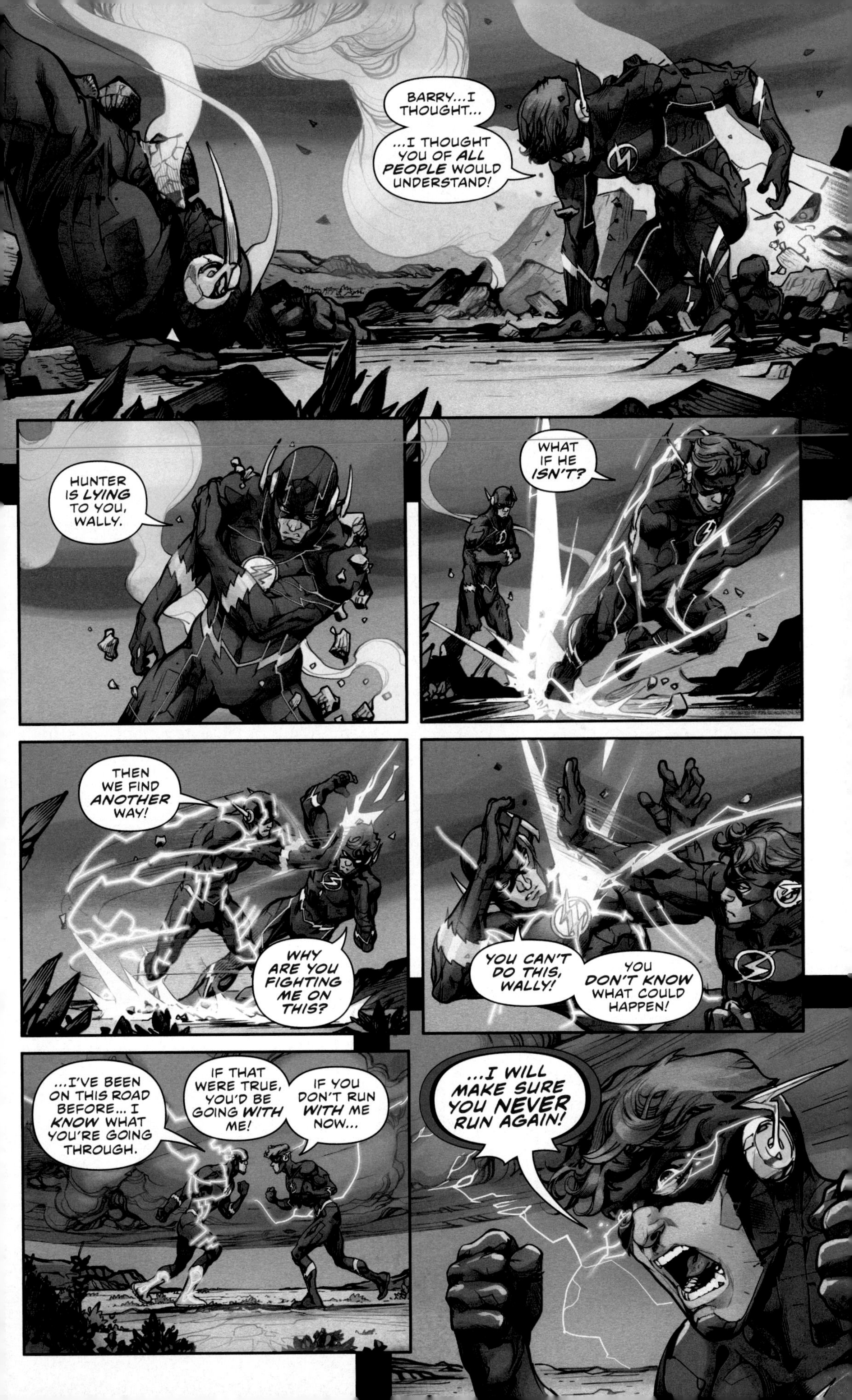
BARRY...I THOUGHT...
...I THOUGHT YOU OF ALL PEOPLE WOULD UNDERSTAND!
HUNTER IS LYING TO YOU, WALLY.
WHAT IF HE ISN'T?
THEN WE FIND ANOTHER WAY!
WHY ARE YOU FIGHTING ME ON THIS?
YOU CAN'T DO THIS, WALLY!
YOU DON'T KNOW WHAT COULD HAPPEN!
...I'VE BEEN ON THIS ROAD BEFORE... I KNOW WHAT YOU'RE GOING THROUGH.
IF THAT WERE TRUE, YOU'D BE GOING WITH ME!
IF YOU DON'T RUN WITH ME NOW...
...I WILL MAKE SURE YOU NEVER RUN AGAIN!

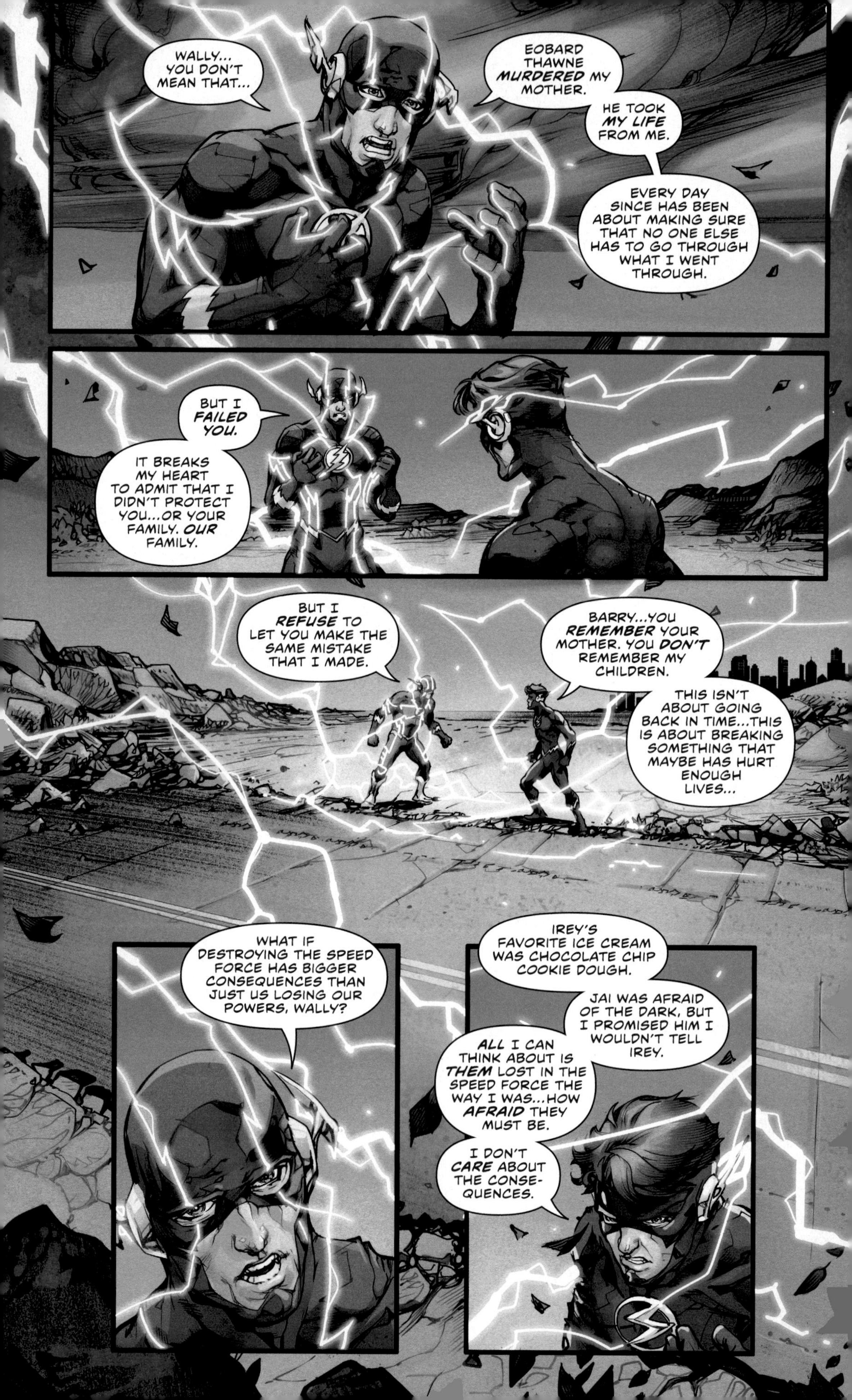
WALLY... YOU DON'T MEAN THAT...
EOBARD THAWNE MURDERED MY MOTHER.
HE TOOK MY LIFE FROM ME.
EVERY DAY SINCE HAS BEEN ABOUT MAKING SURE THAT NO ONE ELSE HAS TO GO THROUGH WHAT I WENT THROUGH.
BUT I FAILED YOU.
IT BREAKS MY HEART TO ADMIT THAT I DIDN'T PROTECT YOU...OR YOUR FAMILY. OUR FAMILY.
BUT I REFUSE TO LET YOU MAKE THE SAME MISTAKE THAT I MADE.
BARRY...YOU REMEMBER YOUR MOTHER. YOU DON'T REMEMBER MY CHILDREN.
THIS ISN'T ABOUT GOING BACK IN TIME...THIS IS ABOUT BREAKING SOMETHING THAT MAYBE HAS HURT ENOUGH LIVES...
WHAT IF DESTROYING THE SPEED FORCE HAS BIGGER CONSEQUENCES THAN JUST US LOSING OUR POWERS, WALLY?
IREY'S FAVORITE ICE CREAM WAS CHOCOLATE CHIP COOKIE DOUGH.
JAI WAS AFRAID OF THE DARK, BUT I PROMISED HIM I WOULDN'T TELL IREY.
ALL I CAN THINK ABOUT IS THEM LOST IN THE SPEED FORCE THE WAY I WAS...HOW AFRAID THEY MUST BE.
I DON'T CARE ABOUT THE CONSE-QUENCES.

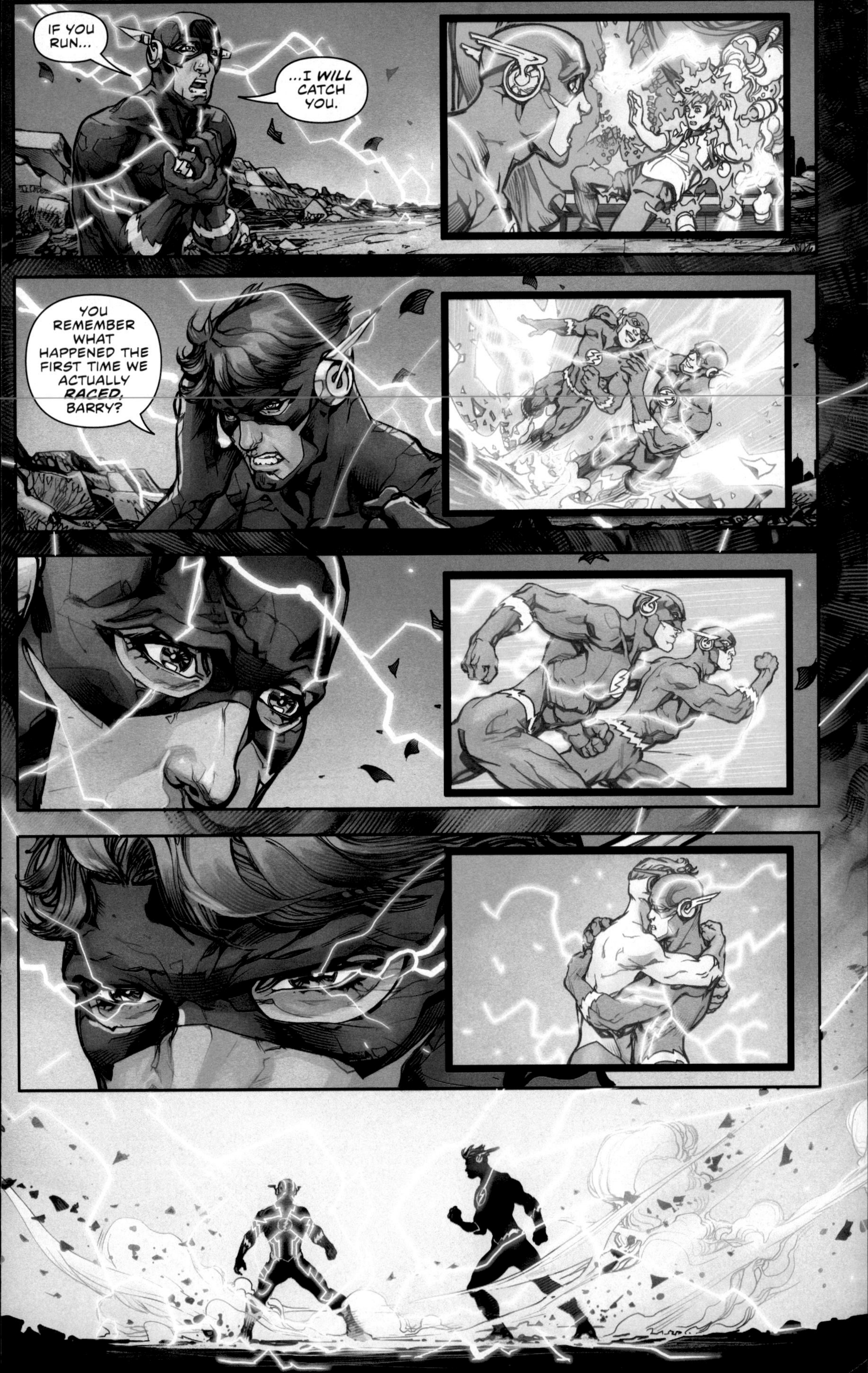
IF YOU RUN...
...I WILL CATCH YOU.
YOU REMEMBER WHAT HAPPENED THE FIRST TIME WE ACTUALLY RACED, BARRY?

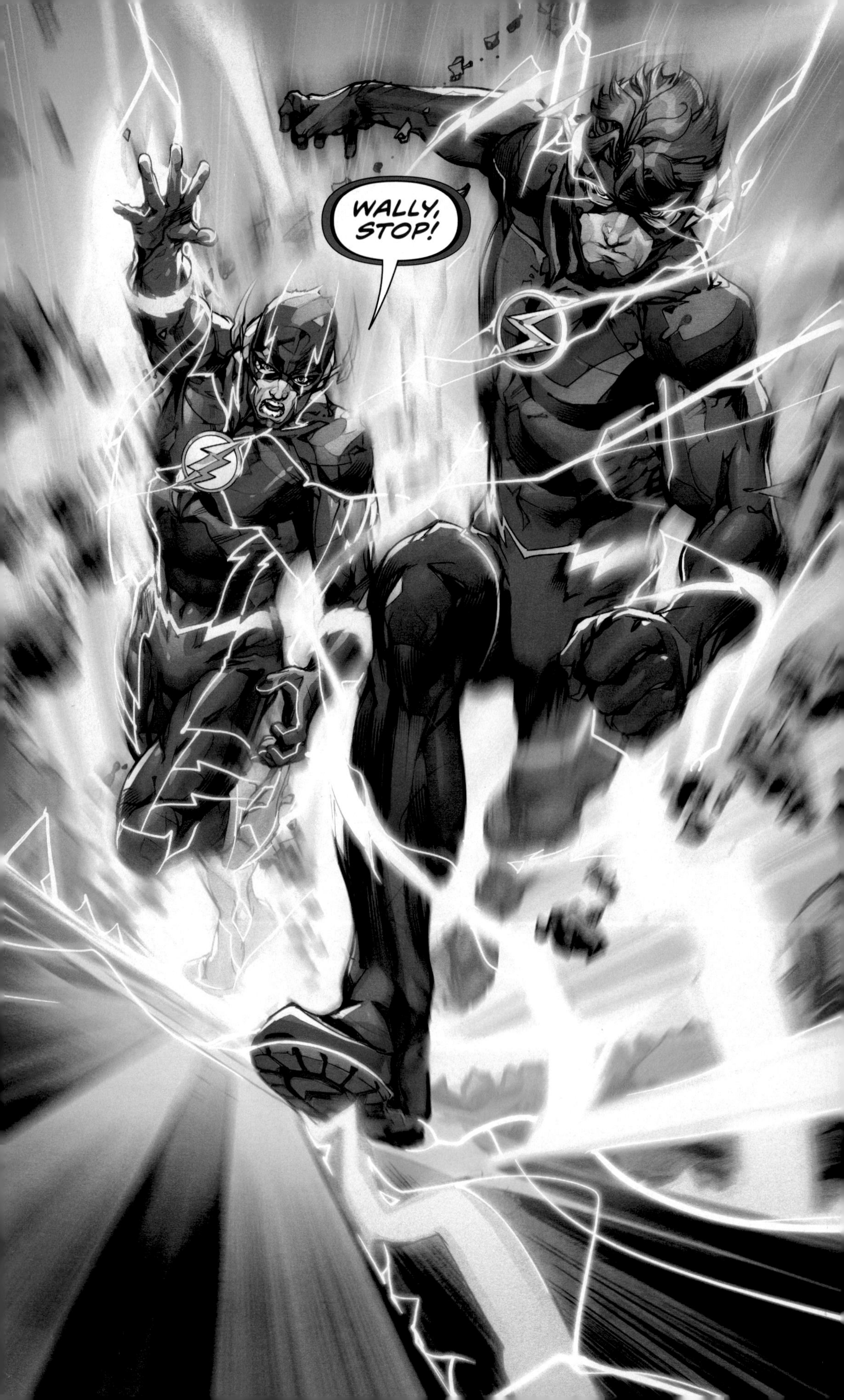
WALLY, STOP!

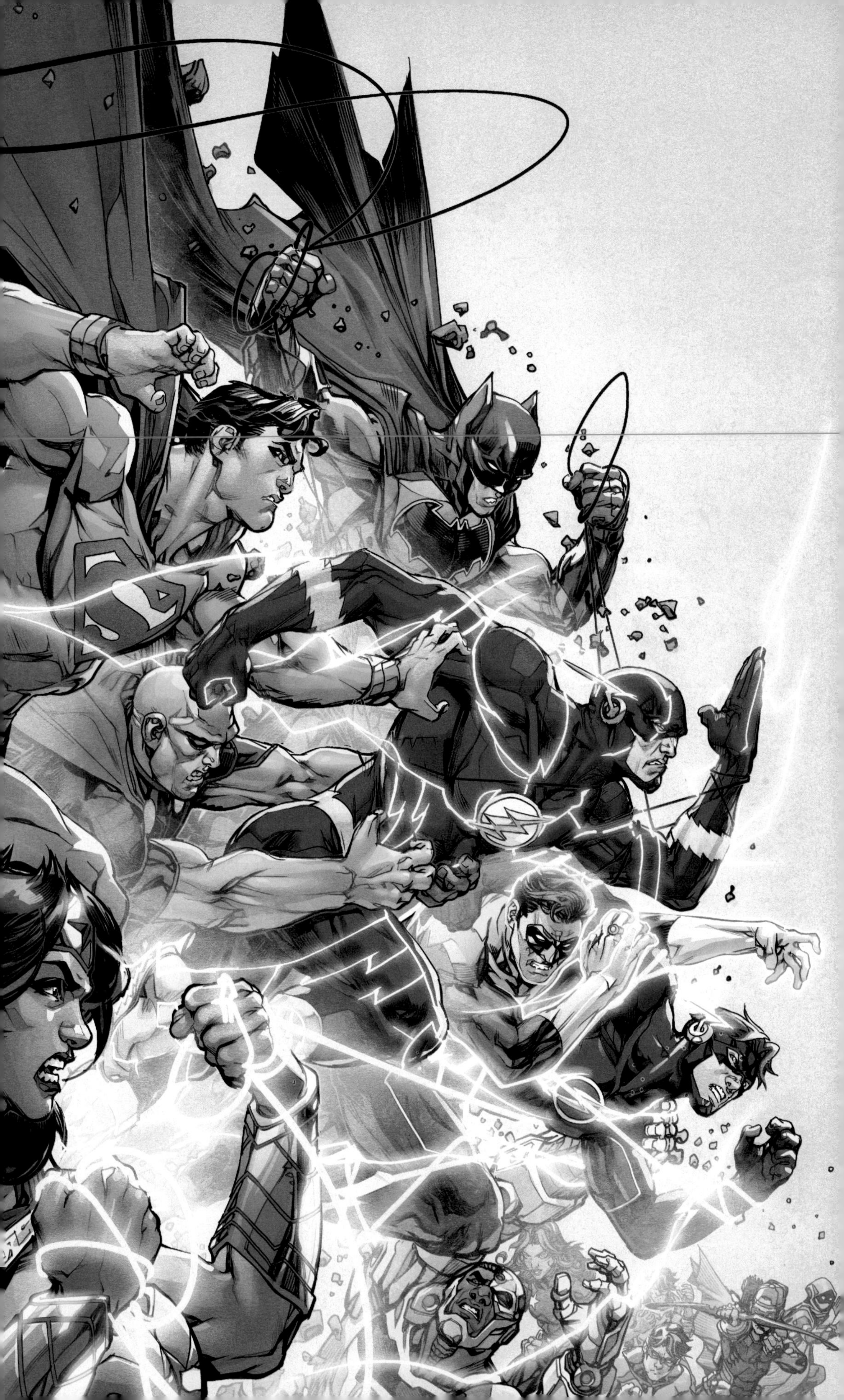

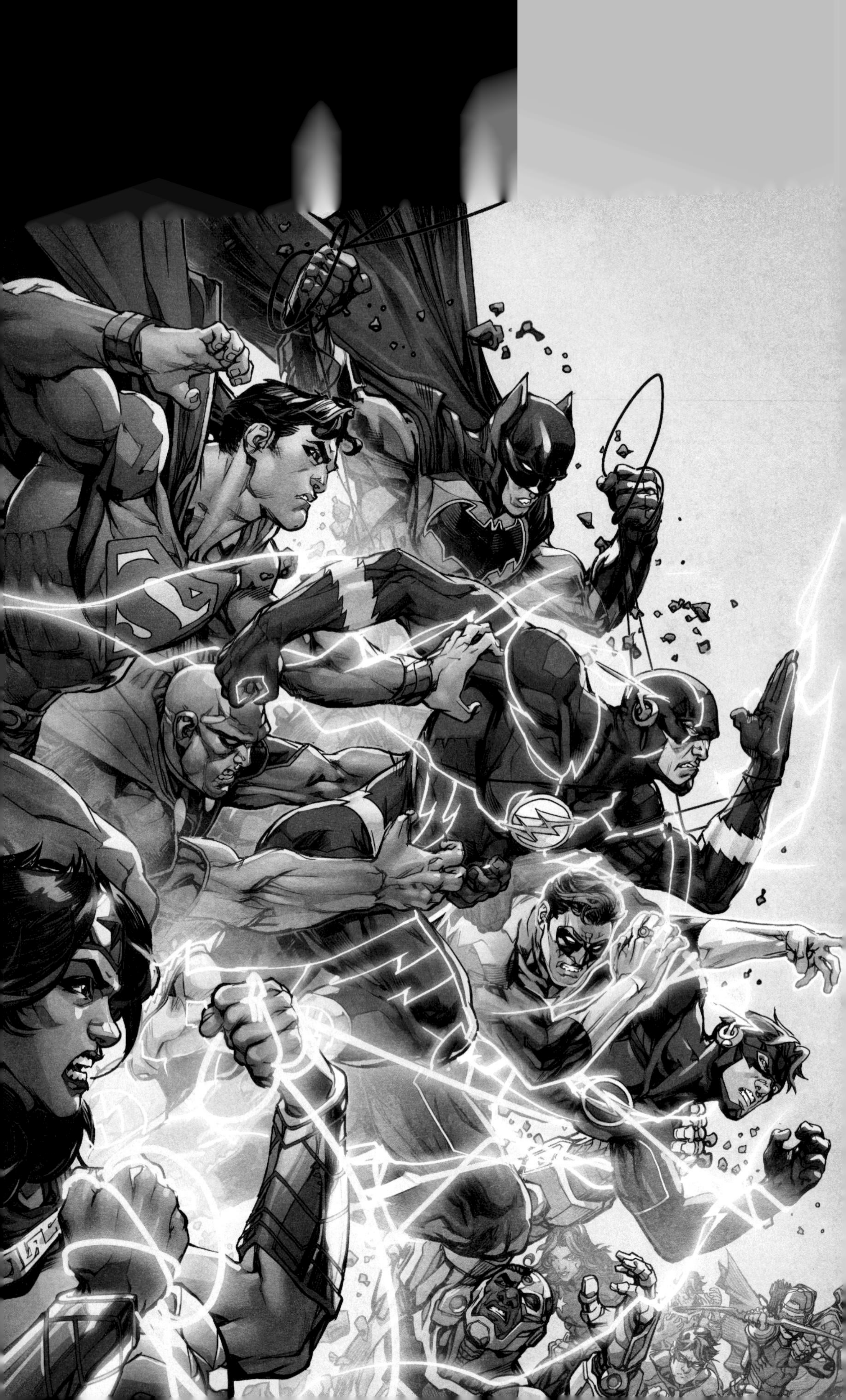

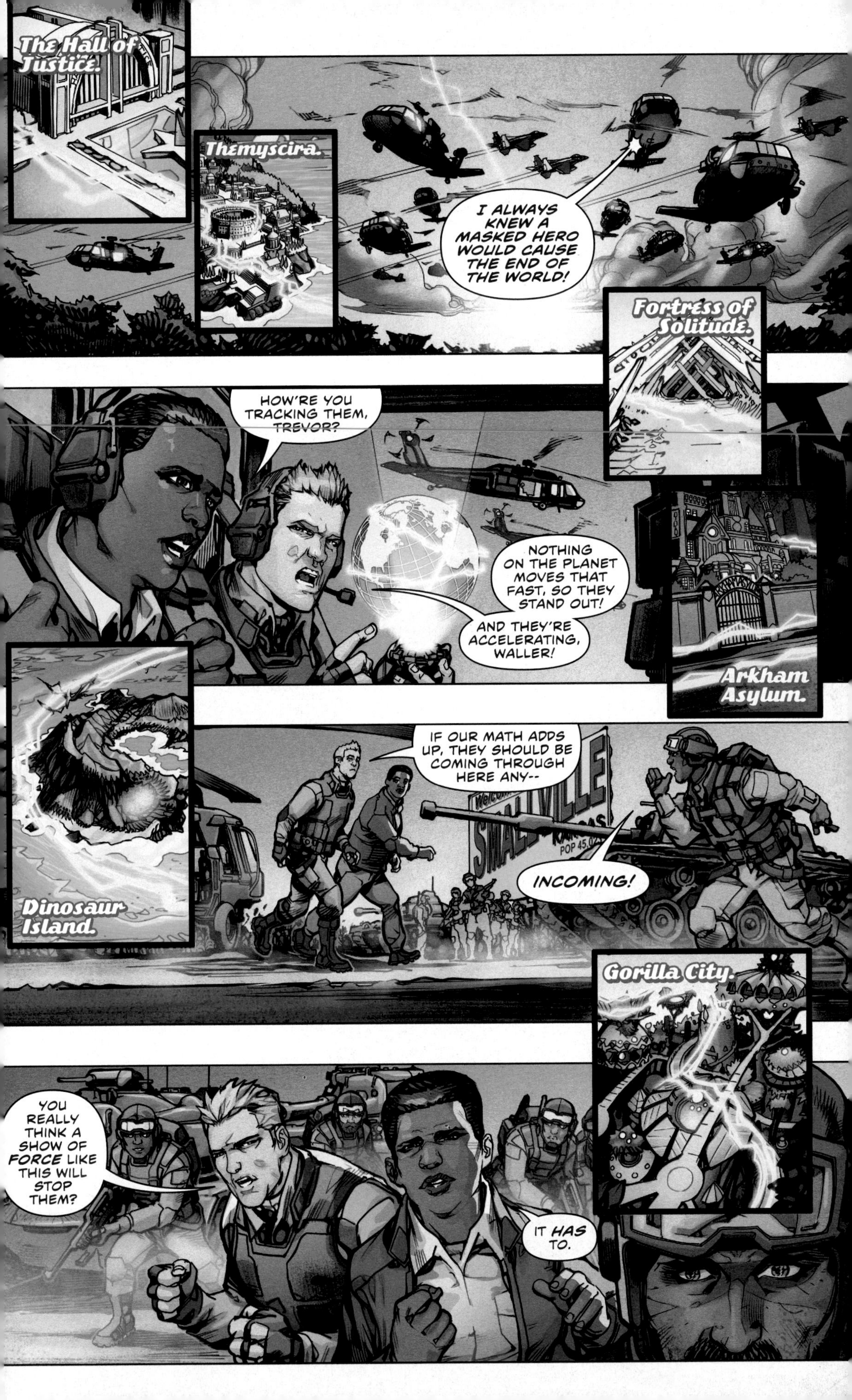
The Hall of Justice.
Themyscira.
I ALWAYS KNEW A MASKED HERO WOULD CAUSE THE END OF THE WORLD!
Fortress of Solitude.
HOW'RE YOU TRACKING THEM, TREVOR?
NOTHING ON THE PLANET MOVES THAT FAST, SO THEY STAND OUT!
AND THEY'RE ACCELERATING, WALLER!
Arkham Asylum.
Dinosaur Island.
IF OUR MATH ADDS UP, THEY SHOULD BE COMING THROUGH HERE ANY--
INCOMING!
Gorilla City.
YOU REALLY THINK A SHOW OF FORCE LIKE THIS WILL STOP THEM?
IT HAS TO.

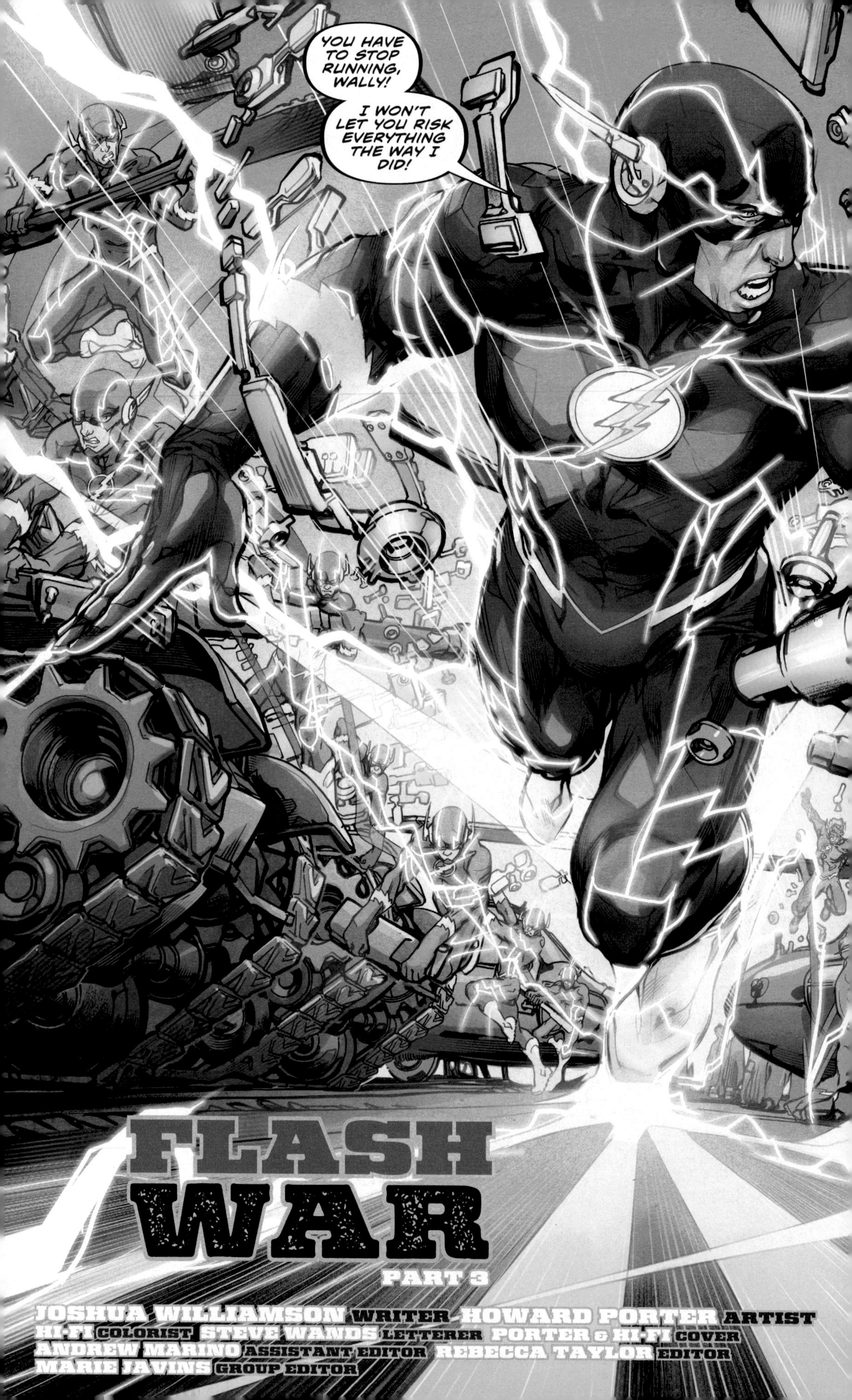
YOU HAVE TO STOP RUNNING, WALLY!
I WON'T LET YOU RISK EVERYTHING THE WAY I DID!
FLASH WAR
PART 3
JOSHUA WILLIAMSON WRITER HOWARD PORTER ARTIST
HI-FI COLORIST STEVE WANDS LETTERER PORTER & HI-FI COVER
ANDREW MARINO ASSISTANT EDITOR REBECCA TAYLOR EDITOR
MARIE JAVINS GROUP EDITOR

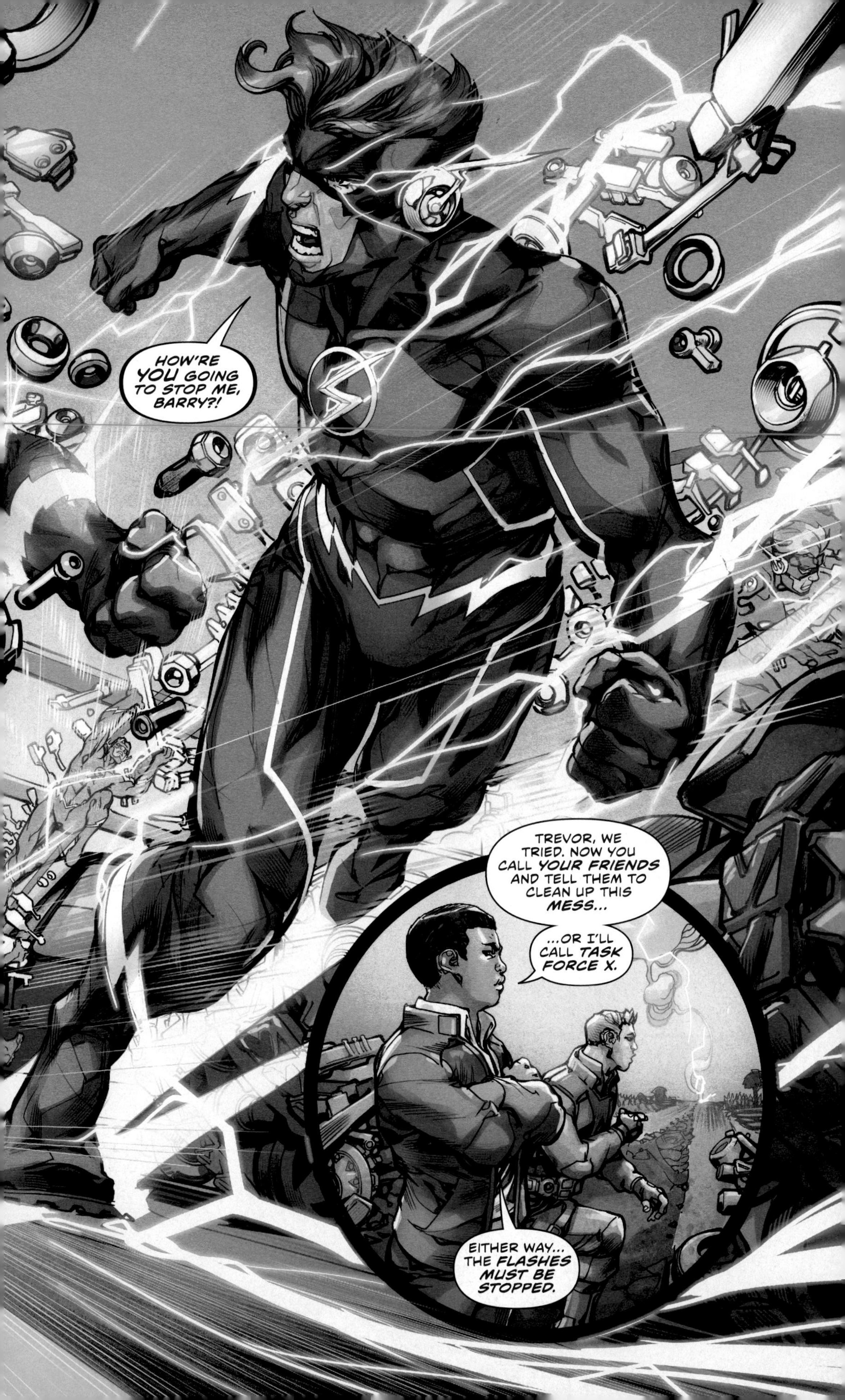
HOW'RE YOU GOING TO STOP ME, BARRY?!
TREVOR, WE TRIED. NOW YOU CALL YOUR FRIENDS AND TELL THEM TO CLEAN UP THIS MESS...
...OR I'LL CALL TASK FORCE X.
EITHER WAY... THE FLASHES MUST BE STOPPED.

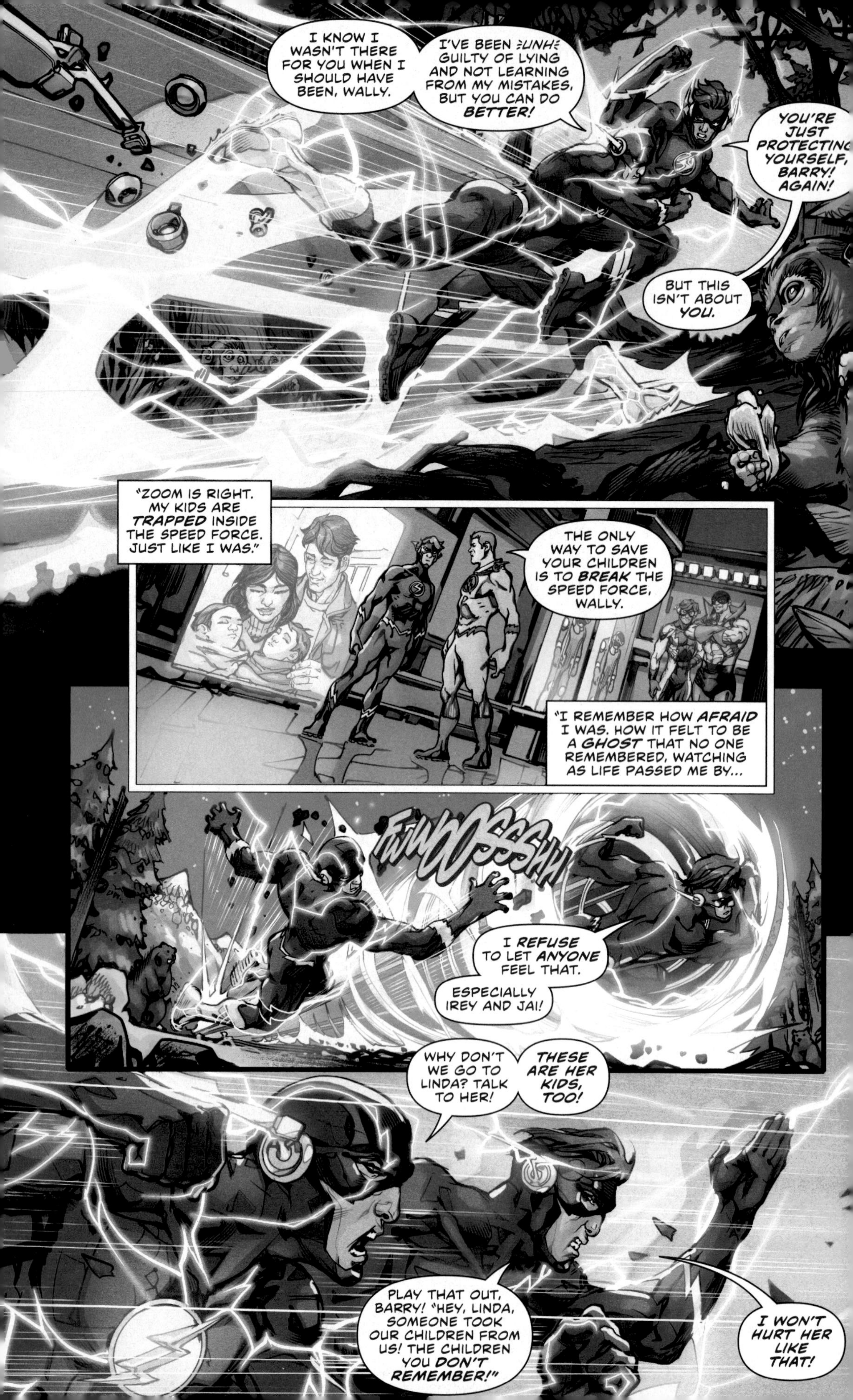
I KNOW I WASN'T THERE FOR YOU WHEN I SHOULD HAVE BEEN, WALLY.
I'VE BEEN GUILTY OF LYING AND NOT LEARNING FROM MY MISTAKES, BUT YOU CAN DO BETTER!
YOU'RE JUST PROTECTING YOURSELF, BARRY! AGAIN!
BUT THIS ISN'T ABOUT YOU.
"ZOOM IS RIGHT. MY KIDS ARE TRAPPED INSIDE THE SPEED FORCE. JUST LIKE I WAS."
THE ONLY WAY TO SAVE YOUR CHILDREN IS TO BREAK THE SPEED FORCE, WALLY.
"I REMEMBER HOW AFRAID I WAS. HOW IT FELT TO BE A GHOST THAT NO ONE REMEMBERED, WATCHING AS LIFE PASSED ME BY...
FWWOOSSSHH
I REFUSE TO LET ANYONE FEEL THAT.
ESPECIALLY IREY AND JAI!
WHY DON'T WE GO TO LINDA? TALK TO HER!
THESE ARE HER KIDS, TOO!
PLAY THAT OUT, BARRY! "HEY, LINDA, SOMEONE TOOK OUR CHILDREN FROM US! THE CHILDREN YOU DON'T REMEMBER!"
I WON'T HURT HER LIKE THAT!

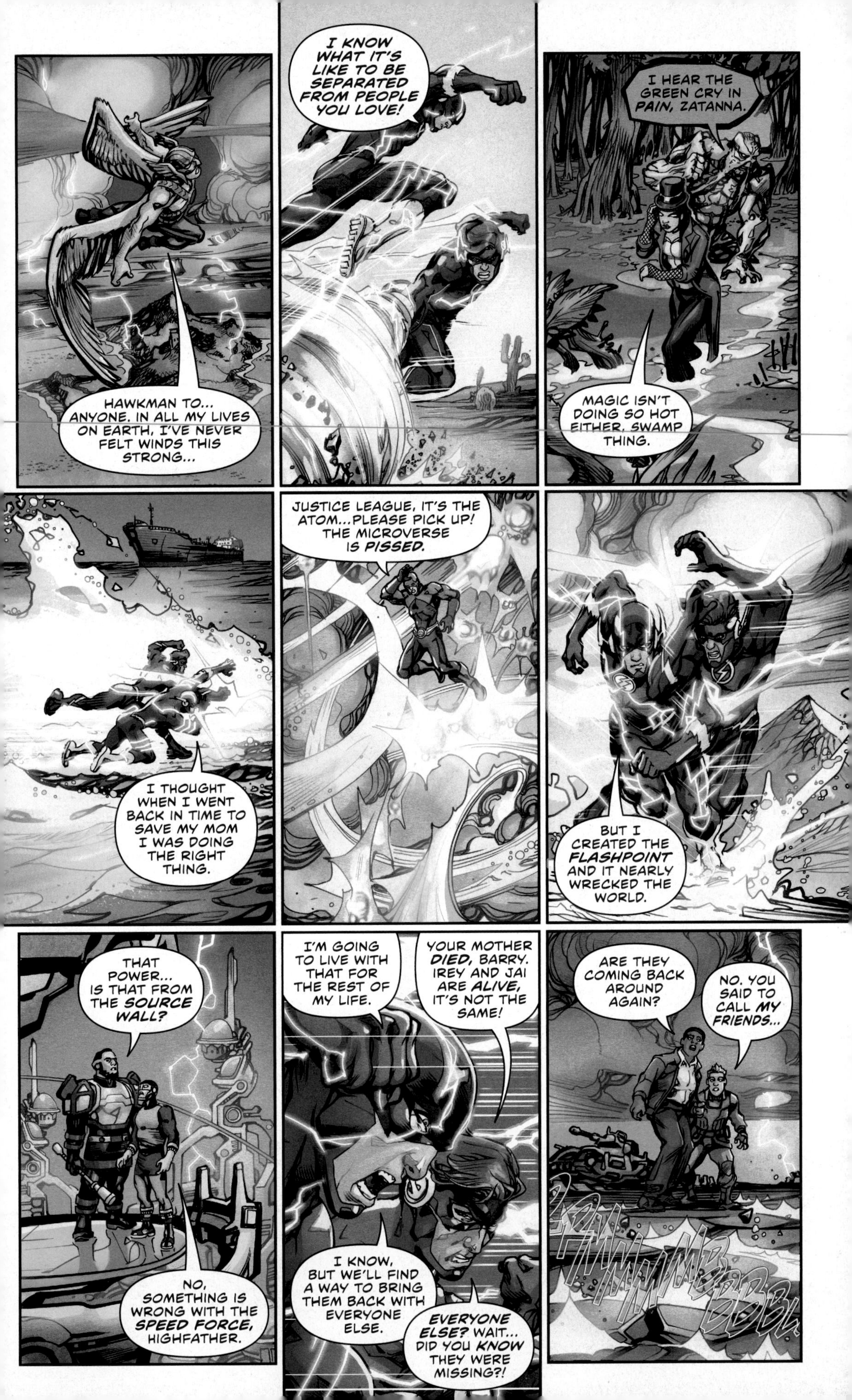
HAWKMAN TO... ANYONE. IN ALL MY LIVES ON EARTH, I'VE NEVER FELT WINDS THIS STRONG...
I KNOW WHAT IT'S LIKE TO BE SEPARATED FROM PEOPLE YOU LOVE!
I HEAR THE GREEN CRY IN PAIN, ZATANNA.
MAGIC ISN'T DOING SO HOT EITHER, SWAMP THING.
I THOUGHT WHEN I WENT BACK IN TIME TO SAVE MY MOM I WAS DOING THE RIGHT THING.
JUSTICE LEAGUE, IT'S THE ATOM...PLEASE PICK UP! THE MICROVERSE IS PISSED.
BUT I CREATED THE FLASHPOINT AND IT NEARLY WRECKED THE WORLD.
THAT POWER... IS THAT FROM THE SOURCE WALL?
NO, SOMETHING IS WRONG WITH THE SPEED FORCE, HIGHFATHER.
I'M GOING TO LIVE WITH THAT FOR THE REST OF MY LIFE.
YOUR MOTHER DIED, BARRY. IREY AND JAI ARE ALIVE, IT'S NOT THE SAME!
I KNOW, BUT WE'LL FIND A WAY TO BRING THEM BACK WITH EVERYONE ELSE.
EVERYONE ELSE? WAIT... DID YOU KNOW THEY WERE MISSING?!
ARE THEY COMING BACK AROUND AGAIN?
NO. YOU SAID TO CALL MY FRIENDS...
FWMMMBBBL

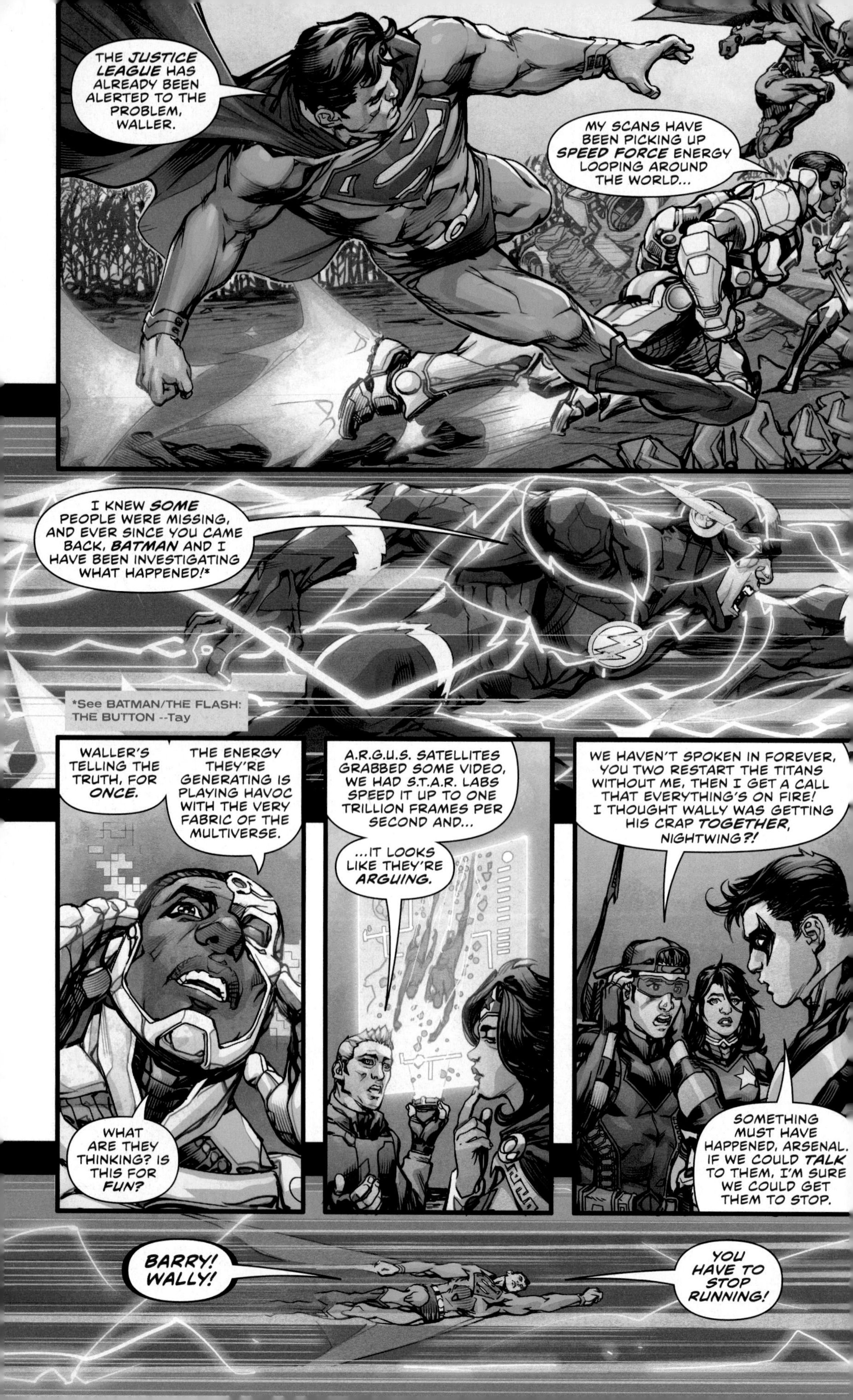

THE JUSTICE LEAGUE HAS ALREADY BEEN ALERTED TO THE PROBLEM, WALLER.
MY SCANS HAVE BEEN PICKING UP SPEED FORCE ENERGY LOOPING AROUND THE WORLD...
I KNEW SOME PEOPLE WERE MISSING, AND EVER SINCE YOU CAME BACK, BATMAN AND I HAVE BEEN INVESTIGATING WHAT HAPPENED!*
*See BATMAN/THE FLASH: THE BUTTON --Tay
WALLER'S TELLING THE TRUTH, FOR ONCE.
THE ENERGY THEY'RE GENERATING IS PLAYING HAVOC WITH THE VERY FABRIC OF THE MULTIVERSE.
WHAT ARE THEY THINKING? IS THIS FOR FUN?
A.R.G.U.S. SATELLITES GRABBED SOME VIDEO, WE HAD S.T.A.R. LABS SPEED IT UP TO ONE TRILLION FRAMES PER SECOND AND...
...IT LOOKS LIKE THEY'RE ARGUING.
WE HAVEN'T SPOKEN IN FOREVER, YOU TWO RESTART THE TITANS WITHOUT ME, THEN I GET A CALL THAT EVERYTHING'S ON FIRE! I THOUGHT WALLY WAS GETTING HIS CRAP TOGETHER, NIGHTWING?!
SOMETHING MUST HAVE HAPPENED, ARSENAL. IF WE COULD TALK TO THEM, I'M SURE WE COULD GET THEM TO STOP.
BARRY! WALLY!
YOU HAVE TO STOP RUNNING!

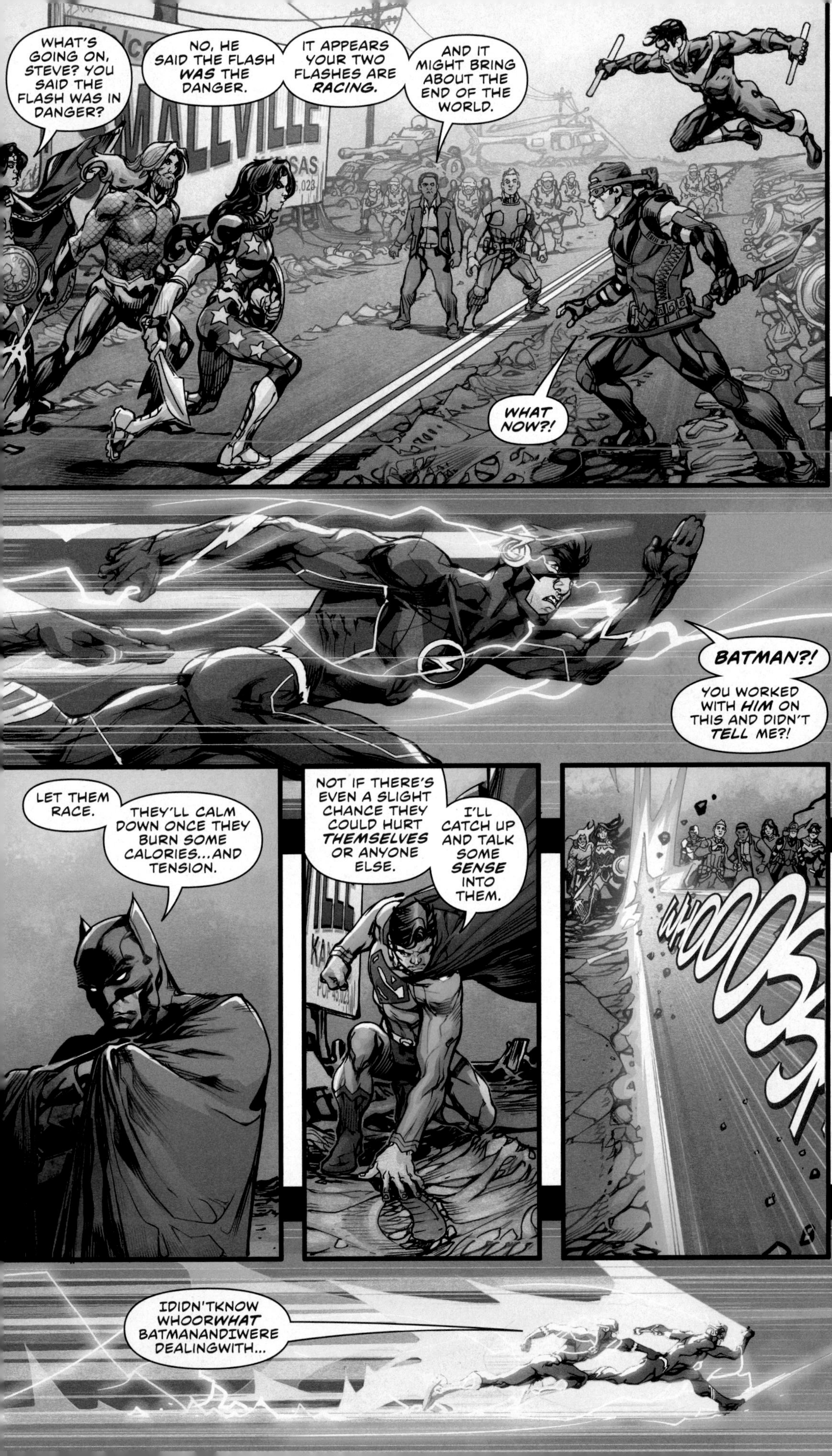
WHAT'S GOING ON, STEVE? YOU SAID THE FLASH WAS IN DANGER?
NO, HE SAID THE FLASH *WAS* THE DANGER.
IT APPEARS YOUR TWO FLASHES ARE *RACING.*
AND IT MIGHT BRING ABOUT THE END OF THE WORLD.
WHAT NOW?!
BATMAN?!
YOU WORKED WITH *HIM* ON THIS AND DIDN'T *TELL* ME?!
LET THEM RACE.
THEY'LL CALM DOWN ONCE THEY BURN SOME CALORIES...AND TENSION.
NOT IF THERE'S EVEN A SLIGHT CHANCE THEY COULD HURT *THEMSELVES* OR ANYONE ELSE.
I'LL CATCH UP AND TALK SOME *SENSE* INTO THEM.
IDIDN'TKNOW WHOOR*WHAT* BATMANANDIWERE DEALINGWITH...

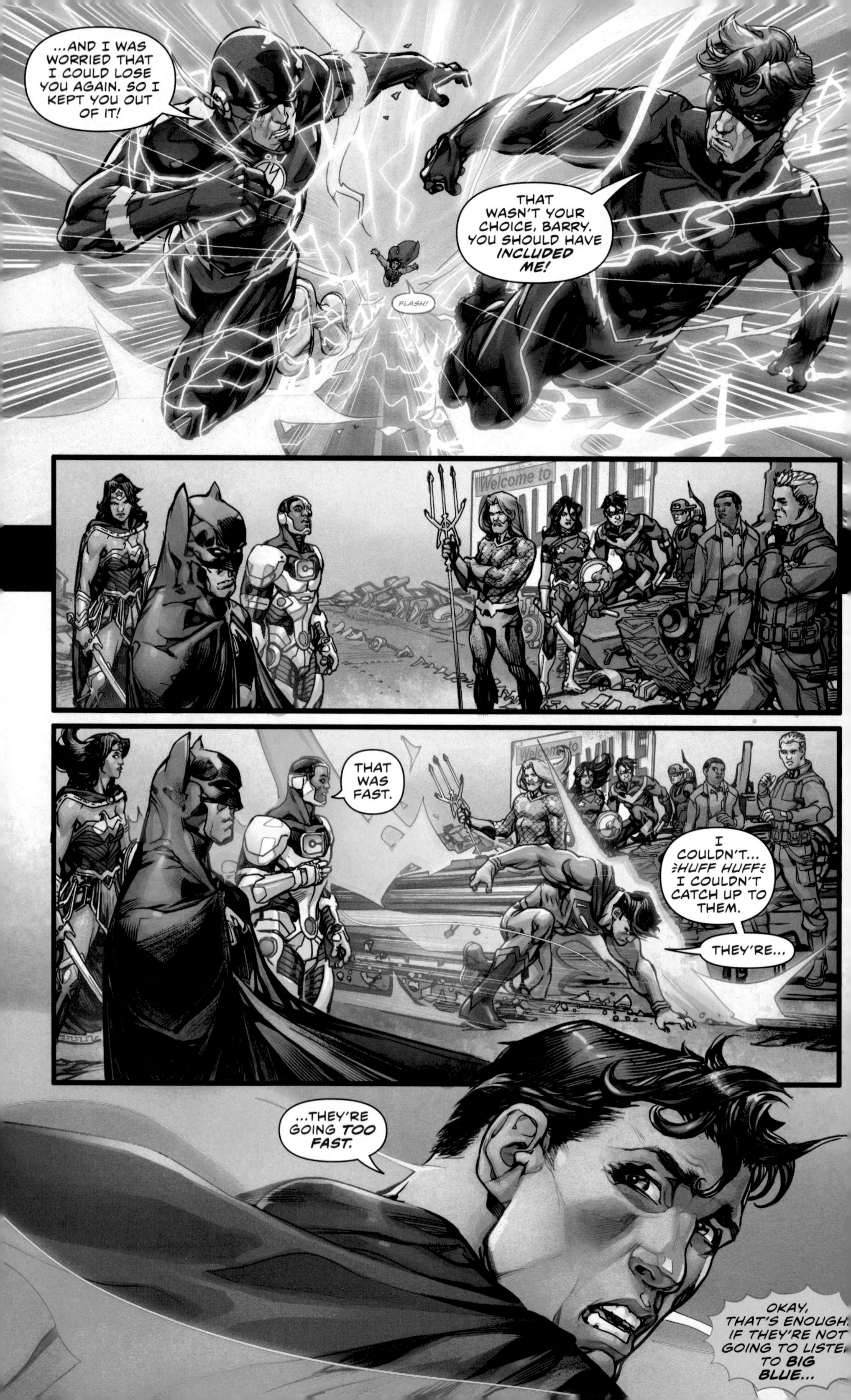
...AND I WAS WORRIED THAT I COULD LOSE YOU AGAIN. SO I KEPT YOU OUT OF IT!
THAT WASN'T YOUR CHOICE, BARRY. YOU SHOULD HAVE INCLUDED ME!
FLASH!
Welcome to
THAT WAS FAST.
I COULDN'T... HUFF HUFF I COULDN'T CATCH UP TO THEM.
THEY'RE...
...THEY'RE GOING TOO FAST.
OKAY, THAT'S ENOUGH. IF THEY'RE NOT GOING TO LISTE TO BIG BLUE...

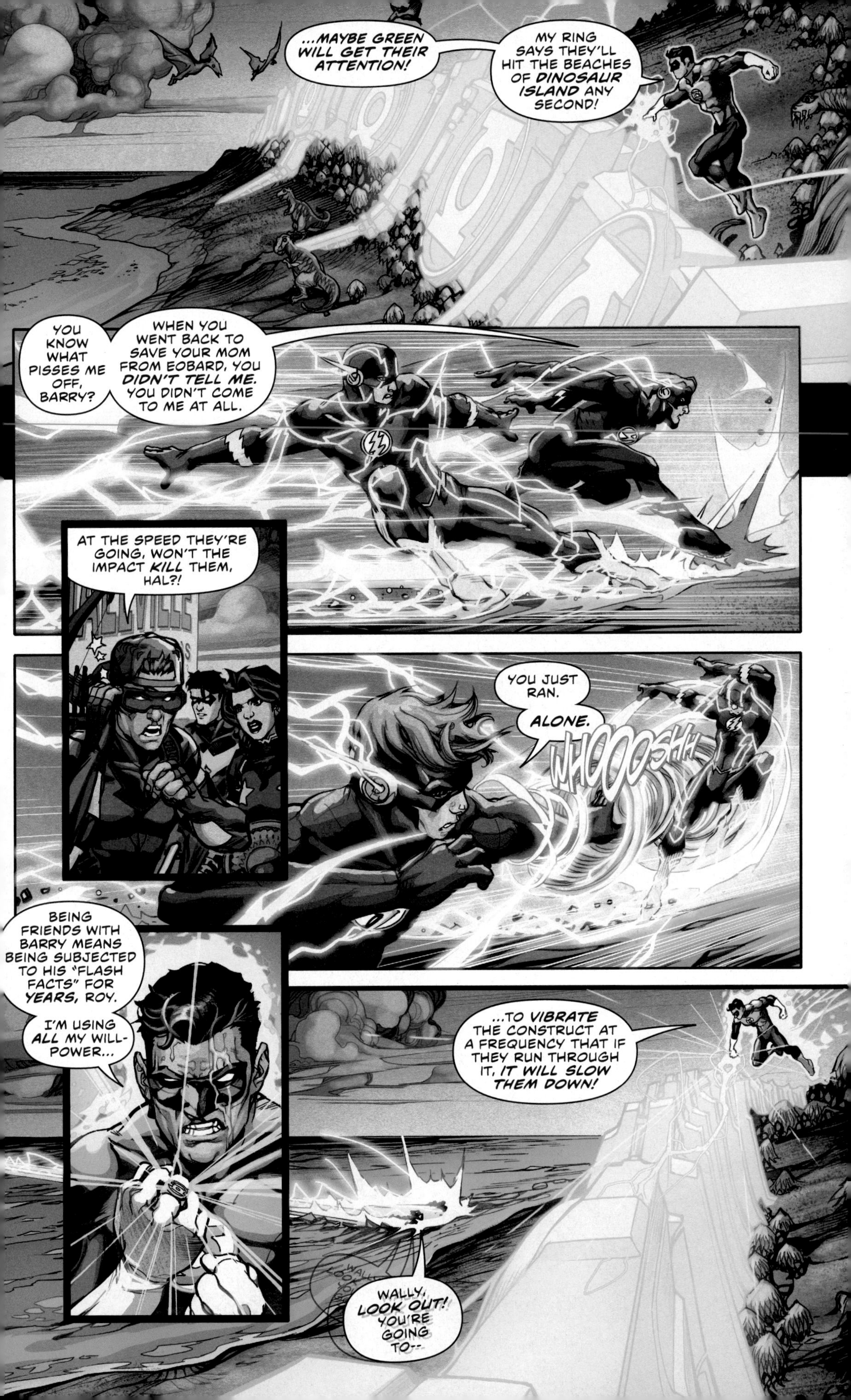

...MAYBE GREEN WILL GET THEIR ATTENTION!
MY RING SAYS THEY'LL HIT THE BEACHES OF DINOSAUR ISLAND ANY SECOND!
YOU KNOW WHAT PISSES ME OFF, BARRY?
WHEN YOU WENT BACK TO SAVE YOUR MOM FROM EOBARD, YOU DIDN'T TELL ME. YOU DIDN'T COME TO ME AT ALL.
AT THE SPEED THEY'RE GOING, WON'T THE IMPACT KILL THEM, HAL?!
YOU JUST RAN.
ALONE.
WHOOOOSHH
BEING FRIENDS WITH BARRY MEANS BEING SUBJECTED TO HIS "FLASH FACTS" FOR YEARS, ROY.
I'M USING ALL MY WILL-POWER...
...TO VIBRATE THE CONSTRUCT AT A FREQUENCY THAT IF THEY RUN THROUGH IT, IT WILL SLOW THEM DOWN!
WALLY, LOOK OUT! YOU'RE GOING TO--

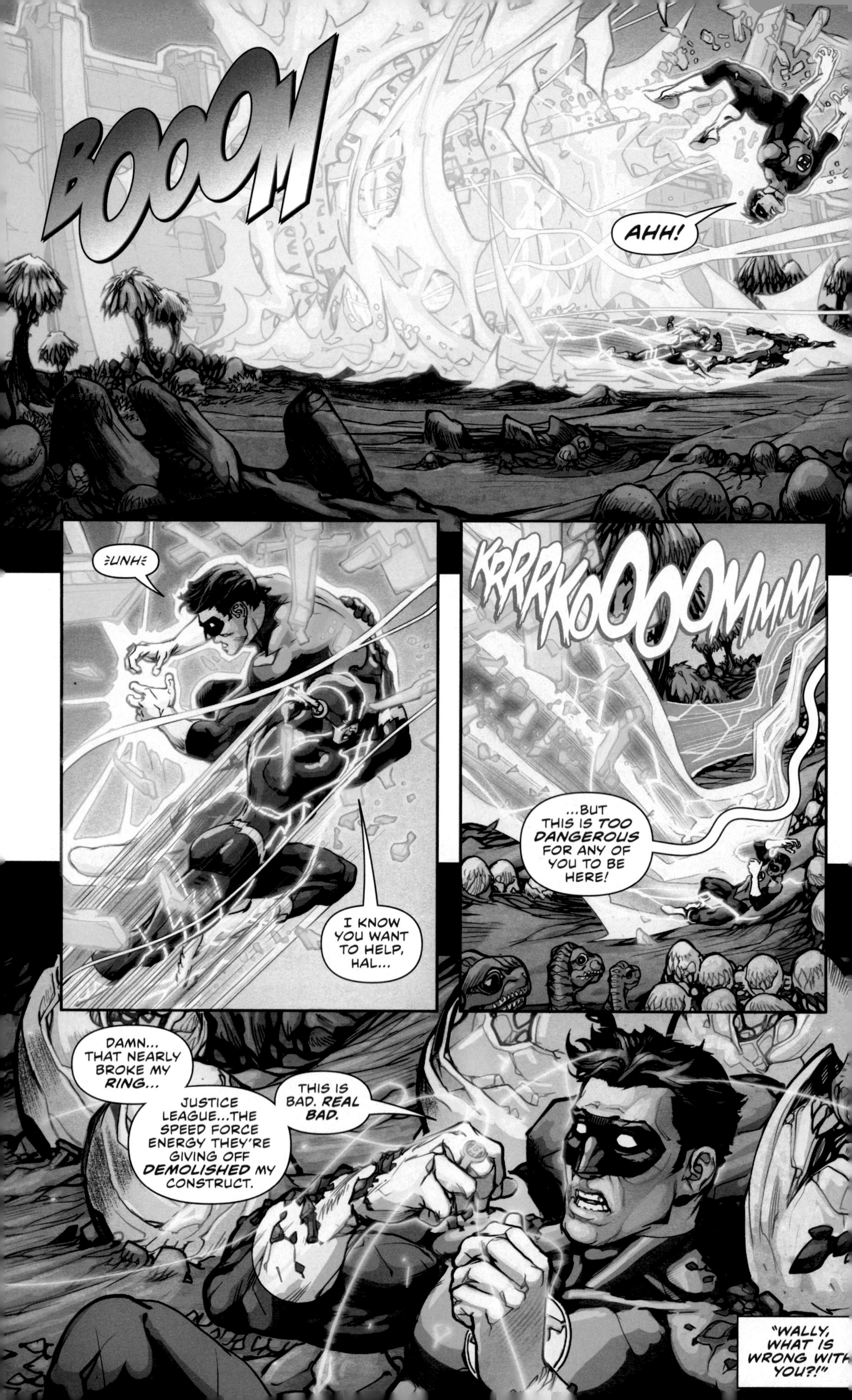
BOOOM
AHH!
UNH
I KNOW YOU WANT TO HELP, HAL...
KRRRKOOOOMMM
...BUT THIS IS TOO DANGEROUS FOR ANY OF YOU TO BE HERE!
DAMN... THAT NEARLY BROKE MY RING...
THIS IS BAD. REAL BAD.
JUSTICE LEAGUE...THE SPEED FORCE ENERGY THEY'RE GIVING OFF DEMOLISHED MY CONSTRUCT.
"WALLY, WHAT IS WRONG WITH YOU?!"

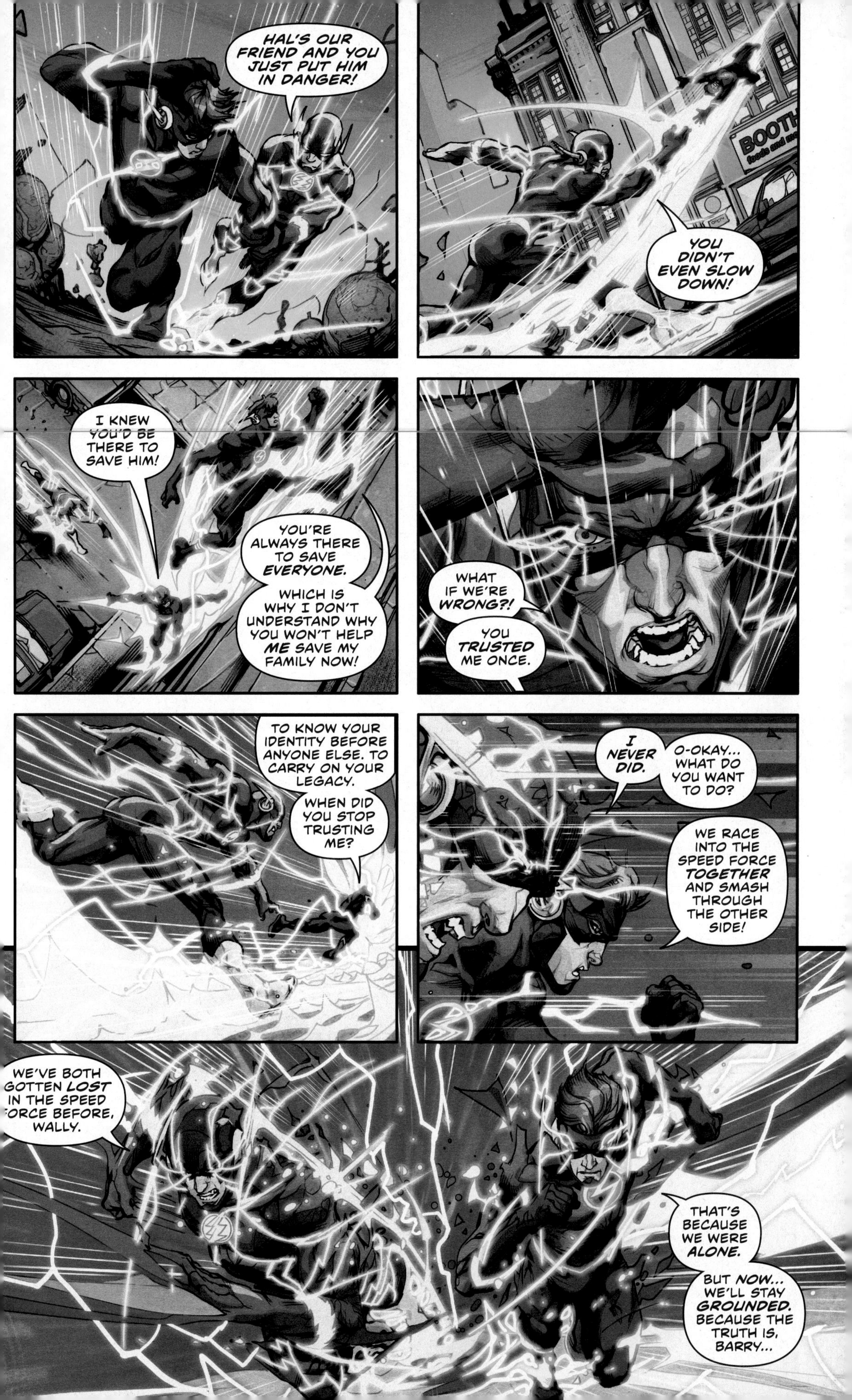
HAL'S OUR FRIEND AND YOU JUST PUT HIM IN DANGER!
BOOTH foods and
YOU DIDN'T EVEN SLOW DOWN!
I KNEW YOU'D BE THERE TO SAVE HIM!
YOU'RE ALWAYS THERE TO SAVE EVERYONE.
WHICH IS WHY I DON'T UNDERSTAND WHY YOU WON'T HELP ME SAVE MY FAMILY NOW!
WHAT IF WE'RE WRONG?!
YOU TRUSTED ME ONCE.
TO KNOW YOUR IDENTITY BEFORE ANYONE ELSE. TO CARRY ON YOUR LEGACY.
WHEN DID YOU STOP TRUSTING ME?
I NEVER DID.
O-OKAY... WHAT DO YOU WANT TO DO?
WE RACE INTO THE SPEED FORCE TOGETHER AND SMASH THROUGH THE OTHER SIDE!
WE'VE BOTH GOTTEN LOST IN THE SPEED FORCE BEFORE, WALLY.
THAT'S BECAUSE WE WERE ALONE.
BUT NOW... WE'LL STAY GROUNDED. BECAUSE THE TRUTH IS, BARRY...

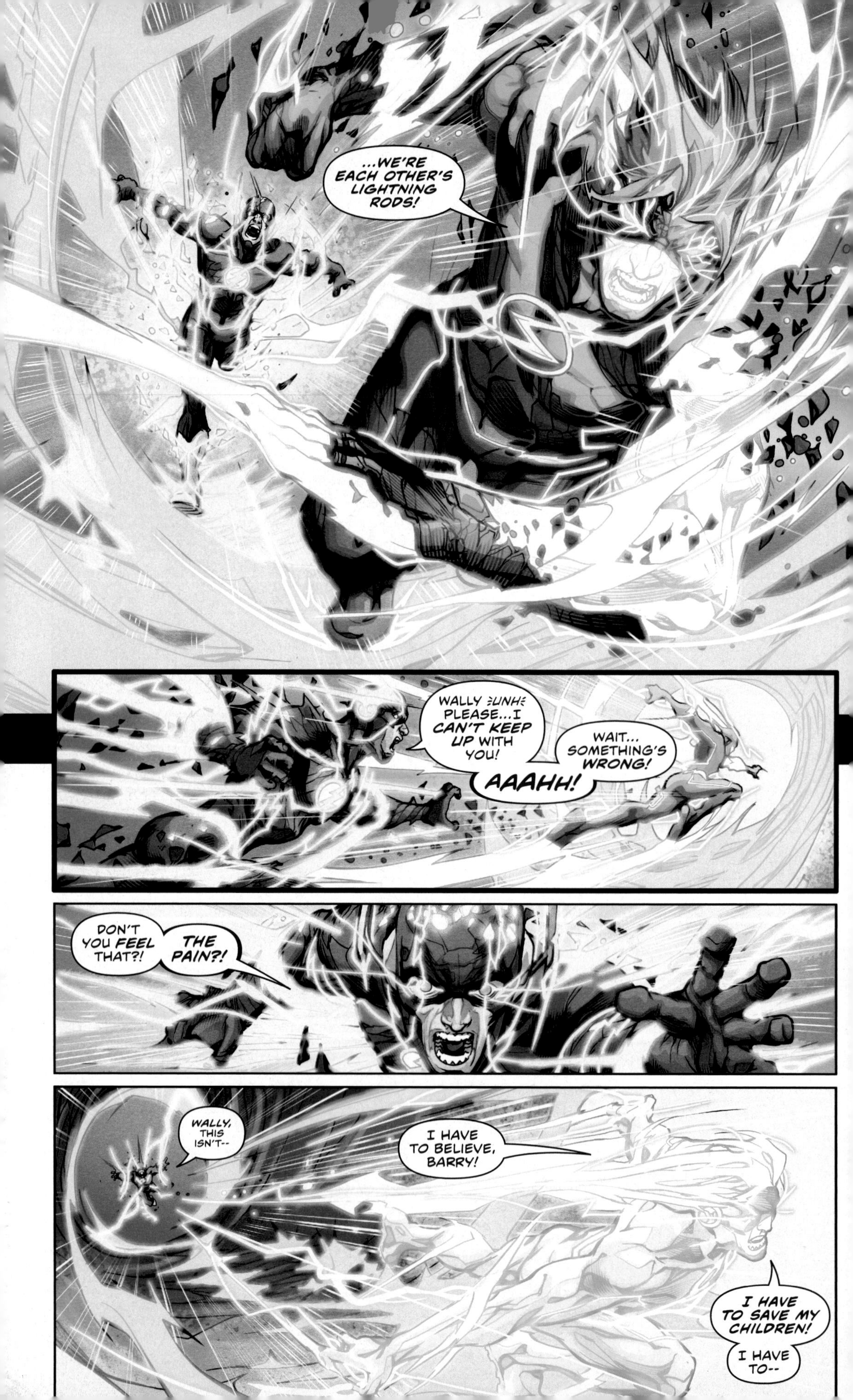

...WE'RE EACH OTHER'S LIGHTNING RODS!
WALLY UNH PLEASE...I CAN'T KEEP UP WITH YOU!
WAIT... SOMETHING'S WRONG!
AAAHH!
DON'T YOU FEEL THAT?!
THE PAIN?!
WALLY, THIS ISN'T--
I HAVE TO BELIEVE, BARRY!
I HAVE TO SAVE MY CHILDREN!
I HAVE TO--

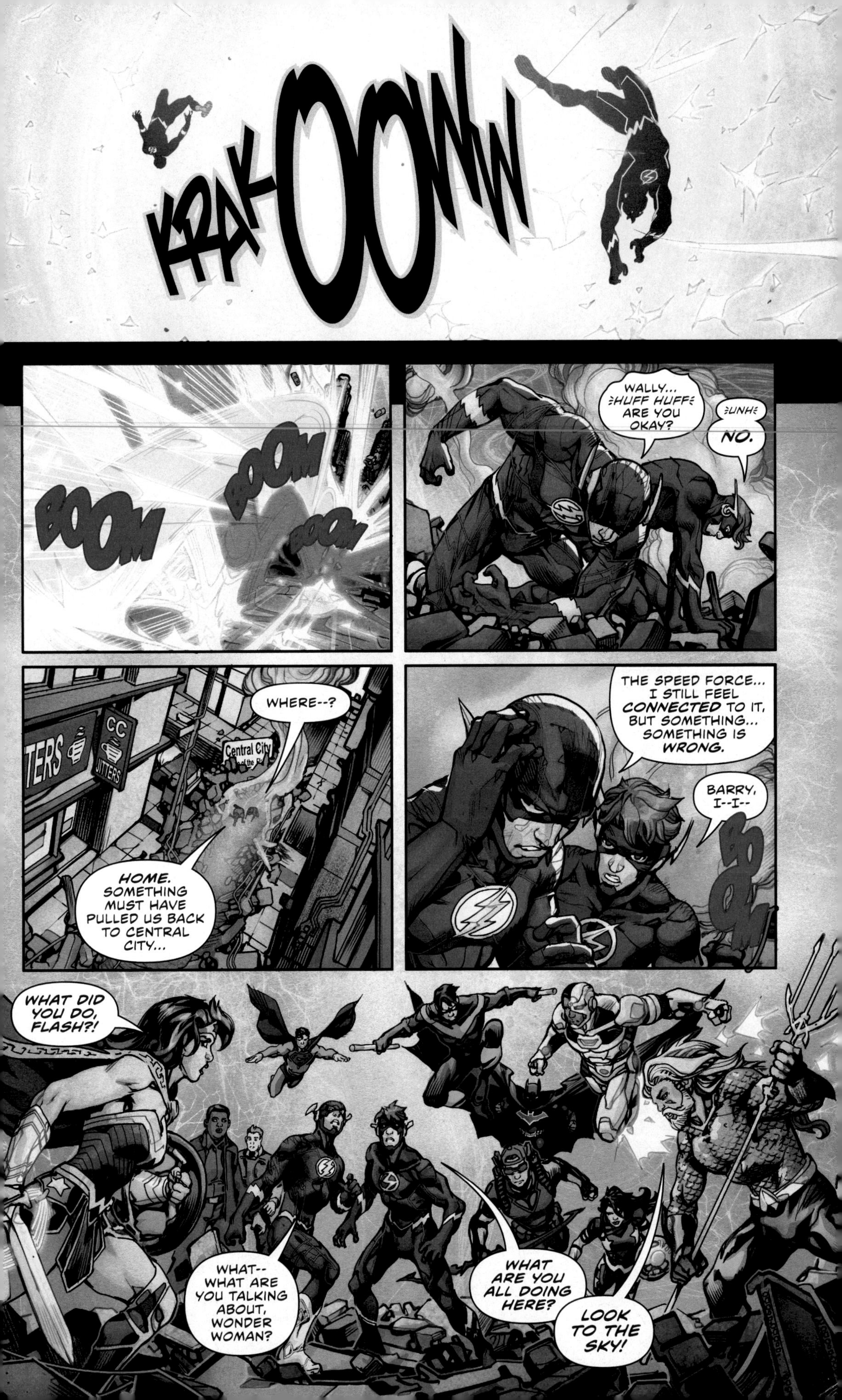
KRAKOOWW
BOOM
BOOM
BOOM
WALLY... HUFF HUFF ARE YOU OKAY?
UNH
NO.
WHERE--?
JITTERS
CC JITTERS
Central City
HOME. SOMETHING MUST HAVE PULLED US BACK TO CENTRAL CITY...
THE SPEED FORCE... I STILL FEEL CONNECTED TO IT, BUT SOMETHING... SOMETHING IS WRONG.
BARRY, I--I--
BOOM
WHAT DID YOU DO, FLASH?!
WHAT-- WHAT ARE YOU TALKING ABOUT, WONDER WOMAN?
WHAT ARE YOU ALL DOING HERE?
LOOK TO THE SKY!

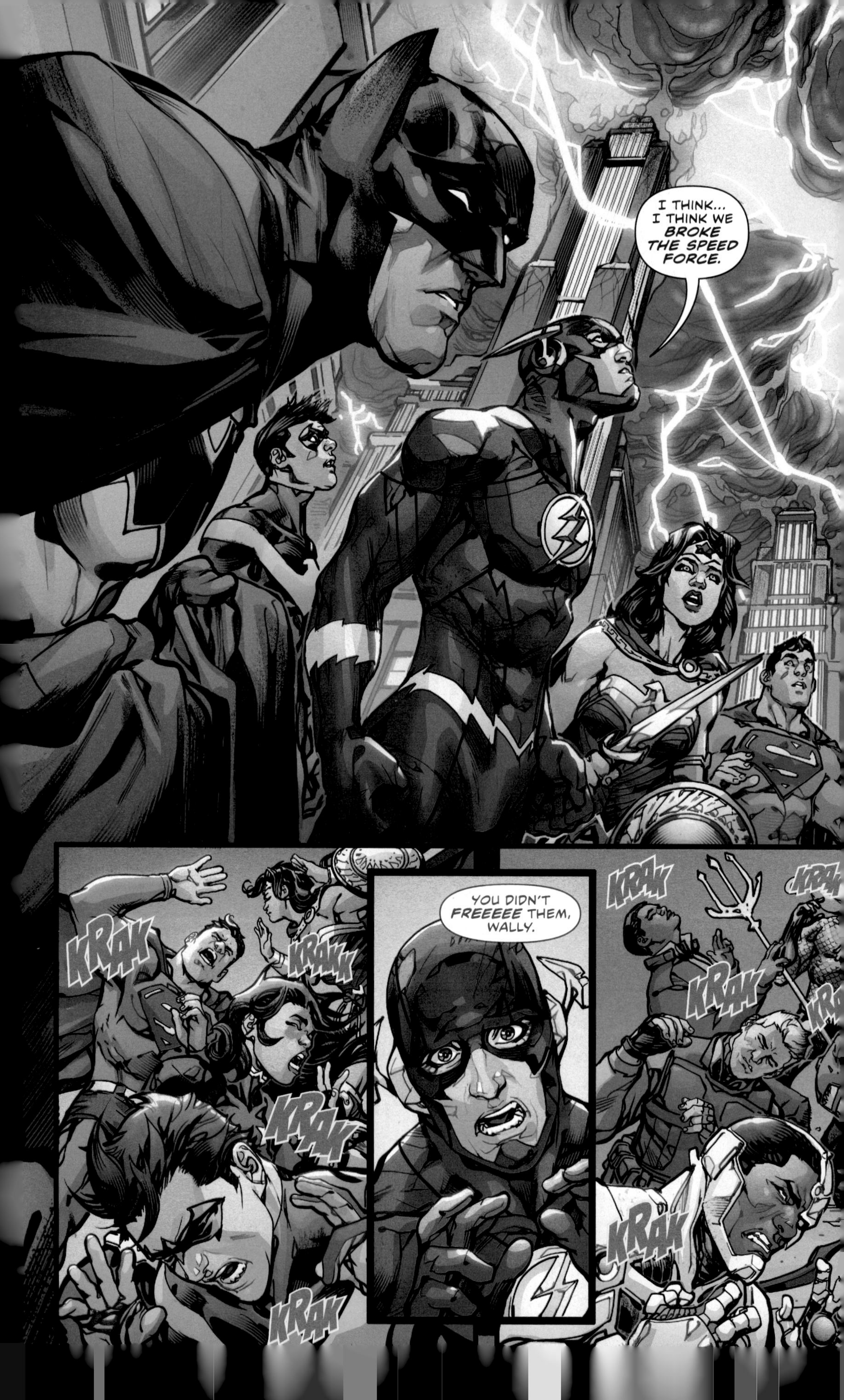
I THINK... I THINK WE BROKE THE SPEED FORCE.
KRAK
KRAKK
KRAK
KRAK
YOU DIDN'T FREEEEE THEM, WALLY.
KRAK
KRAK
KRAK
KRAK

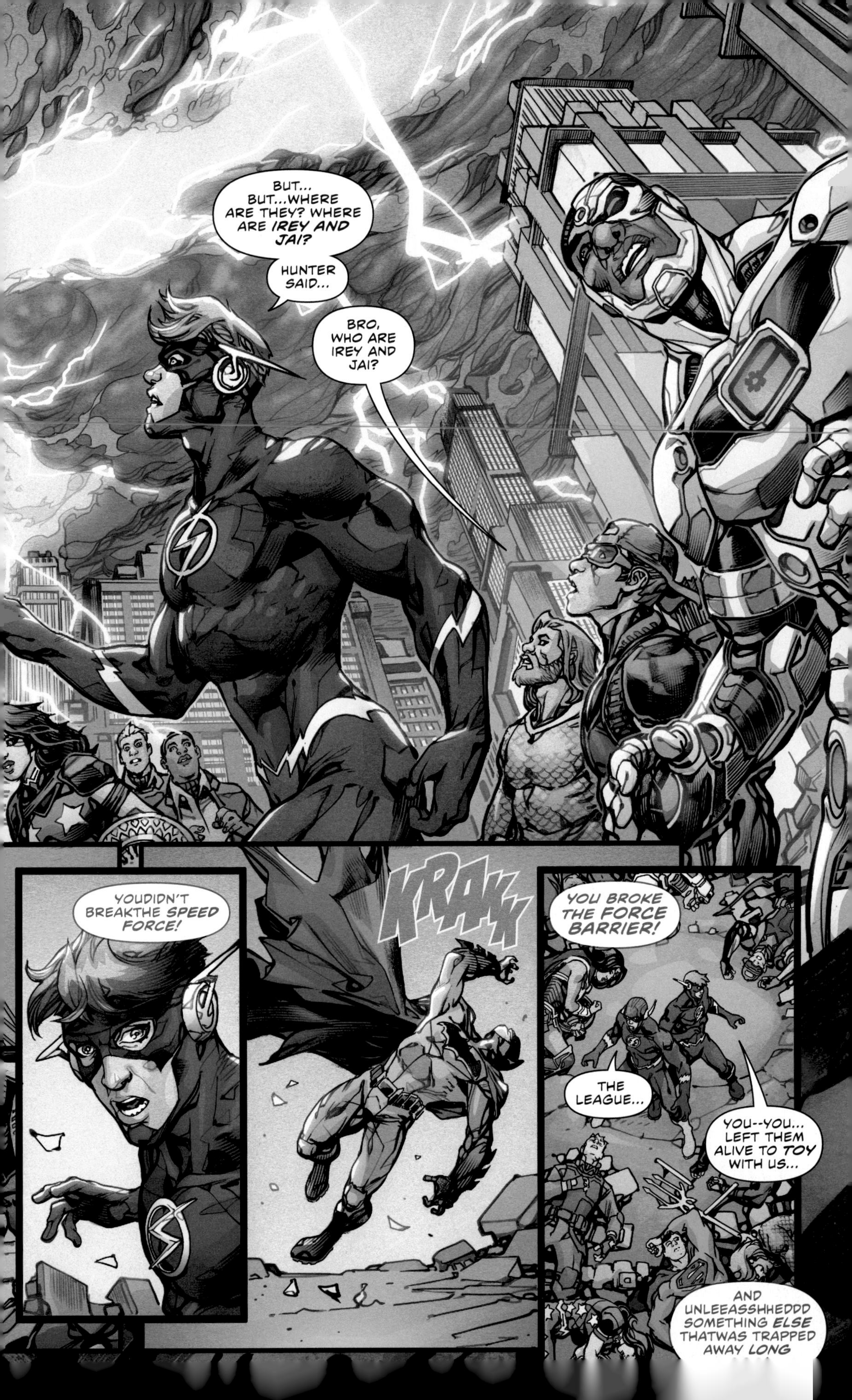
BUT... BUT...WHERE ARE THEY? WHERE ARE *IREY AND JAI?*
HUNTER SAID...
BRO, WHO ARE IREY AND JAI?
YOUDIDN'T BREAKTHE *SPEED FORCE!*
KRAKK
YOU BROKE THE FORCE BARRIER!
THE LEAGUE...
YOU--YOU... LEFT THEM ALIVE TO *TOY* WITH US...
AND UNLEEASSHHEDDD SOMETHING *ELSE* THATWAS TRAPPED AWAY *LONG*

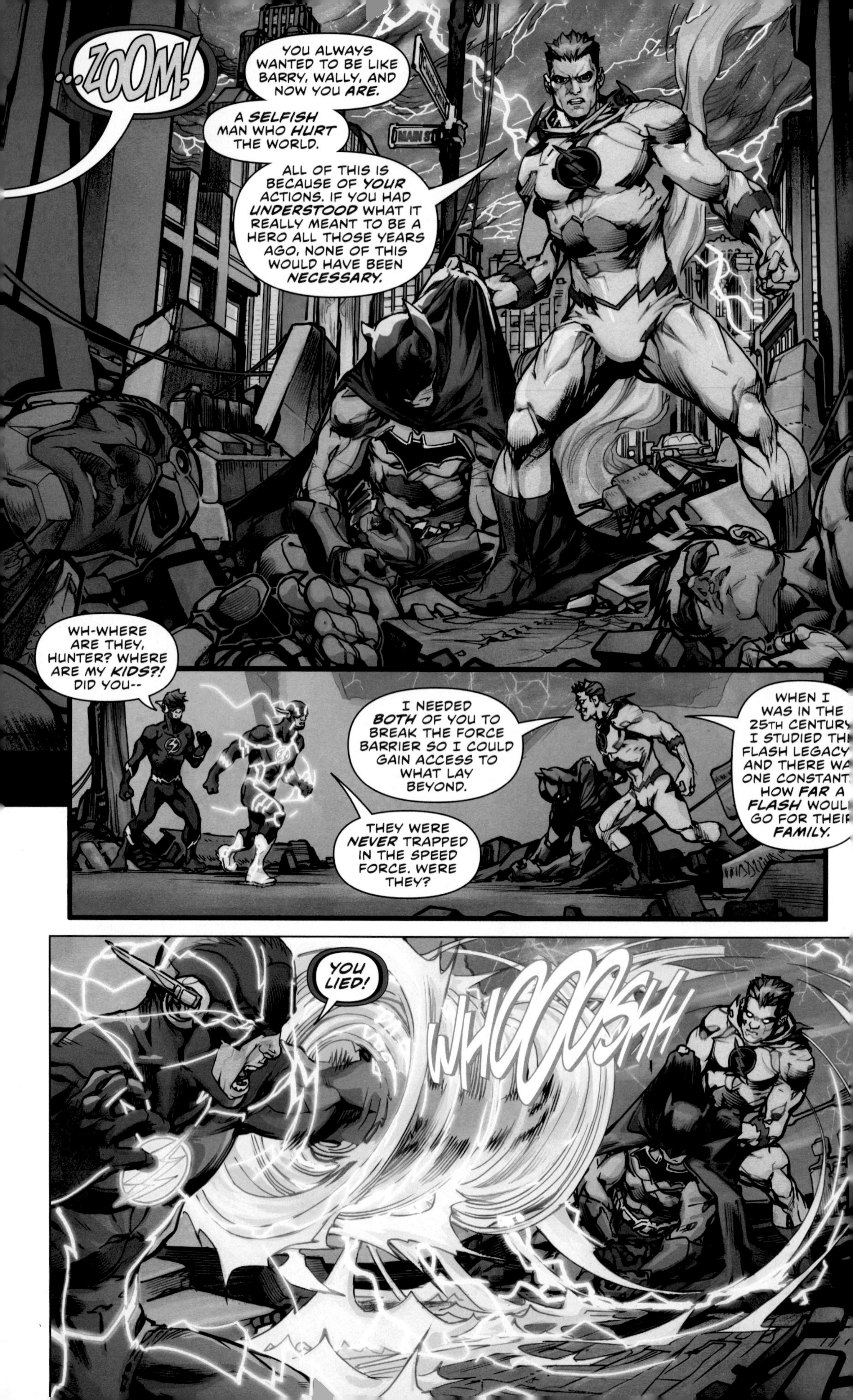

...ZOOM!
YOU ALWAYS WANTED TO BE LIKE BARRY, WALLY, AND NOW YOU ARE.
A SELFISH MAN WHO HURT THE WORLD.
ALL OF THIS IS BECAUSE OF YOUR ACTIONS. IF YOU HAD UNDERSTOOD WHAT IT REALLY MEANT TO BE A HERO ALL THOSE YEARS AGO, NONE OF THIS WOULD HAVE BEEN NECESSARY.
MAIN ST
WH-WHERE ARE THEY, HUNTER? WHERE ARE MY KIDS?! DID YOU--
I NEEDED BOTH OF YOU TO BREAK THE FORCE BARRIER SO I COULD GAIN ACCESS TO WHAT LAY BEYOND.
WHEN I WAS IN THE 25TH CENTURY I STUDIED THE FLASH LEGACY AND THERE WA ONE CONSTANT. HOW FAR A FLASH WOUL GO FOR THEIR FAMILY.
THEY WERE NEVER TRAPPED IN THE SPEED FORCE. WERE THEY?
YOU LIED!
WHOOOSHH

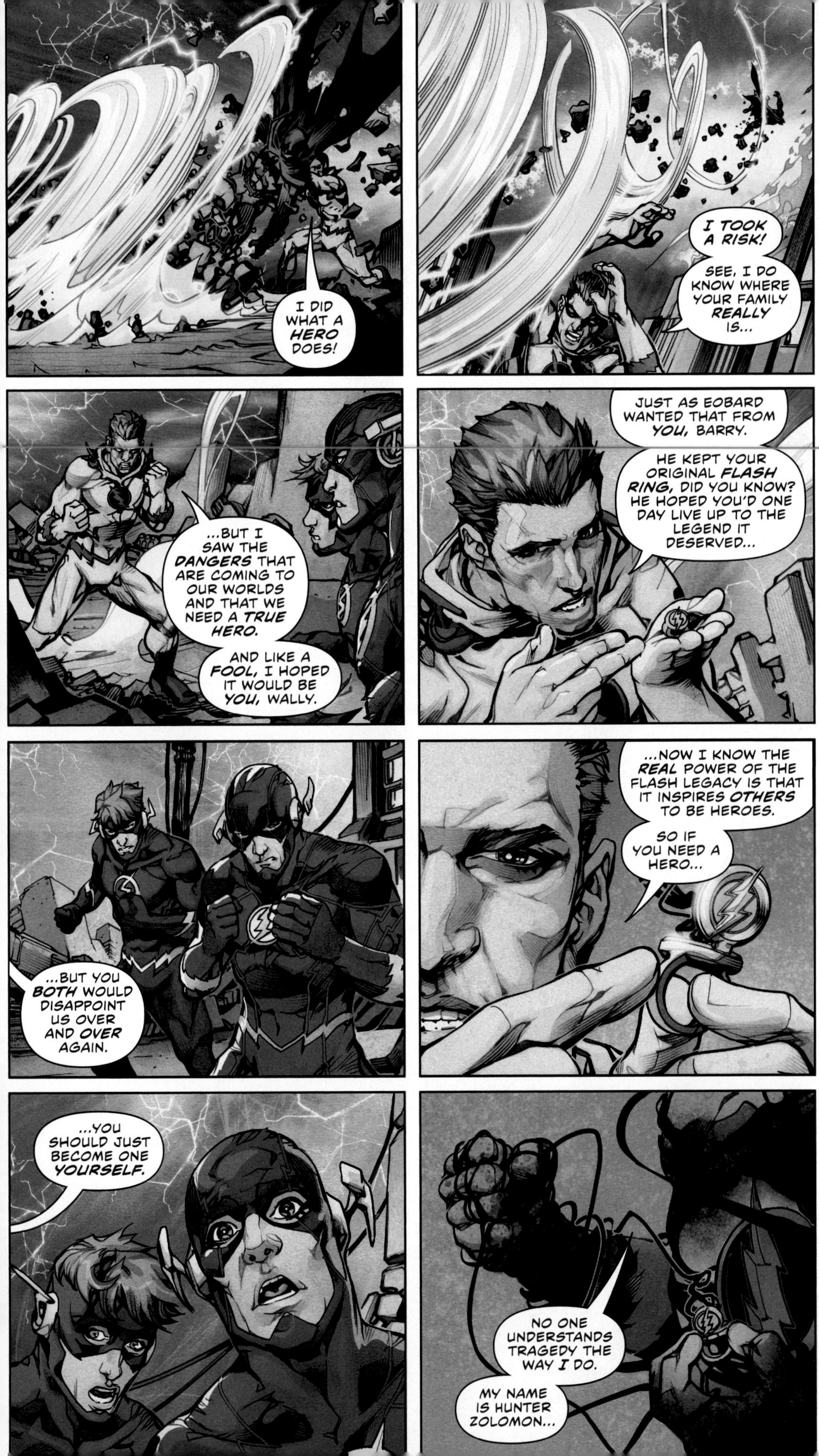
I DID WHAT A HERO DOES!
I TOOK A RISK!
SEE, I DO KNOW WHERE YOUR FAMILY REALLY IS...
...BUT I SAW THE DANGERS THAT ARE COMING TO OUR WORLDS AND THAT WE NEED A TRUE HERO.
AND LIKE A FOOL, I HOPED IT WOULD BE YOU, WALLY.
JUST AS EOBARD WANTED THAT FROM YOU, BARRY.
HE KEPT YOUR ORIGINAL FLASH RING, DID YOU KNOW? HE HOPED YOU'D ONE DAY LIVE UP TO THE LEGEND IT DESERVED...
...BUT YOU BOTH WOULD DISAPPOINT US OVER AND OVER AGAIN.
...NOW I KNOW THE REAL POWER OF THE FLASH LEGACY IS THAT IT INSPIRES OTHERS TO BE HEROES.
SO IF YOU NEED A HERO...
...YOU SHOULD JUST BECOME ONE YOURSELF.
NO ONE UNDERSTANDS TRAGEDY THE WAY I DO.
MY NAME IS HUNTER ZOLOMON...

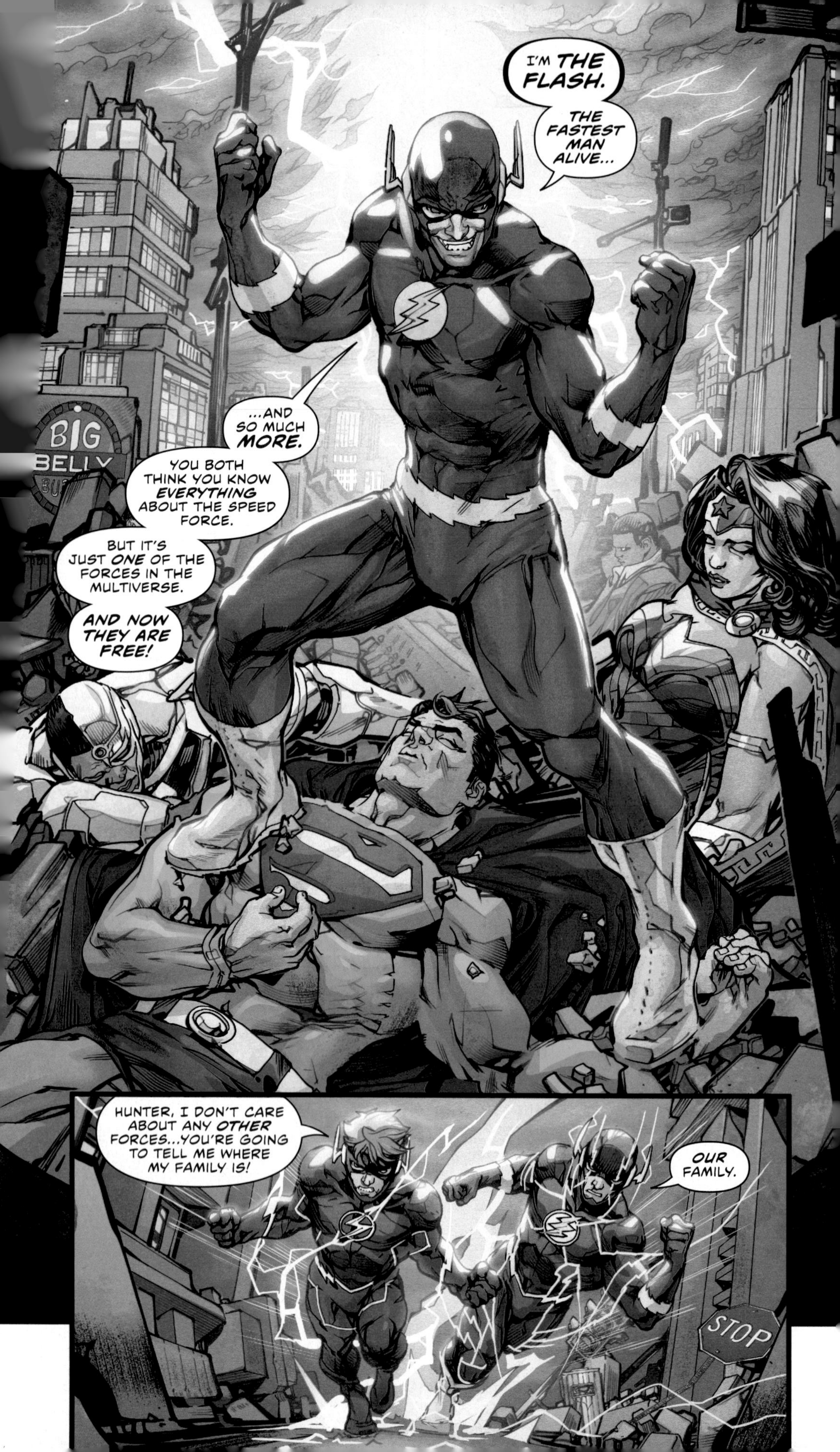

I'M THE FLASH.
THE FASTEST MAN ALIVE...
...AND SO MUCH MORE.
YOU BOTH THINK YOU KNOW EVERYTHING ABOUT THE SPEED FORCE.
BUT IT'S JUST ONE OF THE FORCES IN THE MULTIVERSE.
AND NOW THEY ARE FREE!
BIG BELLY
HUNTER, I DON'T CARE ABOUT ANY OTHER FORCES...YOU'RE GOING TO TELL ME WHERE MY FAMILY IS!
OUR FAMILY.
STOP

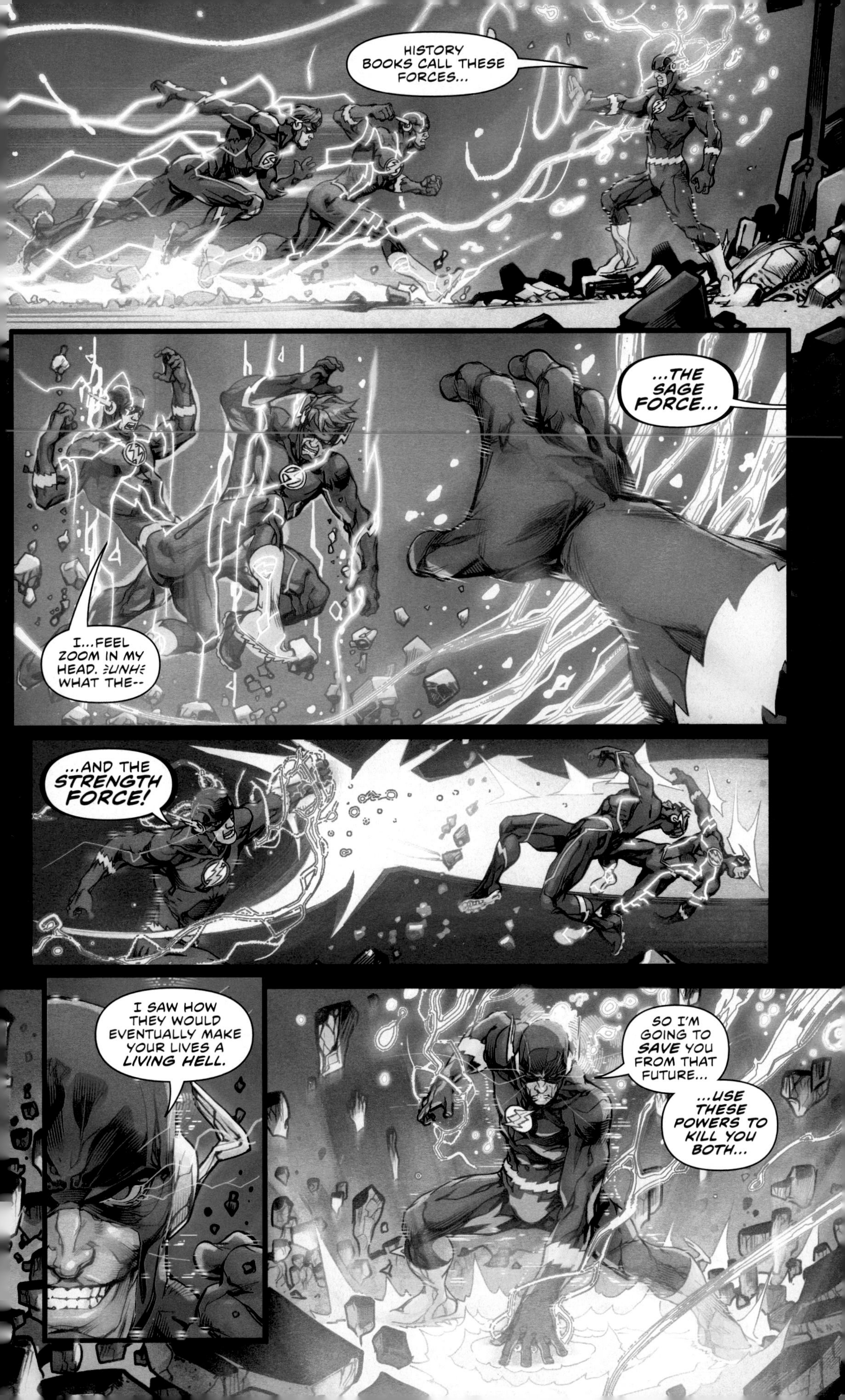
HISTORY BOOKS CALL THESE FORCES...
...THE SAGE FORCE...
I...FEEL ZOOM IN MY HEAD. UNH WHAT THE--
...AND THE STRENGTH FORCE!
I SAW HOW THEY WOULD EVENTUALLY MAKE YOUR LIVES A LIVING HELL.
SO I'M GOING TO SAVE YOU FROM THAT FUTURE...
...USE THESE POWERS TO KILL YOU BOTH...

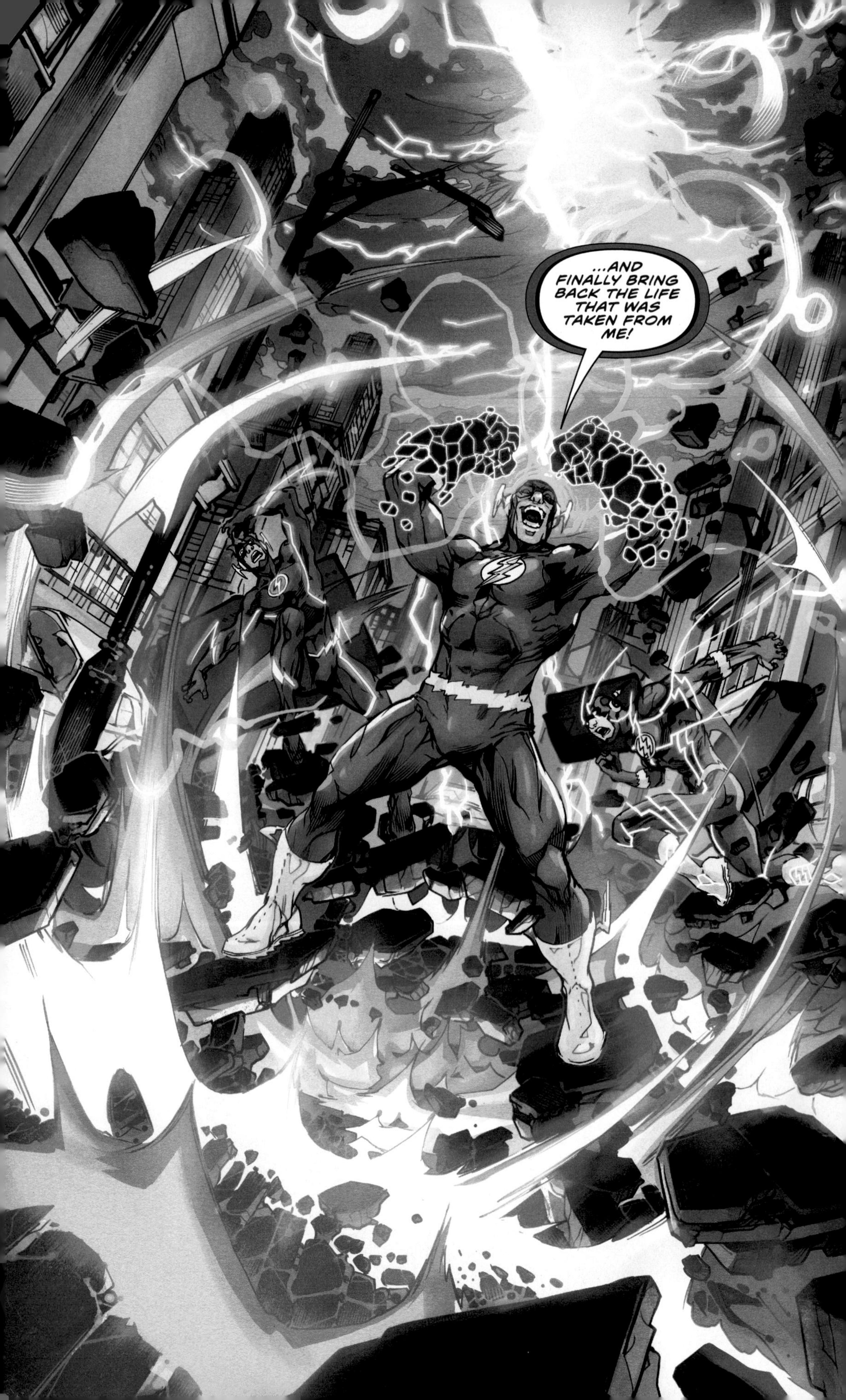
...AND FINALLY BRING BACK THE LIFE THAT WAS TAKEN FROM ME!

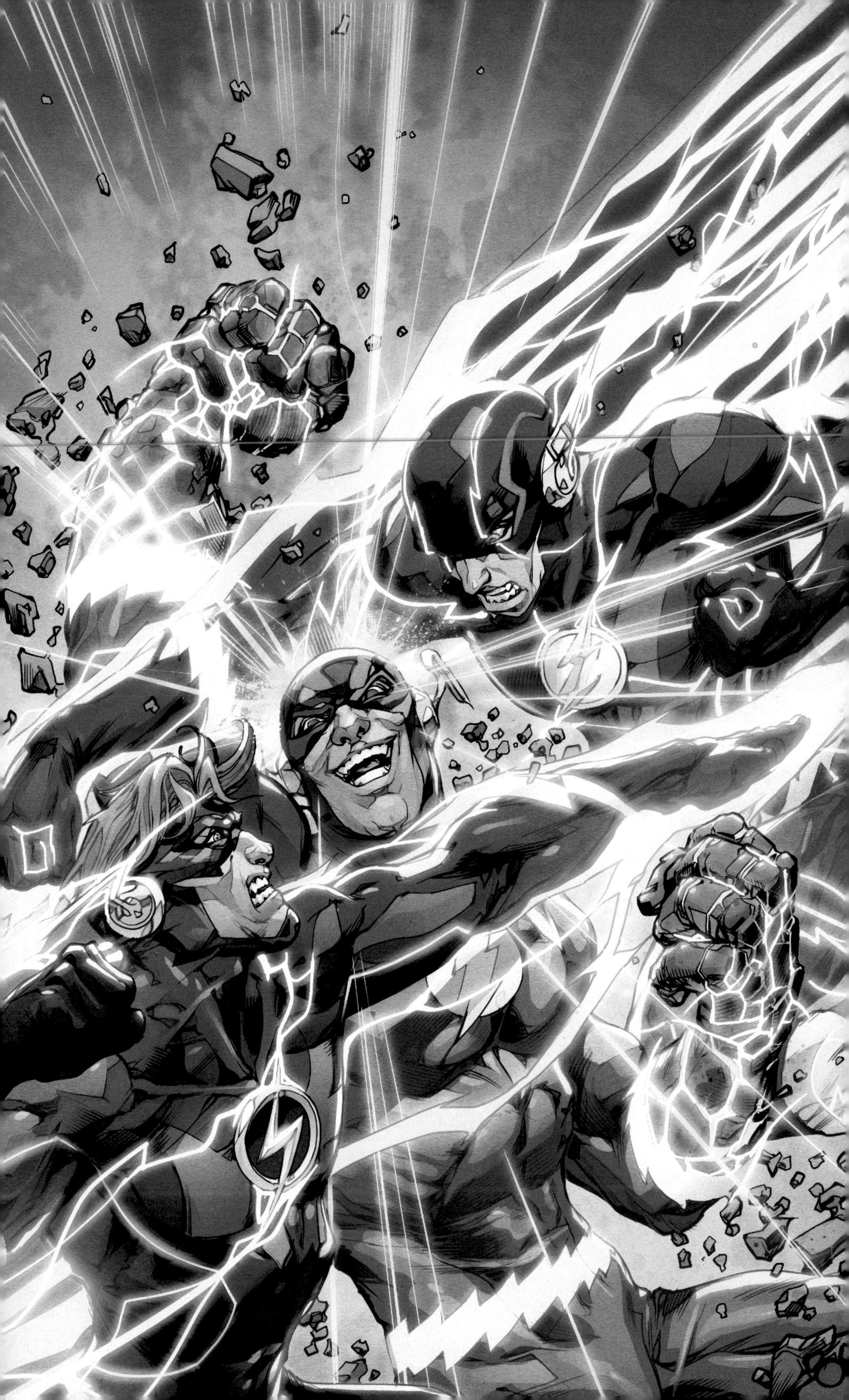

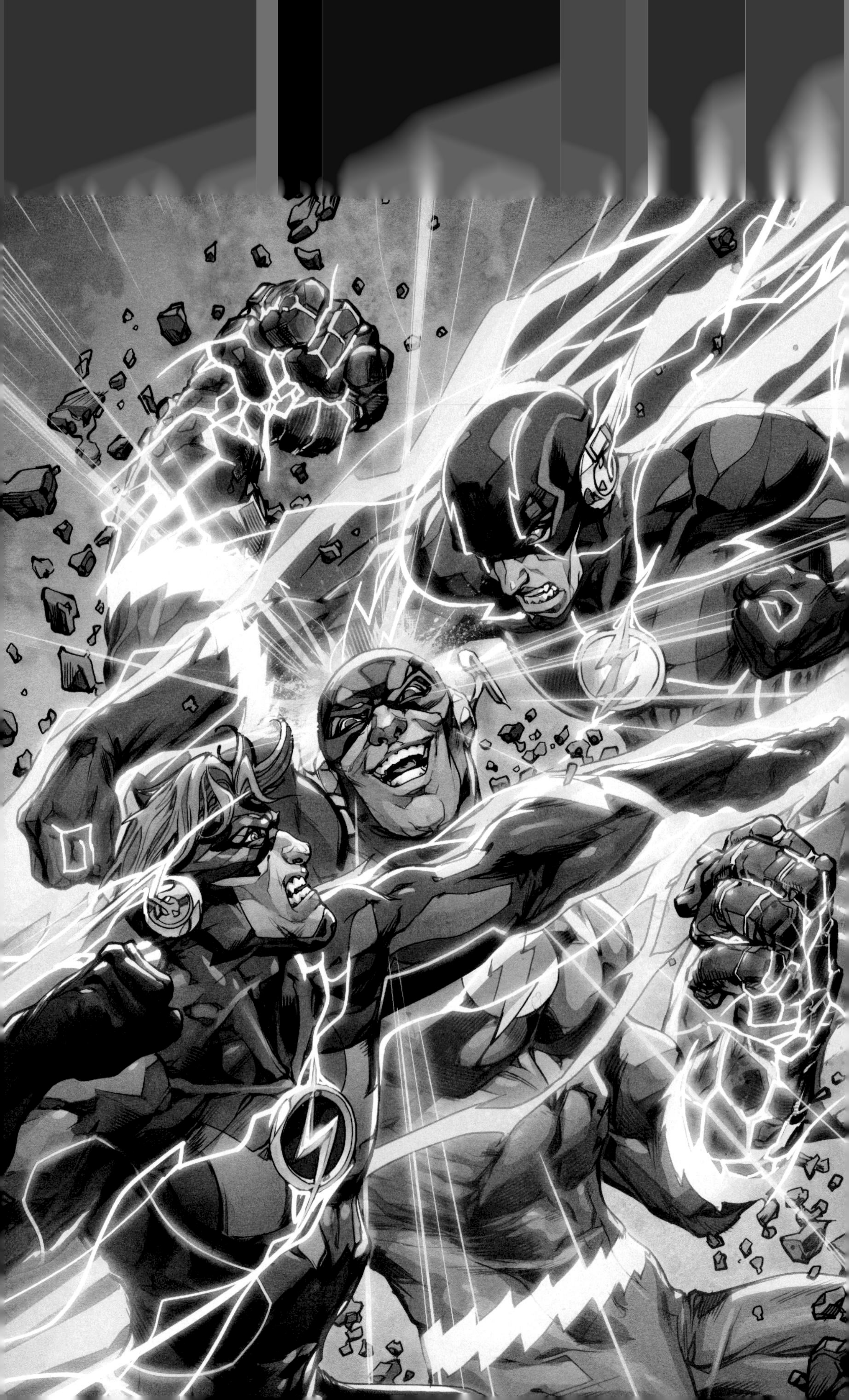

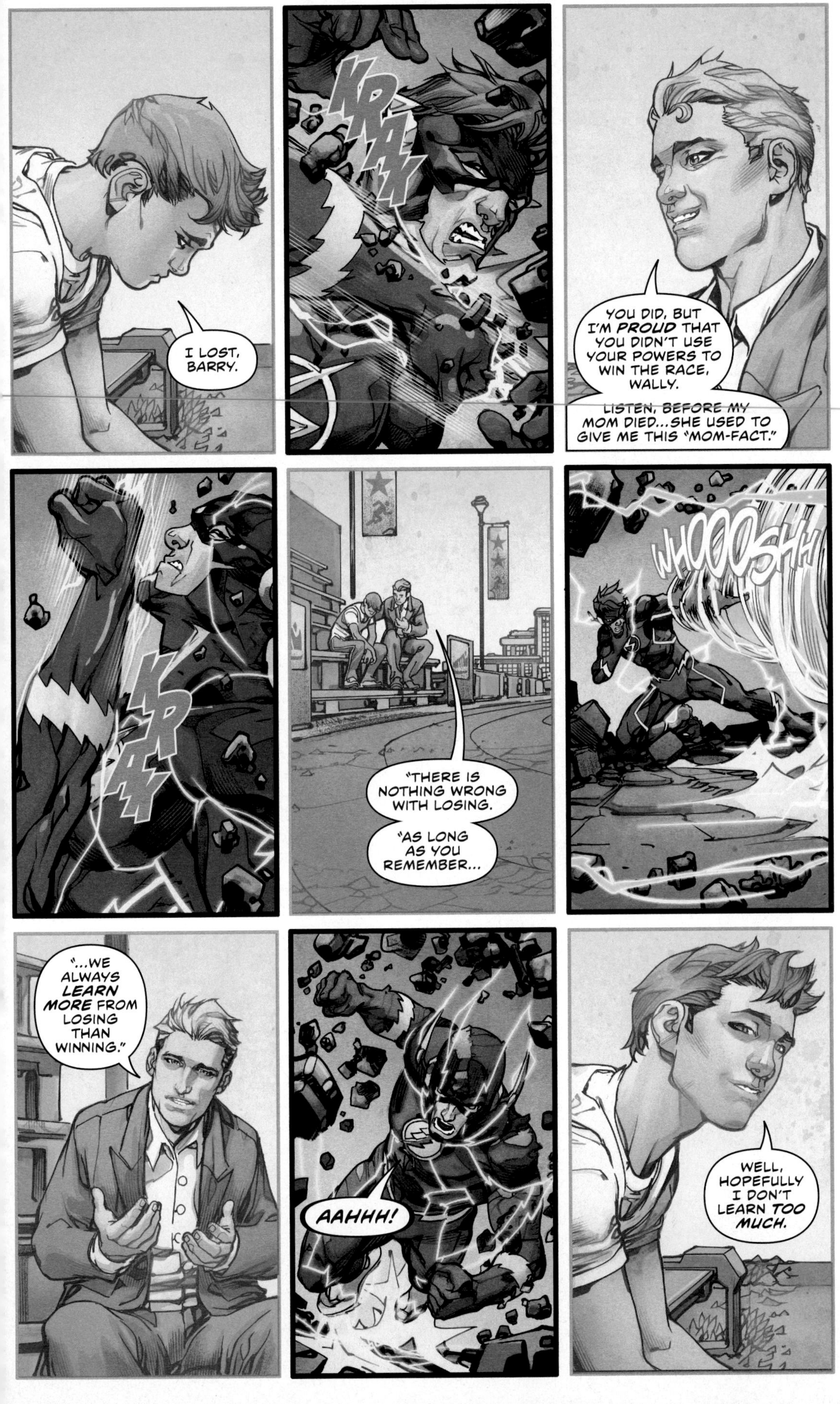
I LOST, BARRY.
KRAAK
YOU DID, BUT I'M PROUD THAT YOU DIDN'T USE YOUR POWERS TO WIN THE RACE, WALLY.
LISTEN, BEFORE MY MOM DIED...SHE USED TO GIVE ME THIS "MOM-FACT."
KRAK
"THERE IS NOTHING WRONG WITH LOSING.
"AS LONG AS YOU REMEMBER...
WHOOOSHH
"...WE ALWAYS LEARN MORE FROM LOSING THAN WINNING."
AAHHH!
WELL, HOPEFULLY I DON'T LEARN TOO MUCH.

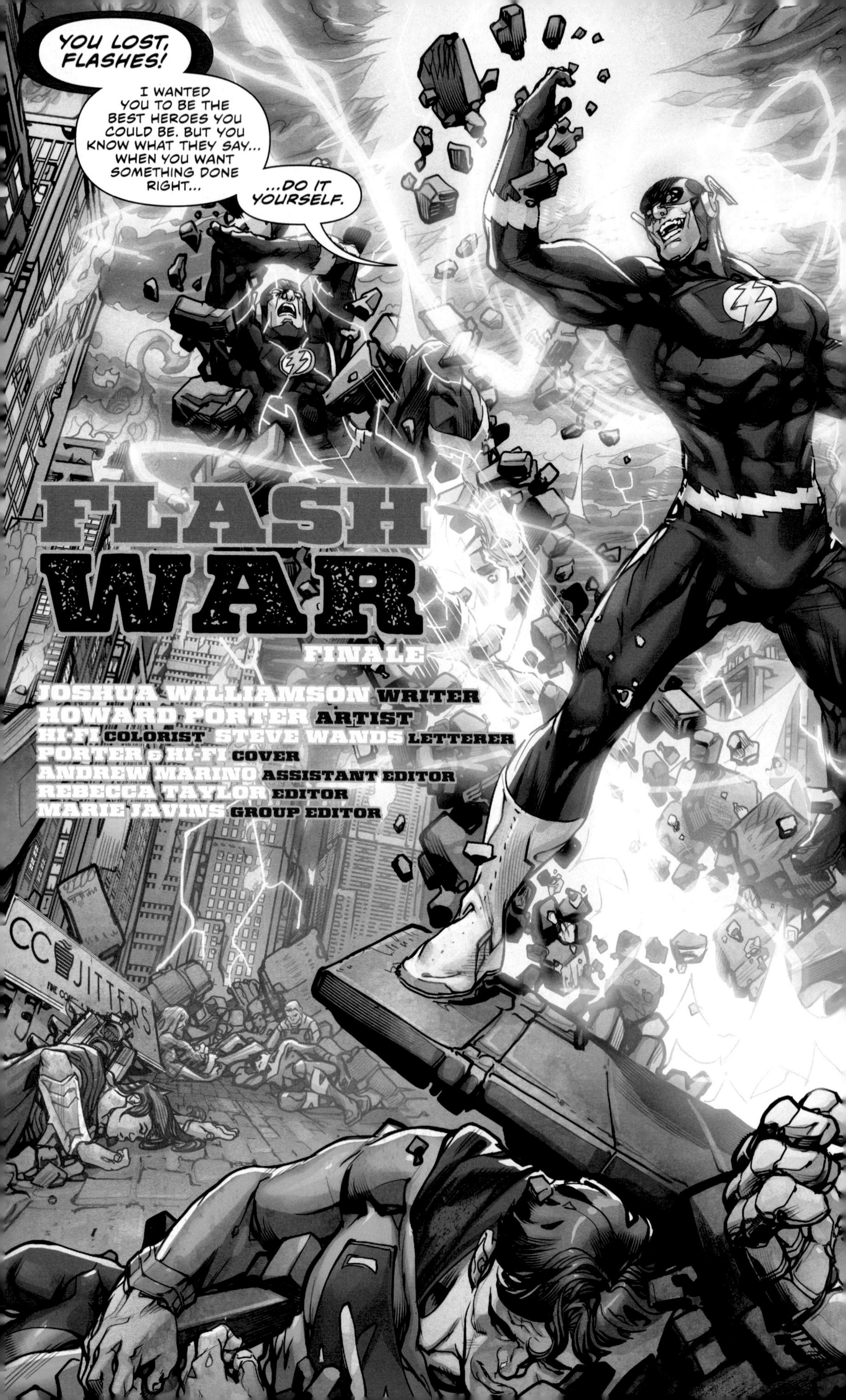

YOU LOST, FLASHES!
I WANTED YOU TO BE THE BEST HEROES YOU COULD BE. BUT YOU KNOW WHAT THEY SAY... WHEN YOU WANT SOMETHING DONE RIGHT...
...DO IT YOURSELF.
FLASH WAR
FINALE
JOSHUA WILLIAMSON WRITER
HOWARD PORTER ARTIST
HI-FI COLORIST STEVE WANDS LETTERER
PORTER & HI-FI COVER
ANDREW MARINO ASSISTANT EDITOR
REBECCA TAYLOR EDITOR
MARIE JAVINS GROUP EDITOR
CC JITTERS

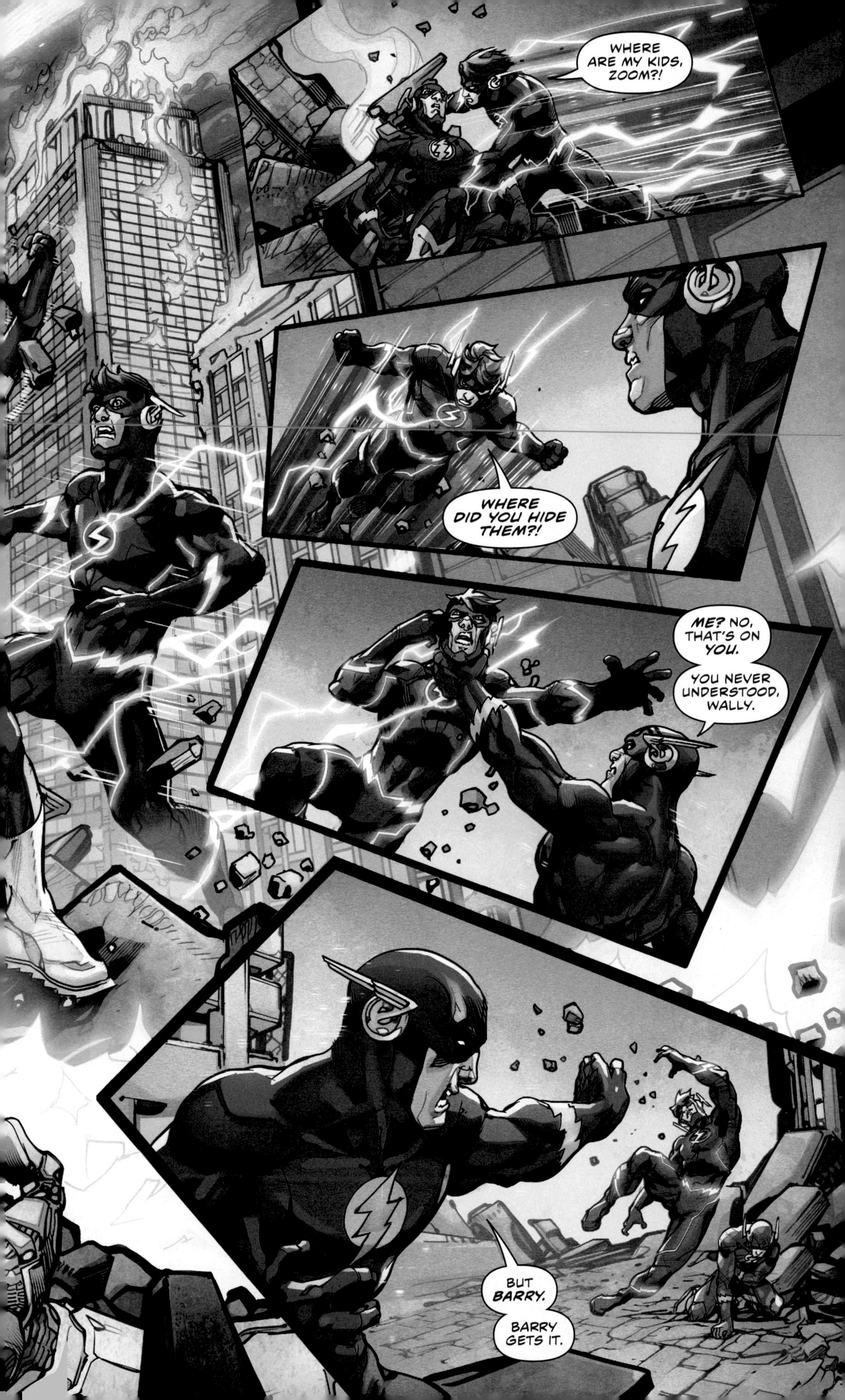
WHERE ARE MY KIDS, ZOOM?!
WHERE DID YOU HIDE THEM?!
ME? NO, THAT'S ON YOU.
YOU NEVER UNDERSTOOD, WALLY.
BUT BARRY.
BARRY GETS IT.

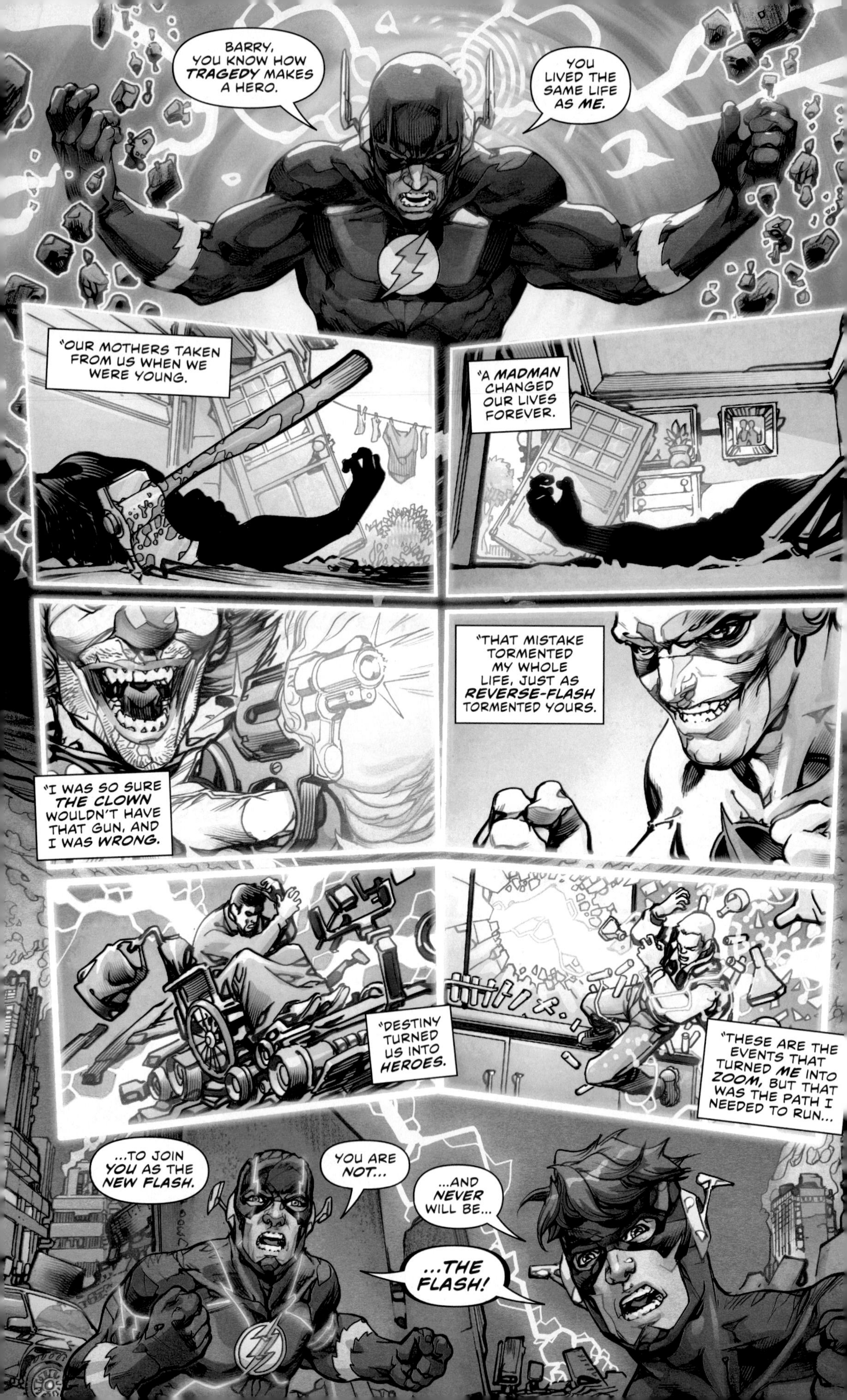
BARRY, YOU KNOW HOW TRAGEDY MAKES A HERO.
YOU LIVED THE SAME LIFE AS ME.
"OUR MOTHERS TAKEN FROM US WHEN WE WERE YOUNG.
"A MADMAN CHANGED OUR LIVES FOREVER.
"I WAS SO SURE THE CLOWN WOULDN'T HAVE THAT GUN, AND I WAS WRONG.
"THAT MISTAKE TORMENTED MY WHOLE LIFE, JUST AS REVERSE-FLASH TORMENTED YOURS.
"DESTINY TURNED US INTO HEROES.
"THESE ARE THE EVENTS THAT TURNED ME INTO ZOOM, BUT THAT WAS THE PATH THAT I NEEDED TO RUN...
...TO JOIN YOU AS THE NEW FLASH.
YOU ARE NOT...
...AND NEVER WILL BE...
...THE FLASH!

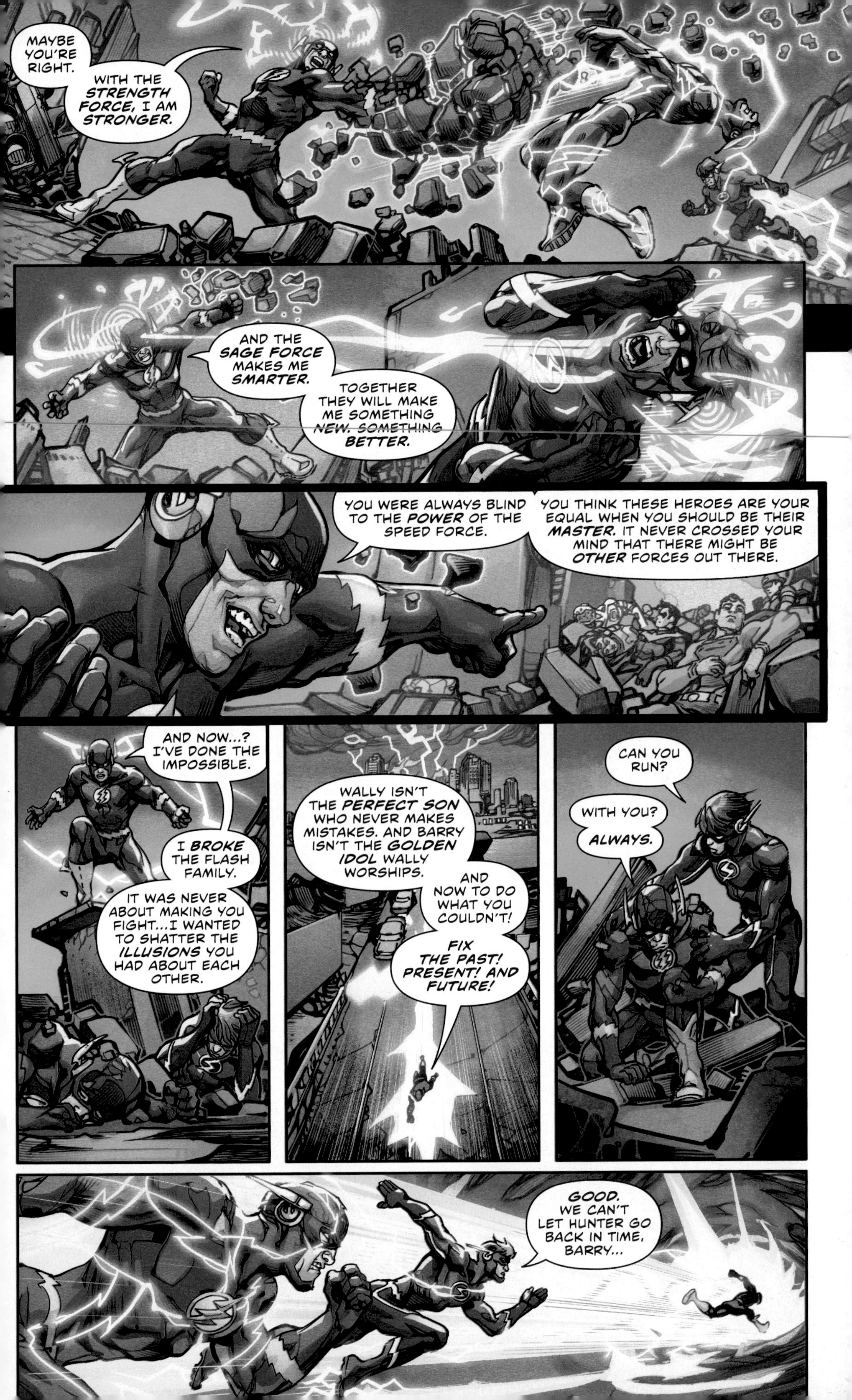
MAYBE YOU'RE RIGHT.
WITH THE STRENGTH FORCE, I AM STRONGER.
AND THE SAGE FORCE MAKES ME SMARTER.
TOGETHER THEY WILL MAKE ME SOMETHING NEW. SOMETHING BETTER.
YOU WERE ALWAYS BLIND TO THE POWER OF THE SPEED FORCE.
YOU THINK THESE HEROES ARE YOUR EQUAL WHEN YOU SHOULD BE THEIR MASTER. IT NEVER CROSSED YOUR MIND THAT THERE MIGHT BE OTHER FORCES OUT THERE.
AND NOW...? I'VE DONE THE IMPOSSIBLE.
I BROKE THE FLASH FAMILY.
IT WAS NEVER ABOUT MAKING YOU FIGHT...I WANTED TO SHATTER THE ILLUSIONS YOU HAD ABOUT EACH OTHER.
WALLY ISN'T THE PERFECT SON WHO NEVER MAKES MISTAKES. AND BARRY ISN'T THE GOLDEN IDOL WALLY WORSHIPS.
AND NOW TO DO WHAT YOU COULDN'T!
FIX THE PAST! PRESENT! AND FUTURE!
CAN YOU RUN?
WITH YOU?
ALWAYS.
GOOD. WE CAN'T LET HUNTER GO BACK IN TIME, BARRY...

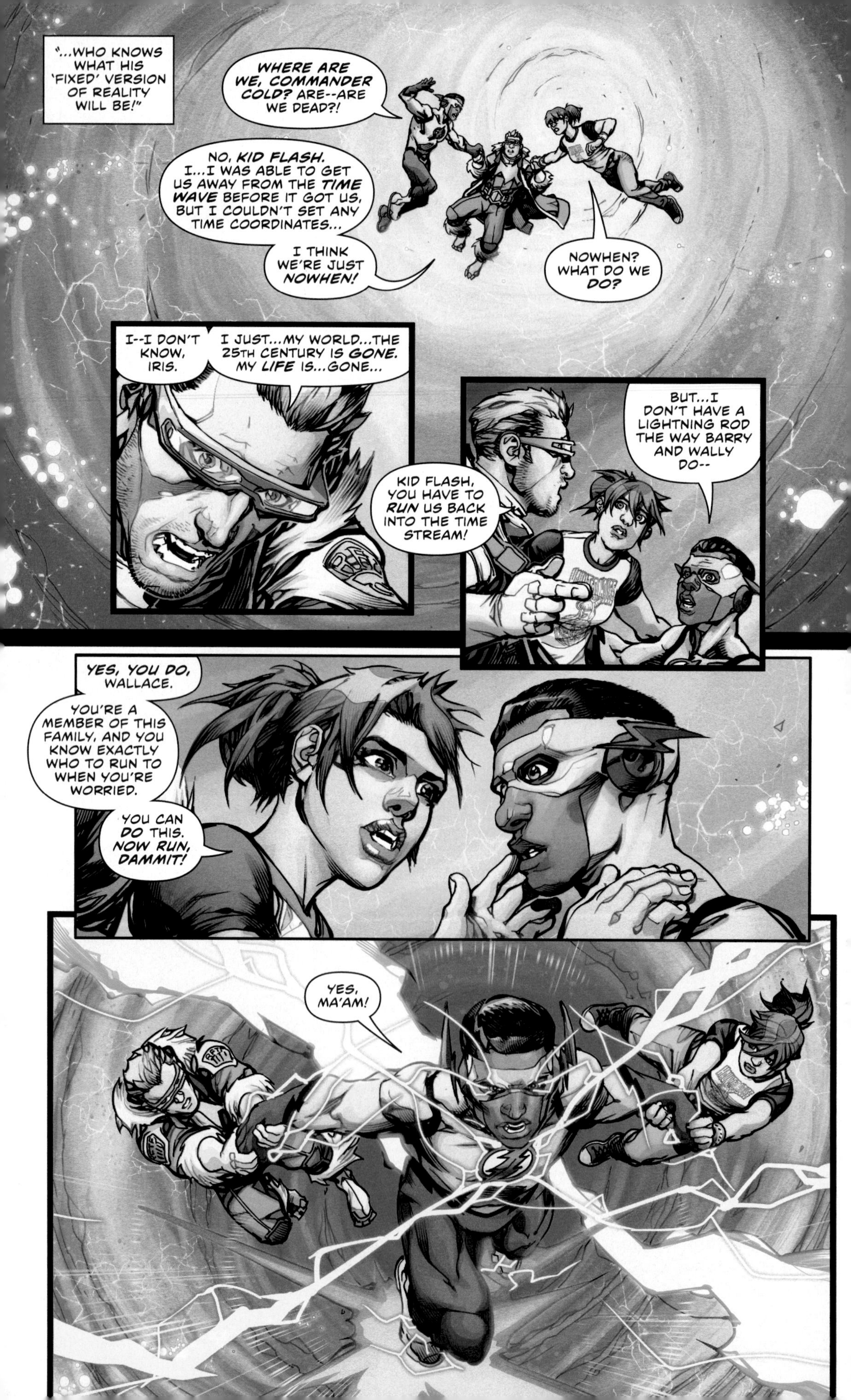
"...WHO KNOWS WHAT HIS 'FIXED' VERSION OF REALITY WILL BE!"
WHERE ARE WE, COMMANDER COLD? ARE--ARE WE DEAD?!
NO, KID FLASH. I...I WAS ABLE TO GET US AWAY FROM THE TIME WAVE BEFORE IT GOT US, BUT I COULDN'T SET ANY TIME COORDINATES...
I THINK WE'RE JUST NOWHEN!
NOWHEN? WHAT DO WE DO?
I--I DON'T KNOW, IRIS.
I JUST...MY WORLD...THE 25TH CENTURY IS GONE. MY LIFE IS...GONE...
KID FLASH, YOU HAVE TO RUN US BACK INTO THE TIME STREAM!
BUT...I DON'T HAVE A LIGHTNING ROD THE WAY BARRY AND WALLY DO--
YES, YOU DO, WALLACE.
YOU'RE A MEMBER OF THIS FAMILY, AND YOU KNOW EXACTLY WHO TO RUN TO WHEN YOU'RE WORRIED.
YOU CAN DO THIS. NOW RUN, DAMMIT!
YES, MA'AM!

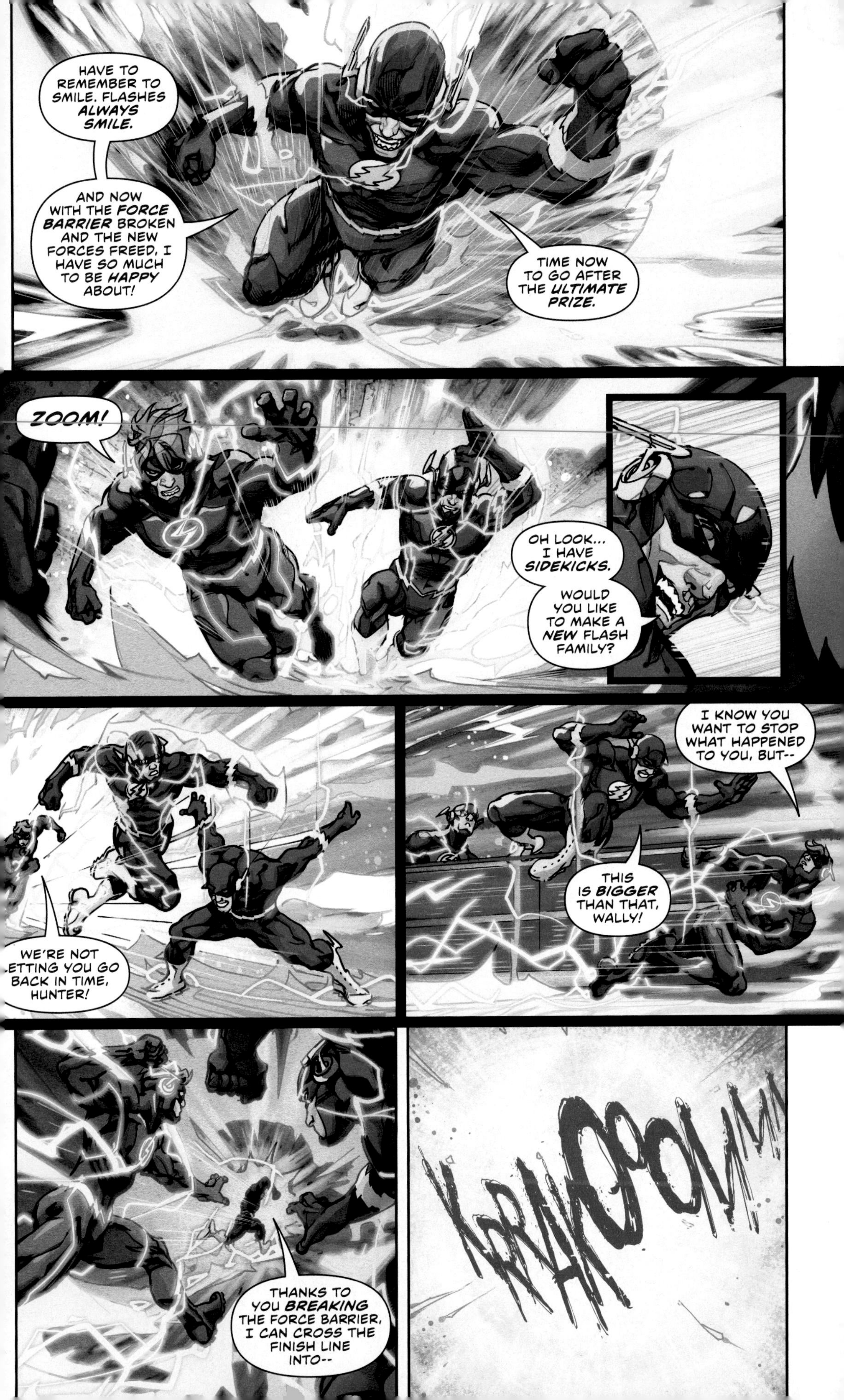
HAVE TO REMEMBER TO SMILE. FLASHES ALWAYS SMILE.
AND NOW WITH THE FORCE BARRIER BROKEN AND THE NEW FORCES FREED, I HAVE SO MUCH TO BE HAPPY ABOUT!
TIME NOW TO GO AFTER THE ULTIMATE PRIZE.
ZOOM!
OH LOOK... I HAVE SIDEKICKS.
WOULD YOU LIKE TO MAKE A NEW FLASH FAMILY?
WE'RE NOT LETTING YOU GO BACK IN TIME, HUNTER!
I KNOW YOU WANT TO STOP WHAT HAPPENED TO YOU, BUT--
THIS IS BIGGER THAN THAT, WALLY!
THANKS TO YOU BREAKING THE FORCE BARRIER, I CAN CROSS THE FINISH LINE INTO--
KRAKOOM

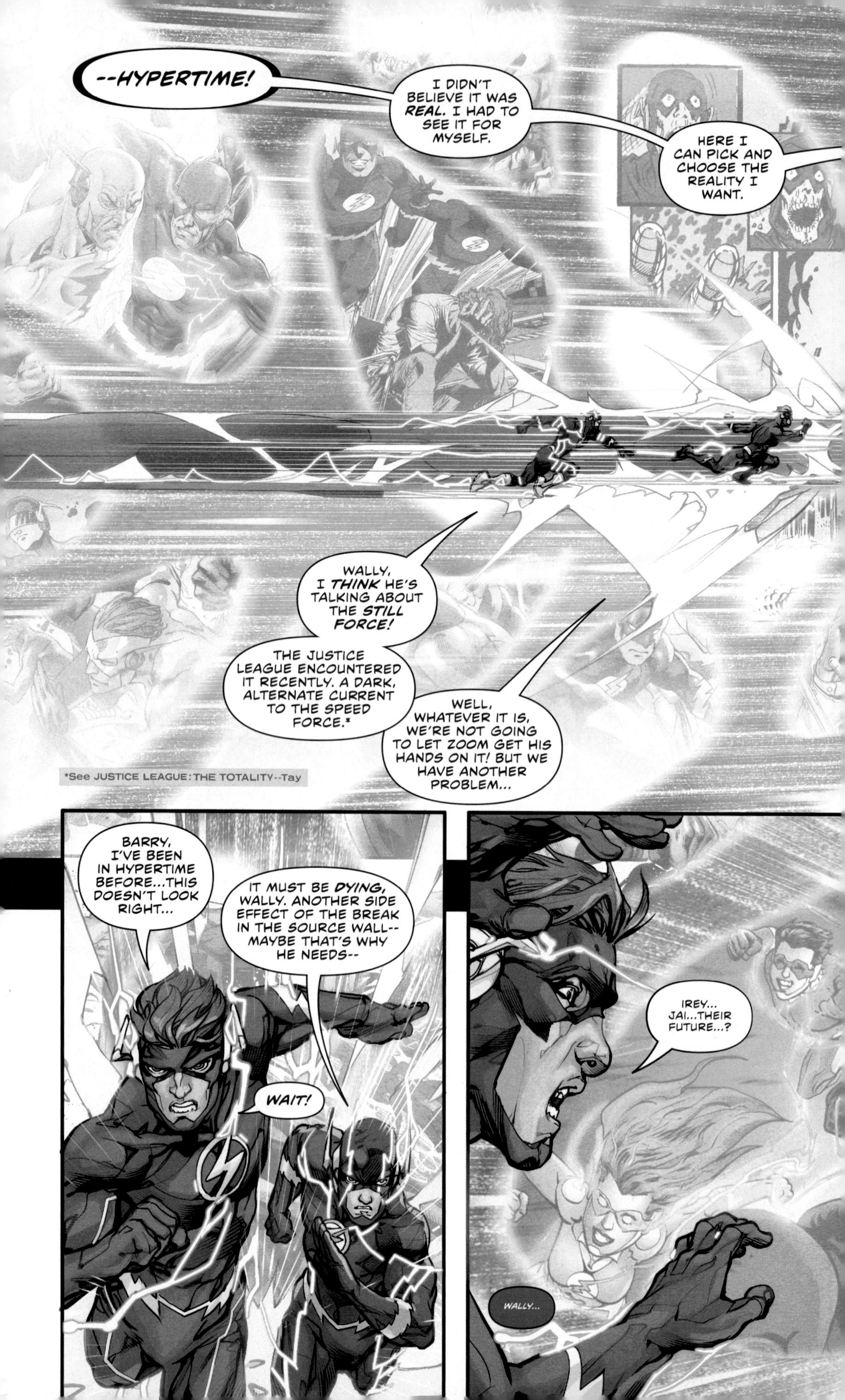
--HYPERTIME!
I DIDN'T BELIEVE IT WAS REAL. I HAD TO SEE IT FOR MYSELF.
HERE I CAN PICK AND CHOOSE THE REALITY I WANT.
WALLY, I THINK HE'S TALKING ABOUT THE STILL FORCE!
THE JUSTICE LEAGUE ENCOUNTERED IT RECENTLY. A DARK, ALTERNATE CURRENT TO THE SPEED FORCE.*
WELL, WHATEVER IT IS, WE'RE NOT GOING TO LET ZOOM GET HIS HANDS ON IT! BUT WE HAVE ANOTHER PROBLEM...
*See JUSTICE LEAGUE: THE TOTALITY--Tay
BARRY, I'VE BEEN IN HYPERTIME BEFORE...THIS DOESN'T LOOK RIGHT...
IT MUST BE DYING, WALLY. ANOTHER SIDE EFFECT OF THE BREAK IN THE SOURCE WALL--MAYBE THAT'S WHY HE NEEDS--
WAIT!
IREY... JAI...THEIR FUTURE...?
WALLY...

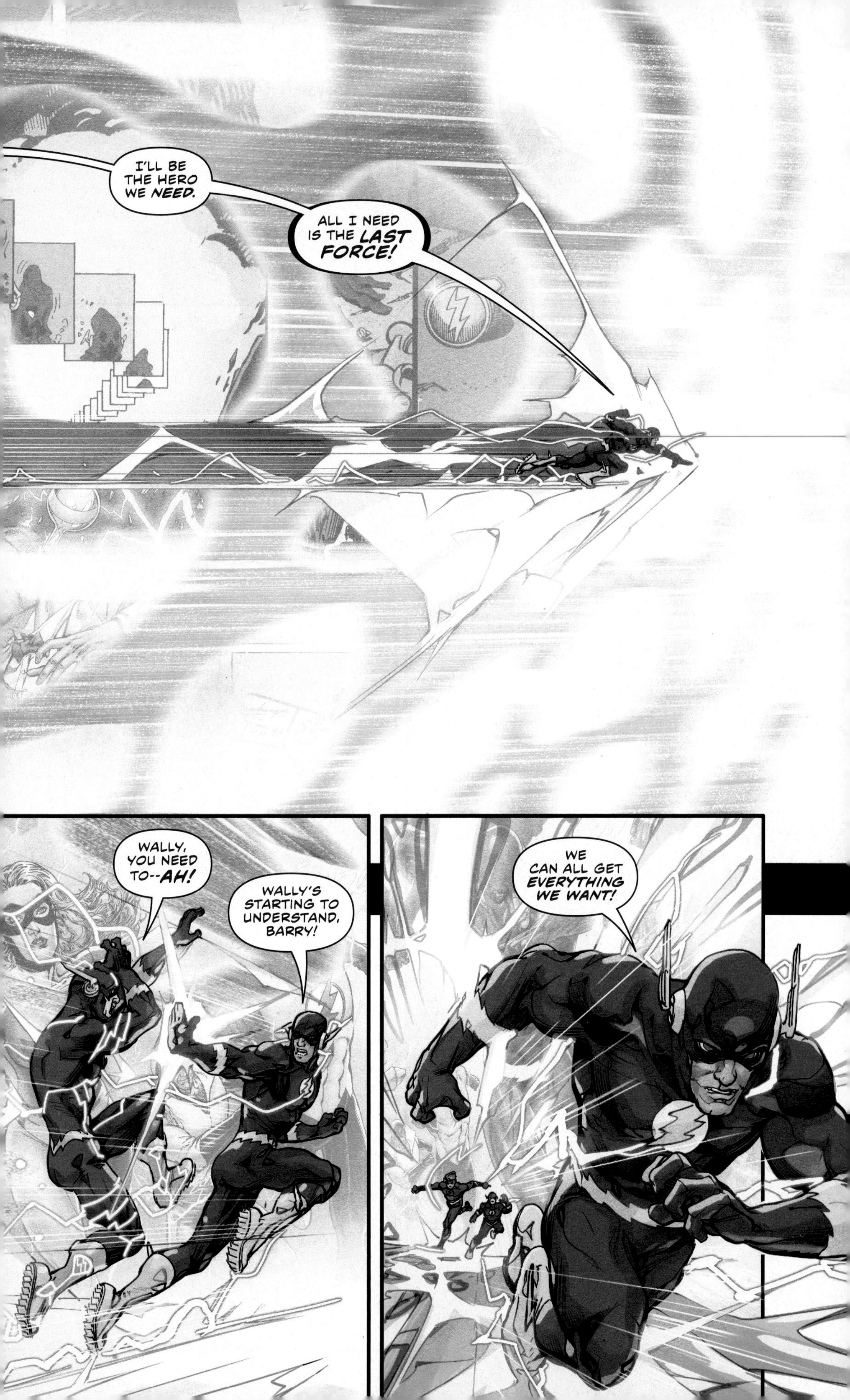

I'LL BE THE HERO WE NEED.
ALL I NEED IS THE LAST FORCE!
WALLY, YOU NEED TO--AH!
WALLY'S STARTING TO UNDERSTAND, BARRY!
WE CAN ALL GET EVERYTHING WE WANT!

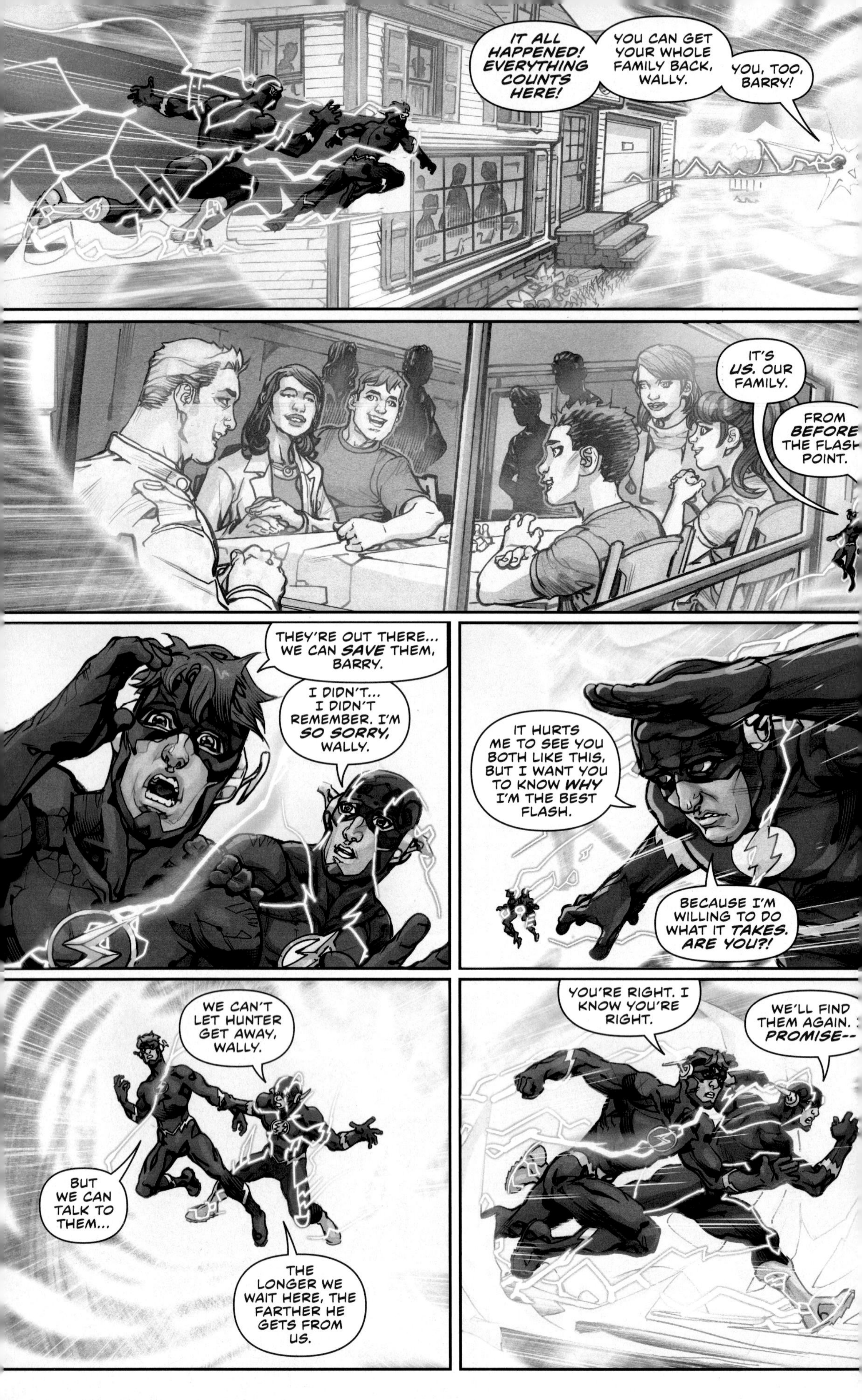
IT ALL HAPPENED! EVERYTHING COUNTS HERE!
YOU CAN GET YOUR WHOLE FAMILY BACK, WALLY.
YOU, TOO, BARRY!
IT'S US. OUR FAMILY.
FROM BEFORE THE FLASH POINT.
THEY'RE OUT THERE... WE CAN SAVE THEM, BARRY.
I DIDN'T... I DIDN'T REMEMBER. I'M SO SORRY, WALLY.
IT HURTS ME TO SEE YOU BOTH LIKE THIS, BUT I WANT YOU TO KNOW WHY I'M THE BEST FLASH.
BECAUSE I'M WILLING TO DO WHAT IT TAKES. ARE YOU?!
WE CAN'T LET HUNTER GET AWAY, WALLY.
BUT WE CAN TALK TO THEM...
THE LONGER WE WAIT HERE, THE FARTHER HE GETS FROM US.
YOU'RE RIGHT. I KNOW YOU'RE RIGHT.
WE'LL FIND THEM AGAIN. I PROMISE--

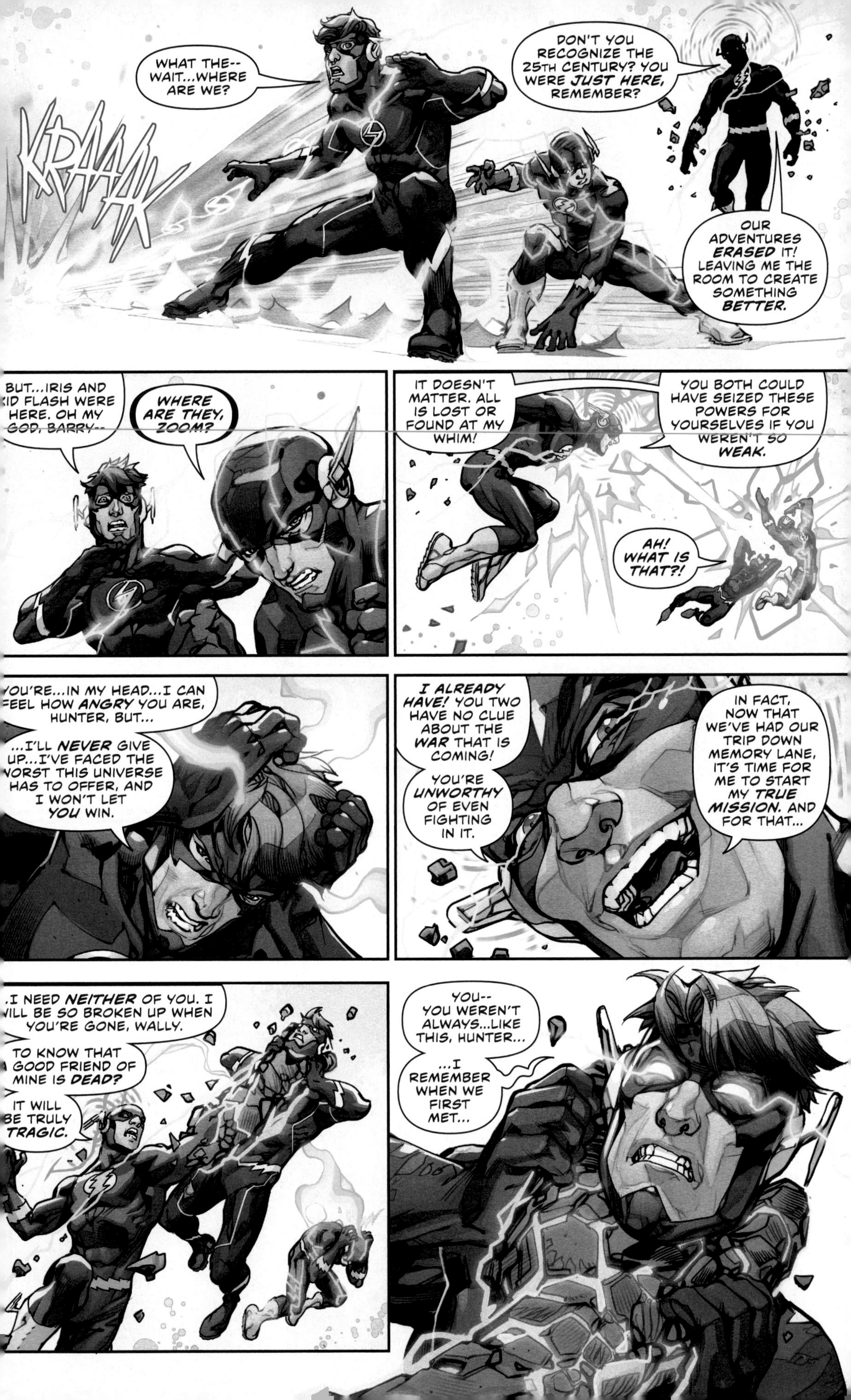
KRAAAAK
WHAT THE--WAIT...WHERE ARE WE?
DON'T YOU RECOGNIZE THE 25TH CENTURY? YOU WERE JUST HERE, REMEMBER?
OUR ADVENTURES ERASED IT! LEAVING ME THE ROOM TO CREATE SOMETHING BETTER.
BUT...IRIS AND KID FLASH WERE HERE. OH MY GOD, BARRY--
WHERE ARE THEY, ZOOM?
IT DOESN'T MATTER. ALL IS LOST OR FOUND AT MY WHIM!
YOU BOTH COULD HAVE SEIZED THESE POWERS FOR YOURSELVES IF YOU WEREN'T SO WEAK.
AH! WHAT IS THAT?!
YOU'RE...IN MY HEAD...I CAN FEEL HOW ANGRY YOU ARE, HUNTER, BUT...
...I'LL NEVER GIVE UP...I'VE FACED THE WORST THIS UNIVERSE HAS TO OFFER, AND I WON'T LET YOU WIN.
I ALREADY HAVE! YOU TWO HAVE NO CLUE ABOUT THE WAR THAT IS COMING!
YOU'RE UNWORTHY OF EVEN FIGHTING IN IT.
IN FACT, NOW THAT WE'VE HAD OUR TRIP DOWN MEMORY LANE, IT'S TIME FOR ME TO START MY TRUE MISSION. AND FOR THAT...
...I NEED NEITHER OF YOU. I WILL BE SO BROKEN UP WHEN YOU'RE GONE, WALLY.
TO KNOW THAT GOOD FRIEND OF MINE IS DEAD?
IT WILL BE TRULY TRAGIC.
YOU--YOU WEREN'T ALWAYS...LIKE THIS, HUNTER...
...I REMEMBER WHEN WE FIRST MET...

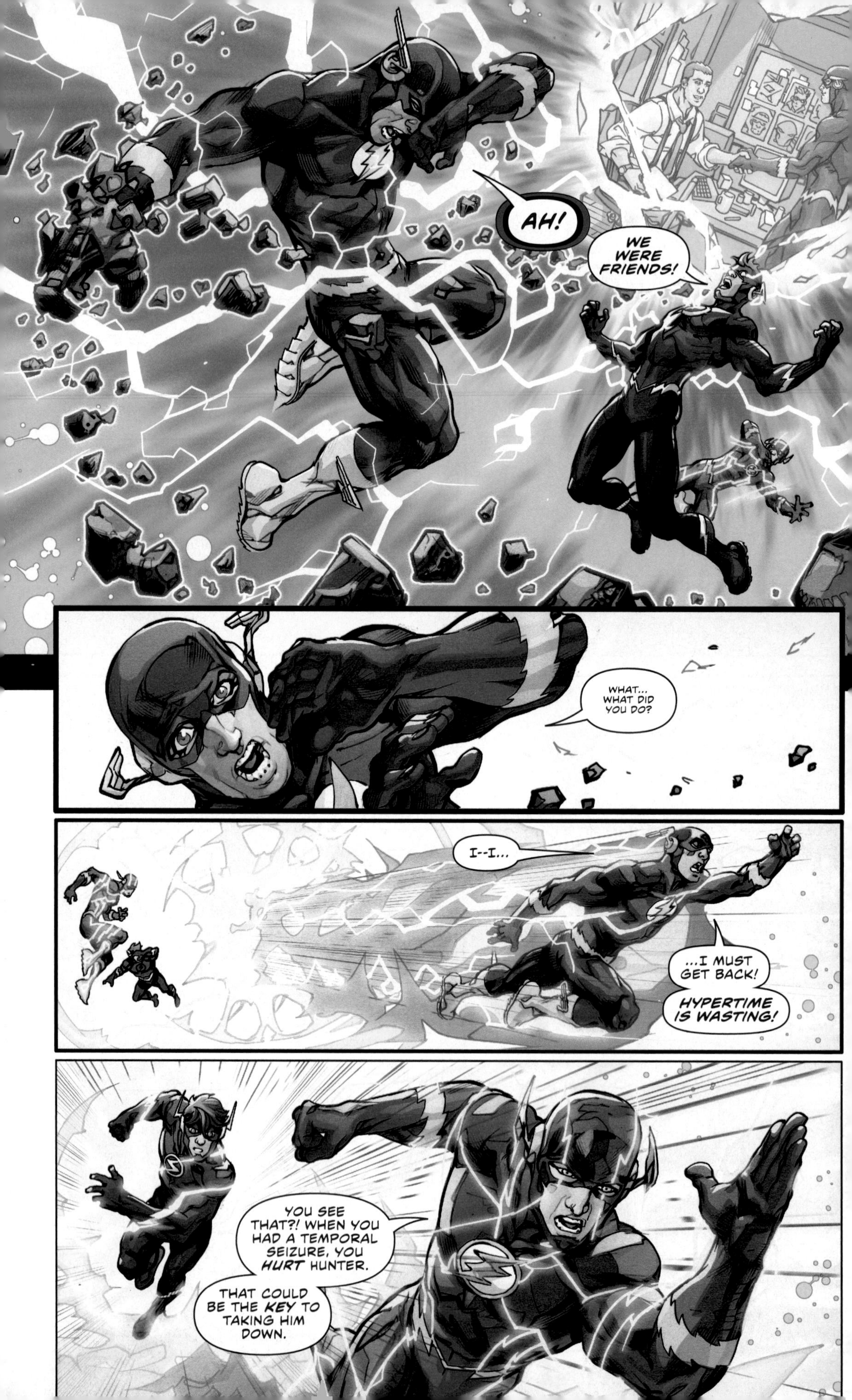
AH!
WE WERE FRIENDS!
WHAT... WHAT DID YOU DO?
I--I...
...I MUST GET BACK!
HYPERTIME IS WASTING!
YOU SEE THAT?! WHEN YOU HAD A TEMPORAL SEIZURE, YOU HURT HUNTER.
THAT COULD BE THE KEY TO TAKING HIM DOWN.

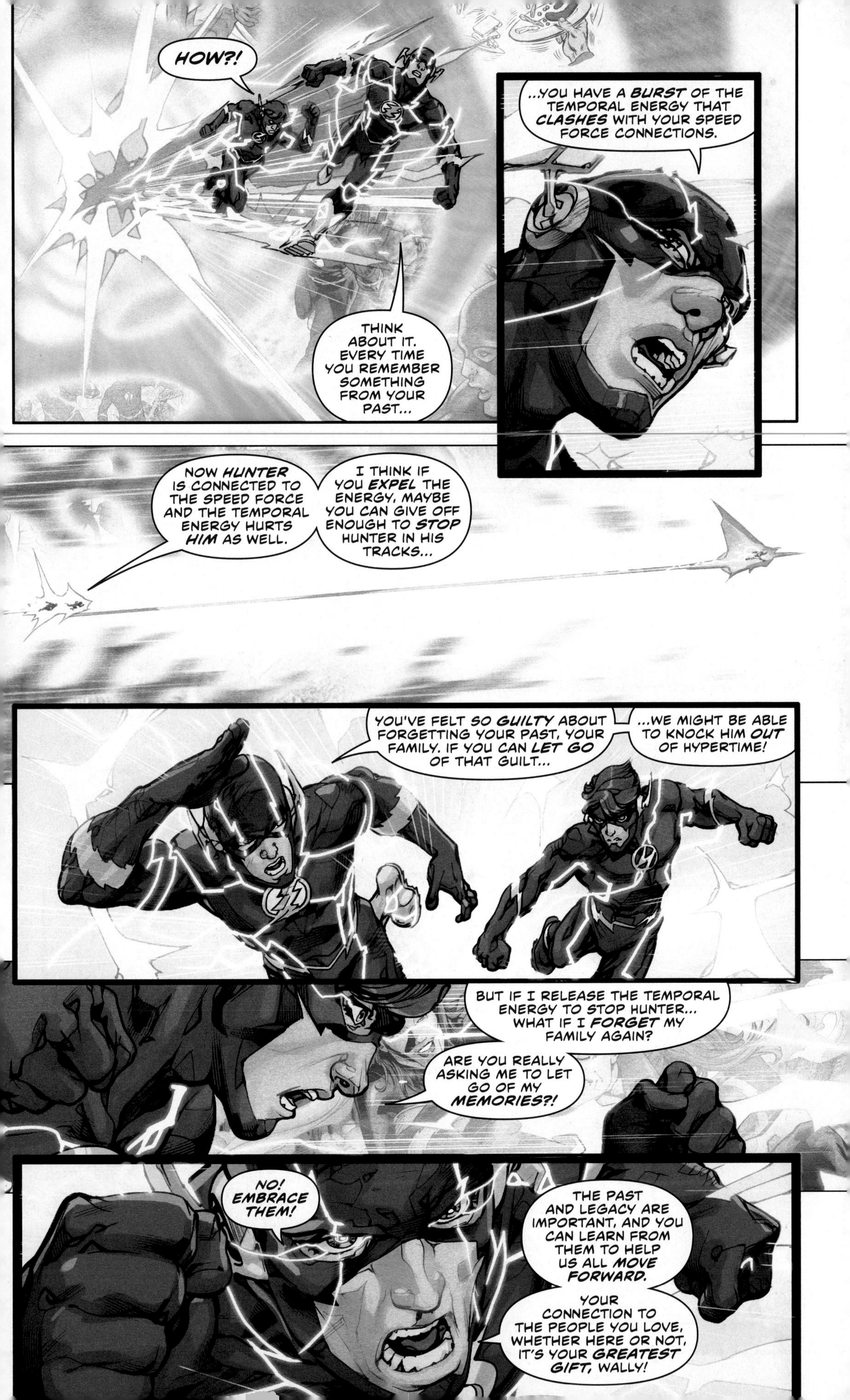
HOW?!
...YOU HAVE A BURST OF THE TEMPORAL ENERGY THAT CLASHES WITH YOUR SPEED FORCE CONNECTIONS.
THINK ABOUT IT. EVERY TIME YOU REMEMBER SOMETHING FROM YOUR PAST...
NOW HUNTER IS CONNECTED TO THE SPEED FORCE AND THE TEMPORAL ENERGY HURTS HIM AS WELL.
I THINK IF YOU EXPEL THE ENERGY, MAYBE YOU CAN GIVE OFF ENOUGH TO STOP HUNTER IN HIS TRACKS...
YOU'VE FELT SO GUILTY ABOUT FORGETTING YOUR PAST, YOUR FAMILY. IF YOU CAN LET GO OF THAT GUILT...
...WE MIGHT BE ABLE TO KNOCK HIM OUT OF HYPERTIME!
BUT IF I RELEASE THE TEMPORAL ENERGY TO STOP HUNTER... WHAT IF I FORGET MY FAMILY AGAIN?
ARE YOU REALLY ASKING ME TO LET GO OF MY MEMORIES?!
NO! EMBRACE THEM!
THE PAST AND LEGACY ARE IMPORTANT, AND YOU CAN LEARN FROM THEM TO HELP US ALL MOVE FORWARD.
YOUR CONNECTION TO THE PEOPLE YOU LOVE, WHETHER HERE OR NOT, IT'S YOUR GREATEST GIFT, WALLY!

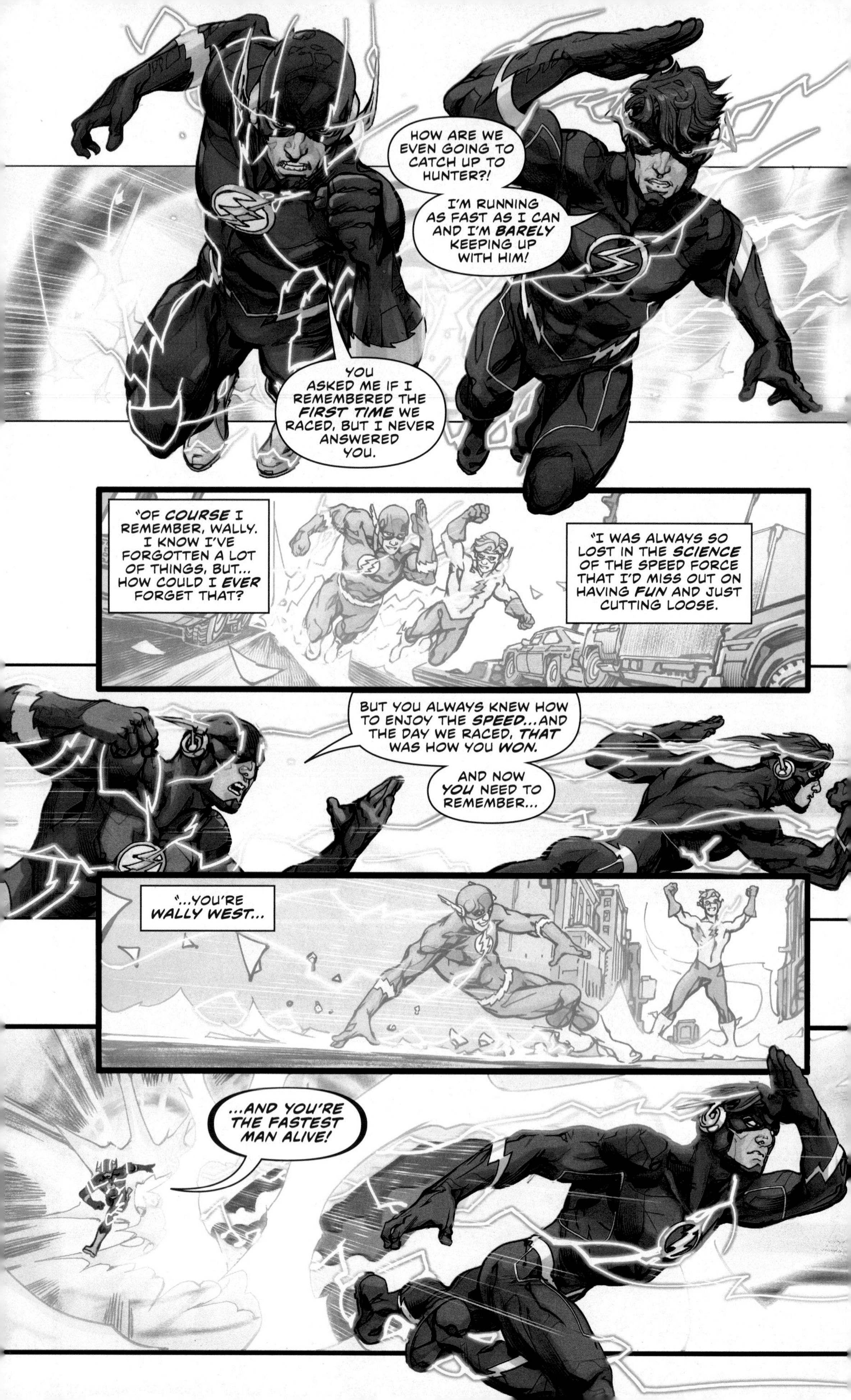
HOW ARE WE EVEN GOING TO CATCH UP TO HUNTER?!
I'M RUNNING AS FAST AS I CAN AND I'M BARELY KEEPING UP WITH HIM!
YOU ASKED ME IF I REMEMBERED THE FIRST TIME WE RACED, BUT I NEVER ANSWERED YOU.
"OF COURSE I REMEMBER, WALLY. I KNOW I'VE FORGOTTEN A LOT OF THINGS, BUT... HOW COULD I EVER FORGET THAT?
"I WAS ALWAYS SO LOST IN THE SCIENCE OF THE SPEED FORCE THAT I'D MISS OUT ON HAVING FUN AND JUST CUTTING LOOSE.
BUT YOU ALWAYS KNEW HOW TO ENJOY THE SPEED...AND THE DAY WE RACED, THAT WAS HOW YOU WON.
AND NOW YOU NEED TO REMEMBER...
"...YOU'RE WALLY WEST...
...AND YOU'RE THE FASTEST MAN ALIVE!

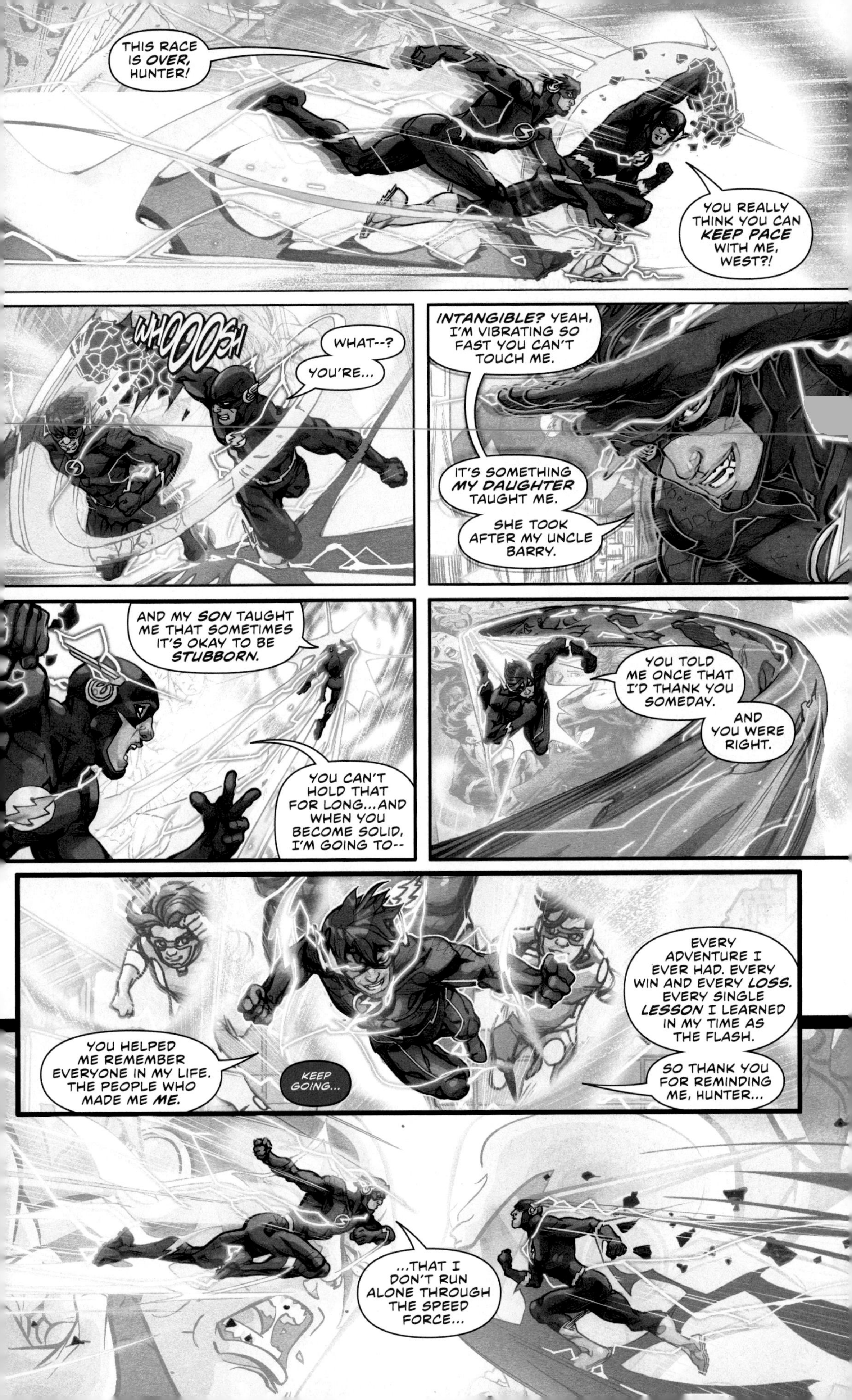
THIS RACE IS *OVER,* HUNTER!
YOU REALLY THINK YOU CAN *KEEP PACE* WITH ME, WEST?!
WHOOOSH
WHAT--?
YOU'RE...
INTANGIBLE? YEAH, I'M VIBRATING SO FAST YOU CAN'T TOUCH ME.
IT'S SOMETHING *MY DAUGHTER* TAUGHT ME.
SHE TOOK AFTER MY UNCLE BARRY.
AND MY *SON* TAUGHT ME THAT SOMETIMES IT'S OKAY TO BE *STUBBORN.*
YOU CAN'T HOLD THAT FOR LONG...AND WHEN YOU BECOME SOLID, I'M GOING TO--
YOU TOLD ME ONCE THAT I'D THANK YOU SOMEDAY.
AND YOU WERE RIGHT.
YOU HELPED ME REMEMBER EVERYONE IN MY LIFE. THE PEOPLE WHO MADE ME *ME.*
KEEP GOING...
EVERY ADVENTURE I EVER HAD. EVERY WIN AND EVERY *LOSS.* EVERY SINGLE *LESSON* I LEARNED IN MY TIME AS THE FLASH.
SO THANK YOU FOR REMINDING ME, HUNTER...
...THAT I DON'T RUN ALONE THROUGH THE SPEED FORCE...

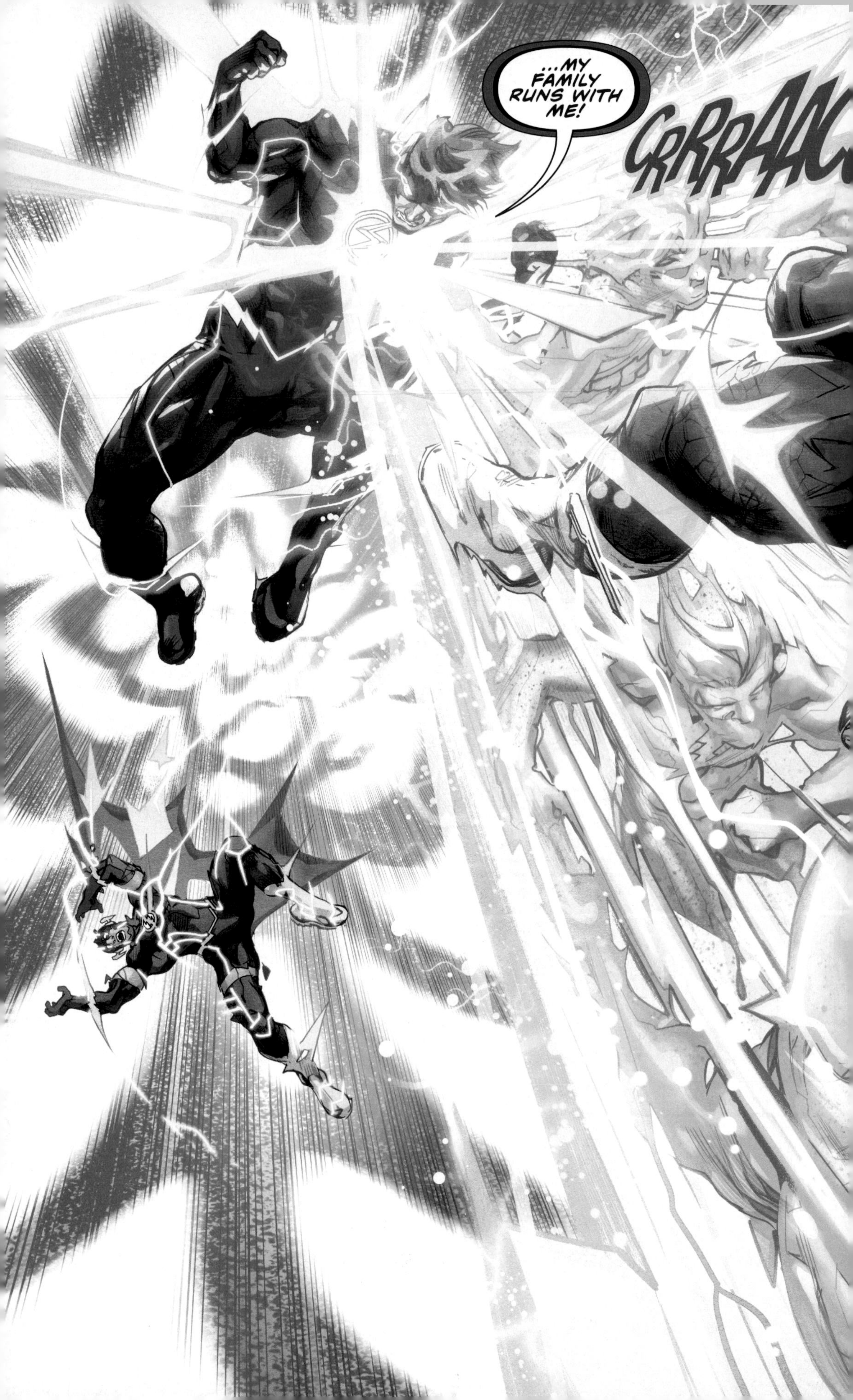
...MY FAMILY RUNS WITH ME!
CRRRAAC

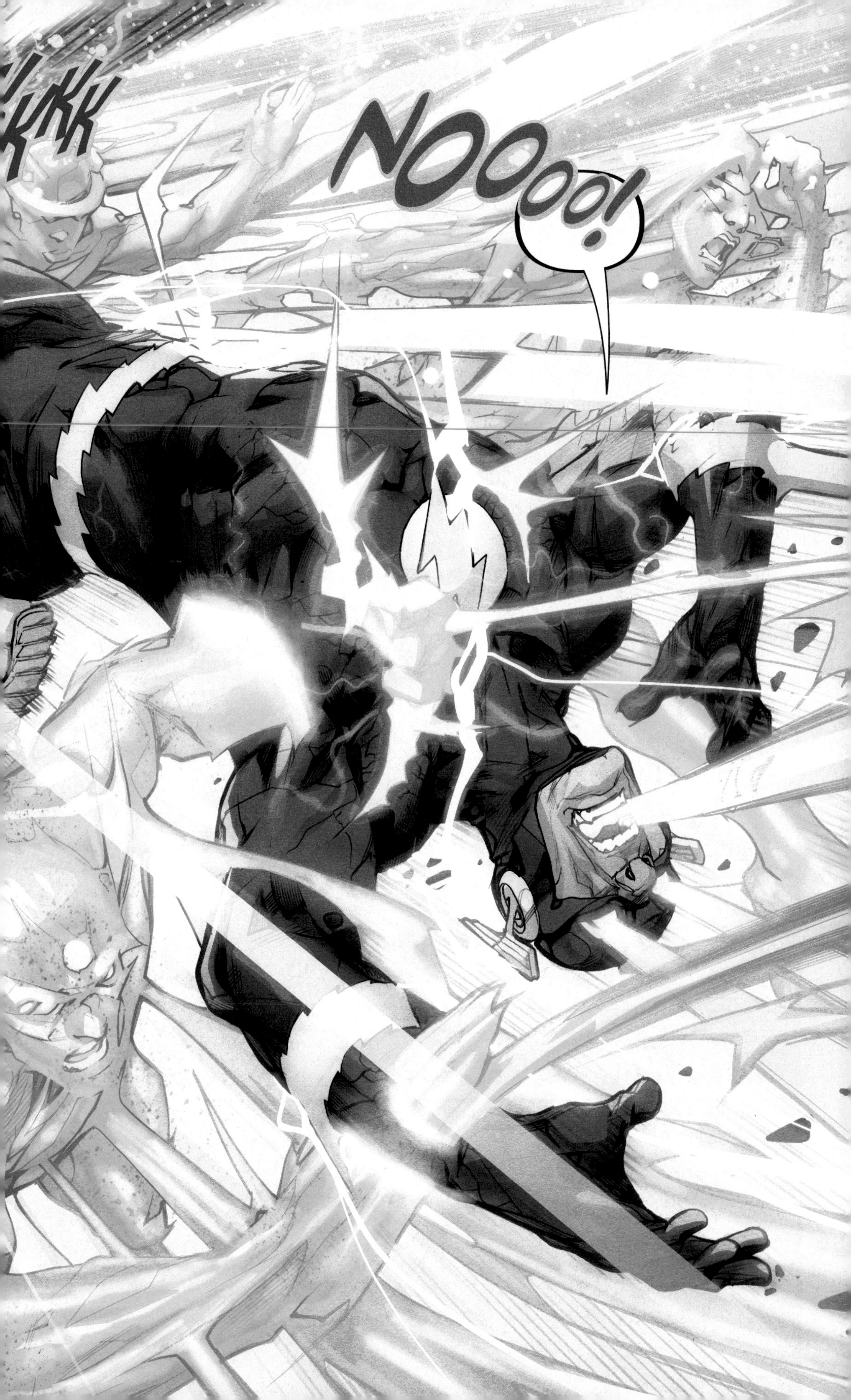
KKK
NOOooo!

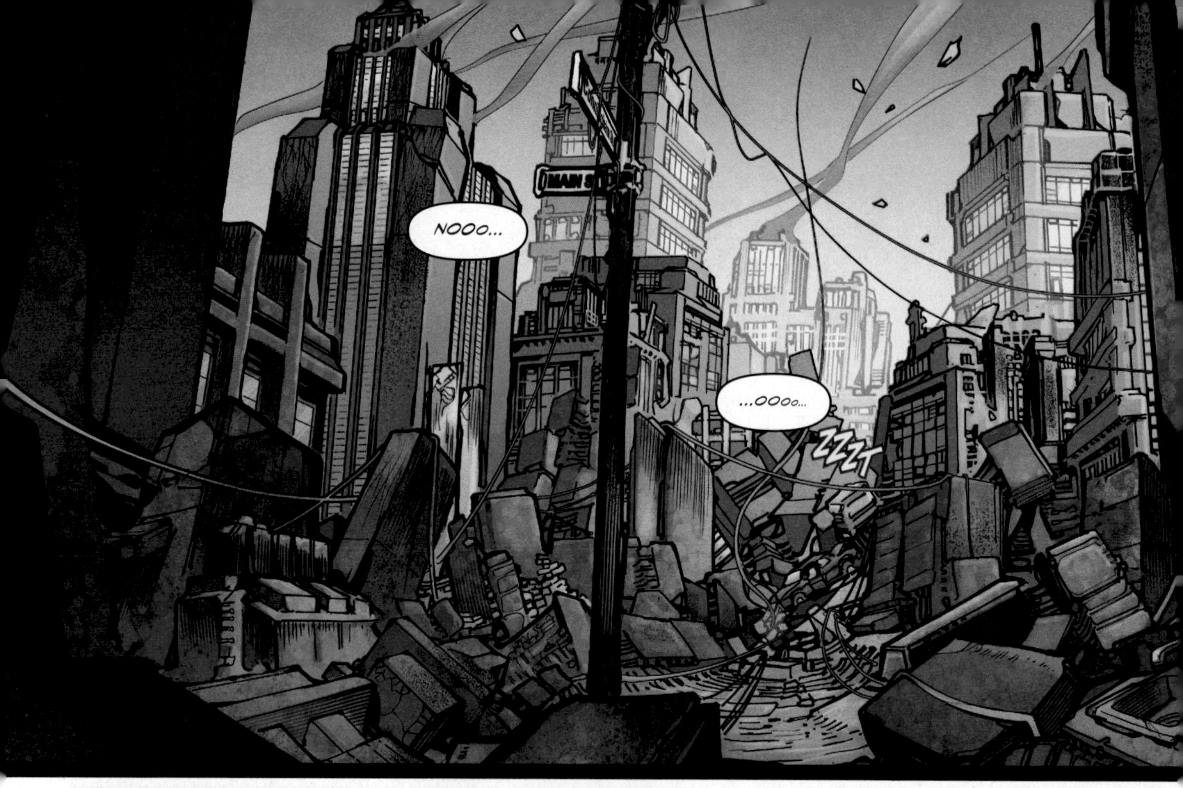
MAIN ST
NOOO...
...OOOo...
ZZZT

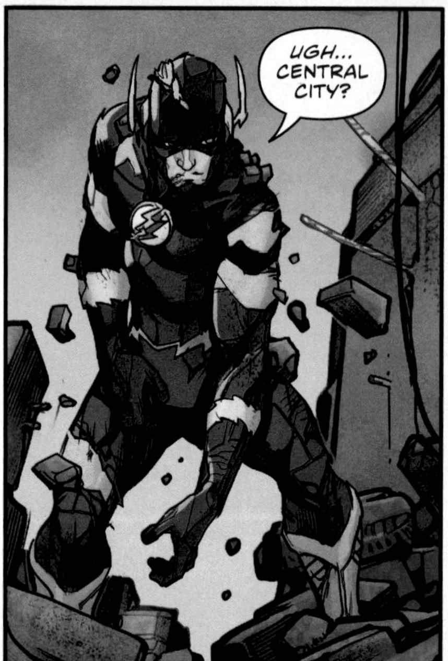
UGH... CENTRAL CITY?

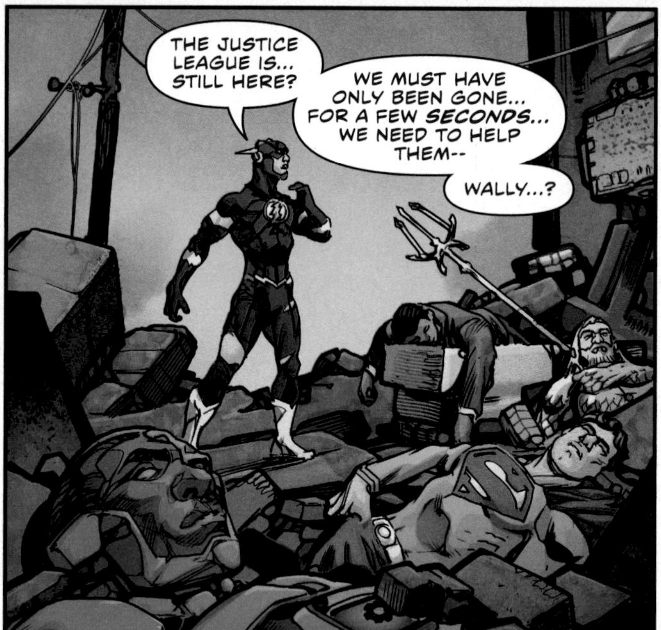
THE JUSTICE LEAGUE IS... STILL HERE?
WE MUST HAVE ONLY BEEN GONE... FOR A FEW SECONDS... WE NEED TO HELP THEM--
WALLY...?

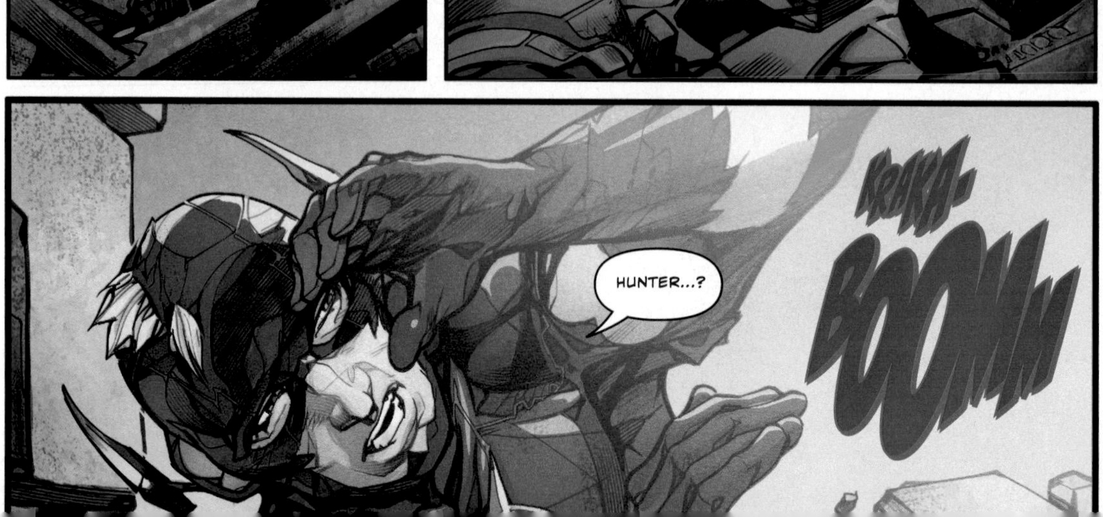
HUNTER...?
KRAKA-BOOMM

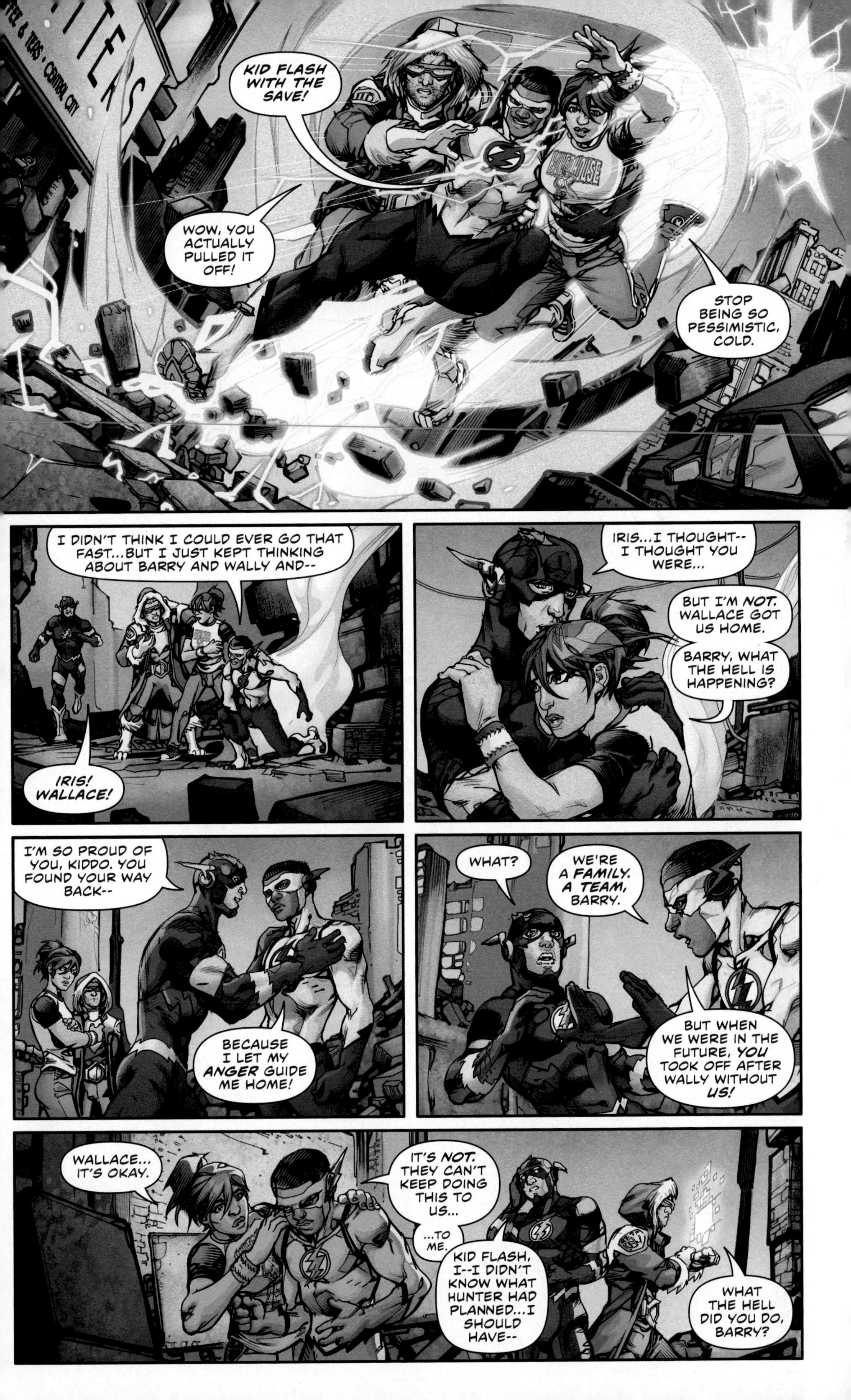
KID FLASH WITH THE SAVE!
WOW, YOU ACTUALLY PULLED IT OFF!
STOP BEING SO PESSIMISTIC, COLD.
I DIDN'T THINK I COULD EVER GO THAT FAST...BUT I JUST KEPT THINKING ABOUT BARRY AND WALLY AND--
IRIS! WALLACE!
IRIS...I THOUGHT-- I THOUGHT YOU WERE...
BUT I'M *NOT.* WALLACE GOT US HOME.
BARRY, WHAT THE HELL IS HAPPENING?
I'M SO PROUD OF YOU, KIDDO. YOU FOUND YOUR WAY BACK--
BECAUSE I LET MY *ANGER* GUIDE ME HOME!
WHAT?
WE'RE A *FAMILY.* A *TEAM,* BARRY.
BUT WHEN WE WERE IN THE FUTURE, *YOU* TOOK OFF AFTER WALLY WITHOUT *US!*
WALLACE... IT'S OKAY.
IT'S *NOT.* THEY CAN'T KEEP DOING THIS TO US...
...TO ME.
KID FLASH, I--I DIDN'T KNOW WHAT HUNTER HAD PLANNED...I SHOULD HAVE--
WHAT THE HELL DID YOU DO, BARRY?

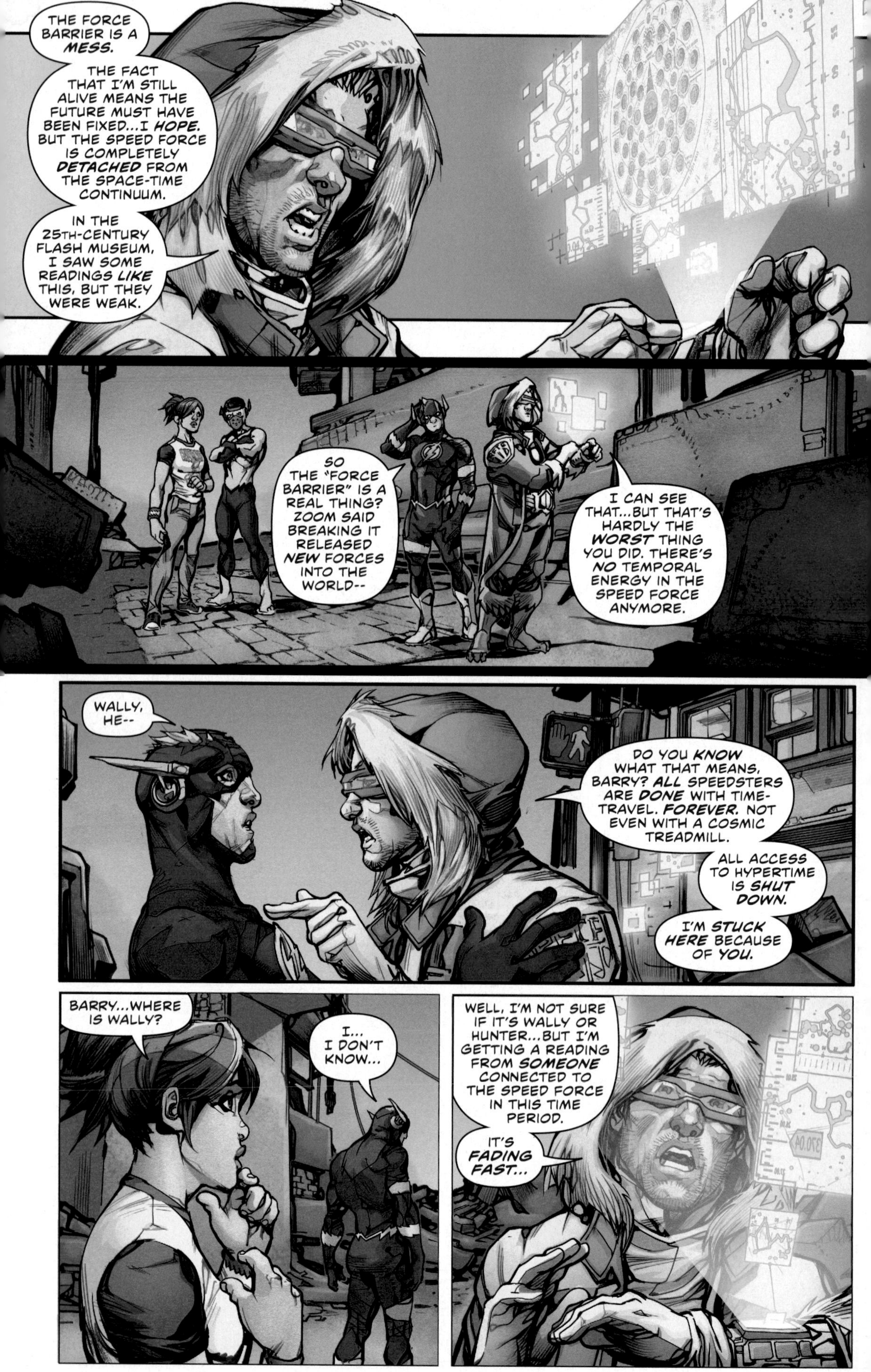
THE FORCE BARRIER IS A MESS.
THE FACT THAT I'M STILL ALIVE MEANS THE FUTURE MUST HAVE BEEN FIXED...I HOPE. BUT THE SPEED FORCE IS COMPLETELY DETACHED FROM THE SPACE-TIME CONTINUUM.
IN THE 25TH-CENTURY FLASH MUSEUM, I SAW SOME READINGS LIKE THIS, BUT THEY WERE WEAK.
SO THE "FORCE BARRIER" IS A REAL THING? ZOOM SAID BREAKING IT RELEASED NEW FORCES INTO THE WORLD--
I CAN SEE THAT...BUT THAT'S HARDLY THE WORST THING YOU DID. THERE'S NO TEMPORAL ENERGY IN THE SPEED FORCE ANYMORE.
WALLY, HE--
DO YOU KNOW WHAT THAT MEANS, BARRY? ALL SPEEDSTERS ARE DONE WITH TIME-TRAVEL. FOREVER. NOT EVEN WITH A COSMIC TREADMILL.
ALL ACCESS TO HYPERTIME IS SHUT DOWN.
I'M STUCK HERE BECAUSE OF YOU.
BARRY...WHERE IS WALLY?
I... I DON'T KNOW...
WELL, I'M NOT SURE IF IT'S WALLY OR HUNTER...BUT I'M GETTING A READING FROM SOMEONE CONNECTED TO THE SPEED FORCE IN THIS TIME PERIOD.
IT'S FADING FAST...

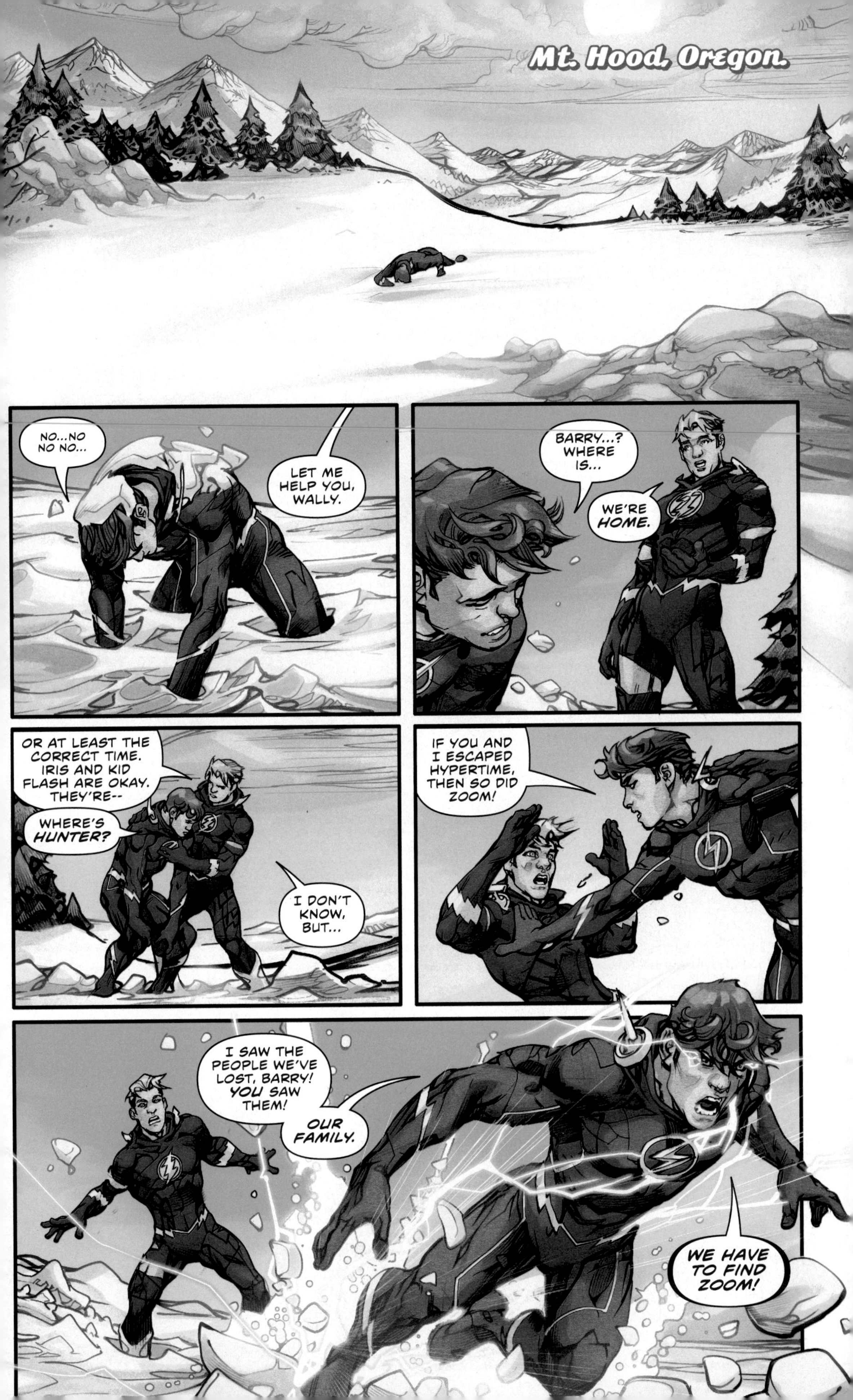
Mt. Hood, Oregon.
NO...NO NO NO...
LET ME HELP YOU, WALLY.
BARRY...? WHERE IS...
WE'RE HOME.
OR AT LEAST THE CORRECT TIME. IRIS AND KID FLASH ARE OKAY. THEY'RE--
WHERE'S HUNTER?
I DON'T KNOW, BUT...
IF YOU AND I ESCAPED HYPERTIME, THEN SO DID ZOOM!
I SAW THE PEOPLE WE'VE LOST, BARRY! YOU SAW THEM!
OUR FAMILY.
WE HAVE TO FIND ZOOM!

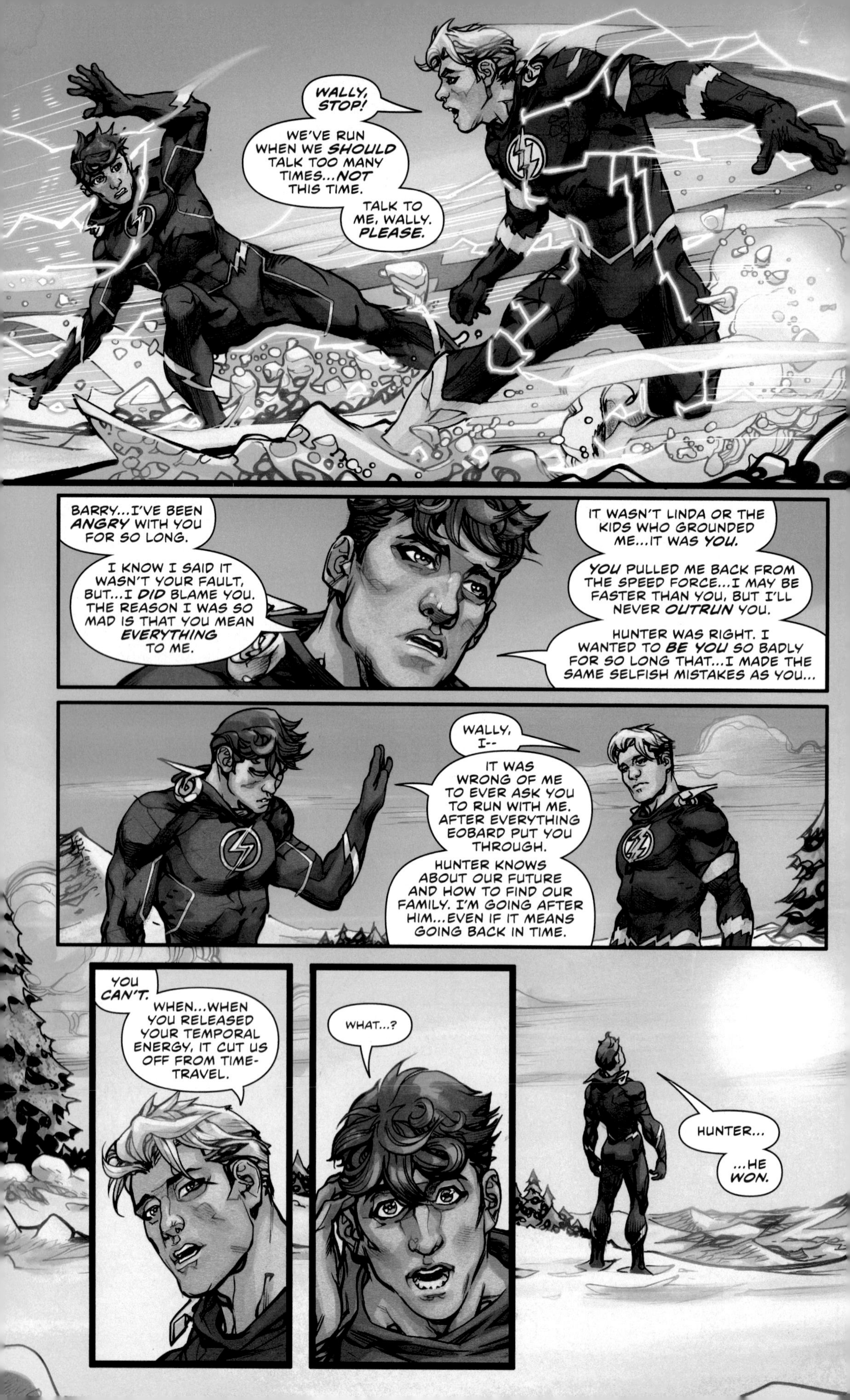
WALLY, STOP!
WE'VE RUN WHEN WE SHOULD TALK TOO MANY TIMES...NOT THIS TIME.
TALK TO ME, WALLY. PLEASE.
BARRY...I'VE BEEN ANGRY WITH YOU FOR SO LONG.
I KNOW I SAID IT WASN'T YOUR FAULT, BUT...I DID BLAME YOU. THE REASON I WAS SO MAD IS THAT YOU MEAN EVERYTHING TO ME.
IT WASN'T LINDA OR THE KIDS WHO GROUNDED ME...IT WAS YOU.
YOU PULLED ME BACK FROM THE SPEED FORCE...I MAY BE FASTER THAN YOU, BUT I'LL NEVER OUTRUN YOU.
HUNTER WAS RIGHT. I WANTED TO BE YOU SO BADLY FOR SO LONG THAT...I MADE THE SAME SELFISH MISTAKES AS YOU...
WALLY, I--
IT WAS WRONG OF ME TO EVER ASK YOU TO RUN WITH ME. AFTER EVERYTHING EOBARD PUT YOU THROUGH.
HUNTER KNOWS ABOUT OUR FUTURE AND HOW TO FIND OUR FAMILY. I'M GOING AFTER HIM...EVEN IF IT MEANS GOING BACK IN TIME.
YOU CAN'T.
WHEN...WHEN YOU RELEASED YOUR TEMPORAL ENERGY, IT CUT US OFF FROM TIME-TRAVEL.
WHAT...?
HUNTER...
...HE WON.

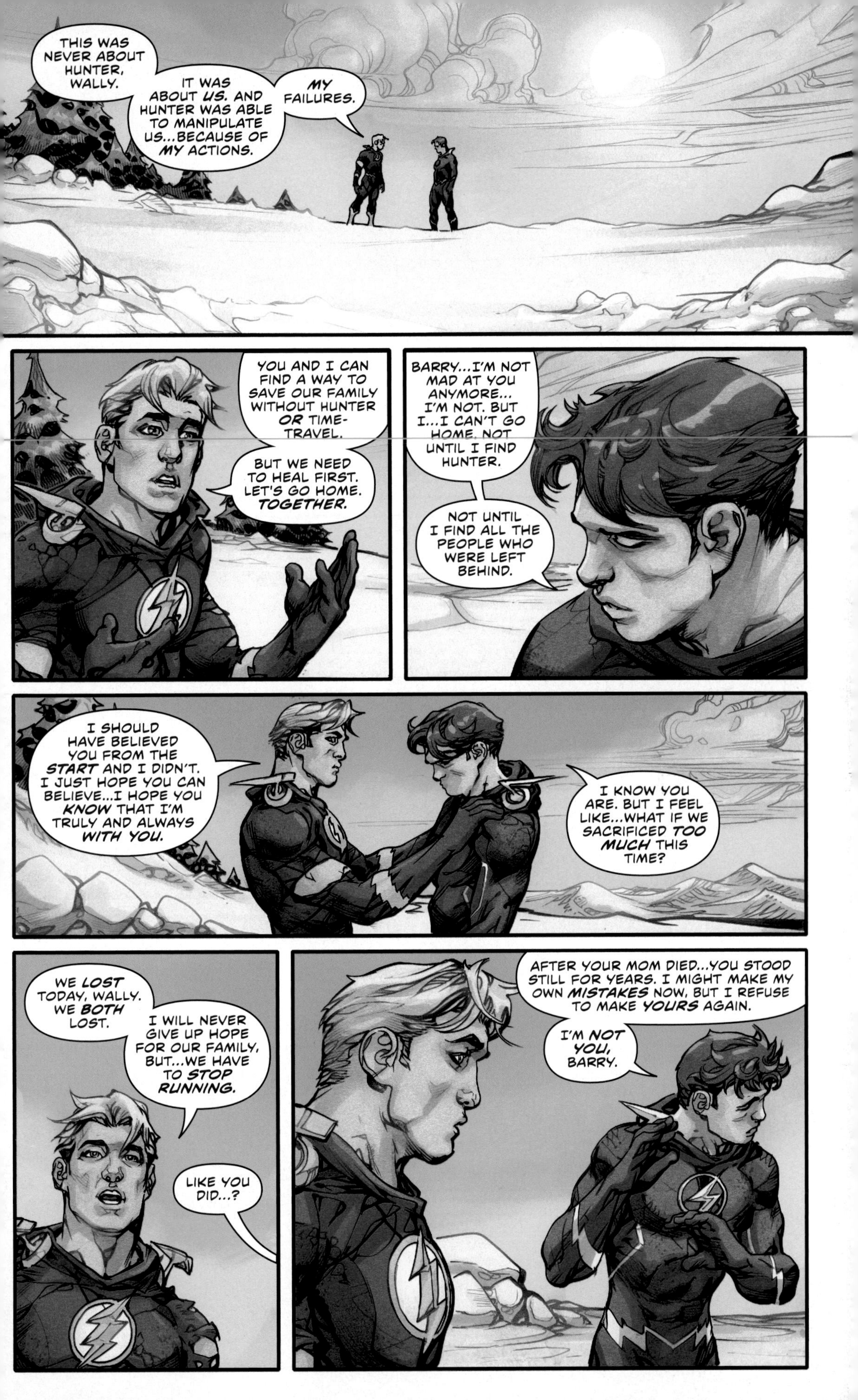
THIS WAS NEVER ABOUT HUNTER, WALLY.
IT WAS ABOUT US. AND HUNTER WAS ABLE TO MANIPULATE US...BECAUSE OF MY ACTIONS.
MY FAILURES.
YOU AND I CAN FIND A WAY TO SAVE OUR FAMILY WITHOUT HUNTER OR TIME-TRAVEL.
BUT WE NEED TO HEAL FIRST. LET'S GO HOME. TOGETHER.
BARRY...I'M NOT MAD AT YOU ANYMORE... I'M NOT. BUT I...I CAN'T GO HOME. NOT UNTIL I FIND HUNTER.
NOT UNTIL I FIND ALL THE PEOPLE WHO WERE LEFT BEHIND.
I SHOULD HAVE BELIEVED YOU FROM THE START AND I DIDN'T. I JUST HOPE YOU CAN BELIEVE...I HOPE YOU KNOW THAT I'M TRULY AND ALWAYS WITH YOU.
I KNOW YOU ARE. BUT I FEEL LIKE...WHAT IF WE SACRIFICED TOO MUCH THIS TIME?
WE LOST TODAY, WALLY. WE BOTH LOST.
I WILL NEVER GIVE UP HOPE FOR OUR FAMILY, BUT...WE HAVE TO STOP RUNNING.
LIKE YOU DID...?
AFTER YOUR MOM DIED...YOU STOOD STILL FOR YEARS. I MIGHT MAKE MY OWN MISTAKES NOW, BUT I REFUSE TO MAKE YOURS AGAIN.
I'M NOT YOU, BARRY.

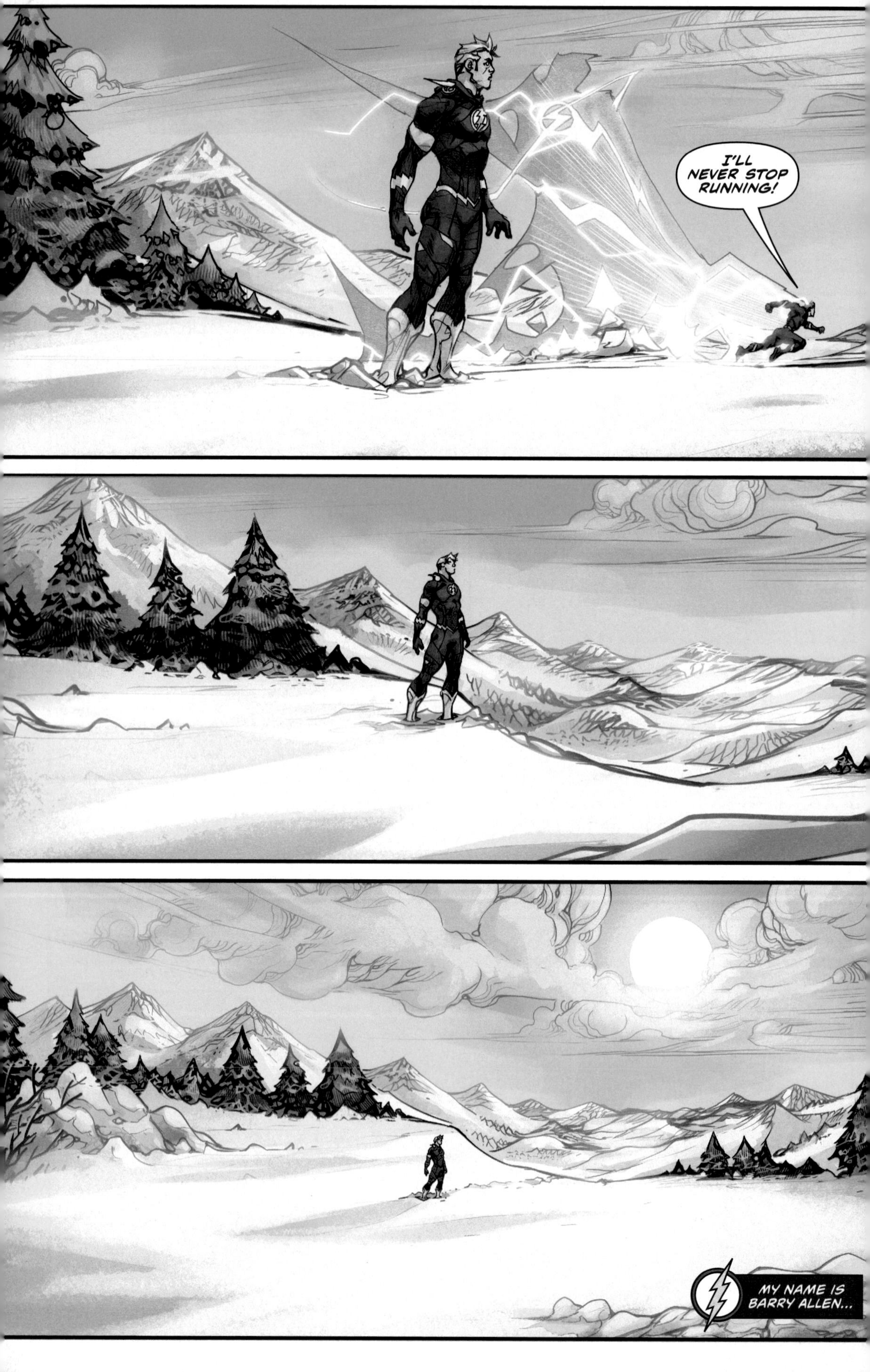

I'LL NEVER STOP RUNNING!
MY NAME IS BARRY ALLEN...

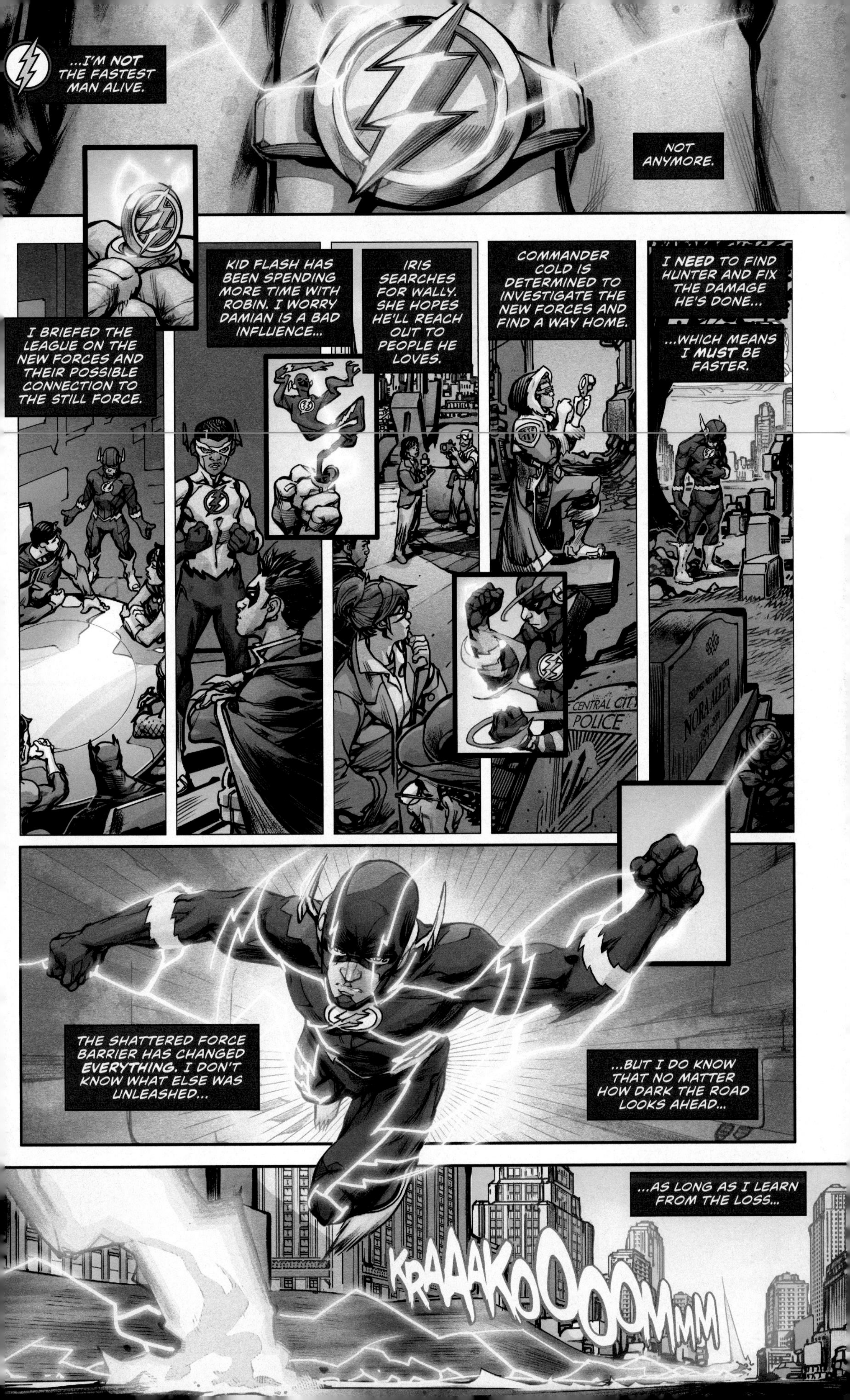
...I'M NOT THE FASTEST MAN ALIVE.
NOT ANYMORE.
I BRIEFED THE LEAGUE ON THE NEW FORCES AND THEIR POSSIBLE CONNECTION TO THE STILL FORCE.
KID FLASH HAS BEEN SPENDING MORE TIME WITH ROBIN. I WORRY DAMIAN IS A BAD INFLUENCE...
IRIS SEARCHES FOR WALLY. SHE HOPES HE'LL REACH OUT TO PEOPLE HE LOVES.
COMMANDER COLD IS DETERMINED TO INVESTIGATE THE NEW FORCES AND FIND A WAY HOME.
CENTRAL CITY POLICE
I NEED TO FIND HUNTER AND FIX THE DAMAGE HE'S DONE...
...WHICH MEANS I MUST BE FASTER.
NORA ALLEN
THE SHATTERED FORCE BARRIER HAS CHANGED EVERYTHING. I DON'T KNOW WHAT ELSE WAS UNLEASHED...
...BUT I DO KNOW THAT NO MATTER HOW DARK THE ROAD LOOKS AHEAD...
...AS LONG AS I LEARN FROM THE LOSS...
KRAAAKOOOOMMMM

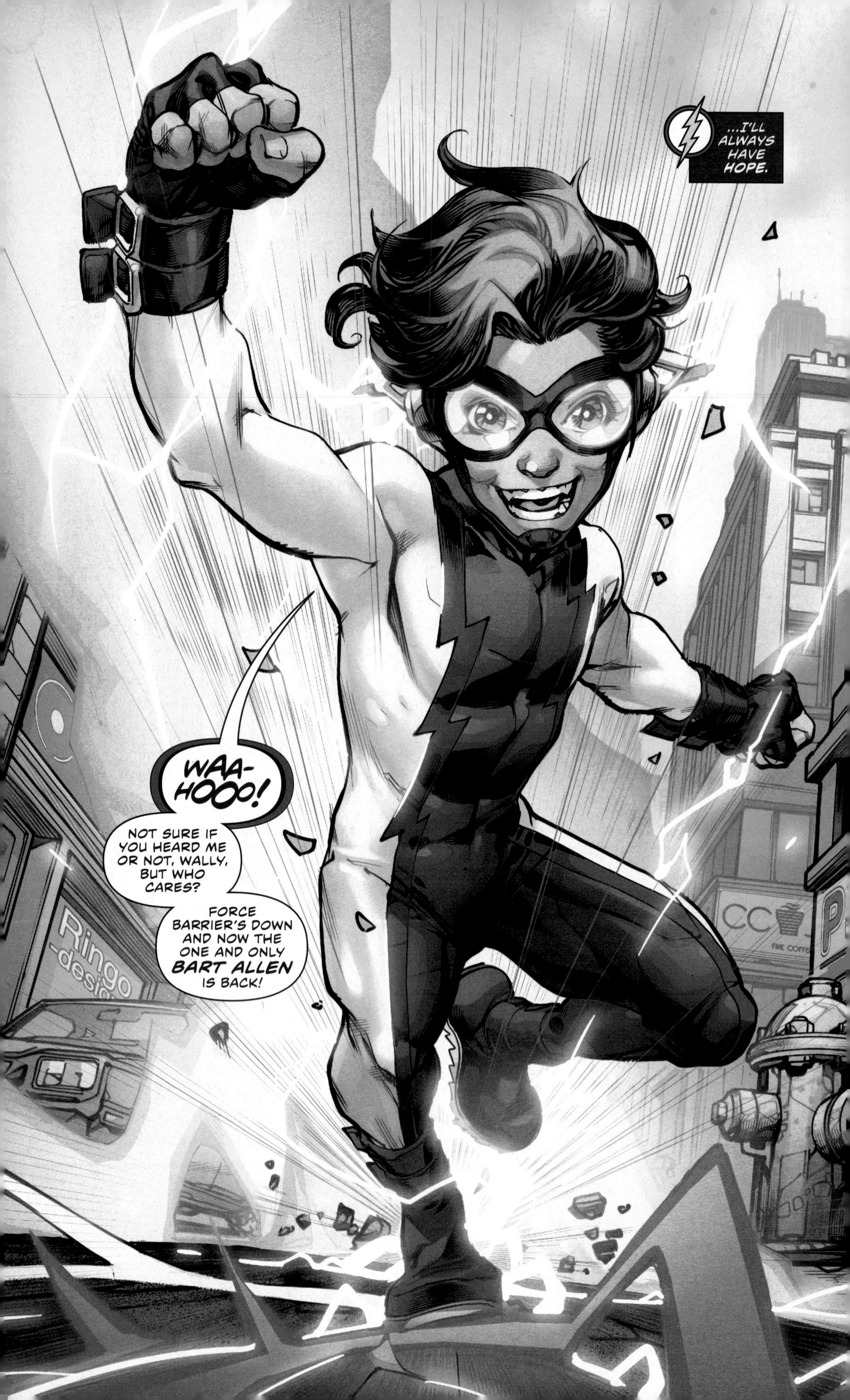
...I'LL ALWAYS HAVE HOPE.
WAA-HOOO!
NOT SURE IF YOU HEARD ME OR NOT, WALLY, BUT WHO CARES?
FORCE BARRIER'S DOWN AND NOW THE ONE AND ONLY BART ALLEN IS BACK!
Ringo -design
FINE COFFEE

E P I L O G U E .

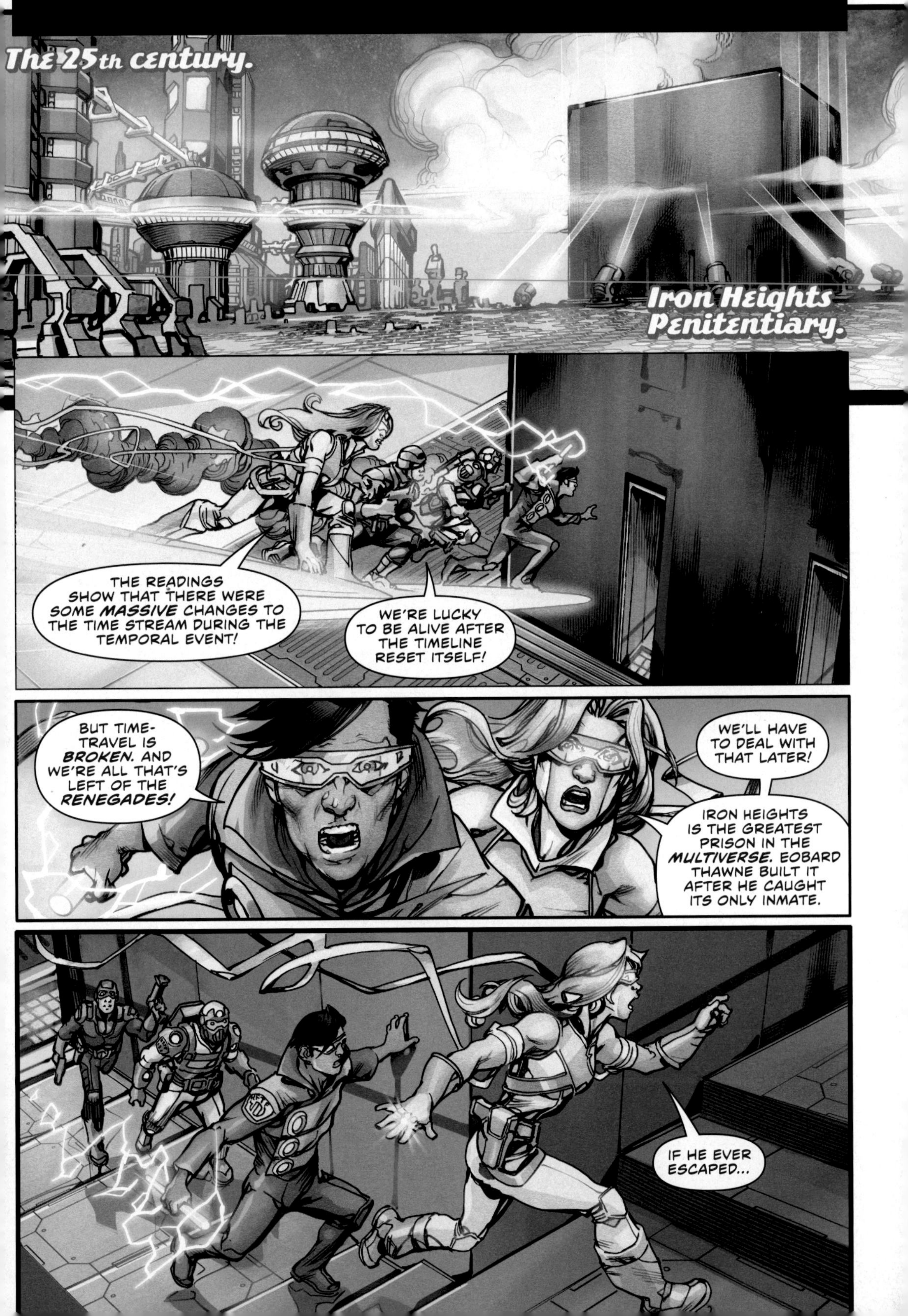

The 25th century.
Iron Heights Penitentiary.
THE READINGS SHOW THAT THERE WERE SOME *MASSIVE* CHANGES TO THE TIME STREAM DURING THE TEMPORAL EVENT!
WE'RE LUCKY TO BE ALIVE AFTER THE TIMELINE RESET ITSELF!
BUT TIME-TRAVEL IS *BROKEN.* AND WE'RE ALL THAT'S LEFT OF THE *RENEGADES!*
WE'LL HAVE TO DEAL WITH THAT LATER!
IRON HEIGHTS IS THE GREATEST PRISON IN THE *MULTIVERSE.* EOBARD THAWNE BUILT IT AFTER HE CAUGHT ITS ONLY INMATE.
IF HE EVER ESCAPED...

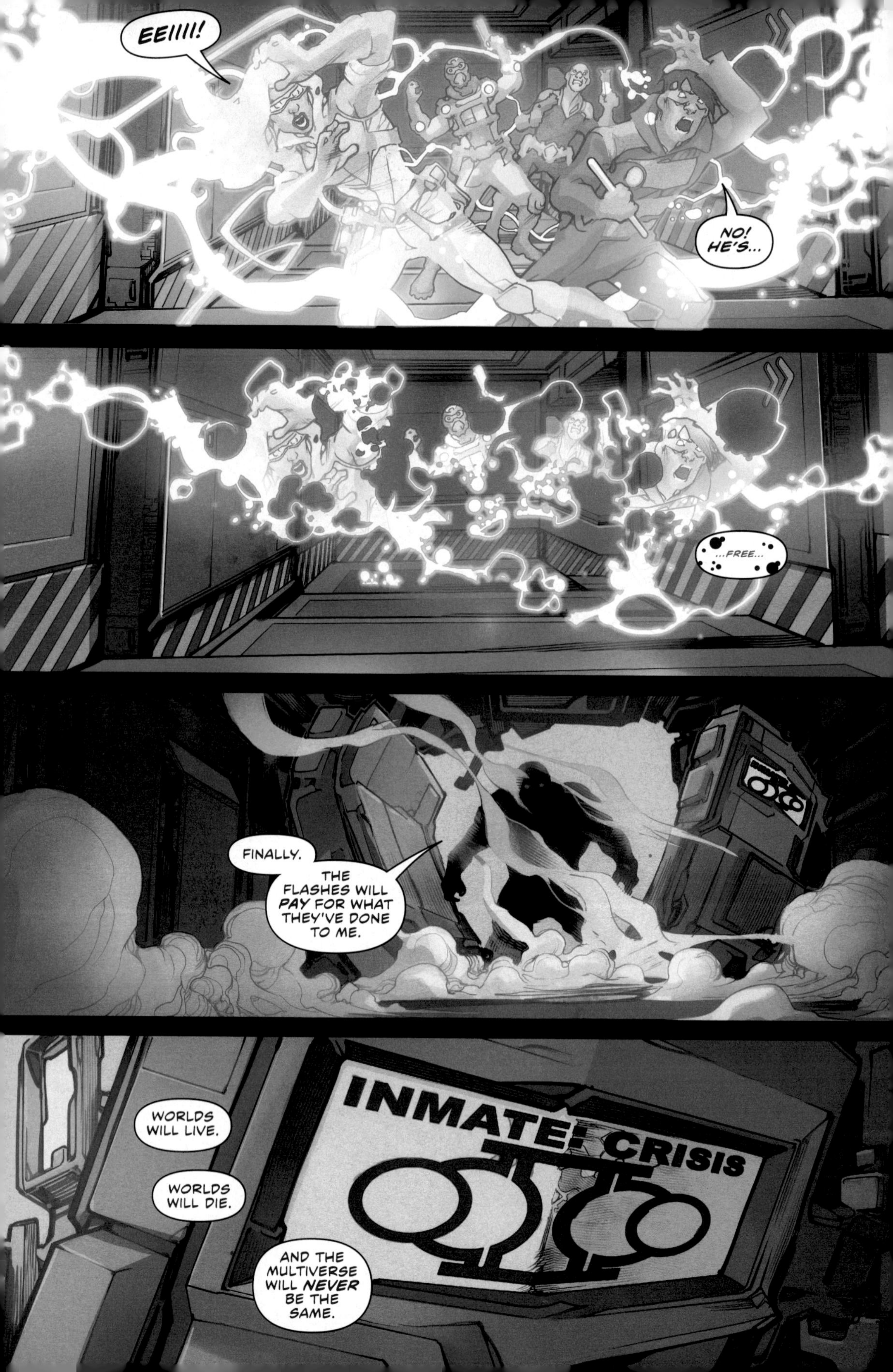
EEIIII!
NO! HE'S...
...FREE...
FINALLY.
THE FLASHES WILL PAY FOR WHAT THEY'VE DONE TO ME.
INMATE: CRISIS
WORLDS WILL LIVE.
WORLDS WILL DIE.
AND THE MULTIVERSE WILL NEVER BE THE SAME.

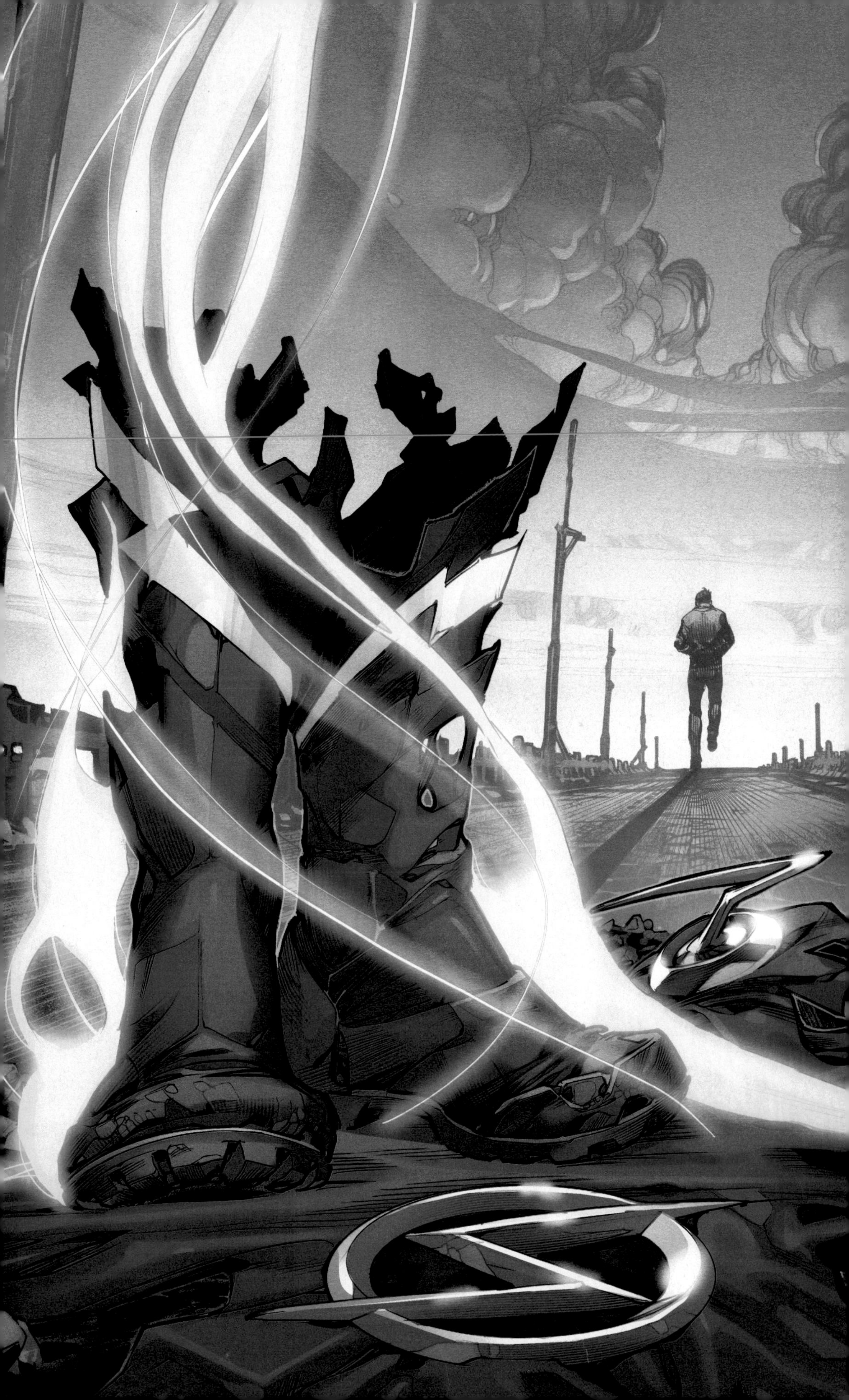

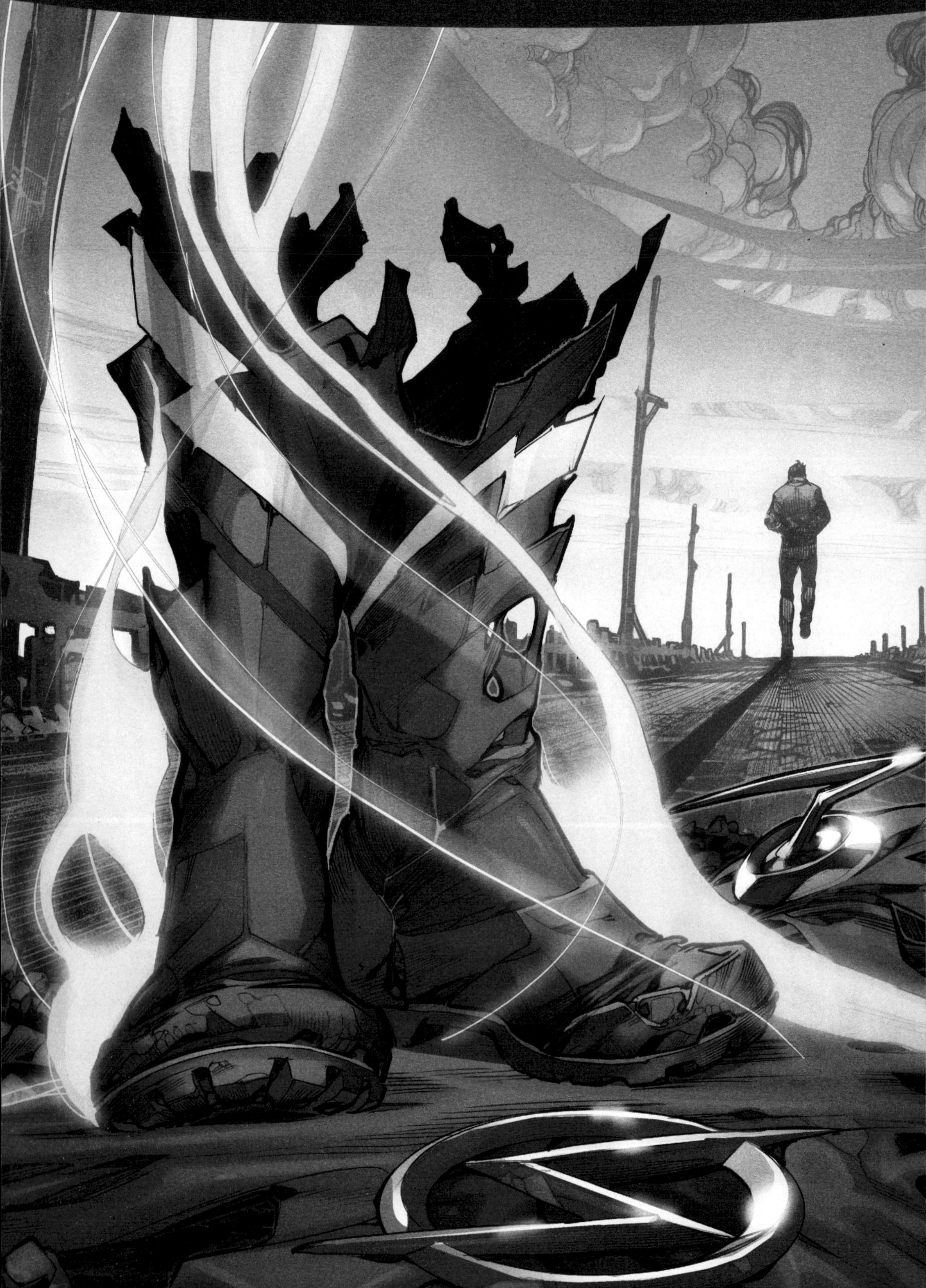

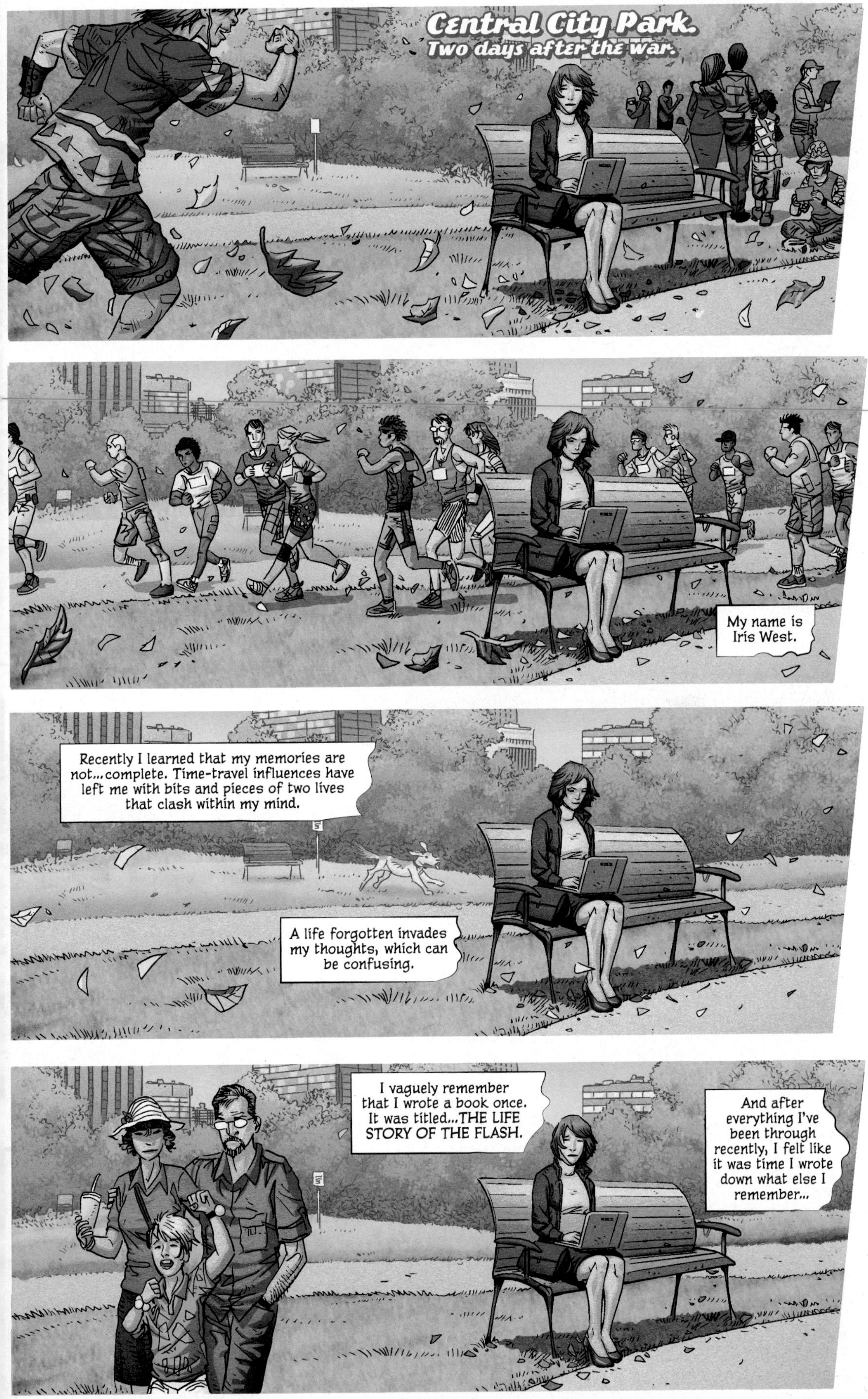
Central City Park.
Two days after the war.
My name is Iris West.
Recently I learned that my memories are not...complete. Time-travel influences have left me with bits and pieces of two lives that clash within my mind.
A life forgotten invades my thoughts, which can be confusing.
I vaguely remember that I wrote a book once. It was titled...THE LIFE STORY OF THE FLASH.
And after everything I've been through recently, I felt like it was time I wrote down what else I remember...

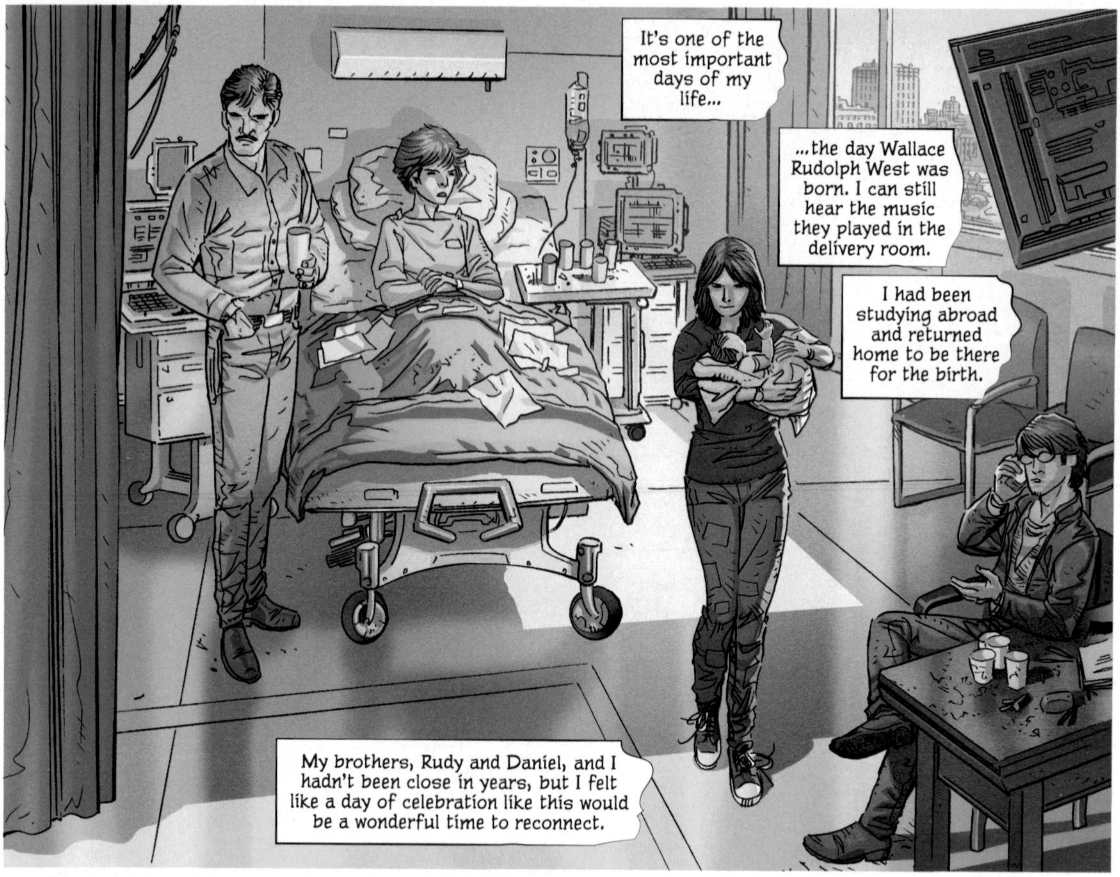
It's one of the most important days of my life...
...the day Wallace Rudolph West was born. I can still hear the music they played in the delivery room.
I had been studying abroad and returned home to be there for the birth.
My brothers, Rudy and Daniel, and I hadn't been close in years, but I felt like a day of celebration like this would be a wonderful time to reconnect.

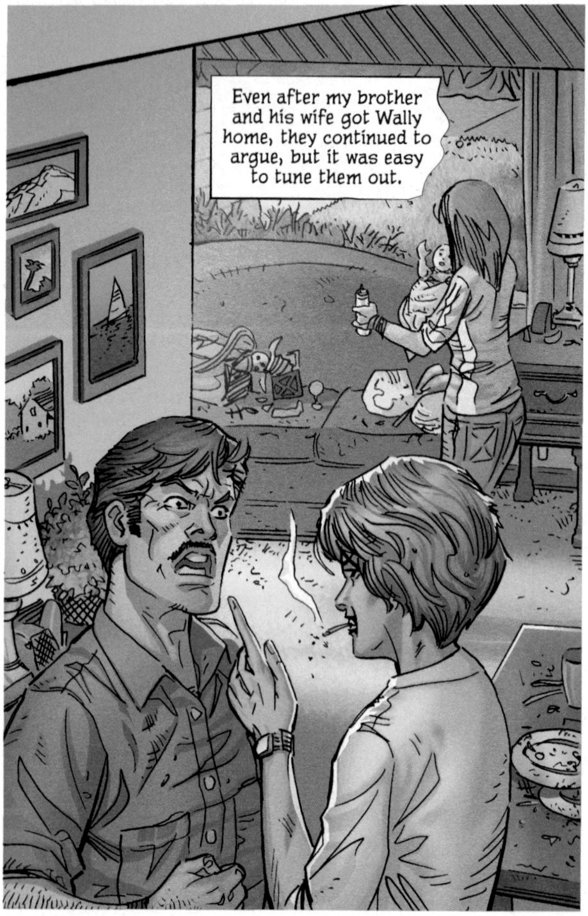
Even after my brother and his wife got Wally home, they continued to argue, but it was easy to tune them out.

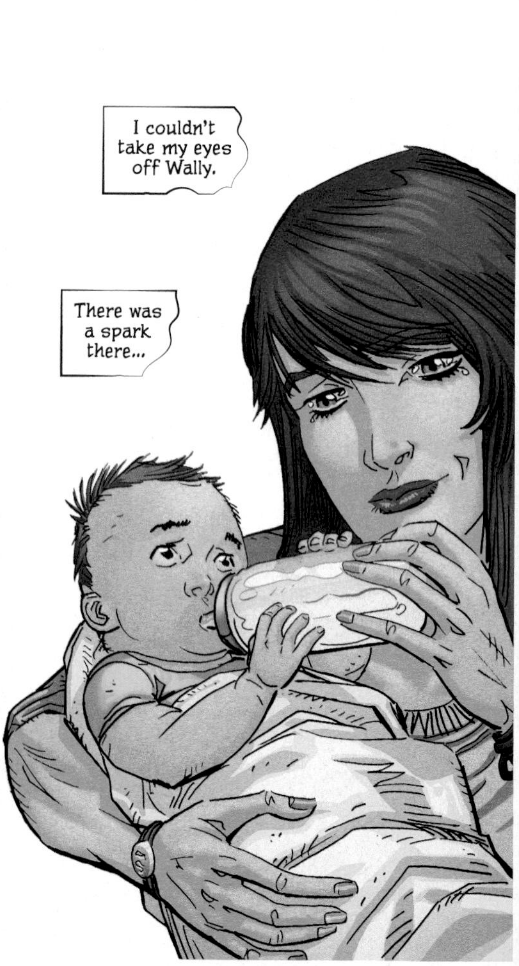
I couldn't take my eyes off Wally.
There was a spark there...

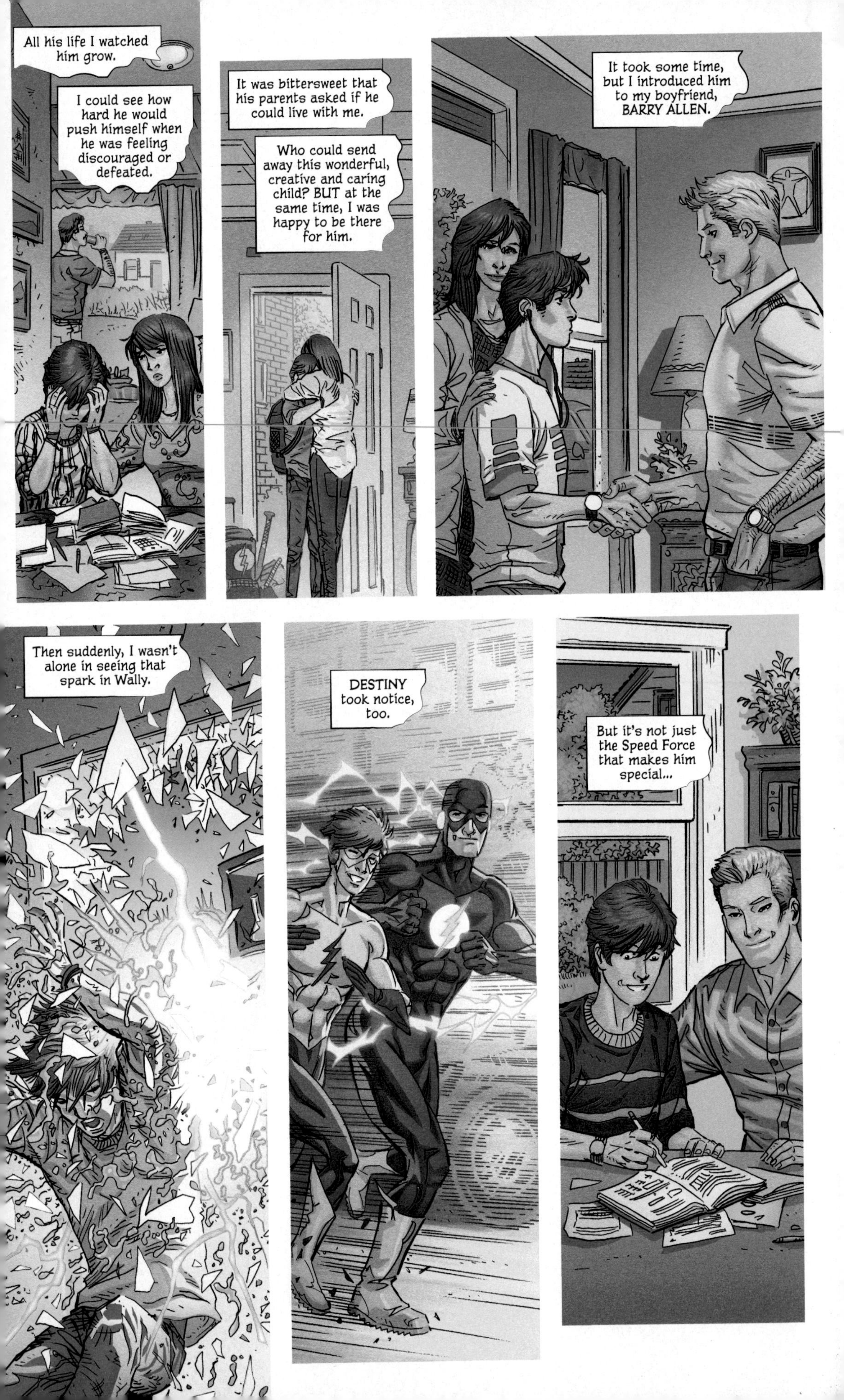
All his life I watched him grow.
I could see how hard he would push himself when he was feeling discouraged or defeated.
It was bittersweet that his parents asked if he could live with me.
Who could send away this wonderful, creative and caring child? BUT at the same time, I was happy to be there for him.
It took some time, but I introduced him to my boyfriend, BARRY ALLEN.
Then suddenly, I wasn't alone in seeing that spark in Wally.
DESTINY took notice, too.
But it's not just the Speed Force that makes him special...

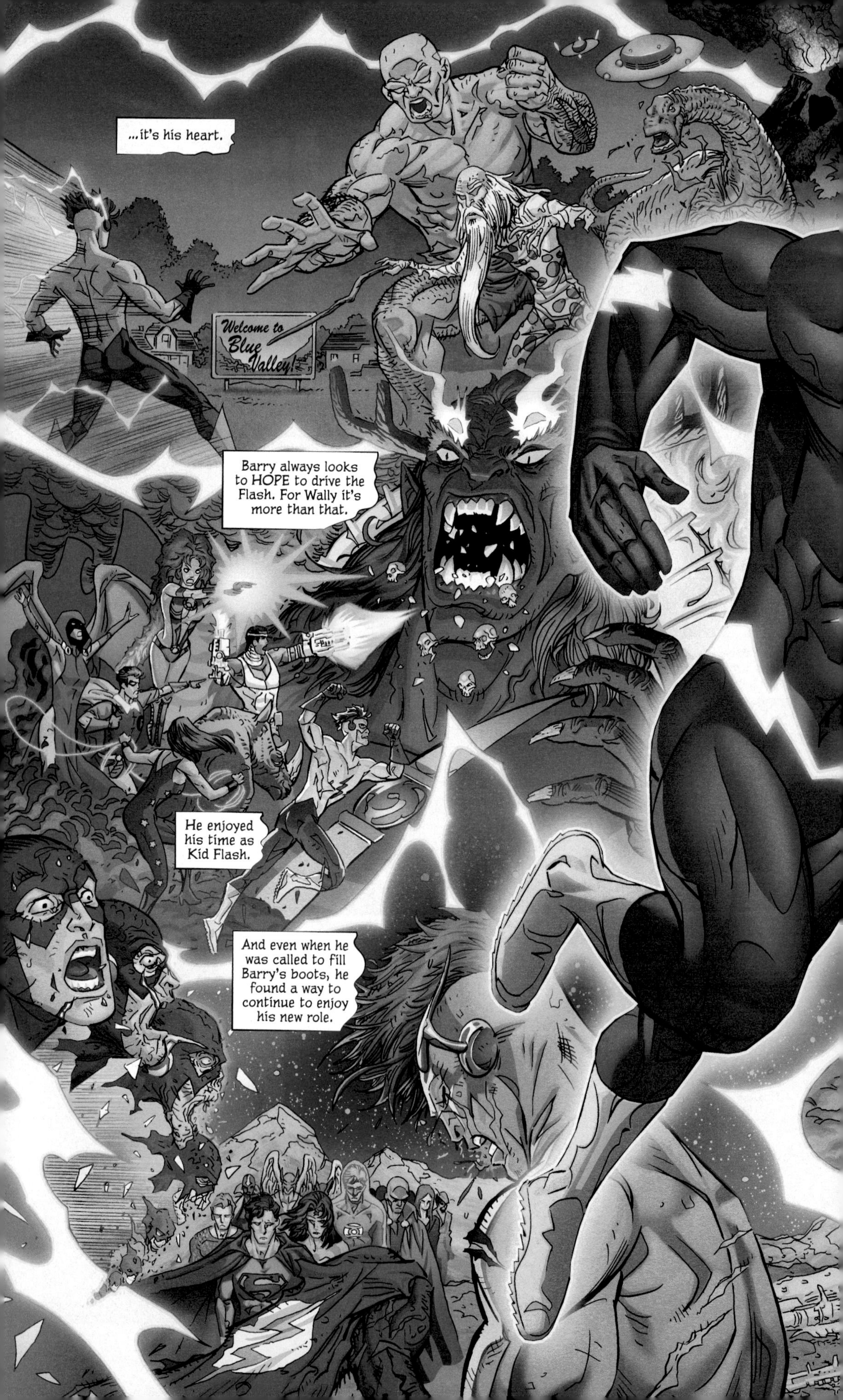
...it's his heart.
Welcome to Blue Valley!
Barry always looks to HOPE to drive the Flash. For Wally it's more than that.
He enjoyed his time as Kid Flash.
And even when he was called to fill Barry's boots, he found a way to continue to enjoy his new role.

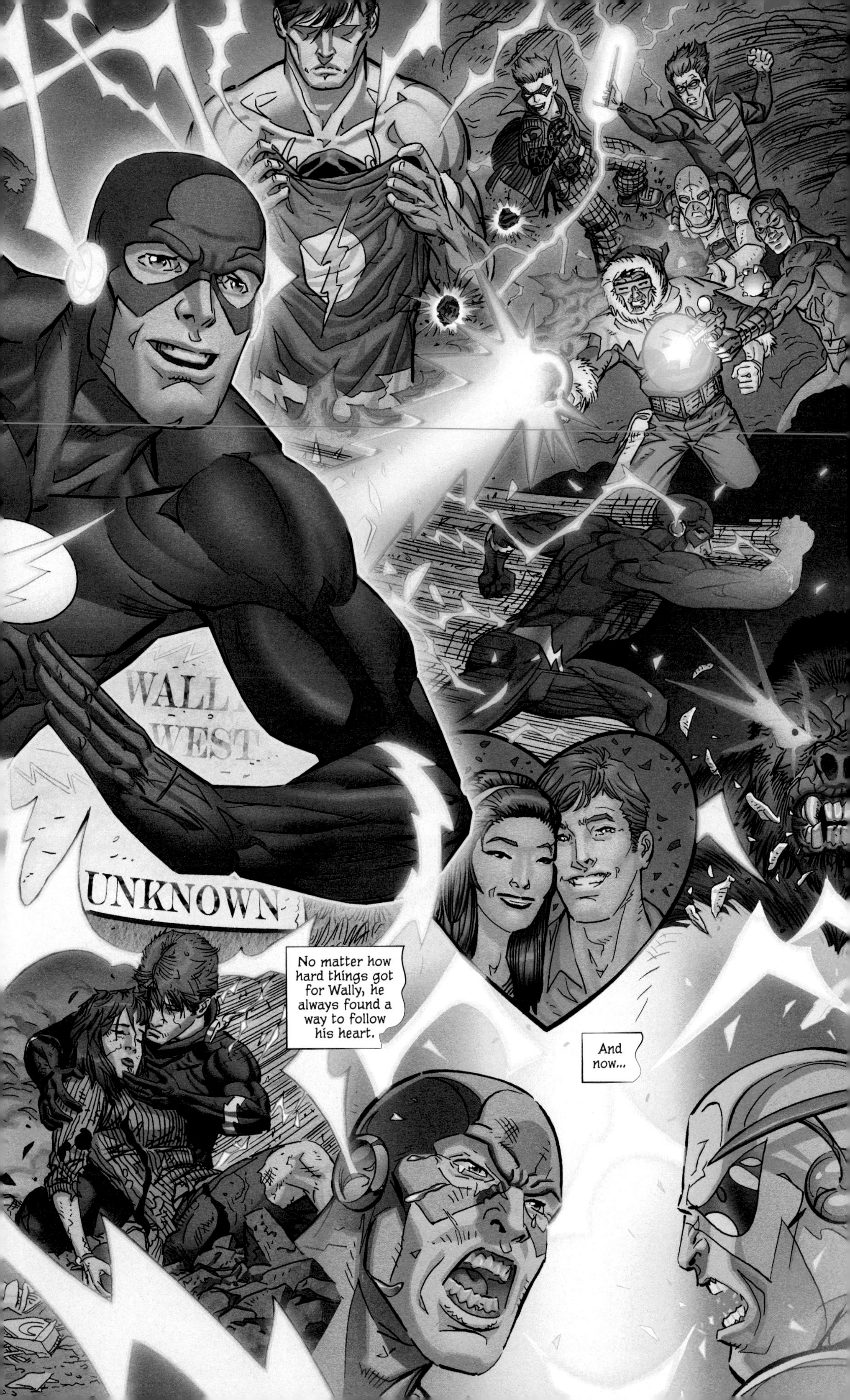
WALLY WEST
UNKNOWN
No matter how hard things got for Wally, he always found a way to follow his heart.
And now...

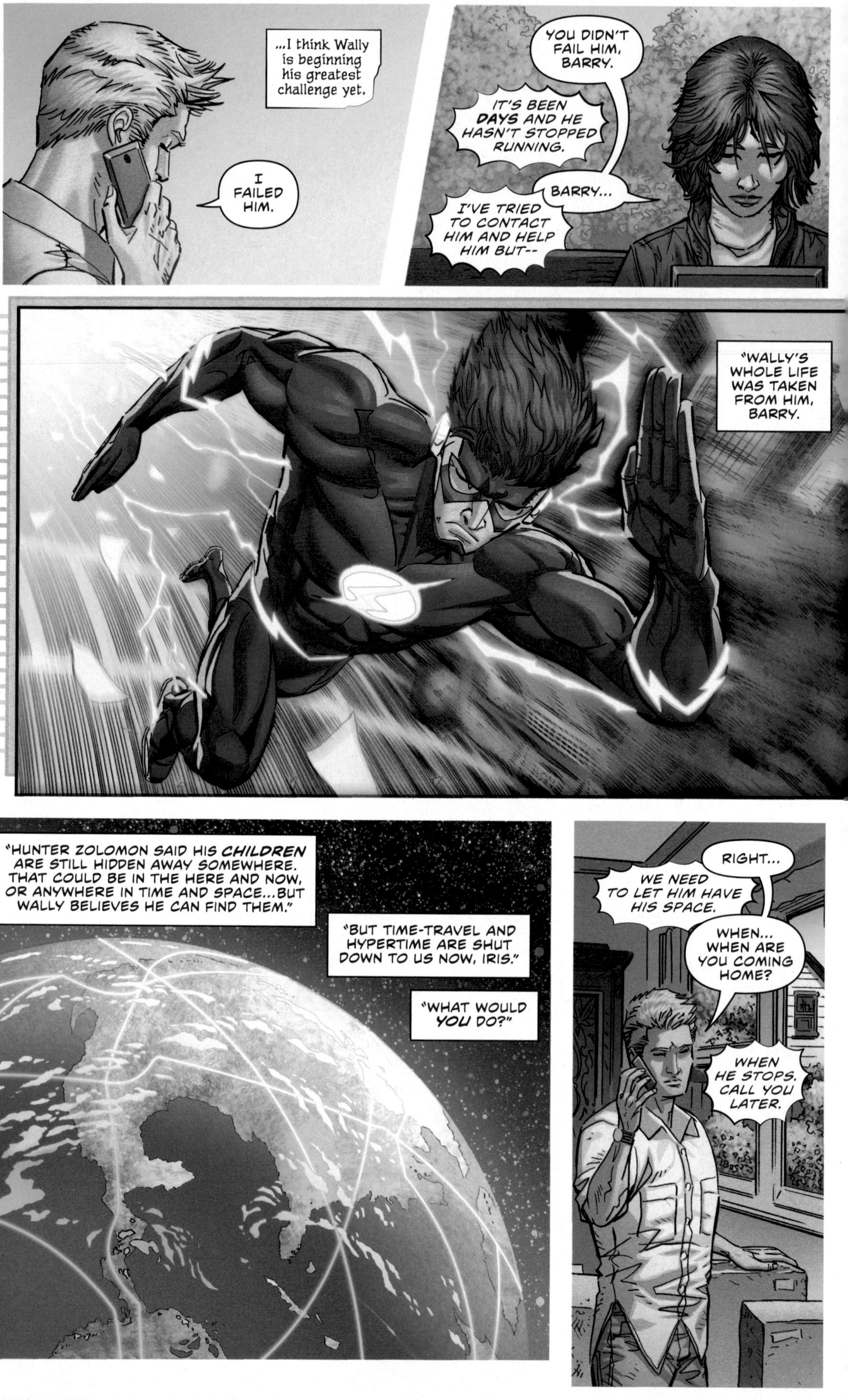
...I think Wally is beginning his greatest challenge yet.
I FAILED HIM.
YOU DIDN'T FAIL HIM, BARRY.
IT'S BEEN DAYS AND HE HASN'T STOPPED RUNNING.
BARRY...
I'VE TRIED TO CONTACT HIM AND HELP HIM BUT--
"WALLY'S WHOLE LIFE WAS TAKEN FROM HIM, BARRY.
"HUNTER ZOLOMON SAID HIS CHILDREN ARE STILL HIDDEN AWAY SOMEWHERE. THAT COULD BE IN THE HERE AND NOW, OR ANYWHERE IN TIME AND SPACE...BUT WALLY BELIEVES HE CAN FIND THEM."
"BUT TIME-TRAVEL AND HYPERTIME ARE SHUT DOWN TO US NOW, IRIS."
"WHAT WOULD YOU DO?"
RIGHT...
WE NEED TO LET HIM HAVE HIS SPACE.
WHEN... WHEN ARE YOU COMING HOME?
WHEN HE STOPS. CALL YOU LATER.

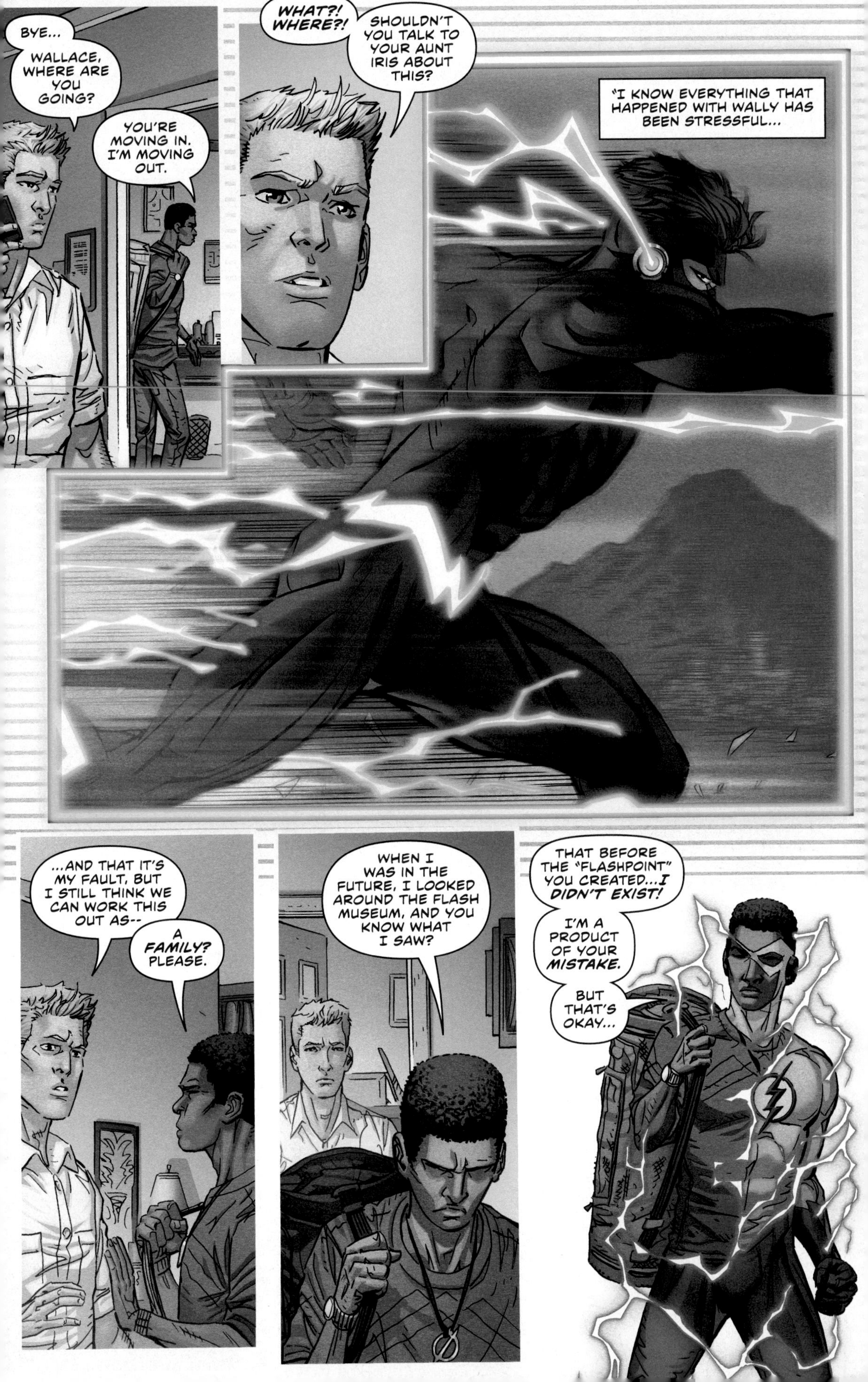
BYE...
WALLACE, WHERE ARE YOU GOING?
YOU'RE MOVING IN. I'M MOVING OUT.
WHAT?! WHERE?!
SHOULDN'T YOU TALK TO YOUR AUNT IRIS ABOUT THIS?
"I KNOW EVERYTHING THAT HAPPENED WITH WALLY HAS BEEN STRESSFUL...
...AND THAT IT'S MY FAULT, BUT I STILL THINK WE CAN WORK THIS OUT AS--
A FAMILY? PLEASE.
WHEN I WAS IN THE FUTURE, I LOOKED AROUND THE FLASH MUSEUM, AND YOU KNOW WHAT I SAW?
THAT BEFORE THE "FLASHPOINT" YOU CREATED...I DIDN'T EXIST!
I'M A PRODUCT OF YOUR MISTAKE.
BUT THAT'S OKAY...

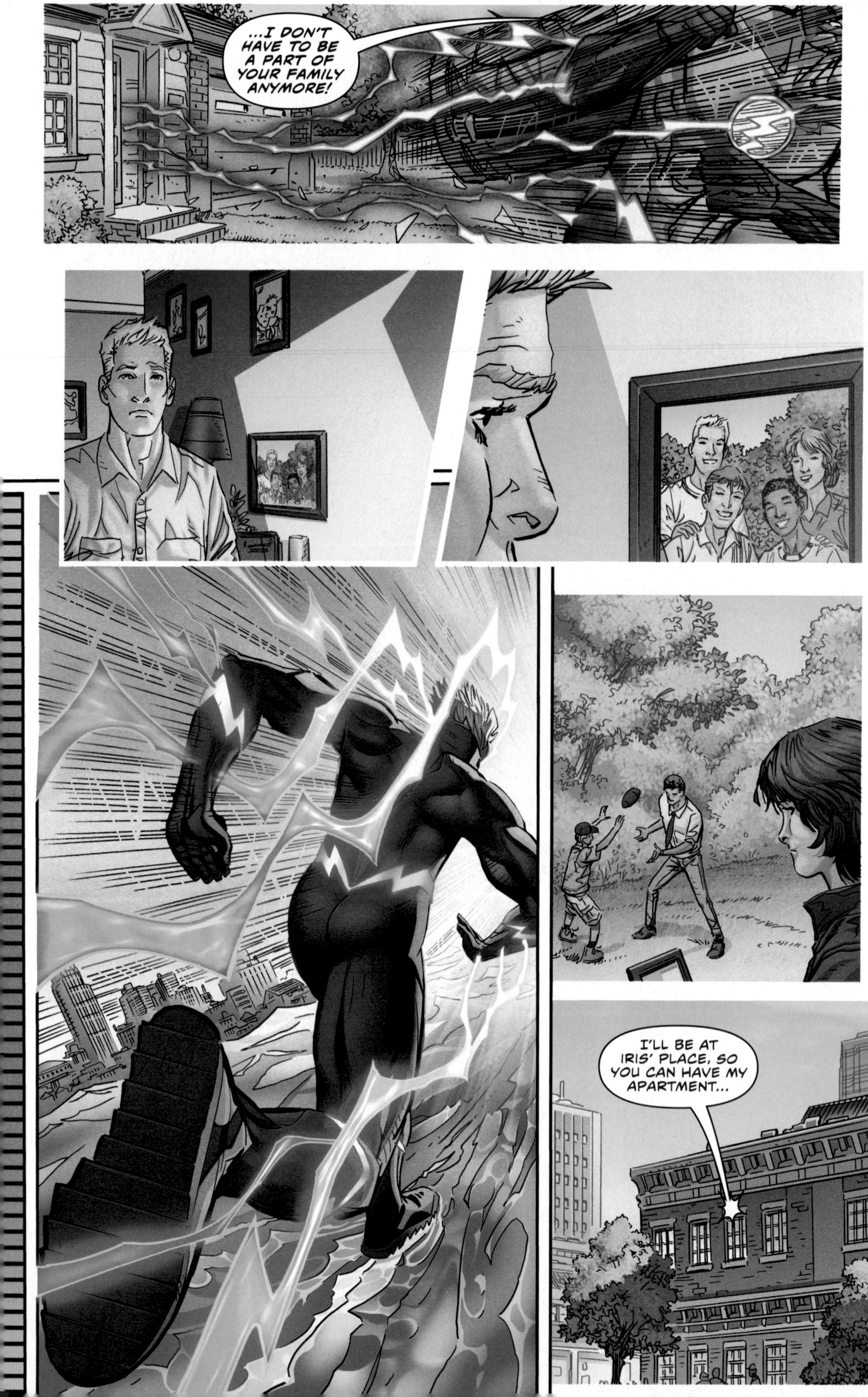
...I DON'T HAVE TO BE A PART OF YOUR FAMILY ANYMORE!
I'LL BE AT IRIS' PLACE, SO YOU CAN HAVE MY APARTMENT...

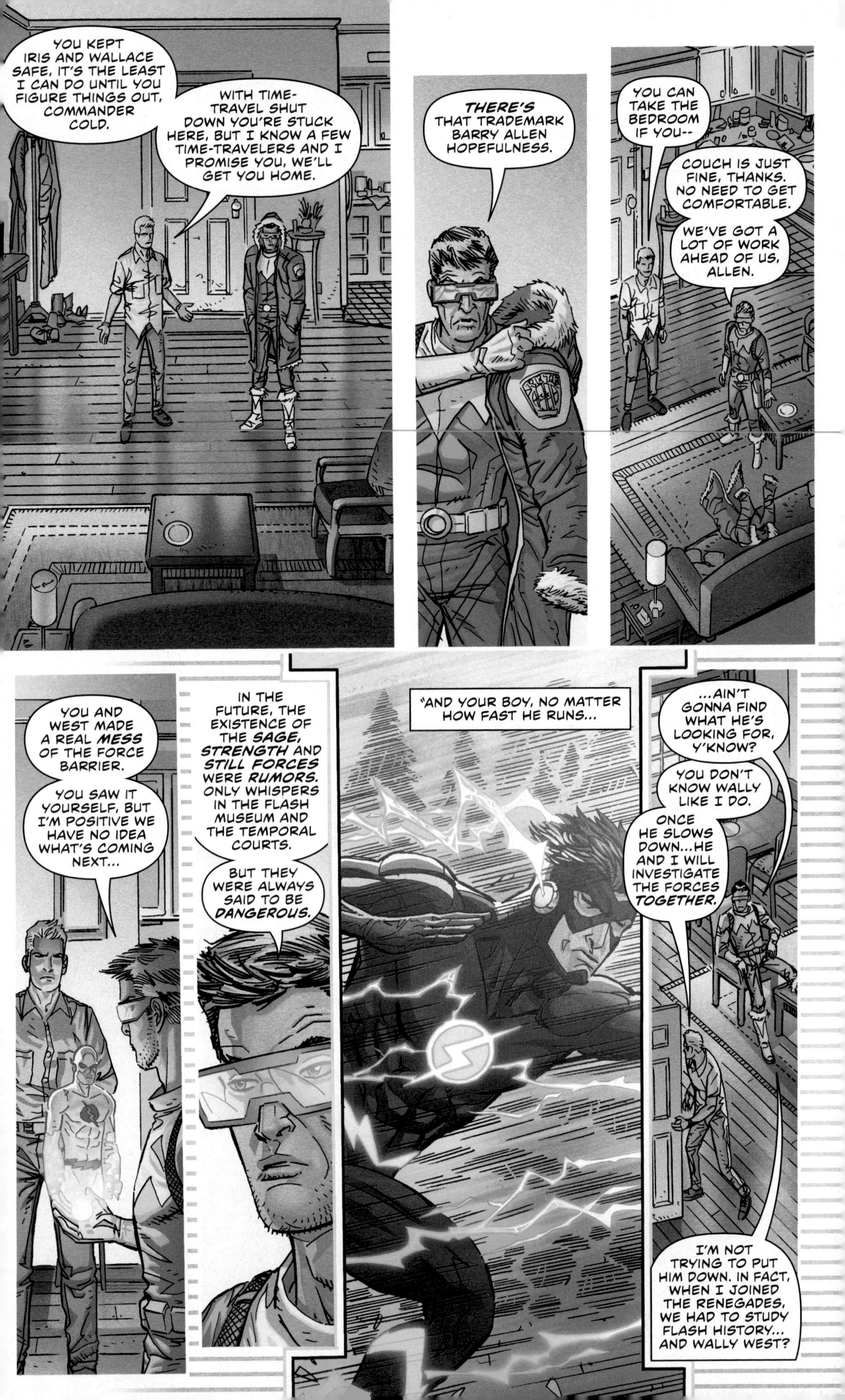

YOU KEPT IRIS AND WALLACE SAFE, IT'S THE LEAST I CAN DO UNTIL YOU FIGURE THINGS OUT, COMMANDER COLD.
WITH TIME-TRAVEL SHUT DOWN YOU'RE STUCK HERE, BUT I KNOW A FEW TIME-TRAVELERS AND I PROMISE YOU, WE'LL GET YOU HOME.
THERE'S THAT TRADEMARK BARRY ALLEN HOPEFULNESS.
YOU CAN TAKE THE BEDROOM IF YOU--
COUCH IS JUST FINE, THANKS. NO NEED TO GET COMFORTABLE.
WE'VE GOT A LOT OF WORK AHEAD OF US, ALLEN.
YOU AND WEST MADE A REAL *MESS* OF THE FORCE BARRIER.
YOU SAW IT YOURSELF, BUT I'M POSITIVE WE HAVE NO IDEA WHAT'S COMING NEXT...
IN THE FUTURE, THE EXISTENCE OF THE *SAGE, STRENGTH* AND *STILL FORCES* WERE *RUMORS.* ONLY WHISPERS IN THE FLASH MUSEUM AND THE TEMPORAL COURTS.
BUT THEY WERE ALWAYS SAID TO BE *DANGEROUS.*
"AND YOUR BOY, NO MATTER HOW FAST HE RUNS...
...AIN'T GONNA FIND WHAT HE'S LOOKING FOR, Y'KNOW?
YOU DON'T KNOW WALLY LIKE I DO.
ONCE HE SLOWS DOWN...HE AND I WILL INVESTIGATE THE FORCES *TOGETHER.*
I'M NOT TRYING TO PUT HIM DOWN. IN FACT, WHEN I JOINED THE RENEGADES, WE HAD TO STUDY FLASH HISTORY... AND WALLY WEST?

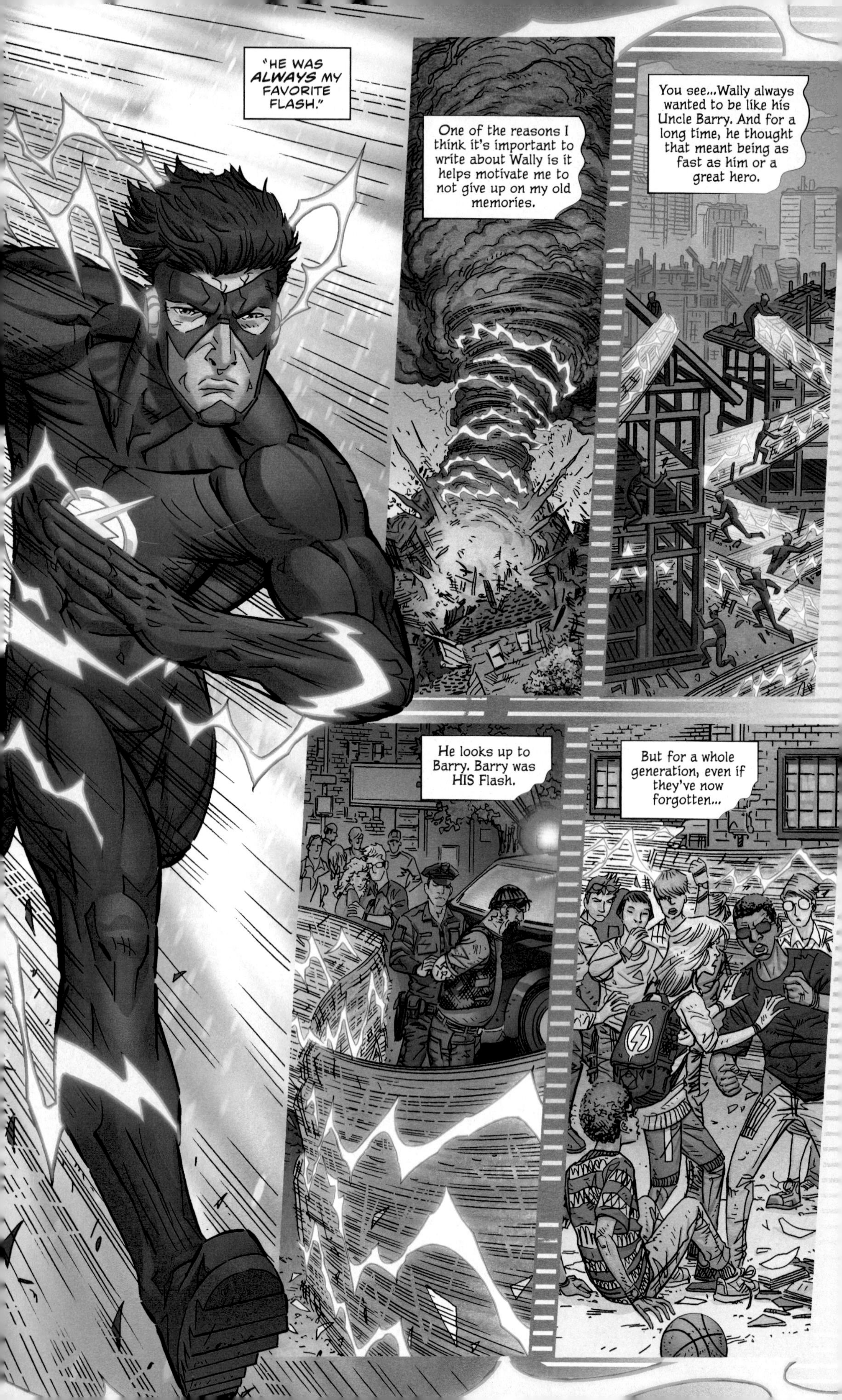
"HE WAS ALWAYS MY FAVORITE FLASH."
One of the reasons I think it's important to write about Wally is it helps motivate me to not give up on my old memories.
You see...Wally always wanted to be like his Uncle Barry. And for a long time, he thought that meant being as fast as him or a great hero.
He looks up to Barry. Barry was HIS Flash.
But for a whole generation, even if they've now forgotten...

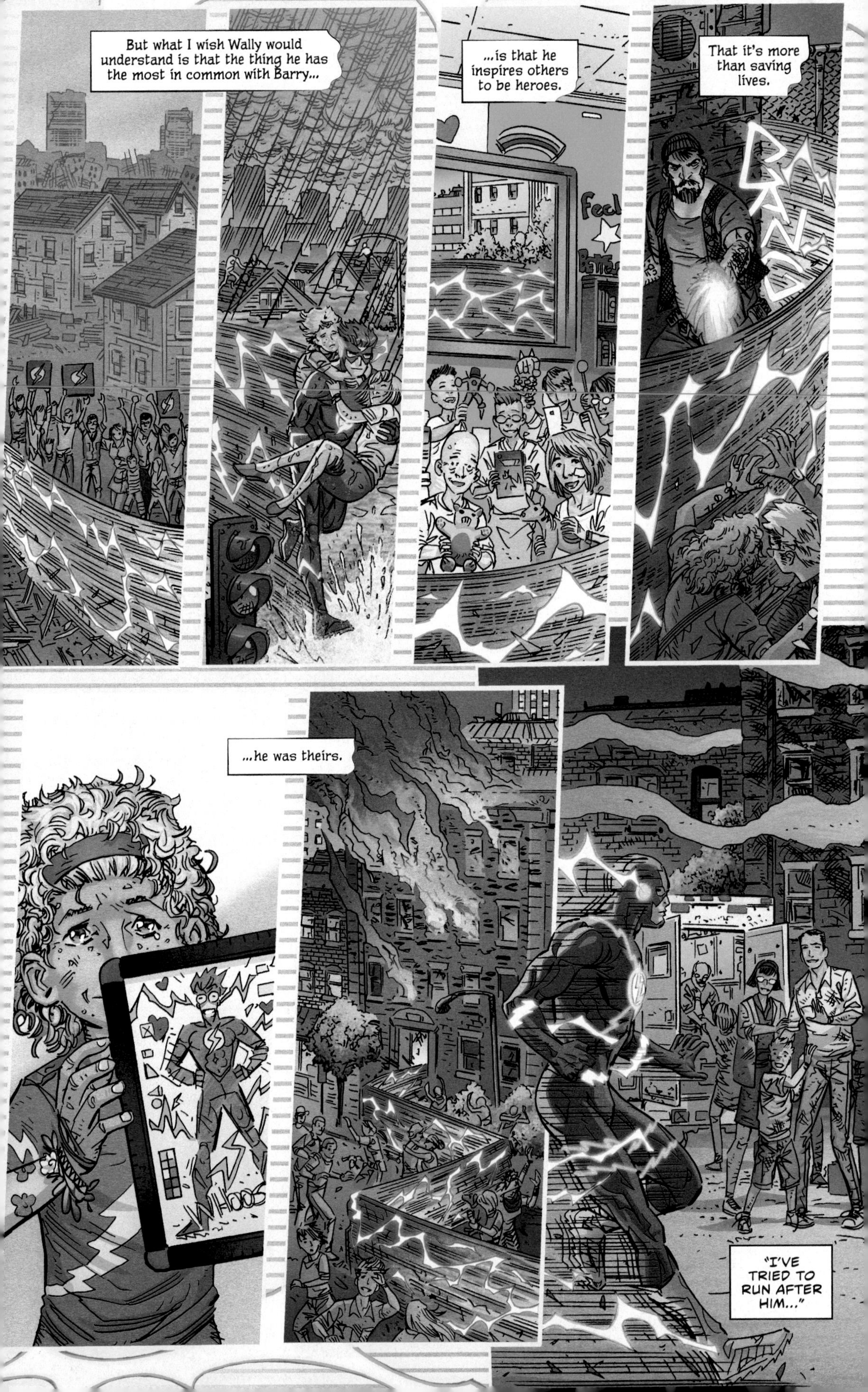
But what I wish Wally would understand is that the thing he has the most in common with Barry...
...is that he inspires others to be heroes.
That it's more than saving lives.
...he was theirs.
"I'VE TRIED TO RUN AFTER HIM..."

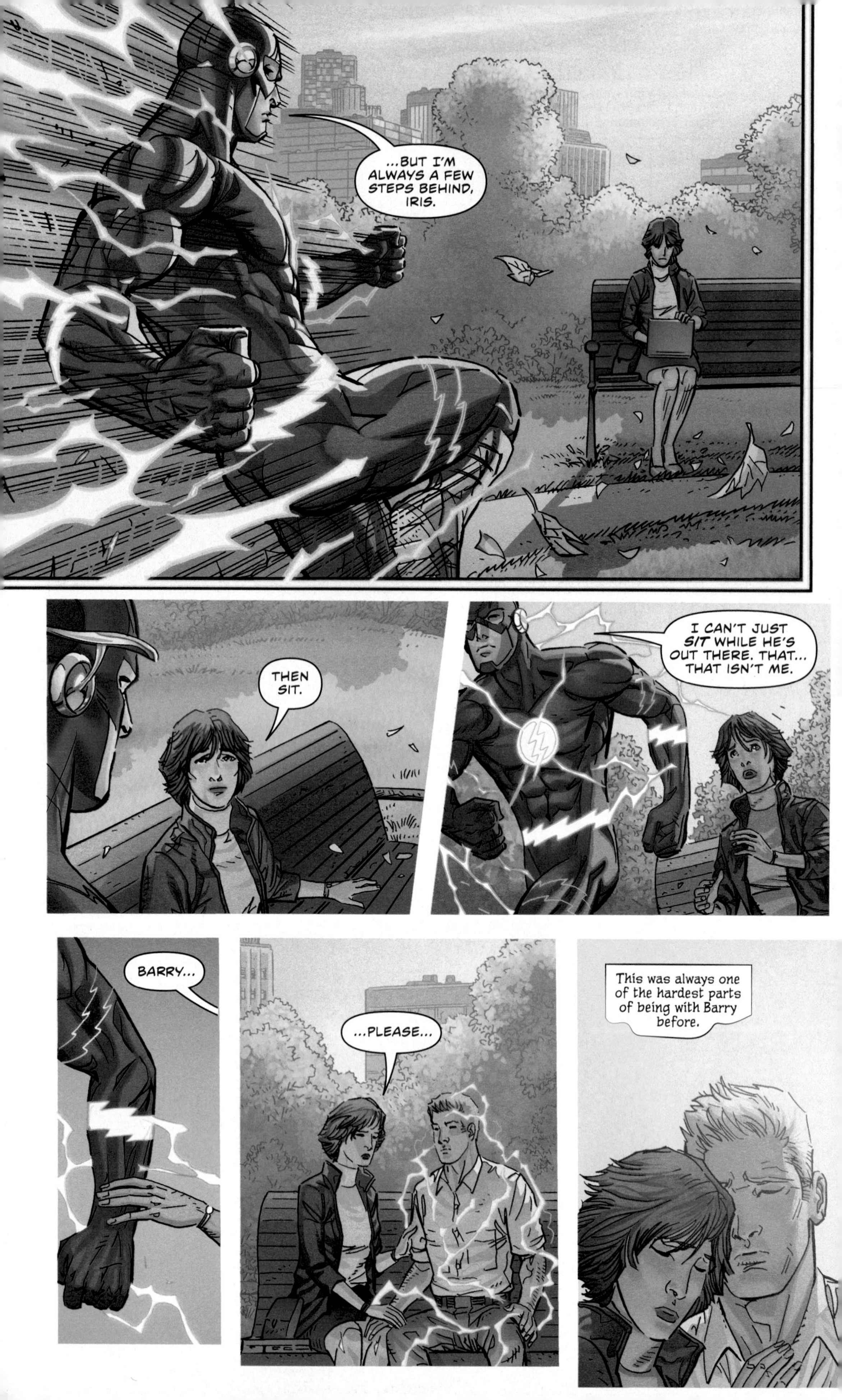

...BUT I'M ALWAYS A FEW STEPS BEHIND, IRIS.
THEN SIT.
I CAN'T JUST *SIT* WHILE HE'S OUT THERE. THAT... THAT ISN'T ME.
BARRY...
...PLEASE...
This was always one of the hardest parts of being with Barry before.

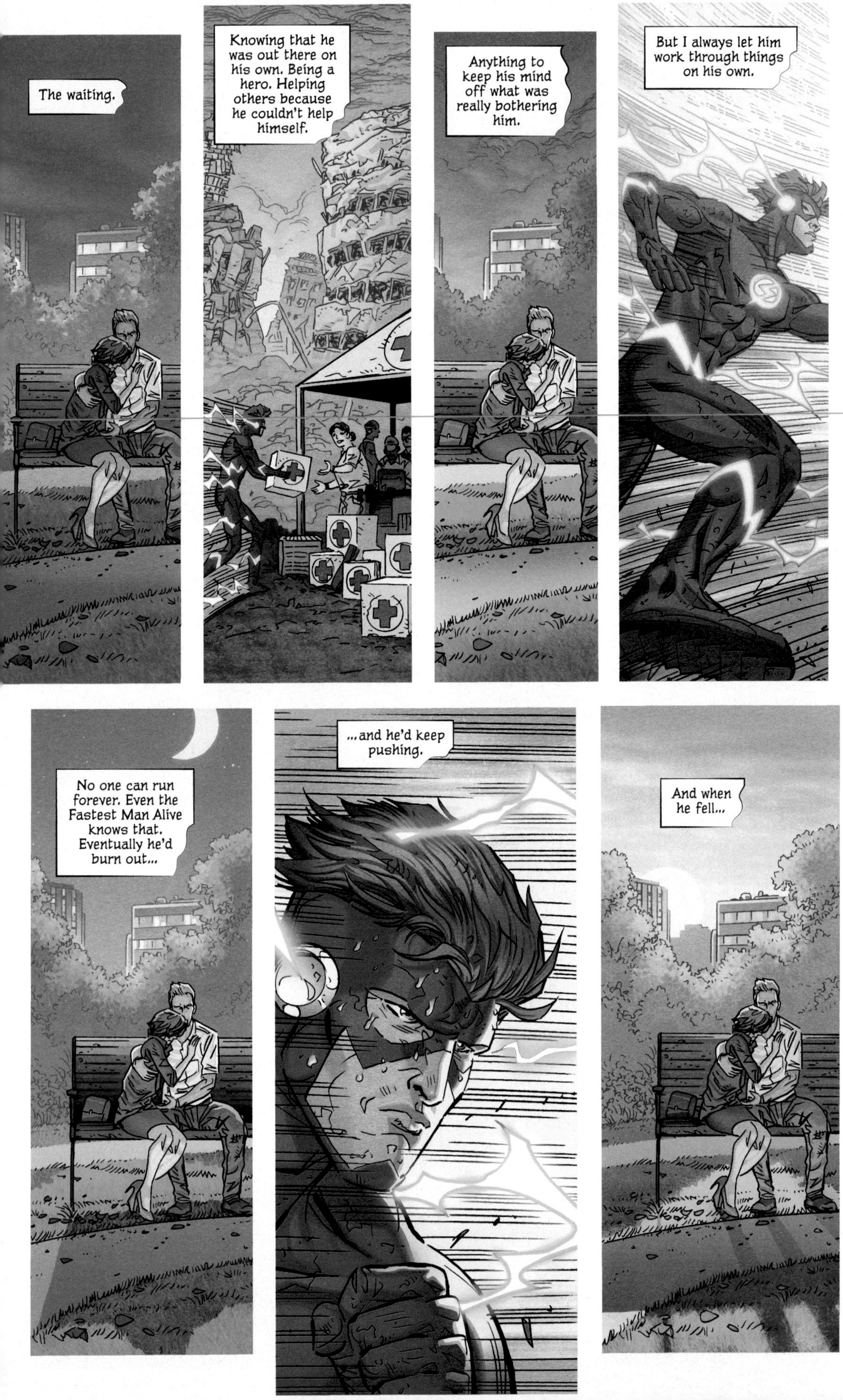
The waiting.
Knowing that he was out there on his own. Being a hero. Helping others because he couldn't help himself.
Anything to keep his mind off what was really bothering him.
But I always let him work through things on his own.
No one can run forever. Even the Fastest Man Alive knows that. Eventually he'd burn out...
...and he'd keep pushing.
And when he fell...

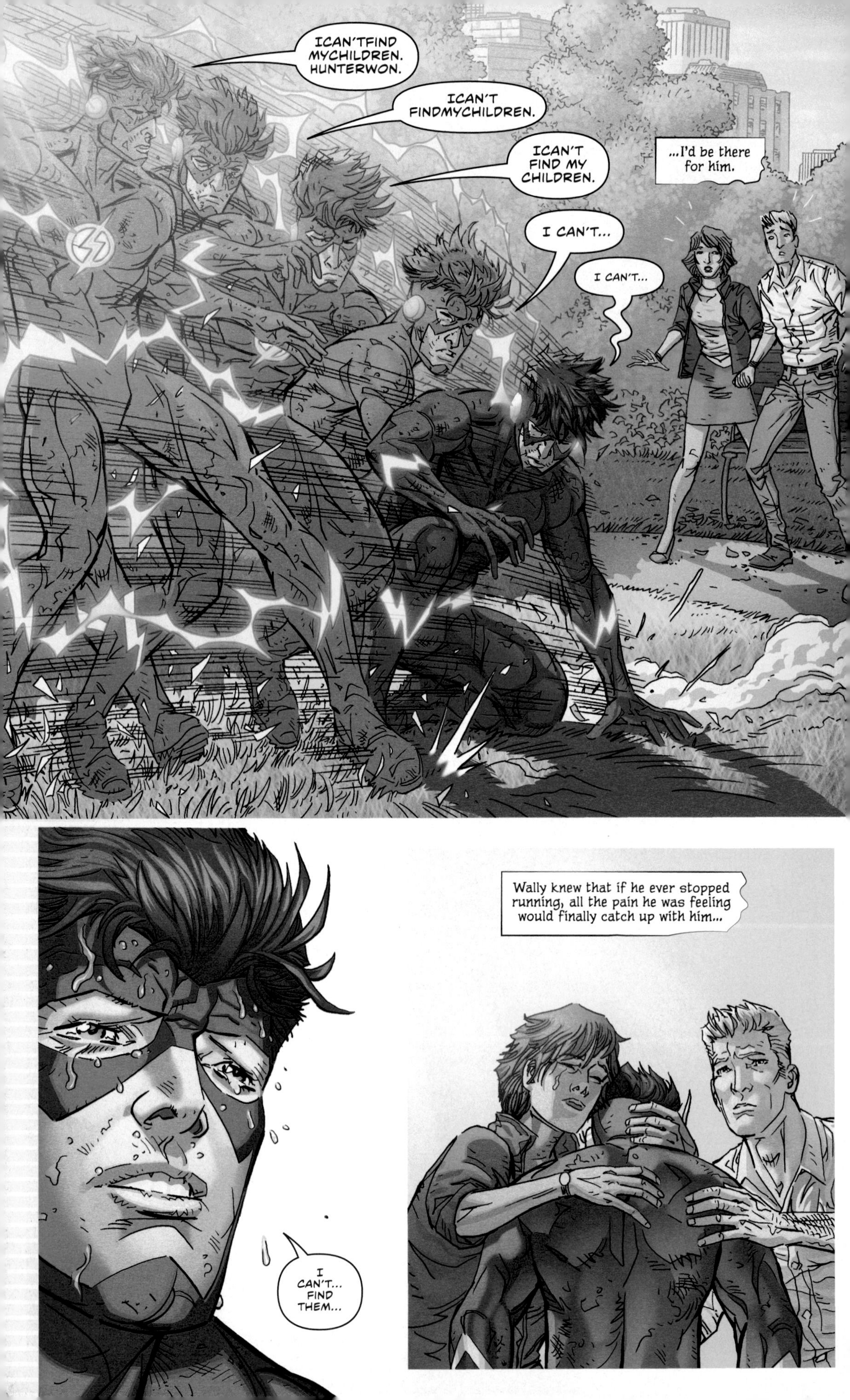
ICAN'TFIND MYCHILDREN. HUNTERWON.
ICAN'T FINDMYCHILDREN.
ICAN'T FIND MY CHILDREN.
I CAN'T...
I CAN'T...
...I'd be there for him.
Wally knew that if he ever stopped running, all the pain he was feeling would finally catch up with him...
I CAN'T... FIND THEM...

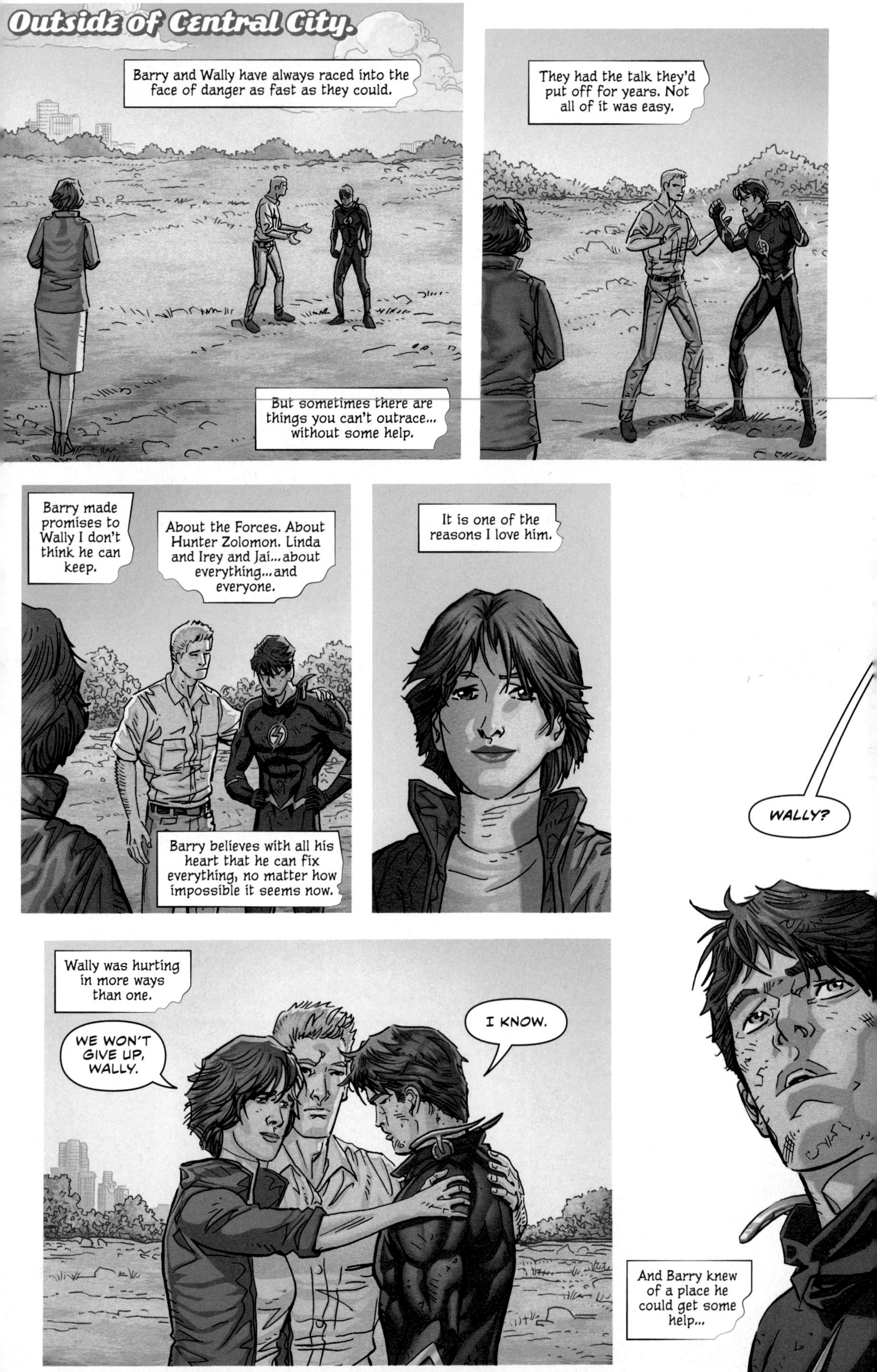
Outside of Central City.
Barry and Wally have always raced into the face of danger as fast as they could.
But sometimes there are things you can't outrace... without some help.
They had the talk they'd put off for years. Not all of it was easy.
Barry made promises to Wally I don't think he can keep.
About the Forces. About Hunter Zolomon. Linda and Irey and Jai...about everything...and everyone.
Barry believes with all his heart that he can fix everything, no matter how impossible it seems now.
It is one of the reasons I love him.
Wally was hurting in more ways than one.
WE WON'T GIVE UP, WALLY.
I KNOW.
WALLY?
And Barry knew of a place he could get some help...

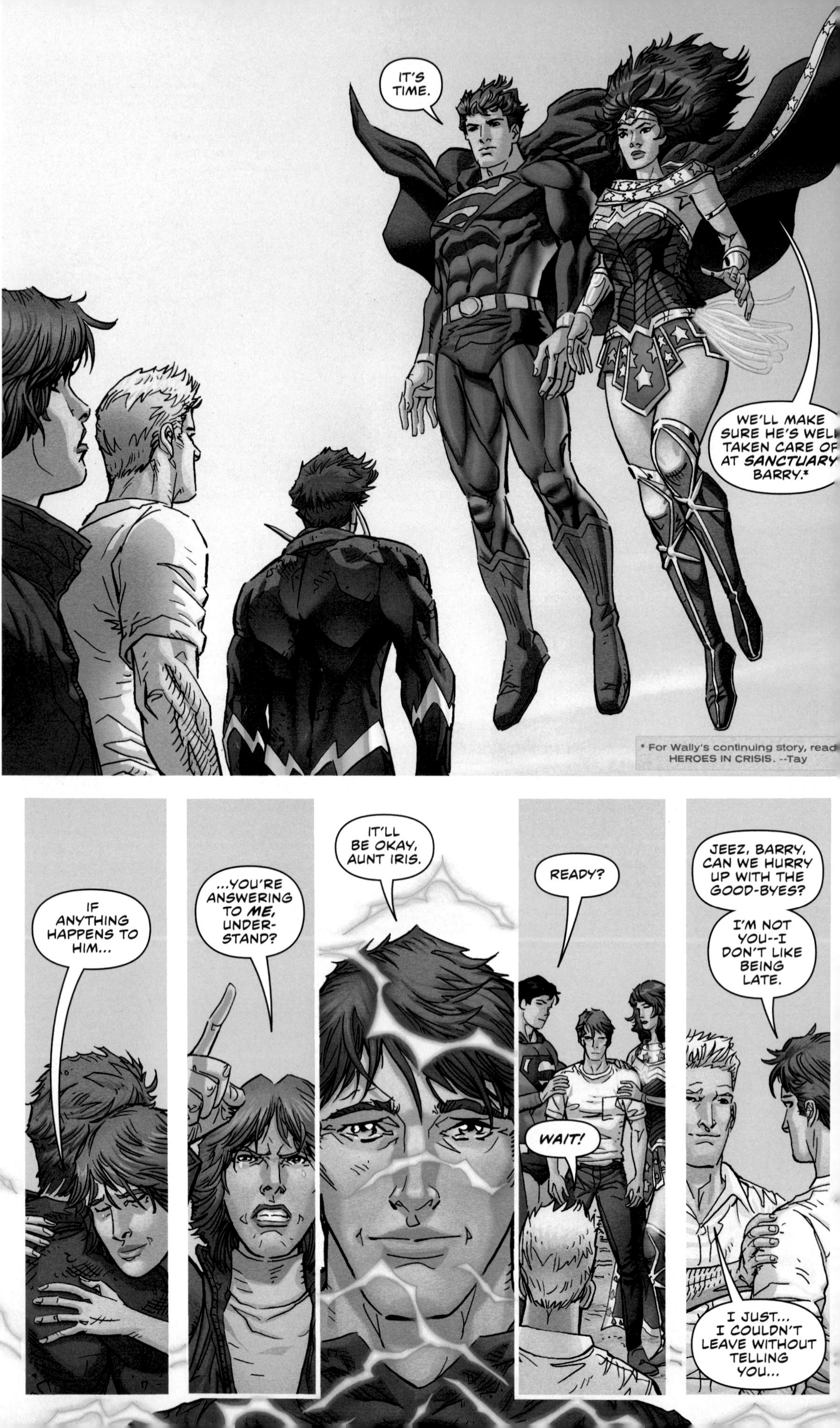
IT'S TIME.
WE'LL MAKE SURE HE'S WELL TAKEN CARE OF AT SANCTUARY, BARRY.*
* For Wally's continuing story, read HEROES IN CRISIS. --Tay
IF ANYTHING HAPPENS TO HIM...
...YOU'RE ANSWERING TO ME, UNDER-STAND?
IT'LL BE OKAY, AUNT IRIS.
READY?
WAIT!
JEEZ, BARRY, CAN WE HURRY UP WITH THE GOOD-BYES?
I'M NOT YOU--I DON'T LIKE BEING LATE.
I JUST... I COULDN'T LEAVE WITHOUT TELLING YOU...

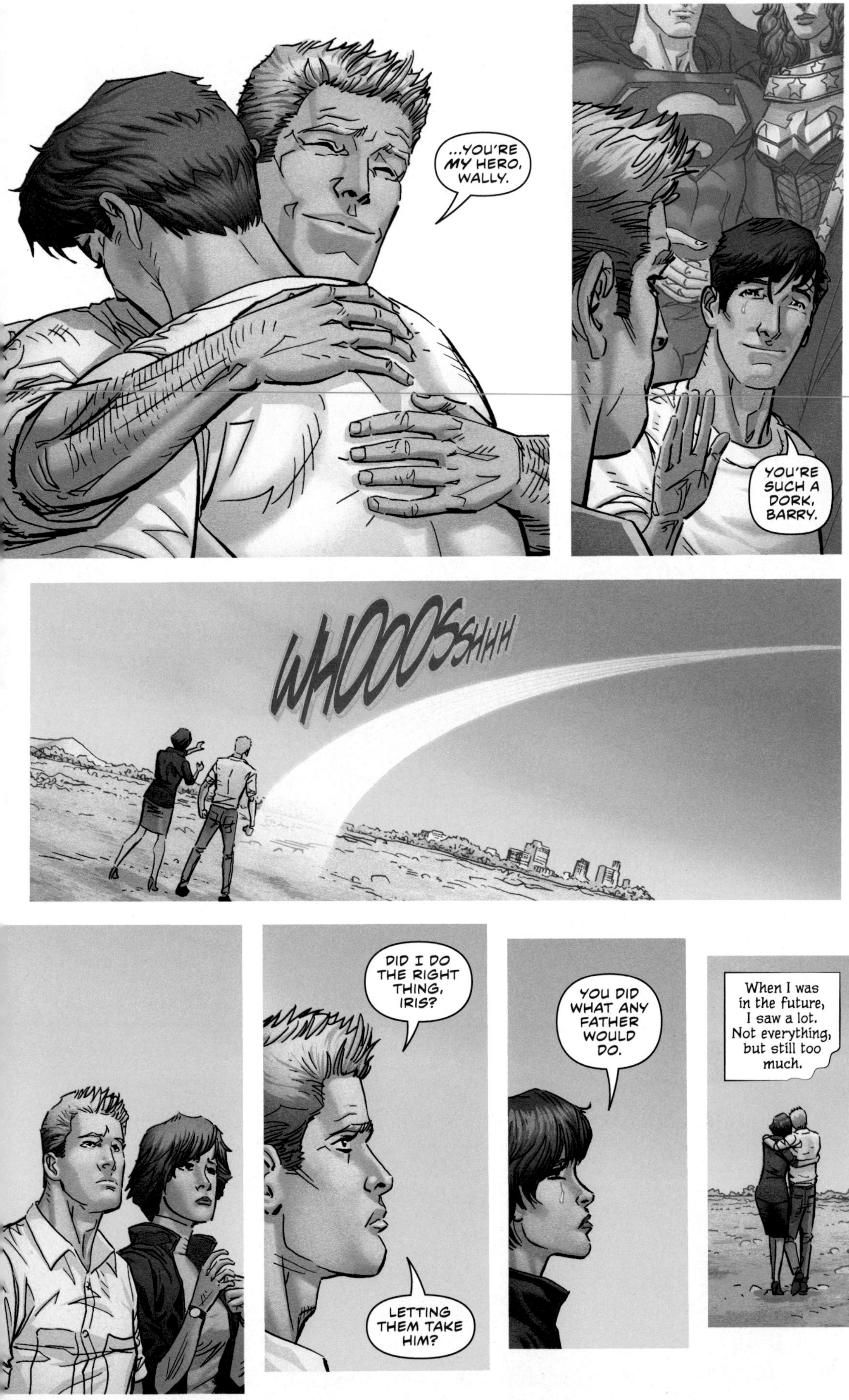
...YOU'RE MY HERO, WALLY.
YOU'RE SUCH A DORK, BARRY.
WHOOOSHHH
DID I DO THE RIGHT THING, IRIS?
LETTING THEM TAKE HIM?
YOU DID WHAT ANY FATHER WOULD DO.
When I was in the future, I saw a lot. Not everything, but still too much.

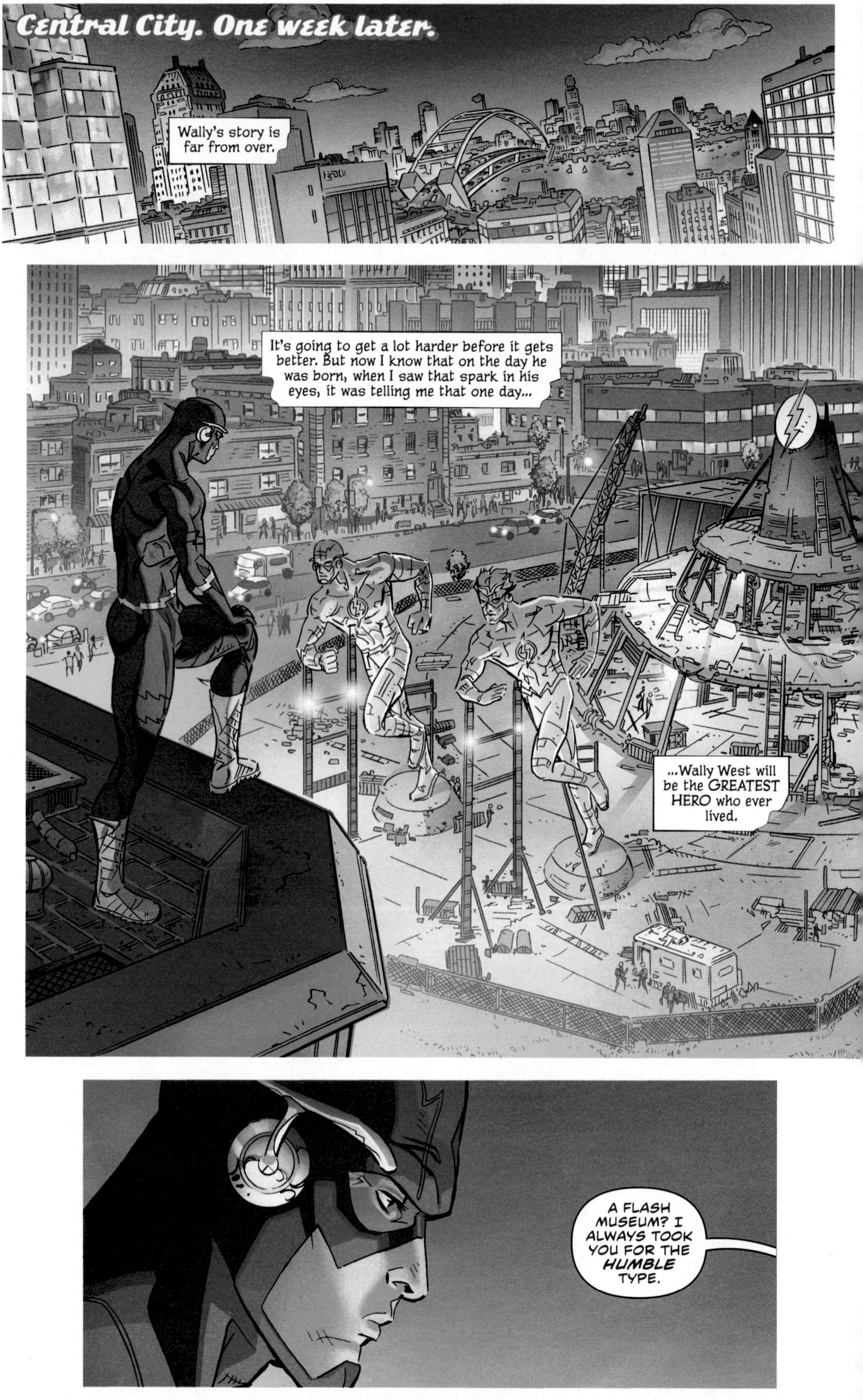
Central City. One week later.
Wally's story is far from over.
It's going to get a lot harder before it gets better. But now I know that on the day he was born, when I saw that spark in his eyes, it was telling me that one day...
...Wally West will be the GREATEST HERO who ever lived.
A FLASH MUSEUM? I ALWAYS TOOK YOU FOR THE HUMBLE TYPE.

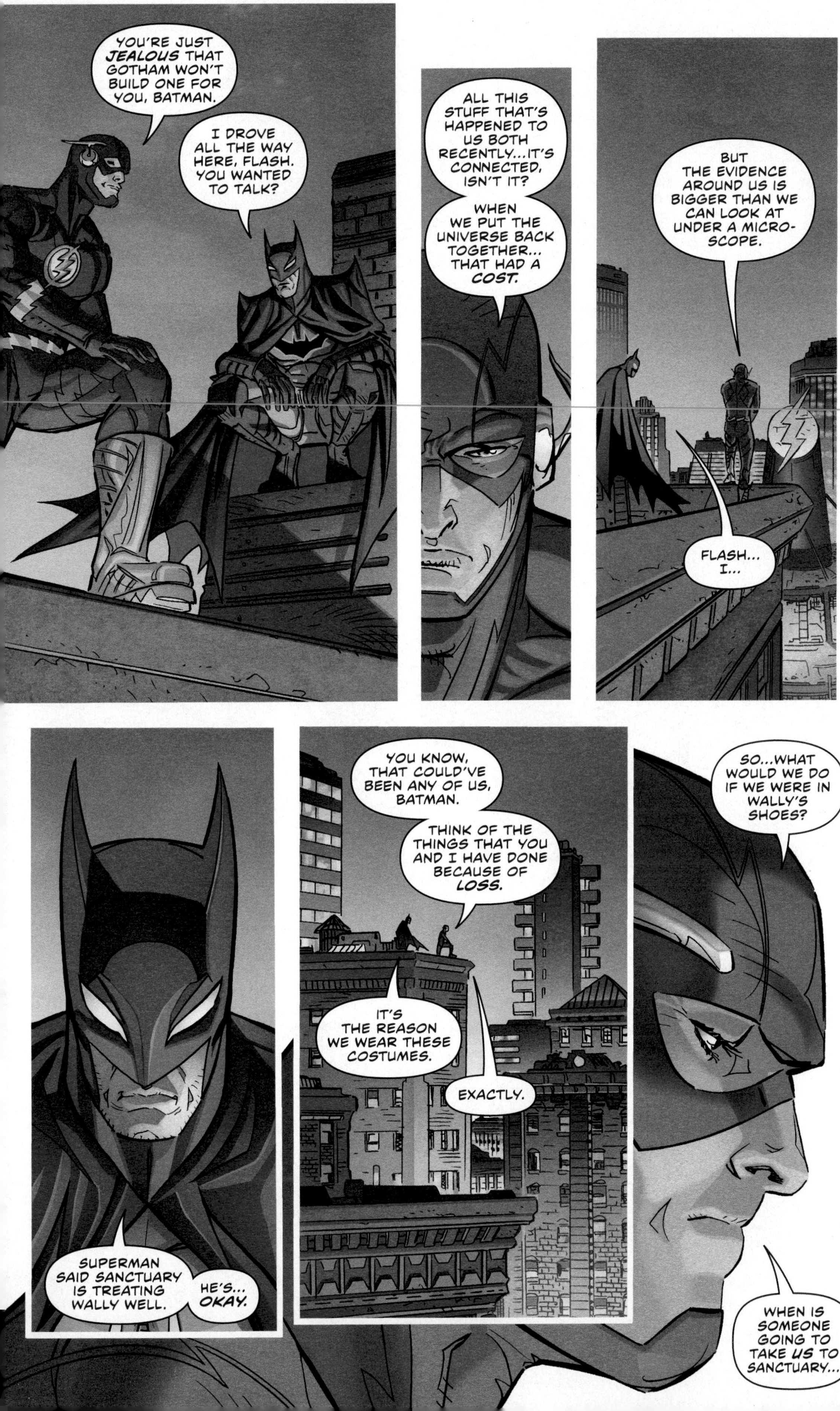
YOU'RE JUST JEALOUS THAT GOTHAM WON'T BUILD ONE FOR YOU, BATMAN.
I DROVE ALL THE WAY HERE, FLASH. YOU WANTED TO TALK?
ALL THIS STUFF THAT'S HAPPENED TO US BOTH RECENTLY...IT'S CONNECTED, ISN'T IT?
WHEN WE PUT THE UNIVERSE BACK TOGETHER... THAT HAD A COST.
BUT THE EVIDENCE AROUND US IS BIGGER THAN WE CAN LOOK AT UNDER A MICRO-SCOPE.
FLASH... I...
SUPERMAN SAID SANCTUARY IS TREATING WALLY WELL.
HE'S... OKAY.
YOU KNOW, THAT COULD'VE BEEN ANY OF US, BATMAN.
THINK OF THE THINGS THAT YOU AND I HAVE DONE BECAUSE OF LOSS.
IT'S THE REASON WE WEAR THESE COSTUMES.
EXACTLY.
SO...WHAT WOULD WE DO IF WE WERE IN WALLY'S SHOES?
WHEN IS SOMEONE GOING TO TAKE US TO SANCTUARY...

THE LIFE STORY OF
WALLY WEST

JOSHUA WILLIAMSON WRITER
SCOTT KOLINS ARTIST

LUIS GUERRERO COLORIST   STEVE WANDS LETTERER
HOWARD PORTER & HI-FI COVER

ANDREW MARINO ASSISTANT EDITOR   REBECCA TAYLOR EDITOR
MARIE JAVINS GROUP EDITOR

"...WHEN IS IT GOING TO BE OUR *LAST RACE?*"

THE FLASH #46 variant cover by FRANCESCO MATTINA

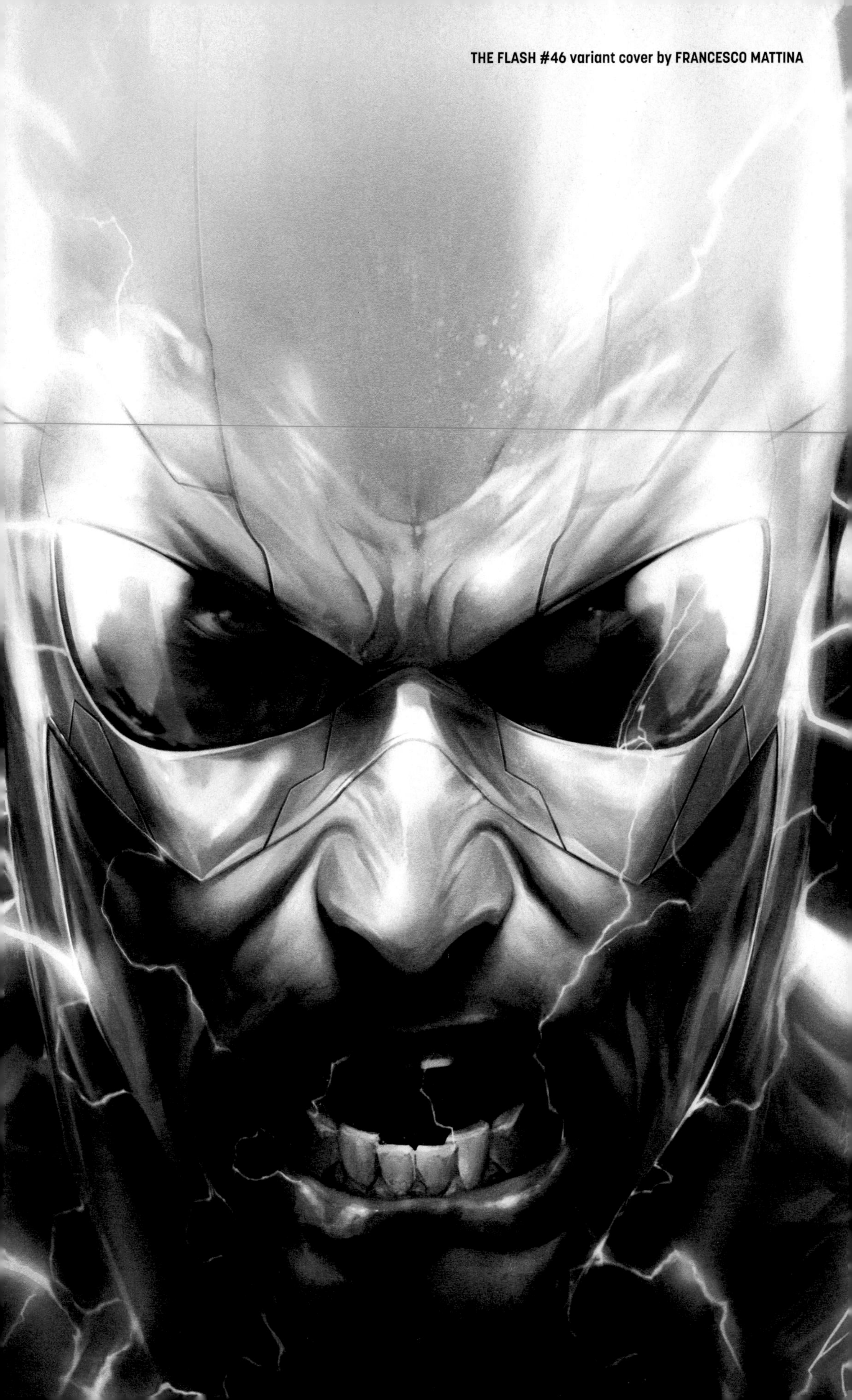

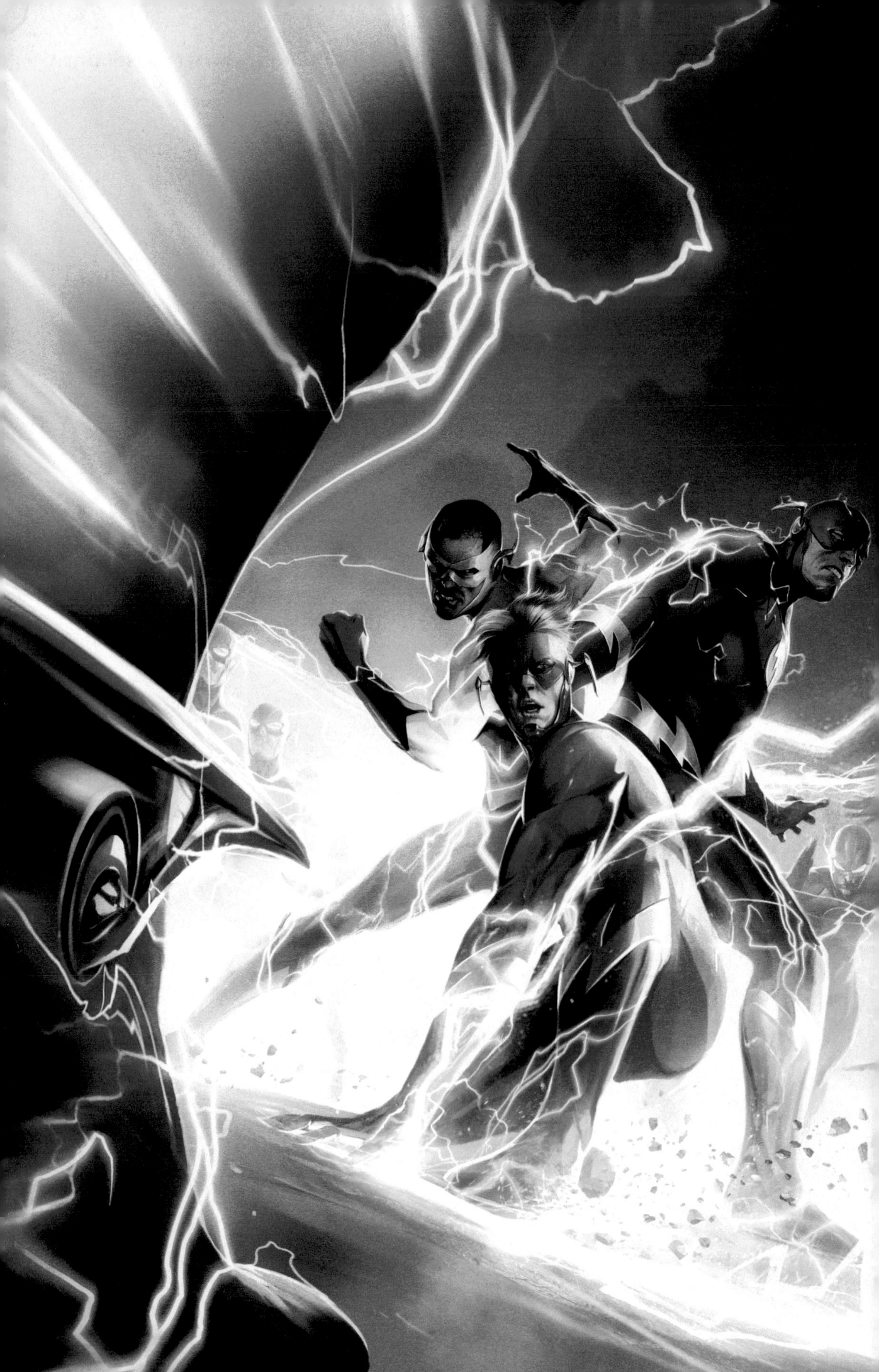

THE FLASH #47 variant cover by FRANCESCO MATTINA

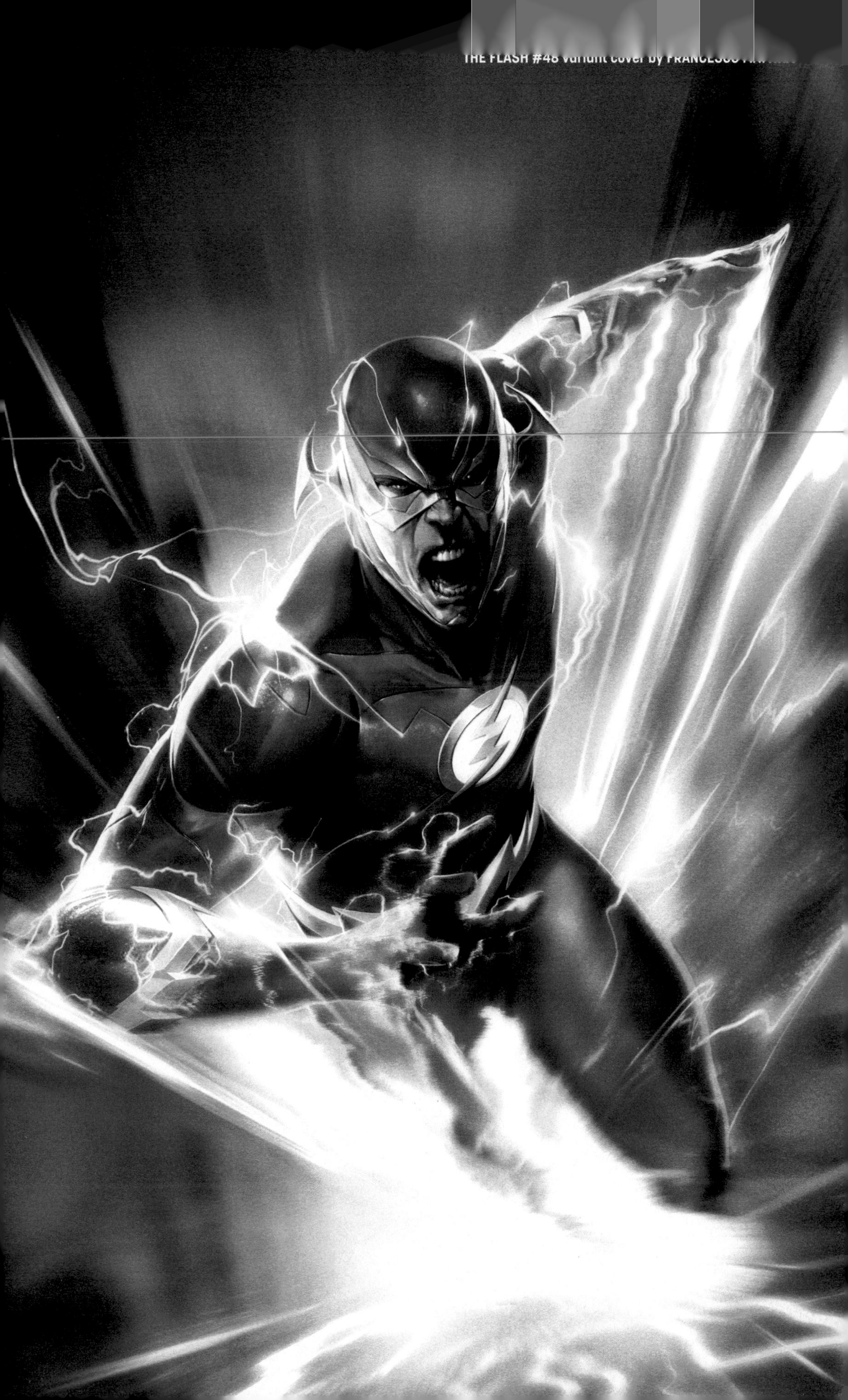

THE FLASH #48 variant cover by FRANCESCO

THE FLASH #49 variant cover by FRANCESCO MATTINA

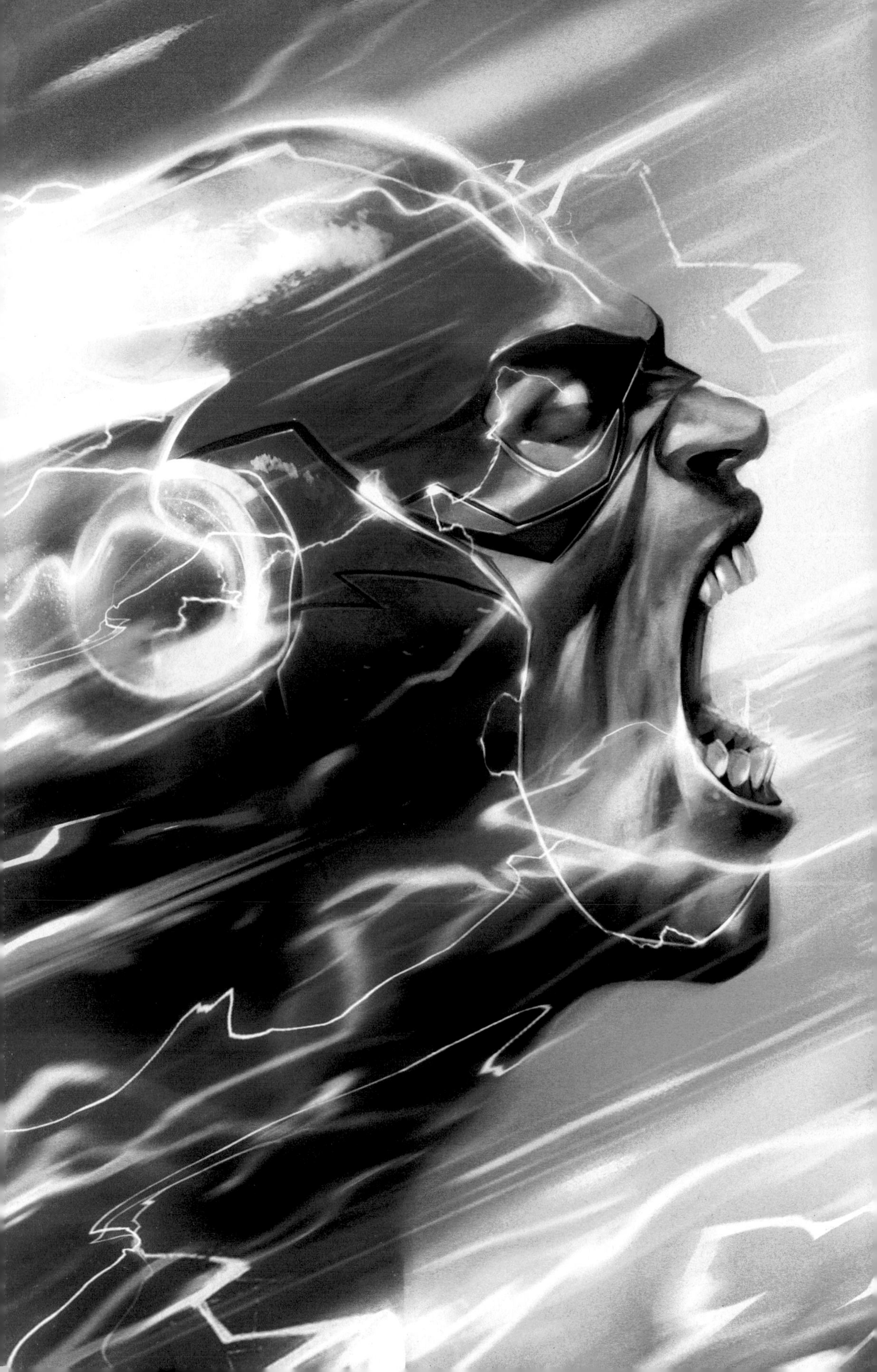

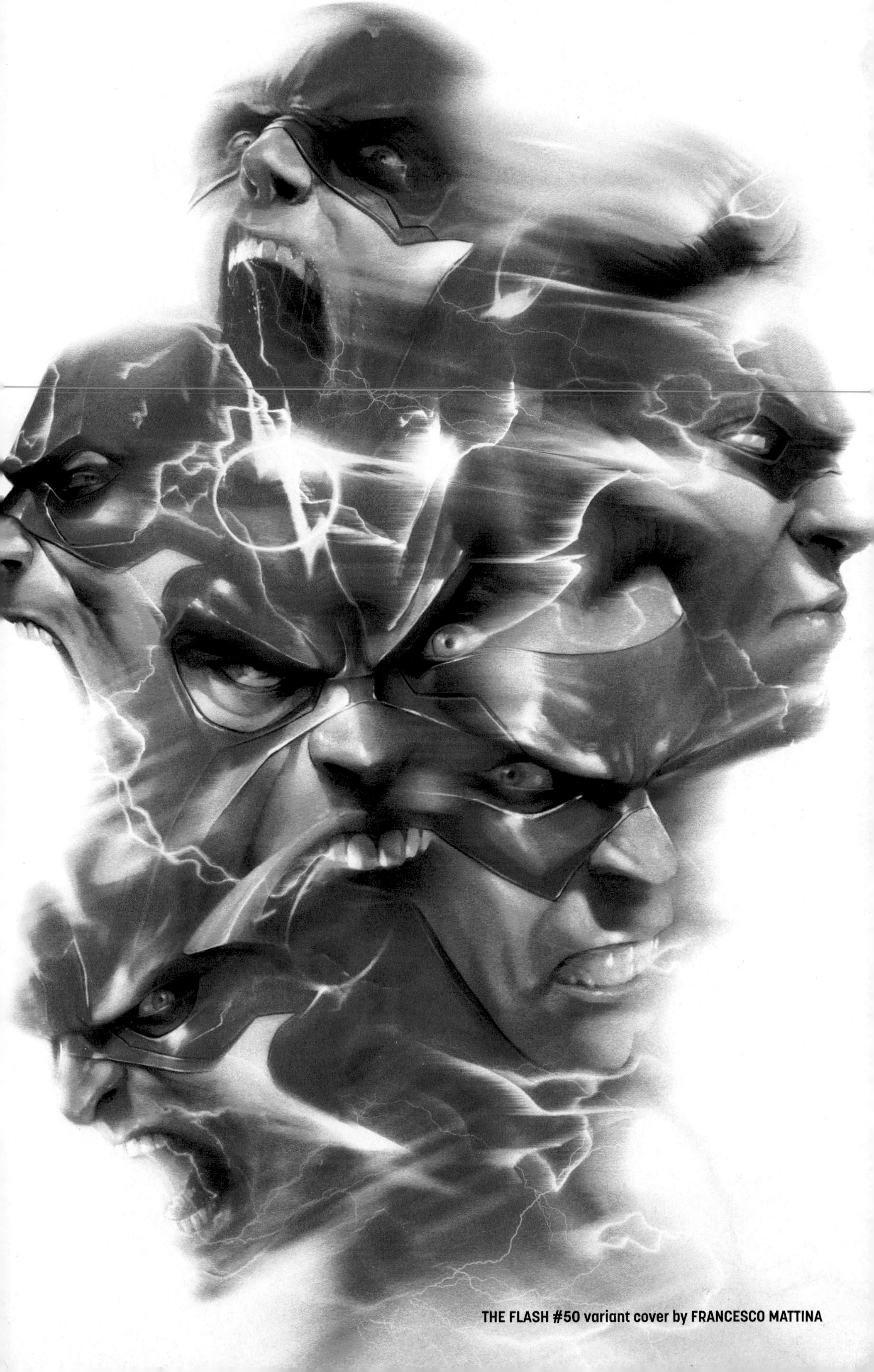

THE FLASH #50 variant cover by FRANCESCO MATTINA

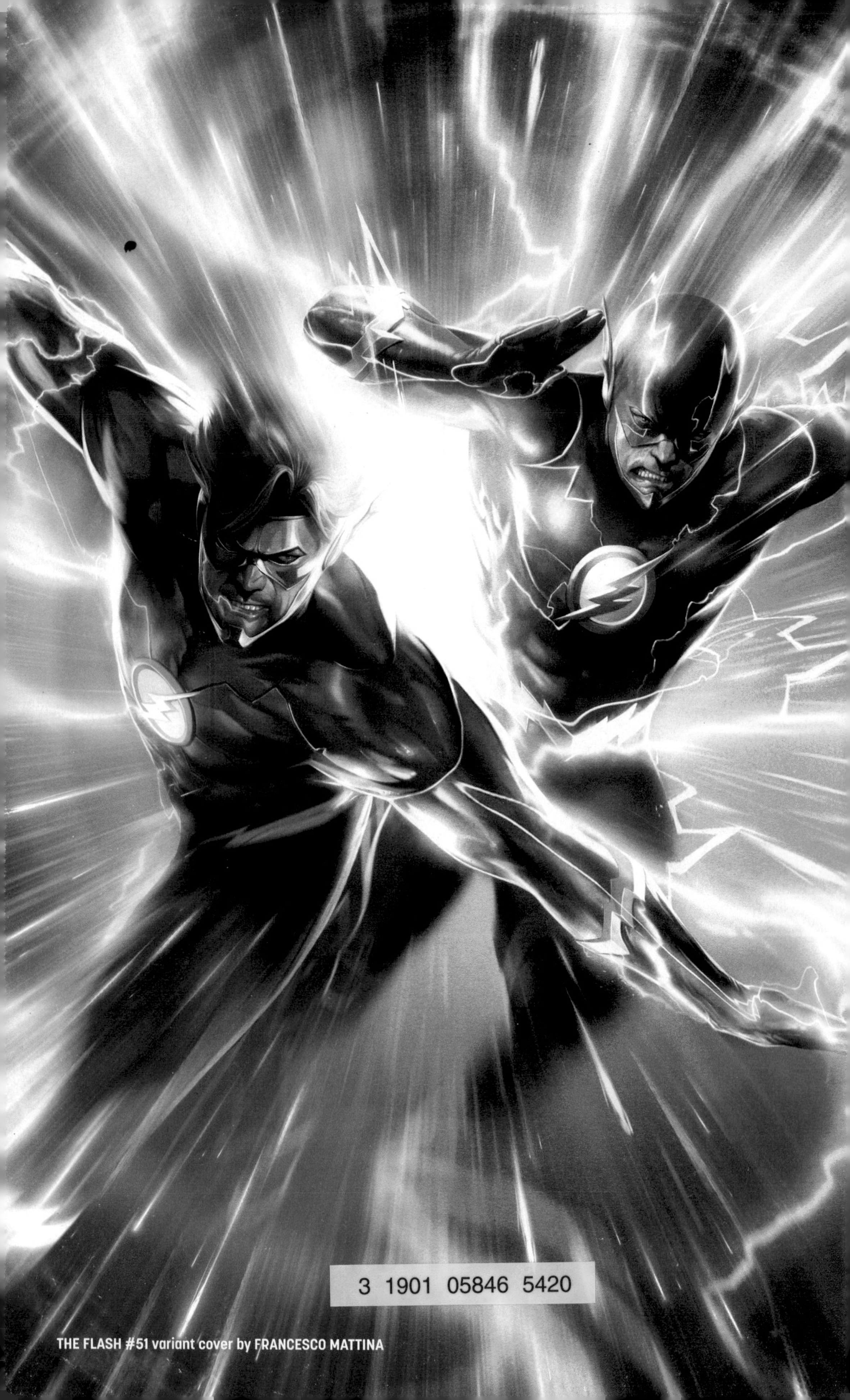

THE FLASH #51 variant cover by FRANCESCO MATTINA